The Realistic Imagination

George Levine

The Realistic Imagination

English Fiction
from Frankenstein to
Lady Chatterley

The University of Chicago Press
Chicago and London

GEORGE LEVINE is chairman of the English
department at Rutgers University and has
written and edited numerous books and
scholarly articles.

The University of Chicago Press, Chicago 60637
The University of Chicago Press, Ltd., London

©1981 by The University of Chicago
All rights reserved. Published 1981

Printed in the United States of America
88 87 86 85 84 83 82 81   5 4 3 2 1

Library of Congress Cataloging in Publication Data

Levine, George Lewis.
    The realistic imagination.

    Includes index.
    1. English fiction—19th century—History and
criticism.   2. Realism in literature.   I. Title.
PR868.R4L48   823'.7'0912   80-17444
ISBN 0-226-47550-6

For Dr. Harris J. Levine
in loving memory

Contents

Acknowledgments

Several chapters of this book are based on materials previously published. An earlier version of chapter 2 appeared as *"Frankenstein* and the Tradition of Realism" in *Novel*. Chapter 4 draws on my article "Sir Walter Scott: The End of Romance," first published in *The Wordsworth Circle*. Chapter 5 is revised from my article "Scott's *Bride of Lammermoor*," which appeared in *Nineteenth-Century Fiction*, Vol. 32, No. 4 (March 1978): 379–98, ©1979 by the Regents of the University of California. Chapter 10 is based on "High and Low: Ruskin and the Novelists," from *Nature and the Victorian Imagination*, the volume edited by Tennyson and Knoepflmacher and published by the University of California Press. Finally, chapter 3, in slightly different form, has appeared in the volume *George Eliot: Centenary Essays and an Unpublished Fragment*, edited by Anne Smith, © Vision Press 1980. I want also to thank the now scattered but always memorable participants in a seminar I taught at Indiana University in 1967–1968. They may be surprised to learn that they provided the seed for this exhausting and now aged growth, and it is a pleasure to write their names again: Robert Abrams, Martin Bidney, Willis Buckingham, Mary Flannery, Barbara Garland, Jim Helgeson, Dean Hartley, Arlene Hersch, Ann Hofstra, Penny Laurans, Peter Parisi, Stephen Rounds, Stuart Schneiderman, Bob Scarola, Ruth Lincoln. Since that seminar my life has been transformed, with my ideas about realism, by a remarkable, often flawed, often trying experiment in education, Livingston College, Rutgers. Although it diverted me from these speculations on the "real," it gave me a profounder education. In addition, I have a continuing debt to Richard Poirier, who brought me East again, and whose loyalty and support and intelligence have helped me through both Livingston and this book. Obviously, I owe a great deal to U. C. Knoepflmacher, whose work has preceded mine and who has been unfailingly supportive as critic, collaborator, and friend; to Alexander Welsh, whose name recurs throughout this text because he seems quietly to have anticipated me in all my best ideas and because he, too, has constantly supported my work; to Tom Edwards, upon whom I inflicted too much of the manuscript in its fragments. But of the friends who have followed this work, advised, criticized, and indulged me through the years, none has been more lovingly, more creatively critical, more relentless in finding waste, more quick to locate what matters, than David Leverenz, a tough mind, an almost too generous heart. None, perhaps, but Margaret Levine, *sine qua non*, friend and far more.

Parts of this book were written with the support of Guggenheim and National Endowment for the Humananities Independent Research grants.

Part One

Introduction

Idea, Reality, and the Monster

1

Realism

Realism is an unfortunate, an ambiguous word, which has been taken up by literary society like a view-halloo.

Thomas Hardy, "The Science of Fiction"

One could wish, to begin with, that the words realism *and* realist *might never again be used, save in their proper sense by writers on scholastic philosophy.*

George Gissing, "The Place of Realism in Fiction"

To take the word *realism* and the idea of representation seriously entails a challenge to the antireferential bias of our criticism and to the method of radical deconstruction that has become a commonplace. It is to challenge the assumptions about the status of literature variously held by Roland Barthes and Jacques Derrida, and, in the area of Victorian literature, J. Hillis Miller. It is to resist the now well established convention that realism is at best a historically inevitable mistake. I do not attempt anything like a full theoretical confrontation with this way of doing criticism, but choose to avoid extensive speculations on theory in order to keep my eye on the texts whose wonders are the occasion of this study.

Even that choice has important implications for literary theory, and I do not wish to avoid them.[1] They are consonant with the attitude toward realism that I am trying to develop and with the overall argument, theoretically significant, that realism is itself intimately and authoritatively connected to the modernist position. This study, in any case, assumes that criticism has a responsibility both to explication and to history, and this despite powerful epistemological arguments denying the possibility of the referentiality of language, despite semiotic theories that show every sign significant only of other signs within an arbitrary code, despite the indeterminacy of texts. Willy-nilly, criticism addresses itself to something besides itself, even in its most dazzling

3

regressions, and creates communities of meaning (if only to agree on unmeaning). At the risk of ideological and metaphysical complicity with things as they are, criticism must behave at times as though something is really out there after all. These are not questions of either/or: one is not either for realism or against it, as though this were a football game, or a war. Realism posits "mixed" conditions. So do I.

Ironically, when I began this study it was to call Victorian realism into question, but as I proceeded I found the great Victorian realists to be immensely compatible. Their art and their commitments have driven me to see Victorian realism as an astonishing effort both of moral energy and of art, and one that must not be diminished by the historical distortions of contemporary critical method or by the Whiggish view of history (I used to share), that we know better now. Nevertheless, this study was made possible by the criticism it often attacks in notes, by the contemporary insistence on the sheer textuality of fiction and the consequent impossibility of external reference.

Modernist criticism has been invaluable in bringing to focus the fact, extensively argued by Gerald Graff,[2] that modernism is not so modern as it seems, but is at least two hundred years old. Part of my point throughout this study is that nineteenth-century writers were already self-conscious about the nature of their medium, and that there is a direct historical continuum between the realists who struggled to make narrative meaningful and modern critics who define themselves by virtue of their separation from realism and even from narrativity itself. In the face of arguments that where we have seen unity of vision there is only indeterminacy, where we have found reference there is only self-reference, I argue that the historical situation was too complex for such readings.The Victorians, surely, did write with the awareness of the possibilities of indeterminate meaning and of solipsism, but they wrote *against* the very indeterminacy they tended to reveal. Their narratives do not acquiesce in the conventions of order they inherit but struggle to reconstruct a world out of a world deconstructing, like modernist texts, all around them. With remarkable frequency, they are alert to the arbitrariness of the reconstructed order toward which they point as they imply the inadequacy of traditional texts and, through self-reference and parody, the tenuousness of their own. but they proceed to take the risk of believing in the possibility of fictions that bring us at least a little closer to what is not ourselves and not merely language.

The "realism" with which this study is concerned is not that of the Scholastic philosophers. And it is only minimally that once notorious kind with which late-nineteenth-century writers sought to sweep away the pieties and conventionalities of the mid-Victorians and of their popular imitators. Realism in England belongs, rather, to a much more affable and moderate tradition, focusing not on the dregs of society, not on the degradations and degenerations of humans in bondage to a social and cosmic determinism. It belongs, almost provincially, to a "middling" condition and defines itself against the excesses, both stylistic and narrative, of various kinds of romantic, exotic, or sensational literatures. The programatic realism of the late century, with its pseudoscientific connections, its "experimental novels," its assumption that the norm of human experience is the extreme, was part of a rebellious movement against the mid-Victorian real and the art that projected it.

The mark of a less insular and more cynical culture was upon this later realism that Gissing explored, in which George Moore dabbled, and through which the great and not so great French and Russian novelists entered the mainstream of English fiction. But even it can be understood, within the terms I shall be finding for the whole tradition of English realism, as a self-conscious rejection of certain conventions of literary representation and of their implications. Purporting, like all realism, to speak the truth, it in fact invents a truth defined by its almost perfect inversion of mid-Victorian conventions. Thus, where earlier nineteenth-century realists found little incompatibility between "sincere" representation and a conscious attempt to speak helpfully to a sympathetic audience, the later realists insisted, like their more aesthetically inclined contemporaries, on an artistic integrity that alienated them from the traditional novel-reading audience. They imagined that the truth would be offensive to that audience, and found confirmation of their fictions precisely in their offensiveness.

Thus Henry James, in his review of Zola's *Nana*, asks with uncharacteristic Jamesian bitterness, "On what authority does [M. Zola] represent nature to us as a combination of the cesspool and the house of prostitution? On what authority does he represent foulness rather than fairness as the sign that we are to know her by?" [3] And in so speaking, James represents the implicit attitudes, not only of the late-century artists who were fostering a more highly aesthetic literary tradition, but of the earlier realists to whom, however far he developed their art and perhaps transcended it, he owed his primary allegiance. For in their inversion of the very tradition that James was trying to outgrow by a renewed partly Flaubertian preoccupation with the nature of his medium, the later realists rejected not only the predominantly middle class perception of reality that informed the moderate landscapes of the Victorian novel, but also the apparently rarefied and genteel emphasis on form and pattern, as opposed to the hard, cold "truth," in the aesthetic tradition to which, we might say, James, and Pater, and Wilde, and the later George Moore in their various ways belonged.

But the later realism, as an alternative to the earlier and apparently conventionalized realism, had few serious exponents in England, where there are no Maupassants or Zolas or Goncourts. Gissing, Hardy, James, Conrad, Moore himself—they all rejected the "experimental novel": and, despite their great differences, they wrote recognizably within the English tradition and sought to reconcile form and art with an appeal both to truth and to their audiences. Nevertheless, the emergence of late-century realism marks an important stage in the breakdown of the realism with which I am primarily concerned; and that stage further complicates the word *realism,* making it an even more dangerously multivalent one.

It is, nevertheless, an inescapable word, and in what follows I risk the dangers because with all the divergent possibilities of meaning, the word, in its literary application, carries a consistent thrust through all its inconsistent history. Whatever else it means, it always implies an attempt to use language to get beyond language, to discover some non-verbal truth out there. The history of English realism obviously depended in large measure on changing notions of what *is* "out there," of how best to "represent" it, and of whether, after all, representation is possible or the "out there" knowable. The history was further complicated by the artist's sense of responsibility to the audience, by conventions of propriety, and by the nature of earlier literary imaginations of the "real." Moreover, there is the problem that "realistic" did not become a label for novels until rather late, so that while Ian Watt can talk about the "rise of realism" in the eighteenth century, the word in ordinary usage is associated not so much with Jane Austen's kind of novel as with Arnold Bennett's or Gissing's, and even more, of course, with Zola's. Nevertheless, I assume a continuity from Defoe through to the nineteenth century, and I begin this study with Jane Austen.

Nineteenth-century realism was an international phenomenon, with its deepest roots in the transformations of culture and literature that we call by the name "Romantic." Realism presumes that the "ordinary" (another difficult but persistent word) has a value hitherto ascribed almost exclusively to the experience of the select few. What was generically low and comic became, as Erich Auerbach's *Mimesis* has definitively shown, mixed and serious. Realism tended to explode the distinctions between high and low in art, although the traces of a comic and "low mimetic" tradition remain visible even now. In England, realism developed its own conventions as it recoiled from earlier "misrepresentations," so that there are easily recognizable similarities among fictions that are ostensibly shaped primarily by their commitment to plausibility and truthfulness rather than to generic conventions.

My concern here is primarily with the development and disruption and transformation of these similarities as they hardened into conventions that were recognized *as* conventions. That they did so harden is manifest, for example, in Gissing's casual dismissal of them in the midst of an attack on the later realism. Realism, Gissing says, "merely contrasts with the habit of mind which assumes that a novel is written 'to please people,' that disagreeable facts must always be kept out of sight, that human nature must be systematically flattered, that the book must have a 'plot,' that the story should end on a cheerful note, and all the rest of it."[4] That "habit of mind," ironically, was what had become of Victorian realism, so that the "realism" Gissing evokes against it is apparently an altogether different thing. Actually however, this later realism is, in effect, using the earlier ideal of realism, the attempt to represent life sincerely, to dismiss its own hardened conventions.

The sticky self-contradictions latent in this relatively simple use of the word will get even stickier. The great novelists of the nineteenth century were never so naive about narrative conventions or the problems of representation as later realists or modern critics have suggested. If we now can detect the conventionality of their admirable struggles to get at truth without imprisoning it in conventions, we can also see that the attempt allies them with the very writers and critics who defined themselves by rejecting them. The later realism is only one evidence of the self-contradictory nature of realism itself.

My concern, then, is not with a definition of "realism," but with a study of its elusiveness. As an idea realism is one thing (or many things); as a literary practice, it is quite another (or others). I want to focus on the practice. In this case at least, our current emphasis on theory as opposed to practice, and the theoretical arguments against exegesis, are a danger to theory itself. No theory of the novel can stand that is not based firmly in a detailed consideration of what novelists actually did. A theory of realism, for instance, which fails to take into account the way particular novels radically change, in style and "content," the conventions of the past and present that realism is frequently said to affirm, can be no theory at all. The theory of this study is, thus, embedded in and inseparable from the exegeses of texts.

Writers and critics return to "realism," from generation to generation, because each culture's perception of reality changes and because literature requires ever new means to intimate the reality. As we may by now be tired of hearing, language, in representing reality, most forcefully demonstrates reality's absence. At best, language creates the illusion of reality so that our current definitions of realism swerve from implying the possibility of direct representation to focus on the difference between the medium and the reality whose absence it registers. Language, finally, can "represent" only other language. Thus a convenient and slippery definition provided by David Lodge comes close to accommodating both our common sense notion that realism tries to represent reality and our sophisticated awareness that it cannot. Realism, he says, is "the representation of experience in a manner which approximates closely to description of similar experience in non-literary texts of the same culture."[5] The philosophical holes in this are large, but no definition of realism can be quite satisfactory. And insofar as this one attempts to get at the connection between nonfictional and fictional experience, it does good service.

But my focus will be on the struggle inherent in any "realist" effort—the struggle to avoid the inevitable conventionality of language in pursuit of the unattainable unmediated reality. Realism, as a literary method, can in these terms be defined as a self-conscious effort, usually in the name of some moral enterprise of truth telling and extending the limits of human sympathy, to make literature appear to be describing directly not some other language but reality itself (whatever that may be taken to be); in this effort, the writer must self-contradictorily dismiss previous conventions of representation while, in effect, establishing new ones. No major Victorian novelists were deluded into believing that they were in fact offering an unmediated reality; but all of them struggled to make contact with the world out there, and, even with their knowledge of their own subjectivity, to break from the threatening limits of solipsism, of convention, and of language. Some aspects of their continuing struggle make the subject of this book.

Abstractly, their struggles follow the large-scale fate of the word *realism* itself. For realism begins, in Aristotelian and Scholastic philosophers, as the reification of the ideal, belief in the prior reality of universals and in the merely contingent reality of things. The idea exists outside the thinker and before the thing. Yet, by a well-known historical quirk, realism slides over to mean its opposite. The elements are the same: ideas and things. But now things are independent of conciousness, ideas empirically contingent upon things. In commonsense language, this way of imagining the world makes realism a grumpy suspicion of ideas, a hard-nosed facing of the facts and of the power of the external world over dream, desire, idea. Ironically, however, this realism edges back in modern thought and literature toward its beginnings, or toward its own entire elimination. For in the new relationship between idea and thing, they become incommensurate, as in nineteenth-century fiction. Neither can be contingent on the other. The idea is reified again, but phenomenally, as an idea, not as a prior reality or a means to reality. By virtue, then, of the very "realistic" discourse that marks the connection between idea and thing, we are, in the modernist predicament, cut off from things. The idea becomes the clearest indication of the thing's absence. Language, as mediator, can be about only itself, for each predicate modifies not the thing, but another predicate, obeys the rules not of the idea but of its own ordering principles. What language attempts to possess by describing eludes, like Keats's fair maiden of the urn, our longing embrace.[6]

But I do not want to dwell on the abstraction. Although my focus must be on realism as a convention, it is a mode that depends heavily on our commonsense expectation that there are direct connections between word and thing. And hence, of all literary movements, realism is most threatened by the contemporary severing of text from referent. Realism, after all, was initiated out of and against the severance. The coincidence of realism and parody[7] is a well-established idea to which I shall be returning frequently, but that coincidence should remind us of the centrality to realism of a self-conscious rejection of literature. Like Don Quixote's friends, realism seems intent on burning libraries, recognizing the madness of taking what is only a text as though it had the authority of reality. Yet, like the Don's friends, realism never quite burns all the books: it claims for itself a special authority. Part of realism's complex fate has to do with the continuing struggle of its practitioners to avoid the implications of their own textuality, that they are merely part of the Don's library, deserving of burning. Much of the power of nineteenth-century realist fiction derives from the integrity of its pursuit of possibilities that would paradoxically deprive it of its authority and sever it from its responsibility to reality and audience. With the high Victorian ideal of Truth or Sincerity, novelists exposed the artificiality of their own conventions, tested the limits of their own exclusions, and as best they could kept their eyes on their objects.

It is no accident, therefore, that conventionally we speak of "romance" as the most obvious alternative to realism. As we shall see with Austen and Thackeray, much nineteenth-century realism defined itself against romance because that form implied wish fulfillment rather than reality. And the romance/realism dichotomy, classically stated by Richard Chase, variously imagined by writers from Clara Reeve and Walter Scott to Nathaniel Hawthorne and Henry James to Northrop Frye and Leslie Fiedler, does require attention. But "romance" has become almost as confused a term as "realism." At present, the conventional dichotomy may help to suggest an alternative to the way I am imagining the problem of realism. What I shall be calling "contradictions" in the realist's program may be seen as more absolute differences in genre.[8] Edward Eigner's recent study, for example, valuably extends this way of arguing. He distinguishes the predominantly mimetic writers from what he calls the "metaphysical novelists," who describe not so much the "effect of experience on individuals," as "the nature of experience itself."[9]

The value of such a generic distinction is evident in the details of Eigner's excellent study, but its elaboration also runs counter to the very mixed condition of Victorian thought. Victorian nonfiction is rich with instances of arguments, firmly based in the mimetic ideal, that make no distinction between what we might call scientific description and metaphysical speculation. One of the primary efforts of Victorian thought was to reconcile empirical science with metaphysical truth.[10] We find such effort, although unsystematic, in most of Ruskin's work, as it is already implicit in Carlyle's. Moreover the great Victorian system maker, Herbert Spencer, the creator of "The Unknowable," claimed to be creating his system inductively. One of the most interesting and touching fragments of such an effort can be found in G. H. Lewes's five-volume *Problems of Life and Mind*, the last two volumes of which were published posthumously by George Eliot, and about which I shall have much to say later.

As we look over the criticism that attached to realism from the start, we find recurring objections to what Hardy was later to attack as mere "copyism."[11] The antimimetic tradition most forcefully espoused by Bulwer never completely lost out, and in fact occupied an important position in the dominant realistic tradition. Although, retrospectively, we can find little important Victorian fiction validly subject to the complaint of copying, the possibility worried many writers. Reviewers in the *Quarterly*, early in the century, were lamenting the failure of novelists working the new field of the "domestic" to throw over their narratives "the colours of poetry."[12] Ironically, late-century writers were finding Victorian realism too ideal, insufficiently real or faithful in its copying. The opposite of realism, Lewes had said around mid-century, was not idealism but "Falsism."

Lewes's defense of realism implies, nevertheless, a cultural consensus that realism tended to be *un*-poetic and *un*-ideal. But the very lateness with which the word appeared on the literary scene, and the difficulty it had surviving serious criticism[13] from novelists themselves, suggest that in England at least the convention was a symptom not of a realistic school, but of a tendency among very different writers. The ease with which realism was reconciled with other objectives—the ideal, the beautiful—further implies not a single genre but a variety of ways of organizing some special historical perspectives. The isolation of a genre to be called the realistic novel entails a circular inductive method: the abstraction from novels we already presume to be realistic of the qualities that make them so. I prefer to keep the focus on the qualities nineteenth-century writers shared, without worrying about generic labels. In a chapter on Thackeray, I shall discuss many of the qualities in detail.

Whatever qualities are abstracted to produce a definition of genre that would include, say, both James's *The Ambassadors* and Thackeray's *Vanity Fair*, formal differences would subvert the definition. The continuing literary problem that plagued realism from the start was the incompatibility of tight form with plausibility. "The realistic writer soon finds," says Northrop Frye, "that the requirements of literary form and plausible content always fight against each other." [14] James's disapproval of much Victorian fiction is partly a disapproval of the expansiveness of form required to produce a cumulatively effective plausibility.

Whatever its difficulties and contradictions, however, realism was a historical impulse that manifested itself as a literary method and imposed itself on almost every form of prose narrative. It was a method consonant with empirical science in that it was exploratory rather than definitive. The method of realism, George Lukács has argued, is a method of discovery, not of representation of preestablished realities. [15] The quest could lead in the direction of the "metaphysical novelists," but normally only through the exploration of the here and now; and although realism may make the particular typical, it resists using allegorical forms and prefers what we might call a Wordsworthian method of finding in the individual a common human appeal. The truth realism sought was replacing the transcendent reality that had dominated knowledge until the Renaissance, [16] but that truth could lead out from the particular once more to an alternative transcendence—as, say, in the Feuerbachian ideal of George Eliot. In withdrawing a metaphysical sanction from reality, George Eliot immediately replaced it with a "humanist" sanction by seeing the forms of human experience in a Wordsworthian light, as manifestations of a large, morally sanctified community. The secular truth might lead as well to a negative transcendence, as in the structure of Hardy's fiction. There, the Providential patterns are exactly reversed to give to the defeated protagonist an almost transcendent dignity. The variety of possibilities reflects the way the realistic impulse is most precisely located in the historical context of a secularizing movement directed against the falsehoods of earlier imaginations of reality. Because it was an impulse particularly vulnerable to social, scientific, and epistemological transformation, its actual embodiments were polymorphous.

If it were possible to locate a single consistent characteristic of realism among its various rejections of traditional forms and ideals, it would be that antiliterary thrust I have already noted; and this thrust is also—inevitably—antigeneric in expression. The quest for unmediated experience becomes central to the dramatic tensions of most realistic fiction, even where the rhetorical strategy is to establish several layers of mediation—as in *Wuthering Heights*, which is generically a romance, or in *The Newcomes*, with Pendennis narrating a quintessentially realistic fiction. The fate of realism and its complicated relation to all those literary forms in which it confusedly manifests itself are intimately involved with the writer's and the culture's capacity to believe in the accessibility of experience beyond words.

If we agree to take realism in this way, as a historical phenomenon, we can discuss it with some precision, locate those qualities that mark it as anticonventional, and keep it unstably in process. For the label, "realism," sticks. In disentangling the threads that weave the label, I want to insist on three major points. First, realism *was* always in process as long as it was important to nineteenth-century fiction; second, there was no such thing as naive realism—simple faith in the correspondence between word and thing—among serious Victorian novelists; and third and not quite contradictorily, Victorian realists, recognizing the difference between truth and the appearance of truth, did try to embrace the reality that stretched beyond the reach of language. Their eyes and hearts were on Keats's fair maiden.

Despite its appearance of solidity, realism implies a fundamental uneasiness about self, society, and art. It becomes a dominant way of seeing at the time J. Hillis Miller describes as marking "the splitting apart of [the communion] of . . . verbal symbols with the reality they named."[17] While "Nature" had become for Carlyle a "grand unnameable Fact,"[18] poets and novelists were engaged in naming it. But the activity was self-conscious, and truth telling was raised to the level of doctrine. Such intensity of commitment to speaking the truth suggests difficulties where before none had been perceived. The mystery lay not beyond phenomena, but in them. Description, as Lukács argues, begins at the point where things are felt to be alienated from human activity. Realists take upon themselves a special role as mediator, and assume self-consciously a moral burden that takes a special form: their responsibility is to a reality that increasingly seems "unnameable," as Carlyle implies mockingly in the pseudo-science that opens *Sartor Resartus;* but it is also to an audience that requires to be weaned or freed from the misnaming literatures past and current. The quest for the world beyond words is deeply moral, suggesting the need to reorganize experience and reinvest it with value for a new audience reading from a new base of economic power.

The general disrepute into which novel writing had fallen by the beginning of the nineteenth century, although it does not imply disbelief in the power of language to engage reality, does express moral and intellectual outrage at the dominance of literature that trivialized human experience. We see this outrage in Carlyle's puritanical distrust of fiction as a form of lying (picked up and turned upside down by Oscar Wilde in "The Decay of Lying"); in Macaulay's affectionate unease with the appeal of fiction to what is childish in us; in Thackeray's extensive ironies or Austen's amused defense. In the vigor of the dismissal of earlier literature, particularly of the popular novels by women at the end of the eighteenth century, of gothic, sentimental, and silver-fork novels, is an implicit consensus that literature had to be relocated. Although the novel remained an amusement, it often attempted to become (sometimes willy-nilly became) an instrument of knowledge as well.

The relocation entailed a shift of focus from the large to the small, from the general to the particular, and a diminishment of dramatic extremes, as from tragedy to pathos. It is a commonplace to say that realism does not stay at that reduced scale, but the criterion of plausibility requires at least that the beginnings be here, where the characteristic mid-century novel struggles to remain. The shift and the transience of the shift are captured as early as *Sketches by Boz,* where Dickens can be seen learning his craft by learning how to give to the particular and ordinary the resonances traditionally to be found in the universals of an earlier philosophy and literature.

In the first sketch, as published in book form, Dickens's opening words might be taken as a metaphor, or a thesis sentence, for realism's effort to make the ordinary significant: "How much is conveyed in those two short words—'The Parish!' And with how many tales of distress and misery, of broken fortune and ruined hopes, too often of unrelieved wretchedness and successful knavery are they associated!"[19] Already, Dickensian melodrama is present, the impatience with limits; yet the means of transcending limits is "the parish," not a religious organization but a commonplace secular society—Austen's kind of geography. Crude as Dickens's method may be, the means of transcending limits is the exploration of the known as though it were unknown. Dickens will not merely copy the parish; he will see it with a freshness and clarity that will at once make it recognizable to the new popular audience who might take it seriously as a subject, and transform it. The particular, under the pressure of intense and original seeing, gives back the intensities normally associated with larger scale, traditional forms. That such a passage as this sounds now like a cliché and belongs to the "Our Town" convention implies much about the fate of mid-century realism. In any case, by looking intensely at doorknobs, and walls, and old clothes, and cabmen, Dickens uses his *Sketches* to bring together the particular and the conventional, the ordinary and the extreme, making experience amusing, as George Eliot would say of art, by enlarging our sympathies and our knowledge.

Dickens, certainly, was less easy with the limits of realism than most of his contemporaries, but he shares here its mimetic and exploratory tendencies. And his example suggests, perhaps more than the examples of, say, Thackeray, Trollope, and George Eliot, that it is perverse to apply to realism a critical method that assumes the separation of language from its object and the irresistibly conventional nature of literary forms. In his essay on the *Sketches,* J. Hillis Miller attempts precisely to apply such a method: "Any literary text is both self-referential and extra-referential, or rather it is open to being not seen as the former and mistakenly taken as the latter. All language is figurative, displaced. All language is beside itself."[20] Yet surely the figurativeness of the *Sketches* appears to be asking to be taken as "extra-referential." Surely, too, to treat as conventions of literature such references as that to "broken fortunes and ruined homes" does violence, if not to the experience of reading, than to the historical force of the language. Laurence Lerner speaks directly to this difficulty:

> To treat romance, fable, or comedy in terms of a set of literary conventions, devices for noticing some things and not others, is to say nothing unacceptable to the practitioners of these modes; but to treat realism in this way is to knock the bottom out of its programme. . . . To treat realism as merely another set of conventions is to display such a lack of sympathy with its aims as to be virtually incapacitated from appreciating its products.[21]

Such sanely antitheoretical arguments belong in the tradition of realism they defend. Lerner, moreover, understands many of the difficulties of his position. Nevertheless, although Miller carries the argument beyond its historically justifiable place, and Lerner has a firm historical sense of the realist's position, no historical perspective that ignores the problems posed by modern epistemology and criticism can entirely sustain itself. E. H. Gombrich's classic discussion of this kind of problem demonstrates that in spite of a deep commitment to the external real, the artist must use conventions for the representation of reality from which nobody working the medium can too widely depart,[22] and that representations of reality normally change through more or less subtle variations on other representations in the medium—like Constable's on Cozens's clouds, like Austen's on the gothic novel. All perception is mediated by the culture into which one is born so that the Heaven that "lies about us in our infancy . . . fade[s] into the light of common day." "There is no reality," says Roland Barthes, "not already classified by man."[23] And while every beginning, like Dickens's own, is a discontinuity, discontinuity produces, as Edward Saïd argues, a "difference which is the result of combining the already-familiar with the fertile novelty of human work in language."[24] Beginnings and discontinuities can be understood only by way of relationship. And the beginning, for writers in the tradition with which I am concerned, implies differences within a range so recognizably shared that they seem, in their very unconventionality, conventional. While Victorian realists strained to be extrareferential, and must be read as though they were, the nature of their "references" or "representations" is comprehensible only if we also see its conventionality.

We get close to the texture of realism, however, if we recognize that narratives touched by the realistic impulse try to resist or circumvent the formal conventions of narrative. The primary conventions of realism are its deflation of ambition and passion, its antiheroism, its tendency to see all people and things within large containing social organizations and, hence, its apparently digressive preoccupation with surfaces, things, particularities, social manners.[25] Committed to treat "things as they are and not as the story teller would like them to be for his convenience"[26] realists assume the possibility of making the distinction and thus save meaning at the sacrifice of pleasure. Realism further complicates itself because in requiring a continuing alertness to the secret lust of the spirit to impose itself on the world—if not as hero, then as martyr—and in resisting the romance forms that embody those lusts, it is always on the verge of another realism: the recognition that the reality it most adequately represents is a subtly disguised version of its own desires.

There is, then, a continuing tradition of self-consciousness in realistic fiction, a tradition formally initiated in *Don Quixote*. The self-consciousness marks realism's awareness both of other literature and of the strategies necessary to circumvent it, and—at last—its awareness of its own unreality. The complex fate of realism as it unfolds through the century is latent in that self-consciousness. Ironically, the self-consciousness itself becomes a convention, and we can detect it in realism's most overt anti-literary manifestos. A look at a few of these provides a useful starting point.

> If, among those who may be tempted to peruse my history, there should be any mere novel-readers, let me advise them to throw the book aside at the commencement of this chapter, for I have no more wonderful incidents to relate, no more charges at the muse, no more sudden turns of fortune. I am now become a plodding man of

business... [Maria Edgeworth, "Ennui, or Memoirs of the Earl of Glenthorne" (1804)]

I do not invite my fair readers, whose sex and impatience gives them the greatest right to complain of these circumstances, into a flying chariot drawn by hippogriffs, or moved by enchantment. Mine is an humble English post-chaise, drawn upon four wheels, and keeping his Majesty's highway. Such as dislike the vehicle may leave it at the next halt, and wait for the conveyance of Prince Hussein's tapestry. [Scott, *Waverley* (1814)]

All which details, I have no doubt, JONES, who reads this book at his Club, will pronounce to be excessively foolish, trivial, twaddling, and ultra-sentimental. Yes; I can see Jones at this minute (rather flushed with his joint of mutton and half-pint of wine), taking out his pencil and scoring under the words "foolish, twaddling," etc., and adding to them his own remark of *"quite true."* Well, he is a lofty man of genius, and admires the great and heroic in life and novels; and so had better take warning and go elsewhere. [Thackeray, *Vanity Fair* (1847)]

If you think from this prelude that anything like a romance is preparing for you, reader, you never were more mistaken. Do you anticipate sentiment, and poetry, and reverie? Do you expect passion and stimulus, and melodrama? Calm your expectations: reduce them to a lowly standard. Something real, cool, and solid lies before you; something as unromantic as Monday morning, when all who work wake with the consciousness that they must rise and betake themselves thereto. It is not positively affirmed that you shall not have a taste of the exciting, perhaps towards the middle and close of the meal, but it is resolved that the first dish set upon the table shall be one that a Catholic—ay, even an Anglo-Catholic—might eat on Good Friday in Passion Week; it shall be cold lentils and vinegar without oil; it shall be unleavened bread with bitter herbs and no roast lamb. [Charlotte Brontë, *Shirley* (1849)]

The Rev. Amos Barton, whose sad fortunes I have undertaken to relate, was, you perceive, in no respect an ideal or exceptional character, and perhaps I am doing a bold thing to bespeak your sympathy on behalf of a man who was so very far from remarkable,—a man whose virtues were not heroic, and who had no undetected crime within his breast; who had not the slightest mystery hanging about him, but was palpably and unmistakably commonplace; who was not even in love, but had that complaint favourably many years ago. "An utterly uninteresting character!" I think I hear a lady reader exclaim—Mrs. Farthingale, for example, who prefers the ideal in fiction; to whom tragedy means ermine tippets, adultery, and murder; and comedy, the adventures of some personage who is quite a "character." . . .

Depend upon it, you would gain unspeakably if you would learn with me to see some of the poetry and the pathos, the tragedy and the comedy, lying in the experience of a human soul that looks out through dull, grey eyes, and that speaks in a voice of quite ordinary tones. [George Eliot, "The Sad Fortunes of the Rev. Amos Barton," *Scenes of Clerical Life* (1857)]

The family resemblances are remarkable, and these quotations are un-questionably characteristic of a tone and attitude that dominated in English fiction for the first fifty or sixty years of the nineteenth century. They are kin, for example, to the parodic opening of *Northanger Abbey*, in which Catherine Morland is defined by virtue of her qualities in-appropriate to heroines; to Dickens's explanation of the naturalness of melodrama in *Oliver Twist* (chapter 17); to the mock-heroic language of some passages in *Barchester Towers*, and to Trollope's explanation there of why he abjures surprises in fiction, and has difficulties with happy endings; to the strategy of Mrs. Gaskell in *Mary Barton* of attempting to force upon the reader a recognition of the "hidden romances" in "the lot of those who daily pass you by in the street."[27]

Although such passages had become commonplace by the time of George Eliot, each writer, however sophisticated, writes as though the enterprise of the ordinary in fiction were new and difficult, and that in 1860 as well as 1804, the audience had to be warned and cajoled about it. Yet there are differences in the rhetorical strategies, suggesting that the stakes were getting higher. What light satire remains in the passage by George Eliot (compare Mrs. Farthingale with Thackeray's Mr. Jones) moves into a rhetoric of almost romantic intensity, so that the style insists on the seriousness which, in Austen, Scott, even Thackeray, is one of the immediate objects of derision. Even the awkward satirical thrust of the passage from *Shirley* is intense enough to belie the Thack-erayan gestures in the metaphors of food. Thematically, that is to say, these passages all conventionally assert that fiction should shift its focus from the extreme to the ordinary, and that to do so is morally instruc-tive; rhetorically, they imply that to do so is also to violate the dominant conventions of fiction (implicitly absurd, immoral, or both), but in fact to make fiction more, not less, intense, and to give back with greater authenticity by Wordsworthian strategies the very romantic powers taken away in the rejection of conventions.

The refusal of major realists to acknowledge the conventionality of these strategies has partly to do with the nature of much popular fiction of the time, but more important, the refusal was essential to the con-vention itself. It supported the special authenticity the realist novel claimed by emphasizing its primary allegiance to experience over art. But there is no need to think the emphasis disingenuous. In adopting the technique of the direct address to the audience in order to justify the treatment of ordinary experience, all these writers participate in a cultural project—moral, empirical, and self-conscious—that appears conventional only in retrospect.

The epistemology that lay behind realism was empiricist, with its tendency to value immediate experience over continuities or systems of order, and it was obviously related to the developments in empirical science as they ran through the century. These developments did not, of course, validate either the discontinuities empiricism would seem to imply, or the minimizing of imagination and intuition. Yet in requiring the validation of imagination in the visible world, recognizable to the audience that figures so prominently in these passages, realism posits a tension between imagination (with the faculty of reason, as well) and reality. Values are reversed in that the realistic method proceeds to what is not visible—the principles of order and meaning—through the visible; the *a priori* now requires validation.

But the process does not imply a mere literalism of reportage, or "copyism." The implication of each of these passages, most powerfully developed by George Eliot, is that the aim of the apparently dull record of the humdrum is to discover "the poetry and the pathos, the tragedy and the comedy." The writers all share a faith that the realist's exploration will reveal a comprehensible world. George Eliot requires that her narrative, attaining to tragedy, convey the impression of an empirically shareable experience. Its relation to reality may be mediated by consciousness, but it is authenticated by the appeal of consciousness to the shared consciousness of the community of readers. For the realistic method, it is a matter of balance.[28]

One of the dominant theories about nineteenth-century English realism has pointed misleadingly to a reconciliation of these difficulties. If the reality observed is coherent and meaningful, so the theory runs, so too will be its represented form. Thus, the important distinction between realism of correspondence and realism of coherence, invented (used even by the Victorians) to cope with the difference between the text and its subject, between reality and art's appearance of reality, is lost. Ioan Williams, arguing the standard case, for example, says that "there is no doubt that the mid-Victorian novel rested on a massive confidence as to what the nature of Reality actually was," and that "the most fundamental common element in the work of the mid-Victorian novelist . . . is probably the idea that human life, whatever the particular conditions, may ultimately be seen as unified and coherent."[29] Generally, the quotations confirm this view: they do, after all, conclude with "tragedy and comedy," and the apparent confidence with which they imply the value of the trivial suggests an underlying organicism, characteristic of Victorian thought.

But reflection suggests that what is most striking in these passages is not their unquestioning confidence, but their self-consciousness about the difficulties of the arguments in favor of common sense. They are engaged in a battle parallel to that familiar one, most allegorically handled in *Hard Times*, between life, with all its emotion and vitality, and utilitarianism, with all its analytic calculation. The organic and the mechanical are opposed forces in Victorian fiction, and the deadliness of the struggle is most apparent in post-Darwinian thought. the faith was that science would reveal the organic, the secularist's last hope for meaning and the validation of morality; the fear was that it would yield only the mechanical. The distinction made by G. H. Lewes can make clear how important the struggle was if realism was to retain any contact with the values from which it had cut itself off:

> Theoretically taking the Organism to pieces to understand its separate parts, we fall into the error of supposing that Organism is a mere assemblage of organs, like a machine which is put together by juxtaposition of different parts. But this is radically to misunderstand its essential nature and the universal solidarity of its parts. The Organism is not made, not put together, but *evolved*; its parts are not juxtaposed, but differentiated; its organs are groups of minor organisms, all sharing in a common life.[30]

The mechanical reading of the organs is an implicit threat through much of nineteenth-century fiction. Metaphorically, it is foreshadowed by Victor Frankenstein's creation of his monster, and the terrible threat of the nonrational violence built into that machine lurks behind the human ideals that give meaning to the lives of fiction's protagonists, as Pip's ambitions are the reverse image of murderous, Orlick-like desires. For Lewes, the emphasis on organism is part of an argument that leads to metaphysics through science, necessary because common perception and common sense fail to yield the truth visible under the microscope.

None of the novelists uses a microscope, of course, although George Eliot is driven to the analogy herself; but the passages I have quoted all suggest an uneasiness about what unaided vision can yield. The self-consciousness manifests itself in the self-denigrating language with which they refer to the reality they are to describe: the production of "a plodding man of business," "trivial, twaddling, and ultra-sentimental," like "cold lentils and vinegar," or "an utterly uninteresting character."

We need to shift the balance in our appraisal of realism. It was not a solidly self-satisfied vision based in a misguided objectivity and faith in representation, but a highly self-conscious attempt to explore or create a new reality. Its massive self-confidence implied a radical doubt, its strategies of truth telling, a profound self-consciousness. In a culture whose experience included the Romantic poets and the philosophical radicals; Carlyle and Newman attempting to define their faiths; Charles Lyell telling it that the world reveals "no vestige of a beginning, no prospect of an end"; the Higher Criticism of the Bible from Germany; Hume, Kant, Goethe, Comte, and Spencer, with their varying systems or antisystems; non-Euclidean geometry and a new anthropology made possible by a morally dubious imperialism; John Stuart Mill urging liberty and women's equality; Darwin, Huxley, and the agnostics; Tennyson struggling to reimagine faith; Browning, Arnold, Swinburne, Pater—in such a culture it is more than a little difficult to imagine a serious literary mode based on a "massive confidence as to what the nature of Reality actually was." In *Dombey and Son* the railroad produces an "earthquake" and opens up new realities to the insular Dombey (but more important, to his insular audience). In *The French Revolution* Carlyle describes a world in constant process, always burning, and warns of the possible consummation for English society. And Mrs. Gaskell—in *Mary Barton* and *North and South*—maneuvers carefully against what she feared correctly to be a growing breach between the classes.

The confident moralism of which the great Victorian writers are frequently accused turns out almost invariably to be an attempt to rediscover moral order after their primary energies have been devoted to disrupting conventions of moral judgment. The tradition reflected in the passages I have quoted belongs with Wordsworth's attempt to "choose incidents and situations from common life, and . . . to throw over them a certain coloring of the imagination," and with Carlyle's attempt to persuade us to see every drawing room as the crossroads of the infinite. Nineteenth-century realism, far from apologizing for what is, deliberately subverts judgments based on dogma, convention, or limited perception and imagination. Mr. Podsnap is the enemy not only of Dickens, but of all the Victorian novelists. For Stephen Blackpool and Mr. Tulliver it's a "puzzle" or a "muddle." What seems clear becomes cloudy as we see more and from different perspectives. Even as they articulate the social codes, these novels complicate them, engaging our sympathy with lost women, tyrannical husbands, murderers, revolutionaries, moral weaklings, rebellious girls, spendthrifts, and dilettantes. When George Eliot dismisses the "men of maxims," she only articulates what is implicit in the realistic impulse, and when by shifting perspectives she reimagines the nature and worth of her characters, she only acts out formally what Thackeray constantly talked about and what she had already discovered in Scott's novels, as they treated sympathetically both sides of every historical conflict.

The disruptions of moral judgment, of aesthetic patterning, of common sense perceptions have a serious import that we can too easily solemnize. After all, despite the disappearance of God, the potential disappearance of meaning, the mysteries and disruptions, the primary form in which most nineteenth-century English realism manifests itself is comedy. Even these highly moral passages, urging upon us what seems an ascetic renunciation of the glamorous, are partly comic performances. They seem to take pleasure in the details they invoke from outside the patterning conventions of romance. And the great realistic fictions are exuberant with details, even when they are melancholy thematically. The alienation implied by description is partially compensated for by the sheer pleasure of being able to *see*, as though for the first time, the clutter of furniture, the cut of clothing, the mutton chop and the mug of hot rum, the flushed cheeks of Mr. Jones, and the dull grey eyes of Amos Barton. This very vitality of detail is part of the realist's gestures at life, for they will not succumb to the conventions of patterning. James Kincaid finds in Trollope, for example, "a sense that genuine life is to be found only outside all pattern."[31] It is just possible that—as I shall argue in my discussion of Thackeray—the realist's self-conscious rejection of form represents a viable alternative to the Jamesian self-conscious restriction and purification of form. There is a violence implied in the conventions of narrative that wrests resolution from the muddle of experience. If nineteenth-century realism normally succumbs to these wishful thrusts, it also typically indulges in the satisfaction of anticlimactic wisdom, pretending that life extends beyond its pages, that life is only partially reflected in the novel's multitudinous disregard. There is a pleasure in knowing life, and a pleasure in the power to seduce an audience into believing it has seen life too.

As we explore even the most conservative of the classic novels of the nineteenth century, we find continuing experiments with forms, styles, modes of valuing. Those experiments are not aberrations from some realistic norm, but intrinsic to its nature. Resisting forms, it explores reality to find them; denying excess, it deserts the commonplace self-consciously asserted as its subject. Positing the reality of an external world, it self-consciously examines its own fictionality. Even as we watch the apparently confident assimilation of reality to comic patterns, we find fissures, and merely "literary" conventions required to imply the reality of those patterns. The realistic novel persistently drives itself to question not only the nature of artificially imposed social relations, but the nature of nature, and the nature of the novel.

Realism exists as a process,[32] responsive to the changing nature of reality as the culture understood it, and evoking with each question another question to be questioned, each threatening to destroy that quest beyond words, against literature, that is its most distinguishing mark. What consistency there may be in the fate of realism is no greater than that we can find among the implications of these passages: pre-occupation with the nature of their own materials; willingness to violate narrative conventions to call attention to themselves; implicit compari-son between the falsities and pleasures of literature and the truths and rigors of life; concern with audience and the moral consequences of the activities of reading and writing; the moral urgency of seeing with disenchanted clarity and valuing the ordinary as the touchstone of human experience. The impelling energy in the quest for the world beyond words is that the world be there, and that it be meaningful and good; the persistent fear is that it is merely monstrous and mechanical, beyond the control of human meaning. Realism risks that reality and its powers of disruption. And while it represses the dreams and desires of the self with the cumulative, formless energies of the ordinary, it seeks also the self's release—sometimes in the very formlessness of the ordi-nary, sometimes in the increasingly complicated elaborations of the conventions and forms of the novel (which need, as Frank Kermode has noted, to become more difficult and less fairy-talish in order to be convincingly satisfying).[33] In the integrity of its explorations, realism increasingly imagined the limits of its power to reinform, the mon-strous possibility of the unnameable, the likelihood that the monstrous lurked in its very desire to see and to make the world good.

In the chapters that follow I shall be elaborating, with reference to many important texts of the century, the ideas about realism I have been suggesting here. The variousness of the manifestations of realism make anything short of a detailed study of all the novels a distortion, yet I think certain patterns are discernible. And although it would be artifi-cial to propose a single coherent history in which the contradictions implicit in realism work themselves out and eventually destroy it, I do believe that a roughly chronological pattern can be offered plausi-bly. I have tried, in any case, to honor the integrity of these rich and complex texts, and while distrusting realism, to find my theory—like a good realist, I suppose—in the details of the art it purports to account for.

2

The Pattern

Frankenstein *and Austen to Conrad*

*B*y God, I hope I shal you telle a thing
That shal by reson been at your liking;
For though myself be a ful vicious man,
A moral tale yit I you can telle.

Chaucer's Pardoner

Beginnings and endings, we have been hearing, are arbitrary, and chronology falsely presumes meaningful traditions and influences. This study borrows from the shape of chronology, primarily because I am more concerned with the way writers in the realist tradition imagined their relation to each other, to the form of the novel, and to their culture's imagination of knowledge, than I am with the antichronological implications of the fulfilled realist intention. Realism leads away from its originating structures, not to closure, but to indeterminacy, not to clarified relation between idea and thing, but to their exclusiveness. To provide a framework for the studies that follow, I offer here something of a narrative, a tale starting with Mary Shelley's *Frankenstein,* which provides both a pattern and a metaphor for the very different realist literature that followed, and taking as its chronological extremes Jane Austen and Joseph Conrad, figures representative of the polarities of the realist impulse. With the figure of some monster emergent from the most stable as from the most volatile realist texts, we find every writer before Conrad touching on the skeptical possibilities he dramatized, every one after Austen seeking the controlling form she imagined in the communal recognition of the ordinary. The critical narrative I imagine here is therefore presented as a fiction whose closure emphasizes the distance between it and the truth it seeks, metonymically, to shadow forth.

23

I

This nameless mode of naming the unnameable is rather good.

Mary Shelley

Frankenstein and his monster will turn up frequently in the chapters that follow because in their curious relationship they enact much that is central to the traditions of realistic narrative, but much that is not quite reducible to discursive prose. Sandra Gilbert and Susan Gubar identify as a characteristic of women's literature the projection of "what seems to be the energy of their own despair into passionate, even melodramatic characters who act out the subversive impulses every woman feels when she contemplates the 'deep-rooted evils of patriarchy.'"[1] *Frankenstein*, of course, provides a perfect model for this; but as I have tried to suggest elsewhere in an extensive analysis of the novel,[2] it provides a model for the whole tradition of realism that I have been identifying. It is true that "even the most apparently conservative and decorous women writers" create such figures. But it is no accident that conservative male writers within the tradition of nineteenth-century realism do so as well. For realism embodies in its very texture the controlling force of the established order of society and history; it is thus a mode particularly available to women writers, sensitive to such force, as Gilbert and Gubar show them to be. It is also, however a mode appropriate to any writers who share women's ambivalence about established authority—needing the very structures that are felt to be oppressive and narrow. Such ambivalence is characteristic of almost every important Victorian writer.

Nineteenth-century realistic fiction tends to be concerned with the possibility of accommodation to established power, and yet, given its inevitable interest in character, it explores with at least equal intensity the possibility of resistance as well. The "madwoman in the attic," to use Gilbert and Gubar's phrase, has her male counterpart; the domesticated man—Pip, Pendennis, or Edward Waverley—has his dangerously rebellious double. Female resistence to the patriarch is echoed in a general Victorian resistance to the tyranny of society, of convention, of the majority.

Mary Shelley's characters, the monster and his creator, reflect the culture's ambivalence about itself, the realist's difficulty with the narrative conventions of realism. As creator, Frankenstein attempts to reach beyond the limits of human possibility, as the realists reached beyond words, into reality. Yet when he finds what his imagination has brought forth, he recoils from it as monstrous, and denies kinship. Thus denied, the monster in effect destroys all that belongs to a recognizably domestic world: the child, the caring friend, the affectionate servant, the all-providing father (whose death he only indirectly causes) and, most important, the bride on her wedding night. The consummation of community, the confirmation of a justly ordered world, the affirmation of consonance between word and action, the marriage turns out to be a murder. All the potential horrors of domestic realism, so carefully averted in the comic tradition, are anticipated here.

The attempt to repress and then destroy the monster leads Frankenstein and his book into a landscape beyond the limits of the domestic realism toward which they had turned for succor. Such landscapes provide the spaces, distant from the centers of realistic drama, in which illicit and uncivilized extremes are acted out. The assumption of most nineteenth-century literature, from Scott forward, is that civilization was indeed advancing. The Macaulayan reading of history implied that savagery had been banished from the centers of Western experience. But in *Frankenstein*, Alps and Arctic wastes are the norm. They are the landscape of isolation from community, Victor's first obsessive choice, and they are the icons of his refusal to bring the monster in from the cold to the communal warmth of the hearth. In the cold, monster and creator enact the futility of their desires in what is almost a ritual and self-destructive parody of the Keatsian quest for the elusive fair maiden. Only Captain Walton returns, and only because he surrenders his Frankensteinian ambition. In its place, he finds an ear for the narrative in his sister, the civilized Mrs. Saville.[3] Telling the story is made possible by the refusal to live it, and is a means to rejoin the community. His position is rather like Mary Shelley's, for she surrenders fully to her imagination, but in the writing she keeps the distance that might save her from it and deny it.

The parabolic neatness of this way of telling the story (certainly a distortion of the novel's instability and ambiguities) suggests why, for the past one hundred sixty years, it has provided metaphors for writers. The monster becomes those sexual, revolutionary, deterministic, or psychic energies that novelists and intellectuals confront even as they try to avert them. It is both rational and irrational, victim and victimizer, innocent and evil. As in the culture at large, Frankenstein and his monster keep turning up in literature—in the face of the uneducated mob in *Mary Barton*, in Magwitch's relation to Pip, his created gentleman, in the laboratories where Ursula Brangwen studies. The power of the myth of *Frankenstein* transcends the limit of the particular narrative because it is, in a way, an antimyth that has embodied in all its ambiguities the modern imagination of the potentialities and the limits of modern consciousness.

Although it takes the shape of traditional myths of the overreacher,

Frankenstein reverses them in ways that suggest its modernity and its kinship to the realistic impulse.[4] In intruding secular science into a traditional gothic framework that normally depends on supernatural machinery, Mary Shelley changes the source of the horror and mystery, and increases their credibility.[5] They come not from evil spirits beyond the visible world, but through secular knowledge. The apparent ideal in *Frankenstein* is the recognizable domesticity that Victor Frankenstein betrays, but the novel lives far beyond the limits of this ideal. It becomes a psychomachia of the extremes of human consciousness aspiring to transcend the limits of thought and language by touching a new reality and to assert the compatibility of that reality with poetic, moral, and religious ideals.

Moreover, *Frankenstein's* preoccupation with "creation"—though connected with literary myths and Mary Shelley's own concern with birth[6]—is more than accidentally related to the problems and responsibilities of writing itself. Mary Shelley obviously belongs in the Romantic tradition of concern about the nature of creativity, about the relation of mind to nature, of mind to itself, and about the possibility that language—particularly poetic language—might live actively in the real world. Belonging to a literature of extremes, *Frankenstein* is nevertheless an act of rebellion against those extremes. It dramatizes, whatever its intentions, the deadliness of Shelley, her husband's, idealizing and rebellion, the consequences of Godwin, her father's, personal tyranny and his antithetic radicalism, the perversion in myths of male creativity and female dependence. In this respect, it is analogous to realism's parodic reaction to romance and to fantasies of extreme power. Like the protagonists to be disenchanted in later novels, Walton, Frankenstein, and the monster all find some radical disparity between what they read and what they experience. Each character must face the consequences of that disparity and come to terms with the limits of dream, yet the text itself is—like much realism—paradoxically Promethean. The realist novel rejects earlier fantasies of power for the limits of the probable, hoping to touch the real.

The duality is *in* the book's drama: Victor, having failed in his quest, never surrenders the dream. He is one of the first in a long tradition of fictional overreachers, of characters who seem to act out the myth of Faust in modern dress, and who transport it from the world of mystery and miracle to the commonplace. He is destroyed not by metaphysical agency—as God expelled Adam from Eden or Mephistopheles collected his share of the bargain (though echoes of these events are everywhere)—but by his own nature and the consequences of living in or rejecting human community. Frankenstein is the indirect father of lesser, more humanly recognizable figures, like Becky Sharp or Pip or

Lydgate, who reject the conventional limits imposed upon them by
society and who are punished, more or less, for their troubles. *Frankenstein* embodies one of the central myths of realistic fiction in the
nineteenth century, even in the contrast between its sensational style
and its apparently explicit moral implications: a simultaneous awe and
reverence toward greatness of ambition, and fear and distrust of those
who act on it. Such ambivalence is almost always disguised in realistic
fiction, where the manner itself seems to reject the possibility of greatness and the explicit subject is frequently the evil of aspiring to it; in
gothic fiction the energies to be suppressed by the realist ideal, by the
model of Flemish painting, by worldly-wise compromise with the possible, are released. Gothic fiction, as Lowry Nelson has observed, "by
its insistence on singularity and exotic setting . . . seems to have freed
the minds of readers from direct involvement of their superegos and
allowed them to pursue daydreams and wish fulfillment in regions
where inhibitions and guilt could be suspended."[7] The mythology of
virtue rewarded, central to English realism, is put to question in the
gothic landscape where more powerful structures than social convention give shape to wish; and, as Nelson suggests, reader and writer
alike were freed to pursue the possibilities of their own potential evil.

It is striking how difficult it is to locate in realistic fiction any positive
and active evil. The central realist mythology is spelled out in characters
like George Eliot's Tito Melema, whose wickedness is merely a gradual
sliding into the consequences of a natural egoism. In gothic fiction, but
more particularly in *Frankenstein,* as Christopher Small argues,[8] evil is
both positively present and largely inexplicable. Although ostensibly
based on the ideas of Godwin's rationalist ethics which see evil as a
consequence of maltreatment or injustice, Frankenstein's story provides
no such comfortable explanation for his own evil. Where did his decision to create the monster come from? Mere chance. Evil is a deadly and
fascinating mystery whose source is in men's minds, an inexplicable
but inescapable aspect of human goodness.

The transposition of the creator from God to man, the secularization
of the means of creation from miracle into science, entail a transposition
of the standard of moral judgment from the external world which ought
to be reflecting a divine order, to the mind which is somehow forced to
establish its own terms. Those terms do not fit the form of discursive or
narrative explanation. *Frankenstein* is full of abrupt discontinuities and
short-circuiting. The monster comes to life although Victor finds an
important excuse not to reveal the fairly simple secret of life that he
discovers, and it acts in the gaps of Victor's consciousness, when he is
away, or feverishly and helplessly ill, or searching in the wrong place.
Frankenstein as a text exercises its appeal in part because it fails to

explain so much. The narrative has a plausibility of images, and the images themselves, not really reflective of a world divinely ordered and intelligible or susceptible to the mind, lend themselves to proliferating and unrestricted interpretations, and can be assimilated to almost any powerful mythology—especially the Freudian. But the horror of the narrative is that, like the monster, it is ultimately uncontrollable. The mind creates life, projects the landscape, but cannot control the imagined world. The landscape of the self and its texts is more frightening and dangerous than the landscape of Milton's Hell—which implies a heaven.

Literally, of course, the narrative encompasses a large part of the Northern hemisphere, and even some of the Near East. But as it wanders across the Alps, to the northern islands of Scotland, to the frozen wastes of the Arctic, *Frankenstein* has something claustrophobic about it. The recurrence of images of ice and cold, the recurrence of patterns of family relations, the recurrence of the preoccupation with isolation and misunderstanding (Justine even admits to a crime she did not commit in order to regain a lost trust, and the gesture is, of course, suicidal): all of these give to the novel a circular and self-enclosed structure, confirmed both by the framing devices and by the ultimate reversal of pursuit. Far more, then, than a conventional realistic novel with thematic restatements, *Frankenstein* invites metaphorical reading by inviting us first to see the epic breadth as a metaphor for a narrower scope—the landscape of a single mind. In *Frankenstein*, ironically, we can see obvious intimations of later writers' attempts to throw all the action "inside." Frankenstein's very creative gesture, a thrust into a world beyond the self, is in part a projection of self upon the world. The novel, in a sense, is about the inevitability of solipsism, the alienation of the self from the world, and the necessity and desperation of the quest to rejoin it.

Some of this novel's remarkable power resides in the way its exploration of the landscape of the mind becomes a rejection of more traditional, Miltonic, ways of writing the myth, and in its preoccupation with literature it threatens to become as antiliterary as realism itself: it finds no satisfying conventions of order, power, or meaning. The monster becomes the disruption that denies any meaning to the natural except what the mind futilely thrusts upon it in the hopeless attempt to make it acquiesce in its dreams of power. The horror of the monster is, of course, its capacity for violence that results from its estrangement from both nature and social reality. That horror is most forcefully and indirectly suggested by the fact that it has no name. Violence erupts where the language fails to control by making meaning. The monster is merely a monster, "a warning," or a showing forth.

The novel's elaborate clarity of structure, Walton's tale enfolding Frankenstein's, which in turn enfolds the monster's, does not reflect a firm moral ordering, but a continuing complicating diminishment of nonverbal reality as it recedes into the distance. The language keeps reinterpreting itself, reaching for that community of understanding that allows us to posit a truth. But satisfaction does not come for any of the three protagonists. Walton would seem the ultimate judge of the experience, as the outsider, yet he explicitly accepts Frankenstein's judgment of it, and largely exculpates him by sharing his ambivalences and by rejecting his injunction to destroy the monster. The monster's own defense and explanation, lodged in the center of the story, are, however, far more convincing. This madwoman in the attic, or monster in the Alps, makes his case very sanely. Frankenstein is forced to confess his failure of responsibility to the creature, and Walton is almost persuaded, deterred only by the nonverbal fact of the monster's hideousness. In the end, however, we are left not with a judgment but with Walton's strangely uncolored report of the monster's last speech and last action. If anyone, the nameless monster has the last word; and that word expresses a longing for self-immolation and the ultimate peace in extinction: an event not narrated. Metaphorically, the Promethean spirit is the ambition to imitate reality, to make an equivalent and yet a better one. In creating the monster, Frankenstein tries to name nature and thus control it.

But he can neither name nor control. He fails to accept his creation, and this failure reflects perfectly the alienation entailed in committing himself to his imitation of nature. His first response to the monster on seeing its hideous but quite touching filial grin is to flee: "He held up the curtain of the bed; and his eyes, if eyes they may be called, were fixed on me. His jaws opened, and he muttered some inarticulate sound, while a grin wrinkled his cheeks. He might have spoken, but I did not hear; one hand was stretched out, seemingly to detain me, but I escaped, and rushed down stairs."[9] The mind here retreats from consciousness of its own ineptitude, or from recognition of its anomalous position in nature. Like a text freed from the intentions of its author, the monster forces that author to take responsibility for him.

Composed as he is of dead bodies (and conventions), the monster is a parody of life and of forms of heroic narrative, but he is also, ironically, the embodiment of the ideal: monster *and* angel. His relation to the world is the reverse of (although it becomes the same as) that of his creator. In his obsession, Frankenstein has cut himself off from the family in which he began. In his reaction to that obsession, he cuts himself off from his creation. the monster begins without family or community and seeks what Frankenstein surrendered in creating him.

Ironically, the quest for the ideal entails the loss of the saving compromises of the human condition. Implicitly, only God should undertake the responsibility of creation: "Oh! no mortal could support the
horror of that countenance" (p. 58). Such is the traditional significance
of the creation/rebellion myth. But the true sin (and the word becomes
more difficult to use, the more we explore the novel) is not the Promethean theft of fire from Heaven, but the sin against self and community. It is the sin of attempting to realize the ideal; the ideal is the
monstrous. This incarnate ideal dies seeking love, and his loving
creator dies hating.

Nevertheless, aside from having these cosmic significances, the monster is also kin to the oppressed women and children of Victorian fiction: like Oliver Twist, Pip, Florence Dombey, and Little Nell, like Jane
Eyre and Lucy Snowe, like Daniel Deronda, Henry Esmond, and Jude
Fawley, the monster is an orphan, rejected by his father, uncertain of
who he is or where he belongs. Naive, well-intentioned, in danger of
being led astray, he is Teufelsdröckh left in a basket, the Wordsworthian child. Where in Frankenstein's story there seems no rational explanation for the entrance of evil into the world, in the monster's the
explanation is clear. The monster assumes that the world makes sense
somewhere beyond the limits of his knowledge, so that education
seems the one thing needful. His story implies the primacy of responsibility to family and community, and his arguments are keenly
rational, Godwinian polemics, in almost every case superior to Frankenstein's, which are ruled by vague emotions. "Yet you, my creator,
detest and spurn me," cries the monster, "to whom thou art bound by
ties only dissoluble by the annihilation of one of us. You purpose to kill
me. How dare you sport thus with life?" (p. 99). Amid all the extraordinary reversals in this novel, perhaps the most startling is the way
the monster becomes, in the dramatized action, the intellectual and
moral superior of his creator. He is the aspiration for meaning in reality,
thwarted by the injustice experience teaches; he is thus kin to the
dreamers of Victorian dreams who are doomed to disenchantment: he is
another anomaly, the true image of their perceived deviance into impossible romantic dreams. The audacity of a murderer accusing his
creator of "sporting with life"!

"Make me happy, and I shall again be virtuous," he pleads (p. 100).
The point is a political one, and much of the monster's experience is
used as an exemplar of the Godwinian view that evil enters the spirit as
a result of the injustice of others. Man is born naturally good, and there
is every evidence that the monster's heart is in the right place (after all,
it was put there by Frankenstein). The monster represents a kind of
Dickensian reading (almost Carlylean, but that Carlyle could not believe

in man's natural goodness) of the French Revolution. Abused, abandoned, maltreated, deprived, he turns, unlike good Victorian children, in vengeance on his master and his master's world.

But none of the characters comfortable in domestic harmony can believe that the world is governed unjustly until the monster strikes. Such blindness makes it evident that domesticity is a deliberately built defense against the disruptive norm of disaster. This is true even for the monster, who enjoys domestic bliss only by peering in the De Laceys' window. When Elizabeth weeps for Justine before the hanging, she is comforted by Frankenstein's father, who says, "If she is, as you believe, innocent, rely on the justice of our law" (p. 81). But in realistic fiction, experience brings knowledge and disenchantment, and one of the novel's themes is an anti-Miltonic version of the danger of knowledge. Disenchantment, a recognition of one's own limits, of the injustice pervasive in society, and of the power of society over one's own ambitions, here is afforded no divine relief. While the characteristic realistic protagonist ends in some sort of compromise, usually eased by marriage to an attractive counterpart, *Frankenstein,* working in a different mode, does not allow secular wisdom and moderation. It deals with the motif of knowledge and innocence and disenchantment on a scale far larger than that of the conventional *Bildungsroman.* Frankenstein's quest for knowledge can be seen as a dramatic metaphor for the universal ambition that leads to lost innocence. It is not merely Frankenstein in this novel who becomes disenchanted: each major character learns something of the nature of his own illusions. As the reality of death (which is really the product of Frankenstein's knowledge) enters the almost idyllic household of Frankenstein's family, the romance of domestic harmony gives way to a deep gloom. What happens to Frankenstein in his pursuit of knowledge happens, inescapably, to everyone no matter how apparently safe or good.

Frankenstein points the Faustian moral to Walton: "Learn from me, if not by my precepts, at least by my example, how dangerous is the acquirement of knowledge, and how much happier that man is who believes his native town to be the world, than he who aspires to become greater than his nature will allow" (p. 53). But this moral—particularly appropriate to the realistic novel—is argued very ambivalently. Even the monster repeats the argument (as he must, being Frankenstein's alter ego): "Increase of knowledge only discovered to me more clearly what a wretched outcast I was" (p. 131). As his knowledge grows, he cries out: "Oh, that I had for ever remained in my native wood, nor known nor felt beyond the sensation of hunger, thirst, and heat!" (p. 120). Yet Mary Shelley knows, as the monster learned, that there is no returning to innocence; the rhetoric implies that the innocence is a lie, and that the disaster that follows its loss is as inevitable as the loss itself. "Of what a strange nature is knowledge! It clings to the mind, when it has once seized on it, like a lichen on the rock. I wished sometimes to shake off all thought and feeling; but I learned that there was but one means to overcome the sensation of pain, and that was death" (p. 120). The monster knows that only silence ends the disparity between word and life. Frankenstein, however, cannot give up the quest or insist unambiguously on the moral of his story. His last speech is a masterpiece of doubt: "Farewell, Walton!" he says. "Seek happiness in tranquillity, and avoid ambition, even if it be only the apparently innocent one of distinguishing yourself in science and discoveries. Yet why do I say this? I have myself been blasted in these hopes, yet another may succeed" (pp. 217–18). Death is the only resolution, and yet it resolves nothing since knowledge and innocence are continuing aspects of human experience. The tension worked out in *Frankenstein* between ambition and natural harmony, as between creator and creature, mind and reality, is not resolved.

This tension is central to realism which, in its parodic and ironic modes, seems sometimes to lend its conventions to the making of an immense cautionary fable, but just as often dramatically belies the fable. Note Frankenstein's cool abstract language and logical balancing of sentences:

> During these last days I have been occupied in examining my past conduct; nor do I find it blameable. In a fit of enthusiastic madness I created a rational creature, and was bound towards him, to assure, as far as was in my power, his happiness and well-being. This was my duty; but there was another still paramount to that. My duties towards the beings of my own species had greater claims to my attention, because they included a greater proportion of happiness or misery. [P. 217]

Frankenstein stands here at a kind of Olympian distance from his experience. He manages to achieve the hero's absolution from responsibility (at least for this moment) by accepting an intolerable dualism. The responsibility to the self's largest desires (its enthusiastic madness) is incompatible with the responsibility to family and society. Any moral calculus reveals an irrational world—one incompatible with the self, and hence unjust and incoherent. Against this sort of dualism the realist novel builds its defenses through the structures of compromise: excess and ambition must be excluded; the prose must be less calculating and abstract, deferring to the flexibility and casualness and *un*-ideality of the quotidian. Realism thus becomes capable of opening new, more fluid, and unstable imaginations of experience, finding

more various—if disguised—articulations of desire, while at the same
time establishing that distance between desire and experience, language and object, that allows narrative to serve equally as a retreat from
experience.

Frankenstein enacts an impasse: the horror of going ahead and the
emptiness of return. By providing an image of satisfied desire, it provides a metaphor for the price of heroism. If heroism is personal satisfaction writ large, it is also monstrous. For that desire turns out to be an
unnameable projection of self onto the world rejected in order to satisfy
it. In attaining the desire one loses it, for it destroys the possibility of contact with another and thus ends by destroying the self.
Alternatively, the refusal to act out the desire is a refusal to test the
limits of the self. Walton at the end is trapped within the prison of social
limits.

This leads to one final point about Frankenstein as a hero, and as a
type of the realist hero. His unattractiveness to the reader follows from
three qualities. The first is precisely his obsession with great action. As
he is obsessed he is also, necessarily, cruel. Like the author of any
narrative, he must exclude, shape, turn secondary characters into
waste. He turns away from his responsibilities; it is with a new sense of
these responsibilities that he dies. The second is that he is really unequal to his own ambitions. He has the technical power to create life,
but he has not the moral power to cope with his technique. In this
respect, he is rather like Dostoyevsky's Raskolnikov although he is
treated without the psychological intimacy that makes us participate in
Raskolnikov's weaknesses. But the third is more central to my immediate concern here. It is the nature of his behavior when he undergoes one of his regular spasms of desire to return to the virtues of
domesticity, "the amiableness of domestic affection." On these occasions, Frankenstein is the passive hero.

If ambition is evil, then, one might think, the absence of ambition is
virtue. And it is one of the curious facts about the most virtuous heroes
and heroines of nineteenth-century English realist fiction that they are
inefficacious, inactive people. Their fullest energies are expended only
(if at all) in response to external threat, in the preservation of familial
and communal ties. Like Dorothea Brooke and Daniel Deronda, they are
somehow incapable of imagining a satisfying action, a way of life which
will allow them seriously to act at all. Alexander Welsh has studied in
detail the nature of Scott's strangely passive hero, and his analysis of
the reasons for that passivity are to the point in considering Frankenstein's actions. For one thing, Scott's characters and his novels are imprisoned, like Walton, by an ideal of prudence, and not a calculating
prudence: "A prudent hero who cannot be deliberately prudent can

have no active role. He can do no deeds of violence; nor can he survive by cunning. He is wholly at the mercy of the forces that surround him, and thus acted upon rather than acting."[10] We recognize something of this both in Frankenstein's commitment to natural feeling (which excludes calculation until the deathbed) and in his persistent blaming of cruel Fate for his difficulties. But, as Welsh points out, "the passive hero only partially admits of a rational explanation."[11] The passive hero, he says, is not neutral, but committed to the ideals—the prudence and superiority—of civilized society. He becomes an observer, then, "committed to the civil state, and observes the uncivil."[12] The application of all this to Frankenstein is striking. As an ambitious hero, he wants to improve things, and in much of the novel, as I have pointed out, the mechanisms of society are regarded as cruel and unjust. But the notion of domestic affections and the needs for communal and family ties run deep. As Frankenstein longs for these, his ambition drops away and he falls into inaction. The whole narrative reveals that Frankenstein, as an active figure, does only two things: he acts obsessively in creating the monster (and it should be noted that even here he insists on his passivity before fate—this provides the moral excuse); and at the end, he acts obsessively (and ineffectually) in pursuing him. The passivity is most painful when he retreats from recognition of the evil he has created and allows Justine to die. But his initial flight from the monster is also a supreme passive act: if you don't see it, it's not there, as Jack Burden says in *All the King's Men*. After he flees from the aborted attempt to create a mate for the monster, he glides into one of the scenes that will become typical of Victorian fiction. He finds himself on a boat which drifts beyond his control in a storm, and he comes ashore at precisely the place where the monster has just killed Clerval. His response is to fall into one of his characteristic illnesses that return him to the helplessness of infancy and to the care of his father and family. In other words, the passivity of this hero is to be explained not only by the ideals of prudence and domestic harmony and natural affection, or by the ideal of the civilized community, but by the irrational need to escape the consequences of adulthood, to retreat to the innocence and helplessness of the womb where the heroic expression of selfhood is denied and replaced by the comfort of dependence and the absorption of love of others. Narratively, it is a retreat from the shaping energies of imagination.

Thus *Frankenstein* provides us with a hero whose being expresses precisely those tensions that will preoccupy later English novelists. Frankenstein enacts not only the role of the realist hero but the alternatives to that role which do much to explain the characteristic shape of realist fiction. The failure of Frankenstein to destroy his knowledge and to retreat to innocence foreshadows, I think, the ultimate self-destruction of realist techniques. Of course, this is a dangerously oversimple generalization, and puts rather a heavy burden on a novel which makes no such claims. But studying *Frankenstein* can help us to understand some of the powerful and inexplicit energies that lie beneath the surface of realist fiction in England and can help explain both the pervasive resistance to and distrust of ambition and energy in its heroes—their strange dulness and inadequacy—and the rebellion against a stifling society, the equally strange and subversive fascination with ambition and evil energies. Who would prefer Amelia Sedley to Becky Sharp, or Little Nell to Quilp, or Daniel Deronda to Grandcourt? The irrational and rebellious are latent in every important English realist novel, and within every hero or heroine there is a Frankenstein—or his monster—waiting to get out. The hero carries the narrative's burden of creation.

II

The delight derived from her pictures arises from our sympathy with ordinary characters, our relish of humour, and our intellectual pleasure in art for art's sake.
But when it is admitted that she never stirs the deeper emotions, that she never fills the soul with a noble aspiration, or brightens it with a fine idea, but, at the utmost, only teaches us charity for the ordinary failings of ordinary people, and sympathy with their goodness, we have admitted an objection which lowers her claims to rank among the great benefactors of the race.

G. H. Lewes, "The Novels of Jane Austen"

Realism got its second full start in the English novel (after Defoe, Richardson, and Fielding) in the work of Jane Austen, and in the historical context of Romantic transformations of experience that reveal the world in a grain of sand. Wordsworth's "little, nameless, unremembered acts" lead eventually to Dorothea Brooke's "unhistoric acts," and to the renewed memories of those who lie in "unvisited tombs." Austen, of course, resisted romantic extravagances of feeling, and did not sentimentalize her miniatures with Carlylean infinitudes; such feelings would have been both disruptive and seductively falsifying in a world dependent on clarity of moral vision. But she assumed the value of her two inches of ivory and her small country villages without Wordsworthian fuss and with an appropriate understanding of the limits of her experience.

In place of the celebration of self in nature, of nature in self, Austen sought primarily to make words conformable to reality, and particularly to the reality of social action. "What is difficult of definition," for Austen's characters and narrative, says Stuart Tave, "is, characteristically, painful."[13] Her art tests Romantic energies against the pragmatic and ordering values of a finely civilized community. These values are undermined by later novelists (while they are only threatened by Austen), but the evaluative force of realism, its critical exploratory definitions of the order in reality are constant in its history. In defining the qualities of Austen's art, early critics were defining the realism whose fate this study is concerned to unravel.

Richard Whately's 1821 essay on Austen (which, along with Scott's on *Emma*, is perhaps the only serious consideration of her until mid-century) serves as a particularly useful definition. It lays out with great clarity the characteristics of what appeared to him to be, and what he calls, following Scott, "a new style of novel." Speaking with the established voice of the *Quarterly Review*, Whately is meticulously *un*-Romantic, judging literature in Aristotelian terms, assuming certain neoclassical values of generality and moral utility appropriate for the archbishop of Dublin. His criticism implies the tension between order and typicality on the one hand and disorder and particularity (of thing and feeling) on the other that marks the drama of Austen's novels. If his terms now seem inadequate, his essay remains an invaluable guide to historical understanding of what, to the sensible contemporary, Austen seemed to be doing, and in what consisted her newness.

Whately intimates from the start a connection between the realistic method and parody. To establish the credentials of the new style, he is required to distinguish it from earlier ones. "Men of taste and sense" can, says Whately, "acknowledge the delights of fiction," for there is a truth in fictions now that was missing in the old. The new fiction grows out of "the exhaustion of the mines from which materials for entertainment had been hitherto extracted"; earlier fictions drew a "false picture of what they profess to imitate."[14] The texture of Jane Austen's novels can be seen as a rebuttal of those false pictures.

As Scott had said in his earlier review, Austen's fiction demonstrated "the art of copying from nature as she really exists in the common walks of life."[15] Whately introduces the analogy, so important in the later realists, with "Flemish painting," a respectable precedent for such copying of "the common walks of life." But there is a Wordsworthian echo here. Although Whately is primarily concerned with truth of representation, he attributes to common life an almost Romantic primacy of value. The argument, not surprisingly, takes Aristotelian shape, but it brings to focus for the first time the relation between particularity and typicality that is so important in the history of realism. Fiction becomes more true than history, but only if it be "perfect in respect of the probability of [the] story," as Austen's novels are.[16]

Whately goes on to distinguish between two disturbing elements, the improbable and the unnatural, both of which must be excluded from the new fiction. The "unnatural" occurs when characters act contrarily to their own natures as well as when supernatural agents are introduced. But the unnatural, says Whately, is less dangerous to a naive audience than the improbable because it is so far from the norm of human experience that nobody could take it as a guide. The improbable occurs when "there is no reason to be assigned why things should not take place as represented, except that the *overbalance of chances* is against it."[17] Even Fielding fails to meet the test of probability. Whately's literalness can be instructive, however, for in attempting to be systematic, he is assuming the centrality of the value of probability in all serious texts. He cannot conceive the possibility that *Tom Jones* is not aspiring to the form of the "new novel" and that, as Robert Alter has argued, Fielding was writing a "self-conscious novel" tied more directly to the problem of writing a novel than to the nature of reality.[18] Nor does Whately consider a more available reading—that *Tom Jones,* like the forms it frequently mocks, is informed by the wish-fulfilling energies of romance. But Whately's focus is directly on the writer's obligation to describe life in accordance with "the existing laws of human affairs."[19]

Whately also evokes the tradition of the realist's preoccupation with audience, which is, like his, a consistently moral preoccupation. The danger of improbability in fiction is not, in his analysis, a literary problem, except in that skill is required to make narratives appear probable. Rather, the danger is that the audience might take the improbable as a guide to life:

> the reader is insensibly led to calculate upon some of those lucky incidents and opportune coincidences of which he has been so much accustomed to read, and which, it is undeniable, *may* take place in real life; and to feel a sort of confidence, that however romantic his conduct may be, and in whatever difficulties it may involve him, all will be sure to come right at last, as is invariably the case with the hero of the novel.[20]

The assumed audience here lacks the intelligence and experience of "men of sense and taste." Consequently, a special responsibility, of a sort we hear in the voices of all the great Victorians, devolves on the novelist of common life. The question is not whether the novelist should instruct, taking the novel as a "guide to life," but how. Although Austen does far less direct talking to her audience than later writers were to do, Whately finds in her art the right sort of speech and concern. She entertains, yet instructs by example as well.

The moral and evaluative commitment is always a part of the realist's contradictory program, and always potentially disruptive. Assuming the possibility of mimesis, Whately himself reveals the massive confidence Ioan Williams attributes to the novelists. But he can do so because the full impact of empiricism and secularity had not touched him. His own method is rationalist, and he assumes an ultimately rational world. "Virtue," he says, "must be represented as producing, at the long run, happiness; and vice, misery; and the accidental events, that in real life interrupt this tendency, are anomalies which, though true individually, are as false generally as the accidental deformities which vary the average outline of the human figure."[21] The novelist need not impose these norms on a narrative, because the norms are the *real* reality, discernible—in an older philosophical tradition of realism—behind the confusions of mere particularities. Strangely, we find that not to record in fiction certain things that do occur in nature is to tell the completer truth.

The reality of untypical particularity will plague realism's progress throughout. Austen's art has little symbolic or allegorical shaping; if she arrives at the kind of typicality Whately thinks he discerns, it is from a thorough understanding of the nature of the experience with which she chooses to deal. Austen's perceptions of social order are informed, that is to say, not by Whately's religious rationalism, but by a rich and mature acceptance of the culture's ideals, ideals that shape her reality as she explores it, even when she finds the ideals missing where she sought them. Particularity in Austen, as almost everywhere in realism, threatens to be disruptive—the "accidental" reality Whately feared. His description of that reality suggests its dangers for him and those who followed:

> when any thing takes place of such a nature as we should call, in a fiction, merely improbable, because there are many chances against it, we call it a lucky or unlucky accident, a singular coincidence, something very extraordinary, odd, curious, &c.; whereas any thing which, in a fiction, would be called unnatural, when it actually occurs, (and such things do occur), is still called unnatural, inexplicable, unaccountable, inconceivable, &c.[22]

The "unnatural, inexplicable, unaccountable, inconceivable" suggests a reality not comfortable to language, which Austen's worlds are constructed to repel or deny. But on the fringes of the most confident realism, even Austen's, is the perception of these monstrous, unnameable possibilities. They threaten the civilized order that the book describes and the narrator's voice implies. Whately is proposing a "new style" of novel that recognizes, with the force of the culture behind him, the moral significance of reality, but he himself misses in

Austen's exuberant good sense the possibility her narratives can suggest that the "unaccountable" is not merely the absurdity of hyperactive sensibility or false feeling, but a continuing possibility and, indeed, the condition for many of the heroines' ultimate successes.

Whately would have accepted Northrop Frye's idea that the requirements of literary form come into conflict with the requirements of plausibility. He is consequently struck by Austen's nearly "faultless fables," which "have all the compactness of plan and unity of action which is generally produced by a sacrifice of probability: yet they have little or nothing that is not probable."[23] Literary form does not, in Austen, seem to fight against plausibility. It is as though, in Whately's view, she has managed to cut through the appearances of the merely singular and aberrant to the truth that lies shapely in the heart of reality.

Yet Whately sensibly notes as one of the primary qualities of Austen's art what we usually take as the realist's dominant stylistic trait, "vivid distinctness of description," "minute fidelity to detail," and "an air of unstudied ease" necessary for the "perfect appearance of reality"[24] In addition, Whately insists that it is possible to be "too scrupulous" in cutting all that has not "some absolute, intrinsic, and independent merit."[25] Without the apparently expendable details, the soul goes out of the work, so that Whately is at once arguing against "anomalies" and "accidental events," and praising Austen for including them.

The latent contradictions are clear. Once the norm of experience shifts from the "common" to the "unaccountable," the "new style" must be shattered. Fidelity of detail becomes the fissure in the realist's program, cracking both the moral significance of experience and the form that makes the significance. The crack in the teacup opens, as Auden has it, "a lane to the land of the dead." Victorian realism, in its continuing moral pursuit of the truth, extends the range of its detail through and beyond the details of domesticity so that—to push the dangerous metaphor—the fissure widens. Compactness of form became difficult in a culture whose empiricist bias required constant trials and errors. Such form awaited another radical transformation in epistemology: the shift of the real from an external, objective, to an internal, subjective, reality. The shape of *The Ambassadors* is the shape of consciousness coming to terms with its own conventions of order.

What Whately leaves out of the experience of realist fiction is finally of larger significance than the surface forms he so well analyzes. One needs a sharper focus on the conventionality of this anticonvention, on the nature of its shaping energies, on its subversive implications; and one needs, for this focus, a way to imagine the continuities and discontinuities that mark its development. As Whately was in no position to argue, although he understands the impelling force of contradiction that helped give rise to Austen's sort of art, realism lives in process and reactions. It responds contrarily to forms and conventions of perception, even to its own evolving ones. And if it begins by parodying different varieties of romance, it does not go long—as witness Thackeray, Scott, Dickens's Mr. Podsnap—without parodying itself. In an analogous, inverse movement, the self-denigrating apologies of Scott and Thackeray transform into George Eliot's claims of tragic significance. What realism may be at any moment depends both on what it has been and on what the culture expects it to be.

Austen, beginning with the "common walks of life," gives us a first heroine in *Northanger Abbey* who is a complex of antiheroic traits. The narrative spins about Catherine Morland's cheerful ordinariness and the absence of the guidance and discipline that would make it possible for her to distinguish the authentic from the merely literary or verbal. The narrative constructs a sensible and civilized alternative to the literature of excess it mocks, while it already implies some of the potential horror of the real that has sanely replaced the horrific fantasies of the gothic. Anne Elliot in *Persuasion* is almost the reverse of Catherine, for Anne is too mature and disciplined to be deluded by the literature of excess. *Persuasion* has little concern with the nature of Anne's reading. She is misled, rather, by the very kind of prudent guidance Catherine needed but never received; maturity and wisdom seem, for a moment at least, to fail, and what is missing is the imaginative power that Catherine so badly misapplies. One could (and should) demonstrate that there are important continuities between the books. *Northanger Abbey*, after all, validates Catherine's genuinely instinctive feeling. But the point is that by *Persuasion* the balance has shifted; prudential reality seems to become a more important danger to the fullest possibilities of life than imagination. As Barbara Hardy puts it, "Up to *Persuasion* [Austen]has been concerned with the dangers of imagination, but *Persuasion* shows us the perceptual and common difficulty of being human"[26] It would not be excessive to suggest that here the initial parodic impulse has turned back on itself.

The particular texts and the large curve of Austen's career make realism's commitment to the "common" seem not quite innocent. The "pleasure" that Whately correctly perceives as a dominant objective of the new style as of the novel in general was only one objective. the particularities and details of the narrative require a continuing reordering and qualifying of moral perspectives, so that if Whately is partly right that the narratives must show virtue and vice properly rewarded, he is also partly wrong in that what constitutes virtue and vice is not easily described or understood. Part of the education of realism is the recognition not of what good and evil are, but of the rigor required to make the discriminations. This is implied in the reversal of perspective between Austen's first novel and her last.

Such reversals are common in realist fiction. The quest for reality is constantly varied, not only as the nature of reality itself changes, but as the frustrated desire to locate it intensifies. As we read a novel like *Emma*, with its marvelously prudential form and its more marvelously mimetic freedom and vividness of detail, it is difficult to resist the heroine whom, Austen feared, none but herself would much like. The comic ending, consistent with early realism's projection of a cultural ideal into the real, is a consequence of realism's small-scale catastrophes. Emma's exuberance turns into cruelty to Miss Bates, and that violation of social responsibility illustrates to her the danger of her power. Yet the texture of the novel almost makes it a celebration and validation of Emma's not quite lawless energies. Indeed, Emma's disenchantment discovers to her the same energy of desire for control she had always exhibited. Unlike later realist protagonists, she does not have to moderate her desires so as to recognize where they have all the time been tending. Joining with Knightley provides her, in all relations except that with Knightley, more power than she would have had as the unmarried Miss Woodhouse. The invariable realist's compromise comes as a realized desire; for a moment, desire and community are one. Yet we enjoy the indiscipline of the blind and witty Emma, and the compromise that reconciles her to society and self through Knightley provides only a short-lived accommodation of realism to the conventions of the comic mode, "the perfect happiness of the union."

Emma, Austen feared, would seem "very inferior in good sense" to *Mansfield Park*.[27] The quiet acquiescence in propriety of Fanny Price has always seemed problematic among the energies of Austen's incipiently rebellious heroines. But Fanny is a figure who tests the implications of a narrative like *Emma*, for Emma has to learn many of the lessons Fanny seems to know from the beginning. Fanny is more "common" than Emma, and is less interesting as a character; her narrative submits less directly to the energy of her desires, and Austen's fiction loses some of its characteristic shapeliness in its reaction against the "confident ironies" of the earlier fiction.[28] But it does more than reassert blandly the moral tradition Austen's heroines had at least partly attempted to escape. In *Mansfield Park*, reality gets a bit more uncertain, and some clarity of definition at least temporarily deserts Austen as her prose develops what Kingsley Amis calls a new "flexibility and awareness."[29]

Fanny Price can suggest two ways that Emma is potentially disruptive. The realist's fidelity to the common walks of life entailed a repression of the extraordinary, as is well known. Yet Emma, that genteel and provincial young woman, has dreams of her own power that do in fact distinguish her radically from her context, that make her very much a heroine—if a flawed one—unlike Catherine Morland. Realism's containment of large ambitions is threatened by so marvelously imagined a character. In addition, Emma threatens what we might call a Whatelyan sense of the compatibility between reality and order. Her disruptions into power threaten also disruptions of the community and of the formal closure of her fiction.

If we move abruptly from Austen to Conrad, we can watch the implications of the reversals within Austen's oeuvre, and within particular texts. Emma's latent disruptions become potent. The repression by things of the dangerous energy of Emma-like desire to control becomes a displacement of desire onto things. Things become animate, as in Dickens, or they leap, as in Conrad, into a chaos of conflicting passions. The implicit contention between the disorder of reality and the order of comedy becomes explicit. Desire and disorder contend and flow together. The vivid imitation of the common walks of life becomes a nightmare or a game.

III

O Aristotle! if you had had the advantage of being "the freshest modern" instead of the greatest ancient, would you not have mingled your praise of metaphorical speech, as a sign of high intelligence, with a lamentation that intelligence so rarely shows itself in speech without metaphor,—that we can so seldom declare what a thing is, except by saying it is something else?

George Eliot, *The Mill on the Floss*

The struggle to sustain meaning and pattern within the limits of Whatelyan realistic style, subject, and structure became elaborate, occasionally devious and elusive, potentially tragic. The monstrous was revealing itself not only in the relentlessly formless surfaces described, the energies repressed, the controls asserted, but in the insistent and averted recognitions that reality was stepping aside from the verbal devices used to fix it and that the strategies of narrative were inadequate to cope with the external world, or perhaps to touch it at all. Thackeray's case is perhaps the most interesting of all as he creates his novels against the irresistible consciousness of reality's side-stepping. But in domestic novel after domestic novel, excess reasserts itself against the realistic style imagined to deny it.

Realism was in part a denial that the excesses of the past could survive, except in occasional barbarous bursts of irrationality, in the context of an ordered and more or less rational civilization. Scott, for example, defined "Romance," with its emphasis on the "marvellous," against the "Novel," whose "events are accommodated to the ordinary train of human events and the modern state of society."[30] Whatelyan "improbability" approximates to the "marvellous"; and probability, then, merges with the modern. But the marvelous also returns in modern dress, and is more dangerous. For the marvelous that is not simply fantastic and part of metaphysical machinery is a part of ordinary human experience uncontainable by principles of ordering. The immediate social solutions were exclusions from modern civilization, particularly in madhouses or prisons. In narrative, the irresistible "marvellous" takes the shape of the monstrous and remains, like the Frankenstein monster, unnamed and unnameable. Once explicit or implicit metaphysical supports for meaning begin to break down, the possibility of identifying and placing—and hence, in a way, controlling—the extraordinary was lost. One might, as an aside, suggest that the Freudian enterprise was precisely the enterprise of naming, of finding labels for the hitherto unnameable in order to reestablish the primacy of order and civilization.

But for the realists, intent on the explorations that would take them beyond the reach of their medium, the balance between the monstrous and the civilized eventually shifted. The monstrous in Conrad's fiction turns out to be more usual than order, and so consistently eludes definition that it ultimately destroys the connection between idea and thing. The real transforms from external thing upon which ideas are contingent, to internal idea or sensation, tenuously or unknowingly linked to the thing, and subject only to its own rules. The very conflict between imagination and society that was so thematically central to realism, and that so richly allowed Austen that sharp definition of language upon which her narratives turn, breaks down. Imagination turns out to be in contest only with another imagination of reality: Frankenstein is doubled by his monster, and the horror of the contest is the horror of psychomachia. In such a condition, the realist turns from the dull grey eyes of the protagonist to be saved by imaginative sympathy, to the protagonist as artist, literal or figurative. For the artist, a Frankenstein in words, is the only figure who might create meaning out of the dead matter of experience (the meaningless other). The only truth-telling realism becomes the realism that faces its own merely created nature. Alternatively, for the artist who distrusts art, or wishes it to do more, the artist-hero can turn out to be only a dilettante antihero—as with Thackeray's Arthur Pendennis, or Conrad's Martin Decoud.

George Eliot's art is central to this whole complex of possibilities. Determined to reconcile her readers to their lots as ordinary and flawed human beings, full of the sense of intellectual discovery that pervaded the avant-garde circles of her time, she believed, like any good realist, that she might make her art speak more truthfully than novelists had hitherto been able. For her, certainly early in her novel-writing career, the moral aesthetic of realism was dominant. She became both its great exemplar and its firmest propagandizer. Yet her career is the clearest demonstration of its impossibility.

The famous, if self-consciously awkward, seventeenth chapter of *Adam Bede* explains that her "strongest effort is to give a faithful account of men and things as they have mirrored themselves in my mind."[31] Even here, there is no simple realism, although fidelity to the actual is the primary focus. For she is aware of the trap of the mirror: "The mirror is doubtless defective; the outlines will sometimes be disturbed, the reflection faint or confused." Yet the narrator's voice sustains the confidence of experience precisely recollected. The clarity of the pastoral images, the sharpness with which place is rendered, seem self-consciously to assimilate a tradition of pastoral comedy to a modern and "civilized" perception of the way reality plays off against the ideal of the virginal milkmaid, or the shepherd/carpenter hero. The mirror that threatens clarity and fidelity recurs opaquely by the candlelight in Hetty's bedroom, but transforms into a window in Dinah's. The dangers of reflection are averted by the powers of imagination to project itself through the glass. And if Hetty suffers from the fatal flaw of realism, the imaginative projection of self on an intransigent reality, the novel itself authenticates another kind of imagination, one that succeeds in its guesses at truth because it tries to remove the self as an obstacle. It can thus see with the realist's eye to imperfection—the hero is too proud and unbending, the villain is only boyish and well intentioned, the clergyman is a gentleman, courteous, generous, and mildly lax in his spiritual work. And it can find in itself those failings and that mixed nature whose discovery creates community and forgiveness and absorbs us into a continuing organic order.

But in *The Mill on the Floss,* George Eliot reaches a point that we might take, symbolically, as a crisis in the process of realism. St. Ogg's is a community built out of tradition but in which almost all power to imagine beyond the self has atrophied. The narrator, oddly present for a moment in the first chapter, speaks with a voice of melancholy nostalgia, "in love with moistness," that becomes irresistibly ironic in the context of what moistness actually achieves in the novel. The voice disappears into a remarkably shrewd and precise observer's, speaking unsentimentally and with vital awareness of the "oppressive narrowness," the banality and cruelty, of the world that evokes the opening nostalgia. The attempt to evoke experience is made in the shape of a saving memory that testifies to the absence of experience.

The narrative of *The Mill on the Floss* resists in almost all of its surfaces the sentimentalizing of which the first chapter seems to be an omen. As we see at the start of book 4, the narrator belongs in the tradition of realism's self-consciousness about its own material, about its audience, about its relation to other literatures. The metaphor is scientific, and the justification for such a petty subject is the scientific enterprise of attempting to "bind the smallest things with the greatest." Victorian organicism, or the quest for it, is here: "There is nothing petty to the mind that has a large vision of relations, and to which every single object suggests a vast sum of conditions."[32] The whole passage provides the most extensive theoretic/moral justification we have of the English realist's enterprise, and it comes in a novel preoccupied with a desire for release from constriction, for some kind of passionate explosion of vital energy: "A vigorous superstition, that lashes its gods or lashes its own back, seems to be more congruous with the mystery of the human lot, than the mental condition of these emmet-like Dodsons and Tullivers" (p. 238). The past, with its barbarities, begins to seem somehow more human than the present with its grotesquely dehumanized traditions of order and respectability. Indeed, *The Mill on the Floss* points forward to the novels in which George Eliot is forced to surrender the continuity between the ideal of community, that saves language and meaning in *Adam Bede,* and the fact of society, whose epitome becomes the monstrous Grandcourt.

The narrative leads to a situation in which satisfactory resolution is unattainable in the terms her adopted realistic mode would allow. Satisfaction must be delayed into "the onward tendency of human things," while the bearers of that tendency cannot endure the facts that are the condition of realistic surfaces and life of St. Ogg's, so clogged with pills and linens and machinery. The progress of Maggie's disenchantment echoes the conventional progress of the disenchanted protagonists of realistic fiction: an excessively romantic and egoistic heroine must learn the relation of desire to possibility, of self to society. But Maggie Tulliver is not allowed to accept the terms available to Catherine Morland or Emma Woodhouse, and marry into society and submit to its restrictions. The resolution George Eliot finds almost authenticates the fantasies of desire (and its perversion, martyrdom) that have been treated consistently with irony, if compassionate irony. The accommodation of protagonist to reality has the shape of another sort of fiction, dominated by the desire that realism's form traditionally represses. The limits Maggie accepts are not, finally, social; they are absolute. If she cannot be absorbed with all her desire into society, she will match herself against nature itself, and against the dream of "moistness" that controlled the narrative from its inception for George Eliot. The death of Maggie is her triumph, a psychological triumph in which, at last, she dominates her brother, and in which the repressed energies of love and anger are manifested in the equivalent of murder, and in the shape of a catastrophe inimical to the realist's enterprise. George Eliot must invoke a natural catastrophe to act out her heroine's need for love and control.

What seems not to have been endurable for George Eliot, in the imagined world of the narrative, was the possibility of Maggie's life's dwindling unclimactically out in the realist's tragedy, as Thackeray called it, of "what you have daily to bear."[33] In the intensity of her exploration of the "real," George Eliot finds herself having to choose between two kinds of monstrousness: the unendurable ordinary, that can be redeemed only by projecting satisfaction into the future; the irrational energies of desire, long repressed by the demands of the ordinary. By the time of *Daniel Deronda,* George Eliot had in effect renounced the limits of realism by renouncing the possibility of satisfactory life within society, the sanction of meaning conferred by a community organically coherent. The ultimate realistic project in George Eliot becomes the projection of community into fictions from which her realist's integrity has banished it. Daniel is sent off, in fact, to create a community, outside the reaches of the society and of the novel whose language can no longer evoke one. The language of realism becomes fit only for that experience of loss and absence that is Gwendolen Harleth's at the end. Meaningful truth must be projected into the distance.

At the risk of some oversimplification, we can say that the later developments in George Eliot's art indicate if not the collapse of a faith in the meaningfulness of the real world, at least a collapse of faith in the dominant reality of the empirically verifiable. Either loss dooms the convention of English realism. But George Eliot never formally stopped being a realist; the nature of her explorations of reality changed, as the elusive figure of reality kept retreating before her rigorous investigation. A developing Victorian science continued to allow her a positive faith in the ultimate accessibility of the real, through an epistemology beyond empiricism. Such an epistemology, however, breaks down the conventions of realism, for what cannot be directly experienced or observed cannot be embodied in realistic forms. The disappearance of the happy ending, and the transfer of marriage from the conclusion to beginning, implies an un-Whatelyan world, where justice is not embodied in reality. Maggie's death in the arms of her brother means that the technique of realism has moved let us say, into very turbulent waters.

IV

Words, as is well known, are the great foes of reality.
The Professor, in *Under Western Eyes*

As reality becomes a kind of destructive and formless flood, we arrive at an art that focuses on individual consciousness, the only remaining source of meaning and order. The culminating crisis in George Eliot's novel becomes the initiating fact of Conrad's: Marlow's voyage to the Congo, Jim's leap, the intrusion in Razumov's rooms. Beginning with the assumption of disaster and creating his drama from the attempt to redeem it, Conrad undermines English fiction's primary traditions; but the attempt at redemption is also an attempt to reassert those traditions. He brings to bear on realism's conventions of moral order and moderation a profoundly skeptical continental intelligence. In those initiating moments in which his protagonists' imaginations of self are belied by reality, he assumes a fuller separation of language from reality than George Eliot's work could intimate.

What feels new in Conrad's skepticism is the stylistically and narratively dramatized distrust of language *qua* language, the developed intuition that mere misuse of language was not the essential cause of the difficulty. Dickens's pleasure in language, for example, was never merely distrust, although his own language, from its polysyllabic Pickwickian comedy to the late bitter detachment, implies a pervasive awareness of the way language obscures the truth.[34] What we have noted in *Sketches by Boz* is intensified in the mystery of *Bleak House*, *Little Dorrit*, or *Great Expectations*. The mystery depends upon closely observed, but opaque, surfaces of ordinary things, which then transform, by metaphor, reiteration, or variation, into something else. Like Conrad, Dickens consistently juxtaposed verbal people, whose language thwarts genuine feeling and disguises moral reality, with inarticulate people, whose gestures or simplicity of statement penetrates the obscurity of surfaces. Magwitch's click in the throat, heard in the first pages of *Great Expectations*, holds the secret of the novel, legible to us but not to Pip.

Such unambivalent significance, however, rarely emerges in any of Conrad's novels, and the "moral disorder"[35] implied in Dickens's chaotic and surfeited worlds is replaced in Conrad by sheer refusal of significance—the vast white emptiness of *Under Western Eyes*. As David Thorburn argues, Conrad was temperamentally hostile to "an expansive conception of fiction that might sanction, even encourage, allegory or fable"[36]—and this hostility is characteristic of the exploratory realistic impulse.

Again, Conrad's self-consciousness about his materials, intensified by the fact that he wrote in his third language, was actually continuous with the self-consciousness we have seen as a mark of nineteenth-century realism. But it seems a long way from any of the manifestos we have already looked at. In Conrad, we can find the same moral urgency as we hear in George Eliot's commitment, in *Adam Bede*, to record the reflection in the mirror of her mind as precisely "as if I were in the witness-box narrating my experience on oath" (p. 178). The desire to make you "see" is similar for both writers. Even the concern for audience, filtered through Conrad's alternative narrators, is present. But while George Eliot writes as though it were possible to get beyond the limits of the mirror, Conrad begins by assuming the unlikelihood of success.

In the preface to a volume of short stories, Conrad speaks with the intonations of a realist, yet a realist troubled in a new way:

> That [romantic] origin of my literary work was far from giving a larger scope to my imagination. On the contrary, the mere fact of dealing with matters outside the general run of everyday experience laid me under the obligation of a more scrupulous fidelity to the truth of my own sensation. The problem was to make unfamiliar things credible. [37]

The reminder of Coleridge's task in *The Lyrical Ballads* is to the point. George Eliot is to Wordsworth as Conrad is to Coleridge; beginning at the periphery of experience Conrad cannot quite find the common language of the Wordsworthian and realist enterprise (it hardly matters for our purposes that, as Coleridge was to argue, Wordsworth never found it either). Conrad speaks without the confidence we have heard in the passage from *Adam Bede*, where the narrator knows she is talking to somebody, that she and her readers form a community and are talking about a community. If George Eliot had been dispossessed of her natural community by her elopement with Lewes, Conrad, the Polish exile, the ex-seaman, in Edwardian London, was yet further from any recognizable center. He talks not of "men and things as they have mirrored themselves in my mind" (with the confidence that somewhere out there men and things *are*), but only of "the truth of my own sensation." The mind is not a means to a world beyond mind; its activity must be the ultimate subject. The one hope, as we hear in his Preface to *The Nigger of the "Narcissus,"* is that the truth of his sensation will reverberate in the separateness of other people's consciousnesses—that an intersubjective community might be built.

Conrad provides an almost "pure" case of the possibilities of the realist impulse because his art is severed from any generally available conventions of meaning. His subject is not a knowable community[38] but an alien world he tries to assimilate to a community he does not quite know. In *Under Western Eyes,* for example, the entire rhetorical strategy is the attempt to make the East—Russia—intelligible to Western European communities. But the effect of the rhetoric is to deny the possibility of knowing not only the East, but the West as well. Conrad's "sensation" is itself alien to the language and to the experience of the reader who traditionally validates the realist's work. Like Razumov, "the label of a solitary individuality,"[39] Conrad understood not only the distortion of reality as it mirrored itself in his mind but the intrinsic impossibility of the magic George Eliot found in the ink at the end of her pen, by which she transports the reader into the world of *Adam Bede* (p. 1). Articulating the impulse of the realist tradition, Conrad could not think of himself as a realist.

In the famous Preface to *The Nigger of the Narcissus,"* Conrad specifically dismissed realism, along with Romanticism, naturalism, even sentimentalism, as "one of the temporary formulas" of the artist's "craft."[40] What for George Eliot was a break with falsifications she had found in sentimental or idealizing fictions had become, by another swing in realism's progress, just another one of the mythifying conventions. Conrad's distrust of the formula, though it drove him from a historically limited realism, did not altogether free him from the mimetic ideal, and certainly not from its formal requirements of verisimilitude and apparent meaning. Against his better knowledge, the novels show him attempting to minimize the distance between language and reality. But he tries to do it through language that does not "mean" so much as suggest silences, gestures, actions, things that exist around the peripheries of the falsities language perpetrates. The truth is in Jim's leap, and not in the endless spinning of words about it; in Razumov's pointing his finger at himself, touching himself, and not in all the Professor's explanatory preliminaries. *Under Western Eyes* dramatizes Razumov's need to bring his language into accord with his being; ultimately, as for Frankenstein's monster, that requires silence.

For Conrad, the disparity between language and being was not only an instinct of a man alienated both from the language he used and the culture in which he lived; it was a position, as I shall be showing in the concluding chapters, sustained by what he understood the new science to reveal. In the tradition of late-century cosmic pessimism, already well developed by Hardy in his novels, Conrad saw reality as incompatible with the human mind itself. Under the pressure of a vision so entirely the reverse of Whately's, Conrad's world loses all the clarity we have found in Austen's. The particularizing, which in the conventions of realism creates a sense of solidity, in Conrad suggests a profound unreality, a slipping of connection not only between experience and dream or desire, but between experience and expectation. In George Eliot, intellectual and moral growth depended on "invariability of sequence," the certainty that one thing leads to another, and does so invariably. Even human character depends on this. If realistic determinism has its enervating consequences and diminishes the power of character to be free,[41] it also makes character as a recognizable and unified entity possible. But in Conrad, nothing is predictable. Everything external—seen with a Dickensian madness of clarity—becomes psychological and disruptive, like the streets of London in *The Secret Agent*, or the jungle in so early a book as *The Outcast of the Islands*. The distinction between inner and outer breaks down, and neither is intelligible. "One's own personality," Conrad wrote to Edward Garnett, "is only a ridiculous and aimless masquerade of something hopelessly unknown."[42]

From *Almayer's Folly* through *Under Western Eyes* Conrad's narratives imply what he metaphorically called an "abyss" beneath the surface of the civilized, intelligible, and ordered world. This old mythic metaphor is, however, misleading in its firm subterranean location of meaninglessness. Even the word *abyss* naturalizes, humanizes, what literally cannot be made human. No description or label can make it intelligible: *abyss* in Conrad is a word that only marks an absence; it is a Conradian gesture at the world beyond words.

As Conrad's characters frequently remind us, reality is "monstrous." Yet though "it" be nameless, we somehow know its lineaments through a prose working with obsessive urgency to evoke and meticulously describe particulars and literal surfaces he teaches us to question as apparition. In its combination of precision in detail with vaguely evocative and menacing adjectives ("inconceivable" and "impenetrable" are among his favorites), the prose suggests that its ultimate "subject" is the contention between realism and the phantasmagoric, between a world accessible to common sense and a world, extreme in its ordinariness, that can only be intimated by Kurtz's "the horror." The language requires us to imagine what it cannot describe.

The way to the unnameable is through the conventions of the nameable, and Conrad works with those conventions as earlier writers made them available. "My task," his manifesto goes in the Preface to *The Nigger of the "Narcissus,"* "is, by the power of the written word to make you hear, to make you feel—it is, before all, to make you *see*" (p. xiv). If this points forward to the antimimetic developments in the twentieth century, it is intricately rooted in the romantic/mimetic art of the nineteenth. The assertion echoes Ruskin's extraordinary declaration that "the greatest thing a human soul ever does in this world is to *see* something, and tell what it *saw* in a plain way."[43] The difference is that Ruskin believes it possible to *tell*, to find the language, and, although he learns different lessons only to reject them once more, he believes that the visible world will answer to Whately's sort of dream of order. The visible world "meant" something to Ruskin, and the meaning was requisite to his continuing his work. The alienation from experience implicit in the overwhelming value attributed to seeing and description was not complete so long as the language struggled to overcome it: the Wordsworthian marriage between mind and nature seemed yet attainable.

For Ruskin, art is the only morality because in making us see, it makes us know God's world. For Pater, whose relation to Conrad is more direct than Ruskin's, art becomes morality because it allows us the fullest intensity of the transitory moment, the richest possible life through the realization of the evanescent impressions that are all that make up our lives. In a letter to R. B. Cunninghame Graham that echoes Pater and anticipates much of his own fiction, even in its self-consciousness about language, Conrad moves into the stark pessimism that Pater's materialist and genteel solipsism entailed:

> Life knows us not and we do not know life—we don't even know our own thoughts. Half the words we use have no meaning whatever and of the other half each man understands each word after the fashion of his own folly and conceit. Faith is a myth and beliefs shift like mists on the shore; thoughts vanish; words, once pronounced, die; and the memory of yeaterday is as shadowy as the hope of tomorrow—only the string of my platitudes seems to have no end.[44]

Not even the transitory moment is more than dream; yet out of this stern extension of Pater's ideas, Conrad pushes back to the Ruskinian and Wordsworthian ideals of community, and of a morality of art built on bleakness of vision.

Somehow, by making us see he may be able to provide us with what the Preface calls that "glimpse of truth for which you have forgotten to ask" (p. xiv). By nourishing, with Paterian intensity, a "passing phase of life," snatched "from the remorseless rush of time," we begin a task that Pater thought was ended in the act of snatching itself. The artist who, in perfect integrity, gives us a "convincing moment" is the one that "may perchance attain to such clearness of sincerity that at last the presented vision of regret or pity, of terror or mirth, shall awaken in the hearts of the beholders that feeling of unavoidable solidarity; of the solidarity in mysterious origin, in toil, in joy, in hope, in uncertain fate, which binds men to each other and all mankind to the visible world" (p. xiv). Here is the realistic and Romantic program, Conrad transforming the faithless vision offered him by his contemporaries into a struggle toward the community at the heart of the rejected realist's dreams.

There is, of course, an uncharacteristic upbeat inflation in the rhetoric of the Preface. It is akin to the whistling-in-the-dark heroism of Bertrand Russell's "A Free Man's Worship," a product of a similar world view. Somehow, Conrad expects language, that foe of reality, to "compel men entranced by the sight of distant goals to glance for a moment at the surrounding vision of form and colour, of sunshine and shadows" (p. xvi). Yet this is not, I think, either the obfuscation it has sometimes been taken to be, or merely disingenuous. Conradian solidarity inheres in the impenetrability of phenomena, in the simultaneous recognition of mutual helplessness, and in the mysterious pleasures of words themselves. Marlow is a performer, who Buddha-like spins out his mysteries and, like Coleridge's ancient mariner, compels attention. His virtuosity constantly makes his ostensible subject—Jim, Kurtz, the Congo, himself—more obscure than it was, constantly reminds us of the arduousness of finding a language that can touch reality, and thus makes us believe in the reality beyond words that his words displace. As a recent critic has put it, "The artist must be engaged in making shapes to prove that shapes cannot be made."[45]

By Conrad's time, then, reality no longer held still for the language realism required. Irrational and mythifying energies intrude everywhere, and become almost the primary validation of the integrity of the realist's enterprise. They are the evidence that it has recognized its own invalidity. Richard Feverel cannot be shaped or systematized, nor can Louisa Gradgrind, or Pip, by his "creator," Magwitch. Hardy's Henchard makes himself most completely only in his death, while survival in his world—the world of the limits of realism—depends upon surrender to phenomena themselves, whose nature is inimical to the human. Before Conrad can surrender meaning, Hardy must invert it.

The emphasis on the mystery of creation justifies Conrad's "unrealistic" subjects. He did not think of the material as separate from the normal human condition. "Subjects," he told Edward Garnett, "never appear revelatory to me."[46] Everything depends on how they are handled. Of course, this has become a cliché of modern criticism, but it was important for Conrad in freeing him from the domestic subjects of traditional realistic fiction. Like Victor Frankenstein, who out of an exemplary and placid bourgeois home in Geneva goes to create his monster, Conrad, in the midst of the literati of London, produced his monsters. An obscure faith in science became the grounds for Mary Shelley's creation; the tradition of psychological and naturalist realism, running parallel to the new science, became the grounds for Conrad's assault on normality. Lydgate's primitive tissue becomes mindless matter.[47] The discovery, instead of leading to a progressive revelation of connections and an ultimate coherence, leads to a capricious, unstable reality in which necessary sequence is transformed into unimaginable indeterminacy. The explorer of reality finds at last that Keats's fair maiden is a monster, better left untouched. Knowledge has learned its incompatibility with its origins.

In Conrad, finally, the realist exploration of reality becomes a necessary and self-destructive act. To attain knowledge is to achieve integrity and stature at the expense of finding oneself the butt of the great cosmic joke:[48] knowledge becomes self-immolation. Frankenstein and his monster cancel each other out. The dilemma is much like George Eliot's, having to choose between the tragedy of what we have daily to bear and the risk of disaster. George Eliot suggests that it might be better, in some cases, *not* to know: "Of scientific truth, is it not conceivable that some facts as to the tendency of things affecting the final destination of the race might be more hurtful when they had entered into human consciousness than they would have been if they had remained purely external in their activity?"[49]

Any fiction that confronts this late, disenchanted, and dualistic vision must, like much late-century fiction, take the shape of romance. It can make no final accommodation, in the realist tradition, to the culture it purports to describe or to the audience it addresses. There can be no community with which to make peace, if only because the ironies implicit in realist presentation have undermined whatever communities there may be. The characters are self-created, and even in the midst of London, or St. Petersburg, they are as isolated a Frankenstein and his monster on the ice.

In almost all of its details, then, Conrad's fiction makes the monstrous, which was so diligently repressed, domesticated, and translated by Victorian realists, into an overt, disruptive, and unnameable presence. Without the solidity of Mary Shelley's monster, the "inconceivable mystery" of Kurtz's "horror" works similar effects through the mediation of the credible. In Conrad, the romantic and gothic become elements of a new high art, the instruments by which their old nemesis, realism, is defeated. Thus, the realism Whately admired as a corrective to excess, the program George Eliot had announced for herself less than fifty years before, and which, she believed, would creatively disturb the complacency of her readers by engaging them with realities they preferred not to see, had become, for Conrad, a mere convention to be disrupted. Realism had become the false complacency of a middle class audience, assuring them of the reality and stability of their culture. The politically conservative Conrad created an aesthetics and politics of disruption, mirrored in the anarchists who wander madly through his pages.

Through all this, there remains in Conrad a touchingly Victorian insistence on finding a public language that might continue the traditions by which language created and expressed community. Ian Watt discusses the way a deep commitment to community existed, unreconciled, with Conrad's alienation.[50] The quest to sustain that impossible commitment requires a radical gesture to reconcile thought and action such as that self-accusatory one imagined for Razumov. The ultimate "realism" of Conrad's art must come in a stripping away of the lies of language as part of a process of creation that will point to an irreducible order and community: an order understood, even in its invention, to be a willed human artifact. The notions of civilization implicit in the realistic method must be denied (because we know they are falsifications and inventions) and asserted (because we cannot live without them). The artist may imagine such a position; he cannot live it.

V

You know how interesting the purchase of a spongecake is to me.

Jane Austen, Letter to Cassandra

The story has a neatness belied by its details. More important, there are alternatives. Conrad's very ambivalence implies something other than the cheerless direction of monstrosity and self-immolation. After all, although it is convenient to take Conrad's special alienation as paradigmatic, it is an extreme instance. Moreover, if the process of realism issues in dualities of the sort we find in Conrad, the Conradian position is no real terminus. One way, for example, to read D. H. Lawrence's art is as a rejection of Conrad's, and an affirmation of the life that lies beyond language. In Lawrence the unnameable monstrous becomes not the tragic evidence of the absence of meaning and horror, but the possibility of genuine life and joy. The gospel of St. John, asserting that in the beginning was the word, has it backward. In the beginning was the life.

There is a tradition, living along with the ones I have been outlining, which makes a direct connection with Whately's neoclassical notion that the primary object of fiction was pleasure. The emphasis on the solemn exploration of the relation between word and thing, between desire and fulfillment, misses the realist pleasure in the visible world. the excess and formlessness of much realism is not merely a manifestation of the disorder of reality (an idea, once again, dependent on the reification of the idea of order), but a simple joy in abundance, in life, and in the endless possibilities of language. Even in Conrad there is a queer humor that results from seeing clearly—Mikulin's wig in *Under Western Eyes*, Stein's butterflies in *Lord Jim*, the contents of the window of Verloc's shop in *The Secret Agent*.

The great Victorian novels are full of "objects," exuberant in their mimetic energy. Thackeray and Trollope, whose fictions can suggest tragic possibilities they deny, self-consciously minimize the significance of their work.[51] But in them, the denial of significance (defensive and self-protective as we may regard it) is no occasion for lamentation. They are professional entertainers who entertain by not making the kinds of aesthetic claims that one of the traditions of Romantic art, so central to some realistic writing, normally makes. Their casualness about art is an affront to Henry James as it must be to critics in a Leavisian tradition who seek moral cogency and rigor.

But I want to suggest, as an alternative to the story as Conrad concludes it, that the tradition of playful and comic exuberance anticipates, with a kind of Austenian sanity, the disruption of traditional forms that we take to be a mark of the movements of literary modernism. Thackeray, for example, was as conscious of the limits of narrative as Conrad. His initial parodies of literary and social forms led him directly toward an antiromantic fiction, but also a fiction that resisted the pulls of literary conventions more effectively than any other writer's. This was precisely because he was not impelled to make meaning out of experience. The very failure of seriousness, which has placed him critically beneath the rank he otherwise deserves by virtue of his remarkable powers with language, allows a freedom implicit in realism but rarely enacted. Thackeray's densely particular narratives roam with astonishing looseness outside of chronology, become self-conscious in the tradition of Cervantes and Sterne, and comic in their willingness not to impose serious and climactic resolutions on the aimlessness of experience.

This kind of self-conscious freedom with literary structures follows logically from realism's rejection of literature. The refusal to take itself seriously would seem to be the consequence of an art that begins in the mockery of forms that take themselves seriously. Indeed, Thackeray's relation to past and contemporary literature is in many ways similar to the relation of modern experimental novelists to the tradition of realism itself. It is not Thackeray's sort of realism that points to the formal purity and coherence of much early modern fiction. His fiction often reads like a critical commentary, not only on the excesses of the fictions he parodies, but on the restrictions of the criticism and literature that followed him.

Long before Conrad, that is, there was a principle of disorder in realism, a principle that was an occasion not for pain but for freedom and celebration. The bric-à-brac density of Victorian fiction, though it is normally enclosed in imposed forms of order and resolution, frequently threatens to run away with the form. While it can be seen as a mode of repressing the violence of desire, it can also be seen as a sort of Victorian erotics, threatened by the discipline of form. Thackeray's details of how to live on nothing a year, with all the moral/formal restrictions imposed by the text upon them, constitute one of the great performances of Victorian art. Maggie Tulliver is destroyed by the formal resolution George Eliot had wisely delayed because she had dwelled so lovingly on the details of the childhood she was reconstructing into a detailed nostalgia.

Traditionally realism is associated with determinism. The anti-romance is the denial of the imagination's power to control circumstance. And thus the characteristic subject of realistic fiction is the contest between dream and reality; the characteristic progress, disenchantment. The single character is implicated in a world of the contingent and must make peace with society and nature or be destroyed. Theoretically, in such a world freedom is entirely restricted by context. Yet—as we pursue one more time the involutions of realism—the failure of the imagination is dramatized in an entirely imagined world. The contingent world is imagined with a vividness of particularity that belies the determinist conception of the powerlessness of the imagination. In Thackeray, what ought to be oppressive frequently becomes a pleasure, and the protagonists of novels like *Pendennis* and *Philip* make their peace with a world obsessed by things, not tragically, with a sense of loss, but pleasantly smoking their cigars and sipping the best wines. Reading Thackeray's fiction can suggest that the determinism we expect from realism emerges formally in the text not by virtue of the cumulative powers of the overwhelming real, but through the formal constrictions of plot, the manifestation in realistic fictions of the most conventional aspects of narrative. The only real determiner is time.

What is unconventional and most exciting about the tradition of realism is its pleasure in abundance, in energy, and the vivid engagement, through language, with the reality just beyond the reach of language. From Emma Woodhouse, concerned about her father's porridge, and shopping in town with her protégée Harriet, to Becky Sharp tossing Johnson's Dictionary from the carriage, to Molly Gibson (in *Wives and Daughters*) attending quietly to domestic duties, realistic novels contain more than they formally need. The antiliterary thrust of realism can be taken either as an assertion of the power of the real over the imagined, and hence of a determined world, or as an assertion of variety and energy against the enclosing and determining forms of art.

But that is another story. As I proceed in the following chapters to examine diverse aspects of realism as they manifest themselves in the art of nineteenth-century novelists, and to fill in some of the outlines suggested in this chapter, it may be that the diversity of possibility will finally unravel the idea of realism altogether. But realism is inescapable, and I hope to suggest that latent in realism is a variety, a self-consciousness, and a complex awareness of the conventions of narrative that anticipate the best of modernism; the realistic impulse to affirm the referentiality of language is a reflection of irrepressible continuing energy for the art and the life that reward us while they threaten at any moment to turn monstrous.

Part Two

Pre-Victorian Realism

Banishing the Monster

3

Northanger Abbey
From Parody to Novel and the Translated Monster

*W*hat have you been judging from? Remember the country and the age in which
we live. Remember that we are English, that we are Christians. Consult your understanding, your own sense of the probable, your own observation of what is passing
around you—Does our education prepare us for such atrocities?

Henry Tilney to Catherine Morland, in *Northanger Abbey*

I

Northanger Abbey was written two decades before *Frankenstein*, but it
was published in the same year, 1818. Its heroine begins her education
at seventeen (her author was already at least twenty-one) when, in the
first chapter, she prepares to leave the village of Fullerton to go to Bath:
"If adventures will not befall a young lady in her own village, she must
seek them abroad."[1] When Mary Godwin was seventeen, she eloped
with Percy Shelley; when she was not much more than a year older than
Catherine Morland, whose education had consisted of fragments of
poetry and intense reading in fiction, particularly of the gothic and
sentimental kind, she began writing *Frankenstein*. On the banks of Lake
Geneva, surrounded by poets, in an imbroglio of passions and under
the eyes of tourists on the hunt for sensation, she brought to bear on her
text not only the experience of excess and alienation, but wide reading
in philosophy, politics, the classics, and, of course, Romantic literature.

The extravagance of the difference between Catherine and Mary—
teenaged girls in search of love and adventure—may be embodied in the
image of the monster. The two first novels (*Northanger Abbey* was Jane
Austen's first completed novel although not the first to be published)
comment on each other in their coincidental proximity intricately and
usefully. One way to talk about *Northanger Abbey* is as a fiction whose
entire strategy is designed to keep at bay that monster, emerging from
the dreams of a risk-taking young girl, who might shatter both the

illusion of order and meaning and the possibility of survival within the community. But the strategy reveals as well as encloses what is hidden.

"At bay," of course, is a loaded phrase, implying that Austen's relation to the monstrous was rather like Victor Frankenstein's. There is a temptation, despite the novel's lighthearted openness, and especially given the long tradition of critical recognition that its movement is self-contradictory (beginning in parody of what in the end it must use), to see it that way. Mark Schorer, for example, notes that Austen "was able to resolve the novel only through the melodramatic means that the very kind of novel she was parodying would itself have depended upon."[2] But this is only part of the truth of what I hope to explore, if a major part. *Northanger Abbey* is not only a parody, and certainly concerned, in its parody, not only with gothic fiction.[3] Its coherence depends in part on the dismissal of earlier fictions, but much more on elaboration through those fictions of the subtle discriminations necessary to distinguish true feelings from false, genuine literature from fake, and to establish a language that will correspond to those discriminations. Such discriminations allow successful mediation between self and society, self and not-self. Like any novel directed by the realist impulse, *Northanger Abbey* seeks to name reality, but in no metaphysical sense. The reality is not "nature" as we understand it in a post-Romantic view, but society and its relations, which comprise all the important manifestations of human nature. For this pre-Romantic nature, language would seem to be perfectly fitted, since the post-Romantic distinction between the artificial and arbitrary constructions of language and the nonverbal constructs of nature does not apply. Language is the natural instrument of social relations.

Avrom Fleishman suggests that Catherine's history through the course of the novel is the history of her acquisition of "abstractions, symbols, and patterns of understanding by which men are made distinctively human in the process of cultural formation."[4] To be distinctively (might one say "naturally") human is to use language effectively and to read it well. And the acquisition of the abstractions entails a definition of self against the narratives and texts that provide one's vocabulary; thus Catherine's narrative, *Northanger Abbey*, constantly maneuvers among other narrative forms. Like the monster at the De Laceys', Catherine Morland learns by reading, by watching how other people use language, by noticing the differences between language and the actions that accompany it.

Northanger Abbey consequently shares with *Frankenstein* an intense preoccupation with literature. But Jane Austen and Catherine Morland, even if as women outside any position of authority they imply an ironic vision of the ideals embodied in literature, read from within the con-

ventions of community. Mary Shelley and her monster do not. Thus the
novel's relations to literature are complicated by the subjectivity of
Frankenstein, expressed through the complicated devices of narration,
and the objectivity of *Northanger Abbey,* whose vision is controlled by a
shrewd and wise narrative voice. When the monster learns the terms of
civilization, he absorbs the ideal embedded in them into a "nature"
naturally, but intensely, loving; and he discovers simultaneously the
disparity between his own being and the ideal: "How was I terrified,
when I viewed myself in a transparent pool! At first I started back,
unable to believe that it was indeed I who was reflected in the mirror;
and when I became fully convinced that I was in reality the monster that
I am, I was filled with the bitterest sensations of despondence and
mortification" (p. 124). The monster's education is to learn that he is *not*
"distinctively human," and he discovers this introspectively. Every
gesture he makes to get beyond his separateness—to put to use the
communal ideal—throws him back more completely on himself. The
ideal of community is for him a condition of separation; his reflection
shows him that he is unworthy of the ideal images the DeLaceys provide him.

Catherine, however, is irresistibly without self-preoccupation, and
hence without morbidity or a sense of separateness. She has little to do
with mirrors, and her relation to any ideal is unself-conscious and un-
questioned. When, like the monster, she makes instinctive attempts to
turn her private sense of justice into a social action, Henry Tilney regards this as a sign of her special excellence as a person. Early in the
novel, when she is disappointed at Tilney's absence (he already having
provided her with a prospective lover and an embodiment of the ideal
of civilization), Catherine does not turn to the mirror to measure her
worth. She finds, instead, her unhappiness taking "the direction of
extraordinary hunger, and when that is appeased, [it] changed into an
earnest longing to be in bed . . . from which she awoke [nine hours later]
perfectly revived, in excellent spirits, with fresh hopes and fresh
schemes" (ch. 9, p. 60). The kind of sensibility that will lead later
novelists to throw all the action inside is thwarted in *Northanger Abbey,*
which steadfastly connects self-preoccupation with distortions of language.[5] The "ideal" is built immediately into the experience as it takes
shape in language so that the narrator is not, like Walton, Frankenstein,
or the monster, a limited seeker of it, but a speaker who literally sees it
in social phenomena and in the activities and language of her characters.

To be sure, Catherine Morland finds, in her progress, a world full of
injustices and radical disparities between word and action. But her
education is the learning that these are immediately discriminable by

the eye of sense (not so much by the eye of sensibility). It is not only General Tilney at the end but the Thorpes throughout who pretend to certain ideal modes of civilization, yet consistently live askew from them; nor is it an accident that the extravagantly inaccurate Thorpe is the source of the general's belief that Catherine is wealthy. Neither Thorpe nor the general reads well; neither has an adequate sense of the objective validity of language. Their readings are determined not by social norms but by selfish preoccupation with their own status. These misreaders threaten the narrative with catastrophe, but for Catherine, the experience of their injustice is not catastrophic. When General Tilney casts her out, as Victor casts out his creation, she is "too wretched to be fearful" (ch. 29, p. 230). But she returns, not to the Alpine wastes, or even to the darkness of her enclosed mind, but only to Fullerton, and a joyful reunion with her family—a reabsorption in the "common feelings of common life" from which she had started (ch. 2, p. 19).

Plausibility, in the novel of common life, requires something other than ideal behavior from Catherine, however; and it is here that we get the novel's fullest explicit confrontation with the irrational. Catherine cannot be genuinely cheered by her mother's arguments about the values of steady friends and loving family: "There are some situations of the human mind," says the comically shrewd narrator, "in which good sense has little power" (ch. 29, p. 239). Having been offered an ideal beyond her common life, by virtue of several misreadings, Catherine fails to come fully to terms with her commonness. Yet the stakes are not nearly so high as they are for the monster. It is a matter, simply, of personal frustration, not of social disruption. The general's monstrous behavior after all can be taken as a mere breach in social manners. *Northanger Abbey* takes into its moderate and sensible reading of literature and experience the monstrosity Mary Shelley so hugely casts on her vast landscapes, but instead of becoming a murderer, Catherine becomes a daughter-in-law.

The moderation and the compromises of the narrative may derive from, but they are something other than, parody.[6] Notoriously, *Northanger Abbey* takes the trouble to praise the very fictions it seems to be mocking, and yet, more interestingly, the narrative dramatizes what the narrator asserts: the characters who most violate common sense, in their self-absorbed egoism, are not the inveterate novel readers. General Tilney, we have seen, is a bad reader. Isabella Thorpe merely talks about reading and has not read *Sir Charles Grandison*. It is only "a particular friend" of Isabella, a Miss Andrews, who "has read every one" of the gothic novels on Isabella's list (ch. 6, p. 40). And it is Isabella, of course, who plays most extravagantly with the truth in the fashion of sentimental novels, even to the extent of deluding herself. Catherine, although absorbed by fiction often, is misled by it only once, and is on the whole a sensible girl. The relation of *Northanger Abbey* to the novels it parodies is complex, not necessarily self-contradictory. If it must resist the catastrophic consequences of a Frankensteinian thrust at the ideal, it is not free—nor does it attempt to be—of the consequences of taking literature seriously (though not solemnly).

For however tightly constricted her narratives seem to be, Austen is certainly in the realist tradition that seeks to push into reality, to explore and discover, not merely to represent, control, and congeal.[7] Her efforts at reality require precisely the power to disentangle various kinds of language and various ways to respond to it, and that power requires a refusal to indulge the extremes which, since not in the landscape of the England she knew, seem to be mere projections of self and selfishness. To remain level-headed is to retain the power to act *with* the power to feel, to make language live in mind, heart, *and* social action.

Austen's reality is, as Whately saw it, objectively in the language which retains a multifaceted relation to reality. It resides not in individual consciousness, which is nevertheless capable of making the necessary discriminations by developing a healthy sense of otherness, but in the sensibly shared understanding of the culture itself. Her heroines, unlike Mary Shelley's monster, will find admission to that culture, but a not at all uncritical admission. Even Catherine, for example, knows the nature of General Tilney's abuse of authority. Since the moral language of the culture is in its literatures, Jane Austen, like the Don's friends, is interested in burning only some of the books. Indeed, the metaphor of Don Quixote cannot quite work with Austen since, while she spoofs a great deal of literature, she does not seem hostile to any of it. Again, her concern is not to respond with an extreme counterstatement, or counter-act, but to make discriminations. The trouble, she seems to suggest, is not so much with the books (which provide so much amusement) but with how we read them. To pick up the metaphor: the problem is with the Don, not with his library.

Austen, after all, knows the difference between a novel and an essay, between literature and life. In the current critical climate, that knowledge, as it appears in so literary a text as *Northanger Abbey*, is a temptation to treat her as though her major enterprise were the self-conscious one of deconstructing texts, and particularly her own, in order to focus on the illusoriness of fiction. The power of such a temptation in *Northanger Abbey* is great because, having sustained a running commentary on literary conventions throughout, the novel closes with a reversed mockery of itself: its readers "will see in the tell-tale compression of the pages before them, that we are all hastening together to perfect felicity" (ch. 31, p. 250). Thus, writes Frank Kearful, "the book ends by denying the autonomy of the illusion it has presented,"[8] and implying the illusoriness of all fictions.

In the bracing sanity of Austen's world, we could hardly expect her to be unaware of the illusoriness of all fictions (or for that matter to think it worth her trouble to write novels to prove it). She would likely have felt herself closer to Whately's arguments that her novels might serve as an excellent moral guide because of the way they conjoined probability with moral justice; while unlikely to quarrel with the substance of Kearful's argument, she seems likely, given the texture of her work, to have denied all its implications. For our very modern self-consciousness about illusion is a reflection of sensibilities utterly foreign to Austen's work. To be sure, *Northanger Abbey* shows that she has the characteristic self-consciousness about her materials that I have suggested one finds in almost all the major realists, yet with all her potential subversions, and ironies that turn every description into a judgment, she knows that a novel like hers, rightly understood, is a source of clarification and a means to a sense of order and stability in language and society. Kearful is askew in arguing from the start that the novel is concerned with establishing the "autonomy of the illusion." Rather, the narrator has, without fuss, made the illusion part of the texture of the novel from the start—in the early allusions to sentimental heroines, in the admission in chapter 5 that she is a novelist.

The ironies of the text do not presume the fictionality of the text; they do imply its authority. The sensible reader, that is to say, understands (as Dr. Johnson said of the audience at Shakespeare's plays) that the novel is only a novel, and finds it pleasurable and true at the same time. Language is not subverted but validated, precisely in the way the text discriminates different kinds of language. The novel offers itself as a social document, an articulation of a social consciousness that, as Fleishman says, embodies the abstractions, symbols, and patterns of understanding that Catherine must develop to be fully civilized and to resist the potential solipsism of the language of misreading. Unlike the brooding *Frankenstein*, *Northanger Abbey*'s turn upon itself is managed in a spirit of play that only confirms the consonance of public language with a meaningful world, of recognized fiction with recognized fact.

Characteristically, then, for nineteenth-century fiction, the self-consciousness about materials is accompanied by a self-consciousness about its relation to its audience, to which *Northanger Abbey* seems an extended address (rather than an autonomous illusion). The opening parody is directed more immediately to the reader than against sentimental or gothic novels. It is a playful version of Charlotte Brontë's later admonition to her readers, "Calm your expectations." In its characteristic deflation of excess, it finds its object not so much in the old

novels as in the false expectations of fictions (and, implicitly, experience) that literary conventions arouse. Every moment in *Northanger
Abbey* signals a minute adjustment of expectations, a short-circuiting of
the introspective and solipsistic tendencies that lead Frankenstein to his
grotesque misreading of nature and critics to their absolutist attempts
to make illusion the object rather than the means. In the writing of a
novel whose direction is a constant clarification of definition through a
narrative whose protagonist turns frequently from heroine to antiheroine, from sensibility to sense, and which dialectically refuses to
eliminate either, Austen was engaged in a complex process of naming.
She did not try to avoid either a recognition of the illusoriness of fiction
or the compatibility of that illusion with the realist's enterprise of attempting to name so complex and myriad-faceted a thing as experience
itself. In naming the reader's expectation she drives out the unnameable
monstrous, and casts a sharper light on a world that she had to believe
was entirely legible (if sometimes difficult to see).

II

Jane Austen is thus truly at the beginning of this study. In her ironic
stance and deflation of excess and of heroism, in her self-consciousness
about her materials, in her concern with audience, in her flexible explorations of human possibility within the context of a carefully defined
society, she works almost all of the elements characteristic of the later
realism. She differs, of course, in the Whatelyan definition of reality,
so that when she reaches beyond the limits of earlier fictional language
into her secular reality, she still writes as though names will find it and
as though the nameless monsters lurking outside the limits of her little
country villages are only the extensions of comprehensible human
greed and selfishness that lead us to call things by the wrong name.
And since parody is the instrument out of which this confident realism
is born, I want to consider here some of the general problems of parody
and some of the parodic elements in *Northanger Abbey*, and to follow
some of the later directions of that parody. Parody is the dialectical
inception—the new defined against a conception of the old—of a dialectical process, both in Austen and in the realists who follow. And we
can see, in the necessary contradictions of literary parody, how the very
attempt to laugh excess and distortions away is a means by which they
recur to be reshaped once more in later fictions.

The newness of Austen is in her voice. A consistently ironic novelist,
she speaks to us in a voice that authorizes itself by virtue of its clarity,
its invulnerability to illusions, its directness and economy. Hers is a
prose unembarrassed by directness and explicitness: "The visions of

romance were over," reads the first sentence of chapter 25 (p. 199). The famous first sentence of *Pride and Prejudice* rings with the authority both of clarity and of correctness: "It is a truth universally acknowledged, that a single man in possession of a good fortune, must be in want of a wife." Near the end of her career, the first sentence of *Persuasion* is also precise, unabashed, funny, and rich with possibilities: "Sir Walter Elliot, of Kellynch Hall, in Somersetshire, was a man who, for his own amusement, never took up any book but the Baronetage." We find an equally direct and characteristic statement at the start of *Emma:* "The real evils indeed of Emma's situation were the power of having rather too much her own way, and a disposition to think a little too well of herself." Such writing is so filled with light, clarity, and judgment implicit or explicit that it would seem there is little room for drama and complexity of imagination. D. H. Lawrence heard this voice as expressing "the sharp knowing in apartness instead of knowing in togetherness" that marks a characteristic English denial of life.[9] But Lawrence is only articulating a modern prejudice that emerges from the absence of experience of "togetherness," an absence more akin to the monster's alienation from a community already perceived as decadent and corrupt than to the sustaining presence of community in Jane Austen's own characters. For the lucidity and apartness of this prose is surely based in a sense of vital and confident community. The voice, with its ironic certainty and directness, seduces us from falling away into the private sensibility of our uniqueness and energy, a sensibility that Austen would see as "unnatural," and alien.

Emma and Sir Walter Elliot, as they are framed by the sentences I have quoted, are imagined, ironically, as too confident within the community according to which they define their power. The "Baronetage" is a text that affirms a community, but Sir Walter uses it to feed an ego that imagines only his superiority to it. Emma is in danger of a similarly separating egoism, her text being not a book but the surrounding community that spoils her and thus encourages her merely private sensibility. *Pride and Prejudice,* contrarily, begins with a widely held maxim of both literature and society, and the novel grows narratively from that maxim. In each case there is a text endorsed by or growing out of a wide community of judgment, and Austen the narrator moves through the experience of the narrative to discover what is essentially and validly communal in the text. Her voice speaks with an authority superior to that of any individual consciousness within her narrative—even that of, say, Henry Tilney—because it can read any text with authority and can, unlike even Mr. Knightley, locate the reverberations of genuine feeling within the language of social sense.

Irony, of course, is not parody, but as parody is a rereading of old texts, so it is predominantly ironic. And *Northanger Abbey*, among Austen's completed novels, is the beginning of the ironic mode that grows to such authority of feeling by the end of her career. *Northanger Abbey* is unusual in Austen's canon only because it is parodic and thus gives us an opportunity to observe directly the not quite hidden literary sources of her characteristic voice, and of the characteristic forms of her major novels.

Parody is a necessarily self-contradictory form. It is not an accident, for example, that in her only direct parody Austen steps into the narrative to give explicit and unequivocal praise to the fiction she seems to be mocking. As we have seen, she does not pretend to be writing a true history, but is a novelist writing a novel. She will not, she says, "adopt that ungenerous and impolitic custom so common with novel writers of degrading by their contemptuous censure the very performances, to the number of which they are themselves adding" (ch. 5, p. 37). Rather, novelists must protect one another, for their works are products of "genius, wit, and taste" which "afford extensive and unaffected pleasure." Parody, that is, implies respect and affection for what it must dismiss, and that duality is built into the entire novel.

The critical commonplace that the book begins in parody and is to a certain extent trapped by the literary gimmickry it rejects is misleading only in the suggestion that the entrapment is an accident of Austen's immaturity at the time. Rather, it is a condition of the form. From the start, Austen exposes the implication of her parody in the form it mocks. For although our attention in the first pages is directed to the delightful spoofing of the reader's expectations of a heroine, by the end of the first chapter, Austen happily allows that Catherine is, after all, a heroine: "But when a young lady is to be a heroine, the perverseness of forty surrounding families cannot prevent her. Something must and will happen to throw a hero in her way" (ch. 1, p. 17). There is, to be sure, some mockery here, and an interesting blurring of the heroine's intentions with those of the author, but the form of the narrative confirms what the narrator here playfully allows. Catherine is, simply, to be rather a different kind of heroine from the one caricatured at the start and in the behavior of Isabella Thorpe. The narrative's investment in Catherine is no less complete than a sentimental novel's in its heroine.

The entrapment in the parodied form is inherent in Austen's imagination, and reflects her consciousness of the way all narrative is at least partly governed by energies and desires not easily contained within the ironies so natural to her. Catherine Morland, that realist antiheroine of the first pages, who eats well, sleeps well, and does not suffer too much, gets her way. The forty families cannot prevent her from growing as pretty as a heroine, acting with a kind of sentimental rightness of feeling, and getting the desired mate. Ostensibly educated into moderation and clarity against the excesses of false fictions, she becomes, formally, the determining energy in her world. Her "irrational" refusal to be comforted requires, finally, its alleviation.

The world Catherine ultimately masters (by virtue, to be sure of some compromises) does not seem irrational, if one seeks there for the kinds of "atrocities" Catherine sought while at Northanger Abbey. One can, however, locate the monstrous in England, in "the country and the age in which we live." But it is a monstrousness translated through parody, and I am interested here in identifying that monstrousness as it reappears in new guise in the work of this sanest and most pragmatic realist novelist. The translation, I want to suggest, is effected by a remarkable play of consciousness which immediately recognizes the false projection of feeling on experience, which, as it were, turns on the lights. Light, indeed, is one of the primary images in realistic novels concerned to dispel the illusions of their protagonists and reveal them in the clarity of solid objects sharply visible.[10] Austen makes Northanger Abbey a clean, well-lighted place, and when she wants most to induce in Catherine the morbid fantasies of monstrosity, she blows out the candle. In *Northanger Abbey*, it is this other, this well-lit and hence objectively present monstrousness that is allowed. It must come naturally in the garb of contemporary England, with no metaphysical trappings. The monstrousness of General Tilney I shall be discussing is enacted formally by his resistance to Catherine's desires. But I will conclude by suggesting another kind of monstrousness in the narrative, one inherited much less self-consciously from the parodied forms. We could see it more clearly if Austen's world were less well-lit, if it remained less frequently outside the consciousness of her heroine, if Catherine, that is to say, looked long and deep in the mirror.

Everywhere in the narrative there are twists that require us to claim for *Northanger Abbey* the devices it seems to introduce entirely for parodic purposes. The laundry list, for example, in the book's last wonderful joke, turns out to have been left there by the servant of the man whose marriage to Eleanor Tilney makes possible Catherine's marriage to Henry. We laugh at the artificiality of the device, but if we can dispense with the connection between Eleanor's husband and the laundry list, we cannot do without the husband as a fictional device. After all, Catherine must, on the terms of the genre Austen adopts, marry the hero; at the same time, the conditions of the world created in the novel make such a marraige very improbable. At ease in the comedy, Austen and her readers allow the rabbit, or the husband, to be pulled out of the hat so that Catherine may become a genuine heroine. We can feel, in this twist, a separation of plot from the primary concerns of the novel that will become more apparent and more damaging in later writers. Here we sense that the true exploratory business of the novel is over before the last chapter. What is required there is only a conciliation between the discoveries made and the initiating desires.

Such twisting is different only in degree from what we find in most of Austen's novels, whose narratives move less arbitrarily toward the "perfect union" at the end of *Emma*. With all of Whately's praise of the "probability" of Jane Austen's narratives, romance devices remain the chief means by which the plots are resolved. The twist normally follows a moment in which the Austenian light finally dawns on the protagonist so that the false and excessive are recognized. "What have you been judging from," asks Henry Tilney, forcing Catherine to see the light at the Abbey. It is a muted version of the old Aristotelian recognition and reversal. If the particular details of the reversal are artificial and, as in *Northanger Abbey*, comically treated as mere conventions, they are certainly meant to correspond to an enlightened reality whose exposition would move beyond the limits of comic narrative. The correspondence is sufficient to guarantee the ultimate probability.

This form, so central to Austen's novels, is what C. S. Lewis has called the form of "undeception," or of "awakening."[11] On the model of Don Quixote, I prefer to call it "disenchantment," primarily because that word implies a loss as well as a gain. The enchantment is the work of the free play of the imagination, uninhibited by critical consciousness. Whatever name we choose, however, the form is recognizable throughout the tradition of the realist novel: the story of hero or heroine who must learn to recognize and reject youthful fantasies (normally first learned from books) in order to accept a less than romantic and more tediously quotidian reality. In this respect, *Northanger Abbey* is a near if rather slight and girlish cousin of *Madame Bovary, Don Quixote, Great Expectations, Pendennis, Jude the Obscure*, and *Emma*.

Parody and this form are frequently conjoined. The form begins in antagonism to falsifications, in literature and society, of the possibilities of personal satisfaction or personal power, of the nature of social relations, of what constitutes true feeling. These falsifications, modeled on fictional conventions, almost always take the shape of excesses in which characters attempt to project the shape of those conventions onto their lives and to stretch beyond the limits of the quotidian. There are real feelings, but you can be sure they are not real if they are expressed in a language that insists on its own high sensibility and on the primacy of the ideal in life itself. Nevertheless, in such fictions, the most attractive moments are usually those that come under the spell of enchantment, in the stretching of the protagonist's reach, or in the comic incongruity that the protagonist cannot quite perceive. The enchantment is indispensable to the narrative. Partly for this reason, novels cannot remain parodies very long, but stretch to find in their own new terms adequate replacements for the rejected enchantment.

Thus parody as a form always seems simpler and less serious than it is likely to become. Not only does it imply respect for what is to be lost in the rejection of the earlier fiction, but it must exist in the medium of its predecessor. The texture of parody is normally comic, while the object of parody is normally a literature allowing too easy triumphs for hero or heroine, that is, literature in a comic form. The logic of rejection would often entail (as in *Northanger Abbey* itself) an unhappy ending. But a comic texture tends to imply a comic form so that to be true to its content, parody would likely be untrue to its form.

Despite these difficulties, parody's centrality to the history of the novel is well established. The classic case has been made by Harry Levin, in *The Gates of Horn*,[12] who traces the novel's history as a series of movements through parody, running from *Don Quixote,* through *Joseph Andrews, Tristram Shandy, Les Liaisons dangereuses,* to *Northanger Abbey,* the early Thackeray, even Joyce, and now Pynchon. Parody, as I have already argued, implies realism somewhere within it. Insofar as we think of parody more generally as any work whose formal principles are determined by self-conscious rejections of earlier fictions—as antiliterary literature—we would probably have to include every novel that makes a real development in fictional technique by freeing itself from the conception of the real currently dominant.

There are not two but three terms in parody, as Levin has shown. There is the past literature; there is its ostensible opposite; and there is the new reality that emerges from their juxtaposition. It is Gombrich's history of graphic representation—first making, then matching, then a revised matching, and so on. Catherine's innocence, an ironic commentary on sentimental novels, allows her to behave with precisely the kind of passionate naiveté that gives her the qualities of a romantic heroine. So the "new reality" emerging from the contest between enchantment and disenchantment participates in and takes much of its shape from the two literary ideas. Very quickly, it becomes itself a literary tradition. Thus, as Austen denies assumptions about heroism for the sake of "useful, plain sense," she also rejects the subjective view of the world as a place where intense private feelings can determine the shape of experience. It cannot be the protagonist, but either the world or the author that satisfies irrational desires, for the heroine cannot embody the necessary energies. Catherine cannot turn herself into a gothic heroine by dreaming it, and she cannot marry Henry Tilney simply because she loves him. But Austen can arrange things so that the general will imagine her as rich (by using the conventions of the older tradition of literature) and thus make the marriage possible. The satisfaction of desire that impels Austen's narrative as fully as it would that of a sentimental novel comes in her fictions through a new reality that allows such resolutions not through large passions but through rational understanding, of the self, and of the necessary conventions of the community.

In its parodic progress through several kinds of fictions,[13] *Northanger Abbey* works to demystify personal and social relations. Catherine's function in all this is surprising if one assumes that she is merely the silly mock heroine of the sequence at the Abbey. In fact, through most of the first half of the book, she is an entirely level-headed young woman whose behavior goes askew only when she is under the pressure of supposedly more mature characters. She is a young woman largely unspoiled by the mystifications in the novels she enjoys, and previously unexposed to people who use fiction's language seriously, and hence dangerously. Thus, for example, when she sees Henry Tilney talking to "a fashionable and pleasing-looking young woman, who leant on his arm," she immediately guesses that the woman is Tilney's sister,

> thus unthinkingly throwing away a fair opportunity of considering him lost to her for ever, by being married already. But guided only by what was simple and probable, it had never entered her head that Mr. Tilney could be married; he had not behaved, he had not talked, like the married men to whom she had been used; he had never mentioned a wife, and he had acknowledged a sister. [ch. 8, p. 53]

Catherine, that is to say, constructs her life on the same rules of probability that govern Austen's novel. The parody here is not at the expense of Catherine; her action is a commentary on a way of imagining relations that complicates where simplicity will do, and, of course, on the fictions that assume the world moves in accordance with such "improbabilities." Here, as almost everywhere, Austen's assumption that human relations can be understood rationally is strongly in evidence. The danger to be avoided is a way of seeing and acting that would destabilize the significances so clearly apparent in behavior. Isabella Thorpe's behavior is a quite serious subversion of the legibility of experience.

The danger of such subversion is implicit in the severity with which Isabella is treated in the denouement, and it is made all the more serious because the novel dramatizes that social relations are complicated enough, difficult enough to read, without unnecessary mystifications. For Henry Tilney, the representative voice of ordered society and of the legibility of experience, violates one of the rules of that society in marrying Catherine. He does so, however, because his father has forced a situation that requires invoking another rule. Henry is described, on the last page of the novel, as feeling himself "bound as much in honour as in affection to Miss Morland, and believing that heart to be his own which he had been directed to gain, no unworthy retraction of a tacit consent, no reversing decree of unjustifiable anger, could shake his fidelity, or influence the resolutions it prompted." Once the general makes an implicit commitment to Catherine, of the sort that *can* be read, by treating her as he did at the Abbey before he expels her, he is morally obliged to accept her as his daughter-in-law even if she has been wrong to aspire above her station, and he wrong in thinking her a social equal. The social order remains always outside any individual consciousness and provides a frame even for self-contradiction.

By invoking two contradictory social and moral principles, however, Austen moves beyond what parody can handle. If the parody be directed at the falsification of excess and the consequent distortion of society, it cannot really function when the heroine has become the victim of distortion and the hero is attempting to set things right again. Thus the last chapters, however self-conscious in their own way, leave parody behind. The logic of parody, in fact, requires that the parodied distortion have painful consequences: otherwise there would be nothing important to parody. But Catherine is not really an antiheroine; she is both too sensible and too capable of genuine feeling. Thus, to satisfy her Austen must use the impossibilities of the world of excess and mystification as though they were possible. Although Henry Tilney acts from sane and strong moral principles, and from a clear understanding of social realities, only luck and the comic-gothic mechinations of James Thorpe and the general make it possible for him to use those principles for the happiness of our new kind of heroine. We know that it is an ordered and sensible world Jane Austen is creating, yet *Northanger Abbey* can remain a comedy only because while the world is morally meaningful, it is not, after all, so simply comfortable to the Whatelyan ideal as the demystifying parody would imply.

The difficulty in *Emma* is, I think, a more sophisticated and impressive version of the difficulty in *Northanger Abbey*. It depends upon the assumption that the real world, into which the heroine is disenchanted, is in fact as firmly ordered as, and ultimately morally better than, the world of illusion she has been forced to abandon. On the basis of this Whatelyan faith, Austen can be a comic realist; through it she can disregard the potential disruptions in the background that are consequent on her heroine's satisfaction and on the formal enclosure of the narrative. Any questioning of that faith—of the sort characteristic of Victorian novelists—will make the mode of parody and disenchantment seem a repressive one, and will drive a wedge between the requirements of plot and the directions of realism.

For the mode Austen develops requires the same sort of chastisement of ambition we have seen in *Frankenstein*. A structure in which social order is ideal is a structure that finds personal ambition disruptive, unless, that is, personal ambition coincides with social need. That is the resolution toward which Austen's novels point, but it is also a characteristic of novels of disenchantment that they harbor, imaginatively, a secret sympathy with aspirations to break from the quotidian, the sensible, the ordinary. After all, the structure of *Northanger Abbey* is designed to fulfill the ambitions that the heroine could not, until the end, quite allow herself to have. She earns it morally by acting with unselfconscious decorum; but the plot awards it to her quite unconvincingly. One of the difficulties of *Mansfield Park* is that it allows itself no secret sympathy with ambition and divides ambition from propriety in the two figures of Mary Crawford and Fanny Price, two alter egos of the innocent Catherine. Mary seems to get less, Fanny Price more than she deserves, but only if one misunderstands Austen's moral commitment in her novels of disenchantment. The attempt to punish ambition in a novel that does not seem to follow the structure of disenchantment, as *Mansfield Park* does not, tends to seem arbitrary and unfair. But Fanny, who has not even the spontaneous honesty of her feelings that Catherine has, is the submissive Catherine Morland in a more serious novel, without the overt structural support of comedy and ironies.

The moral energies begin to edge into conflict with the literary and imaginative energies—to separate themselves out, through the characters and the plots. In the quintessential Austen story, plot and substance are one. Personal ambition, for example, is a form of the very punishment it will induce because it is a distortion of reality which reality must correct. The fullest imagination will, then, detect the distortion, as Emma's imagination finally does, with Knightley's help. But a problem with *Mansfield Park* is that Fanny's imagination seems largely passive and lacks the life and the authenticity one feels in Mary Crawford's. Fanny becomes a sentimental heroine, a Pamela without Pamela's energy, while Mary Crawford seems not to distort reality the way Isabella Thorpe does. Fanny's priggish sense of the moral wrong in acting a play while Sir Thomas Bertram is away, as against the Crawfords' vital willingness to violate decorum for the sake of enspiriting play, seems superior only in a bookish and rule-bound way. Lionel Trilling calls Fanny a "Christian heroine," and Catherine Morland, though less fussily, is a Christian heroine, too. That kind of heroism requires the sort of passive acquiescence in society that Austen's novels tend to belie: the life of *Mansfield Park* is in its Crawfordian resistance to authority; the life of *Northanger Abbey* is in the heroine's active, not passive, growth into the social norms.

I have suggested in the earlier discussion of *Emma* and *Persuasion* how Austen might yet be seen as endorsing an ambition not entirely consonant with this ideal of Christian heroism. The endorsement is, in terms of her chosen form, incomplete, as her moral commitment required that it be. But in the dialectics of development from parody through novel and onward, Anne Elliot's education is not so much in the chastisement of ambition and personal desire, as in the ways to endure the loss that must follow. The narrative form of *Persuasion* must confirm Anne's ambition (as the narrative of *Emma* did not confirm Emma's), but Austen will not have it do so in the solitary contemplation of a disembodied correctness. She still requires a social confirmation.

Once again, it is luck that produces the happy ending, as it is in *Northanger Abbey*. Wentworth comes back a wealthy man, and a series of coincidences reveal to him that Anne still loves him and is both capable and lovable. Anne, then, escapes her unjust punishment as Emma escapes any just punishment, except her formal recognition of the distortions caused by her own subjectivity. Allowing Wentworth to become a good match fudges the nature of the commitment somewhat, but on the whole the novel seems to move to the side of energy and romance, not merely imaginatively, but morally as well. The commitment entails a fundamental change in the novel's structure. There is no disenchantment in *Persuasion*.

Surely, Anne is no Marlovian overreacher. Indeed, she must learn again to begin reaching at all. But that her original ambitions are endorsed by the narrative suggests how Austen's imagination flirted with the opposite of her critical and ironic commitment. There is a continuing tension between personal need and desire and social order. The essential amoral thwarting of all personal ambition, latent in the form of disenchantment, is incompatible with Jane Austen's comic mode, for only if ambition is seen as an unequivocal evil against a society fundamentally sound can the form resolve itself in poetic justice. Among later Victorian novelists the tendency is also to see such ambitions and illusions as evil, but with them it is far more difficult to dramatize the goodness of either the natural or the social order. The form implicit in *Persuasion* keeps struggling to get loose and to grow.

Any shift of authorial endorsement from social order to personal desire is also a wedge between language and posited object. The incommensurateness of language and reality makes Austen's kind of civilizing art impossible. In *Persuasion*, then, she moves very close to a disabling fiction. From the parody of *Northanger Abbey* to the quasi-endorsement of a new kind of "sentimental" heroine in *Persuasion*, Austen marks a wavering progress developed out of the sensible recognition that both sides of the opposition implicit in parody are attractive and have at least potential validity. Anne Elliot is the sensible heroine who acts with the instinct of someone whose imagination is in accord with realities; she is also the heroine of sensibility, whose intensity and vulnerability of feeling mark her off from the merely prudential or the falsely sentimental figures around her.

III

I want to return, at last, to the pursuit of the monstrous in *Northanger Abbey*. Whatever the myriad surface details, the obstructing facts and ironies, realistic fictions and novels of disenchantment and parodies of romance literature are all controlled formally by the needs of the heroes and heroines as their creators imagine them. I have always suggested that not only does Austen assert early on that Catherine is a heroine, but she dramatizes it. The extent of the dramatization will suggest how thoroughly committed to her the narrative is, how monstrous thwarting of her must seem to be, even in comedy, and how great the energy required to avert the thwarting. The demands of the novel form in which the parody lives require that Catherine be more than a token in playful opposition to other kinds of fiction.

She has some of the spontaneous ethical sense that, as Ian Watt points out, was a characteristic of eighteenth-century thought, and that Jane Austen gave to Anne Elliot as well.[14] One of the most moving and effective passages in *Northanger Abbey* deals with material that might, more claustrophobically, have come from Richardson. Catherine is being bullied, cajoled, and threatened by the Thorpes and her own brother to go with them rather than keep her promise to walk with Miss Tilney. However slight and comic the scene, it brilliantly creates an atmosphere of frustration and desperation that at once imitates, laughs at, and uses scenes out of Richardson and later popular novelists. We feel real concern for Catherine, whom the trio has effectively misled into another expedition earlier. Her strength of refusal is both more credible and, perhaps, more moving than Pamela's capacity to keep Lord B. off while she is trapped in his bed. Against Catherine's wishes, James Thorpe tells Miss Tilney that Catherine is otherwise engaged. The speech that follows is short, mature, heroine-like: "This will not do," she says. "I cannot submit to this" (ch. 13, p. 100). The echo of the earlier fiction is intensified because Catherine is restrained physically

—the entrapped heroine after all. She tears herself away from the grip of Isabella and James and dashes to the Tilneys' residence. Breathless, inarticulate, she races past the servant at the door, bursts into the drawing room, and makes her explanation.

This is not merely parody, and there is little comedy in it, the laughter, if any, being mildly and compassionately directed at Catherine, whose motives are entirely right, entirely spontaneous, innocent, and heroic. Catherine is not imitating books; Austen is. And instead of making Catherine seem silly because she acts out a false ideal, Austen makes her seem strong because in her spontaneous feelings she is giving us a true version of the false heroism of romance.

Thus what we observe in *Northanger Abbey* is not the rejection of heroism but its translation into another language. When Catherine feels she is being snubbed by Henry at the theater, she is described in this way:

> Feelings rather natural than heroic possessed her; instead of considering her own dignity injured by this ready condemnation—instead of proudly resolving, in conscious innocence, to show her resentment towards him who could harbor a doubt of it, to leave to him all the trouble of seeking an explanation, and to enlighten him on the past only by avoiding his sight, or flirting with somebody else, she took to herself all the shame of misconduct, or at least of its appearance, and was only eager for an opportunity of explaining its cause. [Ch. 12, p. 93]

Here we have the sentimental conventions, the imagined opposite, and a new sort of reality, which is really a new sort of heroism. Catherine simply has another and a more convincing way to show her innocence than does the heroine of the sentimental novel. But they are both really innocent, really heroines.

Of course, as Henry James might have said, Catherine is too slight a vessel to carry a more ambitious novel. She is a tryout for dramas in which the questions of guilt and innocence and the nature of illusions are more complex, more serious. But it is not a long step from Catherine to Emma, or from Emma to Isabel Archer.

Having discovered the romantic heroine in translation, all that is left is to discover the monster. And, as should already be clear, just as the parodied fiction leaves its residue of romance in Austen's two inches of ivory, so it leaves its residue of villainy. We always need to be reminded that however slight the narrative may seem, there are serious issues involved in Austen's fictions. To be sure, it is a strain for a twentieth-century audience to feel the moral enormity of Catherine's enforced early morning coach ride from the Abbey to her home. But Henry and Eleanor Tilney feel it, and so too does the narrator. The usually generous-hearted Catherine, when told the whole story of the expulsion from the Abbey by the general, comes to feel it. She, "at any rate, had heard enough to feel, that in suspecting General Tilney of either murdering or shutting up his wife, she had scarcely sinned against his character, or magnified his cruelty" (ch. 30, p. 247). Even if there be a touch of irony at Catherine's expense here, the last fluttering of parody, the sentence is largely justified by the narrative. As A. N. Kaul puts it, "The monster of avarice, when she finally recognizes him, turns out to be as cruel and ruthless as any monster she had imagined, and not half so remote."[15] The monster is not so monstrous as Frankenstein's monster, yet the general subverts the moral order as radically, and perhaps more, because he does it from within and from a position of power. In any case, I have been interested here in patterns far more than in literal romances, literal monsters; and the pattern is there.

I have already suggested that there is another sort of monstrousness implicit in the novel, however—one that would be visible if Catherine Morland had examined her lineaments in a mirror. Putting aside the metaphor, what I mean to suggest is that the very structure of narrative, as it embodies both conventions and desires, tends to manifest those disruptive personal energies that the parody and the form of disenchantment are constructed to belie. Through the various devices this essay has considered, Austen quite carefully deflates excess, short-circuits morbid introspection, adjusts personal needs to social order. Yet the very act of doing this entails the final self-contradiction of parody and realism alike. For that act is a large investment of desire— desire for the accommodation of personal need and social necessity.

In a character of our poor heroine, Catherine Morland, that desire is—however lightly—embodied. And as a result, Catherine becomes the shaper of reality. Her dreams, like Mary Shelley's, do give birth to a world. What she wishes is, by convention and need, what takes place. Those who harm her are punished; those who admire her are rewarded. *Northanger Abbey* is a comic novel because its narrative releases Catherine, as Pamela was released by an earlier narrative, from a station in life that promised only tedium and banality. However muted Catherine's ambition, she wants to marry above her station and beyond what Austen's "useful, plain sense" would suggest is possible. She wants more than society allows.

It is worth being reminded that the narrative form through which Austen embodies these satisfied desires is, as I have tried to show, the basic form of her later fictions, as it is of the great majority of novels within the nineteenth-century realist tradition. What is really monstrous in later novels is aspiration beyond the limits imposed by the social and moral order, and thus, in Austen's world, beyond the limits of language to name. Frankenstein's desire to break loose from limits is embodied quite literally in a monster. It has been suggested that Pip, in *Great Expectations,* the quintessential Victorian story of disenchantment, has his double in the murderous Orlick, who acts out in crime what are surely Pip's own unarticulated wishes.[16] Emma manipulates Harriet Smith almost as much as Miss Havisham does Estella, and comes close to ruining her life. Gwendolen Harleth is an accomplice in Grandcourt's death.

In their muted and domestic ways, then, realistic novels contained within their narrative form of disenchantment the very dualism we have seen so starkly and grotesquely worked out in *Frankenstein.* Of course, in so pleasant a book as *Northanger Abbey,* we cannot seriously pursue the notion of Catherine's monstrosity. Catherine's healthy unwillingness to look in the mirror is a refusal of subjectivity and of the imagination of the self's mastery over the objective world. But her story anticipates the increased ambivalence about personal ambition and romantic feeling, the intensifying attraction of the Romantic mirror, that Austen manifests in her later career, and that is so formidable in *Frankenstein.* She surely did enjoy romances, as opposed to the dreary and stilted lessons of *The Spectator,* as she says in chapter 5. Romance, energy, aspiration beyond the congealing limits of ordinary life into a more flexible and pluralist experience are impossible and dangerous. But they constitute an important element even in Austen's fiction. They are, from the perspective of the other Jane Austen, the ironist and spokeswoman for useful, plain sense, monstrous. But they live not only in characters who may be punished; they live at the formal heart of her fictions, balanced delicately against her own incisive ironies, parodied but not dismissed.

Keeping the monster at bay is one part of the realist enterprise. The other is to keep him, or her, alive. Narrative art cannot avoid doing both, for, like *Northanger Abbey,* it must use energy to repress energy, and in reaching beyond words for a truth that will authorize its own language, narrative must confess a disparity between what it can say and what it says it about.

4

Sir Walter Scott
History and the Distancing of Desire

*The numerous vessels of so many different sorts, and destined for such
different purposes, which are launched in the same mighty ocean, although each
endeavours to pursue its own course, are in every case more influenced by the
winds and tides which are common to the element which they all navigate, than by
their own separate exertions. And it is thus in the world, that, when human
prudence has done its best, some general, perhaps national event destroys the
schemes of the individual, as the casual touch of a more powerful being sweeps away
the web of the spider. . . .
But though such an unconnected course of adventures is
what most frequently occurs in nature, yet the province of the romance writer
being artificial, there is more required from him than a mere compliance
with the simplicity of reality . . .*
Sir Walter Scott, Introduction to *The Monastery*

I

Ironically, the first point to be made about Scott as a novelist in relation
to Jane Austen is that he was fundamentally less serious. I do not mean
this as a judgment of their fictional worth or of their importance, but as
a comment on their relation to their narrative materials. Scott almost
never referred to his work without classifying it as "light" literature—a
defensive maneuver, to be sure, but one essential to his achievement
and to the enormous importance of his work. Scott's defensiveness is
reenacted everywhere in his novels: in the elaborate disguises and not
quite sustained anonymity, in his dedications, prefaces, introductions,
intrusions, and, more important, in his narrative style (so frequently
abstract and polysyllabic), in his narrative structures (so arbitrarily
patterned and yet so casual and lax), in his subjects (with their bland
protagonists and their fence-sitting about the clashes between cultures). Scott finds his subjects in the past, and in the past he invested
his fullest, and most disguised, passions. His art, which transformed

81

the history of narrative in Western Europe, both evokes the passions and the excesses he places in the past and protects him from them by placing them there in narratives he refused to take seriously.

Unwilling to imagine himself as serious, he devised a form that radically altered and extended the range of the novel. It was, in fact, an enormously ambitious art, made possible by its own modest commitment to moderation and order and to the exclusion from society of those Napoleonic and monstrous energies his narratives invariably defeat. Scott adored what he could not believe in, and something of the duality of his nature (and his art) is captured in William Hazlitt's brilliant and unsympathetic portrait of him in *The Spirit of the Age:*

> The old world is to him a crowded map; the new one a dull hateful blank. He dotes on well-authenticated superstitions; he shudders at the shadow of an innovation. . . . Our historical novelist firmly thinks that nothing *is* but what *has been*, that the moral world stands still . . . and that we can never get beyond the point where we actually are without utter destruction though everything changes and will change from what it was three hundred years ago to what it is now.[1]

Hazlitt captures the way Scott's incipient historical relativism stops short at the present. Ironically, however, Scott's conservative achievement opened the way for a more thoroughgoing and subversive use of historicism by later realists. For it is this same bigoted Scott of Hazlitt's imagination who, as Karl Kroeber put it, developed the novel into the form that was "best able to express the diversities and complexities of life," and to articulate the post-Augustan sense that life was not "simple, orderly, and rational . . . but wonderfully diverse and complex."[2] His fear of change was the complement of his passion for those figures who were most intently committed to change. The diversity of experience belied his faith in contemporary order and intensified his need for stability; and his narratives always threatened to dissolve into meaningless flux. He invented an art that would honor his passion for the strange and diverse and would avoid the monstrous disruptions these things always threatened.

The excesses that remained for Austen outside the limits of her little country villages are Scott's subject; yet formally, his way into the treatment of those excesses is similar to hers. For *Waverley*, like *Northanger Abbey*, is full of light-hearted and affectionate parody of the traditions of romance. But far more overtly than Austen, Scott indulges the excesses of romance that his hero must outgrow. What Edward Waverley must dismiss, *Waverley* preserves. In Austen, diversity and complexity are elaborated within a single social framework and under the eyes of a shrewdly judgmental narrator. In Scott, there are energies that cannot be contained in such a framework, and they are frequently embodied dramatically in civil war. The narrator, meanwhile, restrains himself from making many Austenian judgments; he gives the act of judgment to history itself. The Whatelyan faith in the meaning and justice of the world is embodied not in the kind of communal consensus we hear in the crisp voice of Austen's narrator, but in a rather Whiggish history, a history that makes its justice, if sometimes rather cruelly.

Scott's parody thus has little of the normative force of Jane Austen's, and parody itself is not a significant element in Scott's oeuvre. But Edward Waverley is a more robust (or perhaps only a more physically active) Catherine Morland, and a more aristocratic one. Like Catherine (or Don Quixote, or Emma Bovary, or Maggie Tulliver) he has read too much in an undisciplined way. His story, then, follows the familiar pattern of disenchantment leading to maturity and compromise.[3] Whereas Catherine is expelled from Northanger Abbey, Edward risks death for rebellion. One is tempted to say that his disenchantment is not so much moral as pragmatic, in part because Fergus MacIvor, the novel's equivalent of General Tilney, is probably less evil while more dangerous. As a rebel, whatever his deviousness, he has a genuine political cause. MacIvor is wrong primarily because he loses. Edward is a pawn in the movement of large historical forces.

Obviously, then, Scott is no mere realistic ironist, and his relation to romance literature is not genuinely parodic. Catherine mistakes ordinary experience for a novel; but Edward's experience is not what Scott described as the subject of Austen's new kind of realistic novel: "nature as she really exists in the common walks of life." Waverley meets and falls in love with a beautiful and daring highland lass, in a setting almost sublime. He meets her brother, who is an imposing and heroic leader of the Jacobite rebellion, and he is honored by the Pretender himself. He participates heroically in the Battle of Prestonpans, and manages to rescue an English officer. Although used by Fergus and the prince, he is hardly mistaken in thinking that the world corresponds to his dreams. Even as he is misled, he is involved importantly in large national affairs, and the narrative seems almost to sanction the romantic dream while making us aware of its absurdity.[4] Edward needs to discover not that his dreams are illusions—though they are for him—but that his nature is not intrinsically romantic after all, and that he sensibly prefers to watch adventure and ambition from the protection of civilized comfort. He must discover also that dreams enacted are counterhistorical: heroism and romance belong to the past,[5] and the consequence of enacting them is the loss of the freedom to dream them. Edward's romance is literary rather than active, a matter of language, not politics. And Scott's art, I will be arguing, as it transforms action into dream, drives a wedge between narrative and desire, between language and action in a way that establishes a pattern for the tradition of realism as it displaces romance.[6]

The separation of language from action in the movement to a more "civilized" society is a major concern of *Waverley*. The playful ironies of Flora MacIvor, talking about Waverley to Rose Bradwardine, are entirely to the point of this separation:

> But high and perilous enterprise is not Waverley's forte. He would never have been his celebrated ancestor Sir Nigel, but only Sir Nigel's eulogist and poet. I will tell where he will be at home, my dear, and in his place—in the quiet circle of domestic happiness, lettered indolence, and elegant enjoyments, of Waverley-Honour. And he will refit the old library in the most exquisite Gothic taste, and garnish its shelves with the rarest and most valuable volumes; and he will draw plans and landscapes, and write verses and rear temples, and dig grottoes; and he will stand in a clear summer night in the colonnade before the hall, and gaze on the deer as they stray in the moonlight, or lie shadowed by the boughs of the huge old fantastic oaks; and he will repeat verses to his beautiful wife, who will hang upon his arm; and he will be a happy man.[7]

Here, Flora the ironist is herself a romantic figure whose language scorns verse making by imitating its romantic conventions. Flora's evocation of the deer "shadowed by the boughs of the huge old fantastic oaks" not only implies the sentimental contemplation of the picturesque so characteristic of the late eighteenth century and so amusingly mocked by Jane Austen in Catherine's view of Bath; it also implies a sharp consciousness of the triviality and emptiness of such insipidly aesthetic romanticism. Implicitly juxtaposed with Waverley's merely verbal or aesthetic romanticism is the high and perilous political enterprise of Fergus—or of Flora herself. Ironically, what Flora describes here is what Scott himself, at Abbotsford, was trying to achieve. In sentimental self-mockery, Scott enacts the movement the whole novel will confirm. Waverley aestheticises the experience that Flora insists on taking practically. The narrative endorses the ineffectual romanticism of Waverley and Scott, just as history (with some help from Scott) has sentimentally romanticized highland life.

In Flora's language, while we mock aesthetic romanticism, we take pleasure in it; and in the narrative as a whole, while we mock Waverley's dreams of an active romanticism, we take pleasure in watching them enacted by Prince Charles, Fergus, Evan Dhu, and Flora herself. Such dualisms, visible in almost all Scott's narratives, are mediated by a narrator who moves ambivalently, even self-contradictorily, between polar oppositions,[8] and sustained in language because they cannot be sustained in action.

Flora's speech can also remind us that the hero of *Waverley* is not much of a hero.[9] No major English writer is more responsible for the death of the hero in fiction than Scott, in spite of Mark Twain's delightfully vicious attack on him for causing the American Civil War. Twain's attack was aimed primarily at Scott's fictions of the Middle Ages (and I will be talking primarily about the Scottish novels); but even the protagonists of the Scottish novels usually appear to have something of the swagger of the chivalric hero. They fight duels (if usually against their wills), are rather touchy on points of honor, in love with the beautiful heroine, involved in dangerous enterprises. Twain accuses Scott of encouraging the dream of chivalry, of celebrating "sham grandeurs, sham gauds, sham chivalries."[10] But the real romance figures—like Flora here—carefully separate the protagonists from the romantic dream as Scott carefully maneuvers them out of the past. Against Scott's false medievalism, Twain sets "wholesome civilization"—"practical commonsense, progressive ideas and progressive works."

But, barring the word "progressive," this is almost the same opposition we find in Scott's novels. The protagonist's heroic qualities of energy, ambition, absolute loyalty, fierce defense of traditional ideas and honor are bedeviled by indecision and passivity. Finally, they must be transmuted into the qualities of a modern, "civilized," gentleman, domesticated and commercially successful. The great chivalric ideals are turned to dream. Language is divorced from action as the hero is from chivalry. If we are to take Mark Twain's description seriously, then, we have to say that the Civil War was not caused by Scott, but by a misreading of him and of his protagonists. Flora would not have made that mistake.

That Scott has managed to have it both ways, even with his critics, is evident in the fact that despite the simplicity of his literary method, his novels are still the subject of radical disagreements, even about their most fundamental literary aims and political and moral commitments. There has been, for example, an inescapable debate about whether Scott was realist or romancer,[11] and this is a literary version of the debate over whether Scott was an idealizer of the past or spokesman for the progress that Twain sought. George Lukács, for example, sees in Scott's fiction the expression, "above all," of a "renunciation of Romanticism, a conquest of Romanticism, a higher development of the realist literary traditions of the Enlightenment in keeping with the new times."[12] If Lukács's emphasis is excessive, he is demonstrably right about Scott's participation in the Enlightenment tradition of antienthusiastic realism.

As James Hillhouse has pointed out, Scott's early reputation depended a great deal on the "reality" of his fictional worlds, and he was perceived as another Defoe, or a latter-day Fielding. Only later, particularly with the writing of his medieval novels and the great popularity of *Ivanhoe*, did the balance of popular approval shift to the "romantic."[13]

The disagreement about Scott probably results from the failure to make a simple distinction between the evident relish with which he portrays the past (and particularly the past irrevocably gone because the historical cause was lost, as with the Stuarts), and his equally evident approval of the present. His narratives frequently remind us (in a style from which Macaulay learned) of the superiority of our civilization to that of the past; yet they relax into the imaginative pleasure of recreating the past well lost and the pain of losing it.

Frederick Pottle offers one of the most illuminating discussions of this ambivalent mode. Scott, he says, "does not, like the more advanced Romantics, believe in the creative imagination as revelatory of truth."[14] Scott saw himself as a practical man of the world, an image Walter Bagehot emphasized: "No man had a stronger sagacity, better adapted from the guidance of common man, and conduct of common transactions. Few could hope to form a more correct opinion on things and subjects which were brought before him in actual life; no man had a more useful intellect."[15] As Pottle argues, Scott had "his perception rooted firmly in the eighteenth century." He sees fiction entirely as make-believe. Hence, "even in his most magnificent writing, he seldom escapes a tone of humorous self-exposure."[16] Scott was neither romancer nor novelist, because he was both. While he called himself a romancer he opposed fact—or history—to fiction, and his obsession with certain kinds of circumstantial reportage is characteristic of English fiction from Defoe on, even though he justifies it through antiquarianism. "It is very interesting," says Pottle, "to see at the basis of his artistic activity this clear, sharp, undistorted, 'realistic' perception of things, and his determination to keep it clear from the play of free imagination."[17] Such determination accounts for much of the antiromantic tone of Scott's narrative style. When the romantic enters, it tends to be defensively wadded about with Enlightenment rhetoric and explanation. Even the young dreamer Waverley is—as Flora perceives—too sensible.

When, for example, Waverley is wounded and treated by a highland "Esculapius," who gives him "to understand that not one of the ingredients had been gathered except during the full moon, and that the herbalist had, while collecting them, uniformly recited a charm," Waverley observed with some surprise, that even Fergus, notwithstanding his knowledge and education, seemed to fall in with the superstitious ideas of his countrymen, either because he deemed it impolitic to affect scepticism on a matter of general belief, or more probably because, like most men who do not think deeply or accurately on such subjects, he had in his mind a reserve of superstition which balanced the freedom of his expressions and practice upon other occasions. [Ch. 24, p. 203]

The superstition is carefully noted; the charm the herbalist spoke while collecting the medicine is carefully transcribed.[18] While we enjoy the mysterious, we are made aware of what people with sense must think about it. Moreover, the implication of Fergus in this primitive absurdity is an important omen that his side cannot win. As Hazlitt knew, the abstract, sensible, explanatory language is justification for including so much superstition and potential mystery: it is a historical *fact* of some importance that, as ballads, charms, folktales imply, people perceived the world superstitiously and romantically. The difference between people then and people now is not intrinsic, but culturally induced. On the verge here of a potentially subversive historical relativism that might threaten the authority of the firm narrative voice—if he chose to look as carefully at the present as he did at the past—Scott is content to retreat to a "tone of humorous self-exposure."

Since the creative imagination does not reveal truth, its primary function is entertainment. The playfulness, sometimes extending into an awkward coyness and tedium, is frequently in the frame of the novels: Jedediah Cleishbotham, Peter Pattieson, and Professor Dryasdust are all part of the game, and where they do not appear, the "Author of Waverley" himself frequently erects elaborate defenses against possible objections. Edward Waverley, we have seen, by sensibly resisting the mumbo-jumbo of the "Esculapius," keeps the Author of Waverley from being implicated in the superstitions. All this playfulness (including Scott's intelligently appreciative review of his own novels)[19] reflects Scott's refusal to "believe in" creative imagination, and thus to risk exposing his desire to the relentless force of history.

It gives to his fictions, moreover, a peculiar, almost modern, sort of self-consciousness. To be sure, modern writers, in their exposure of the fictionality of language and fictions, are far more serious about their play. But while never allowing himself to imagine that fiction could be anything but fiction, Scott gives us a more self-deprecating and amused version of what must happen when any novelists make imaginative forays beyond literature into the real and need to consider the status in truth of what they write.[20]

Scott defensively bolsters his fictions with footnotes and lexicons,[21] urging the possibility of even the most fantastic elements of his narrative, the historical sources for each major incident, the rightness of the decor and the everyday objects that fill his pages. But he suffers no Victorian or modernist anguish in his struggle for the facts; rather, he seems sensibly Johnsonian. Committed to truthfulness, and therefore to assuring his readers that they are reading fictions, he was not concerned, as Henry James was to be, with sustaining illusion. As Dr. Johnson said of the stage audience, Scott might have said of novel readers: "the readers are always in their senses, and know, from the first word to the last, that the page is only a page, and the characters are only characters."[22] He could not see himself as an unacknowledged legislator of mankind, or have sought the esemplastic power. He was only "making things up" for the entertainment of his audience, and the tricks he played on them, the disguises, the self-reflexive games he intruded into the novels, were essentially honest revelations of the fictionality of the fictions.

Like most realists, he had to be sensitive to his audience's expectations, and preoccupied with the conventions of fiction. In the General Preface to the 1829 edition of the novels, and in the first chapter of *Waverley* proper, he amusedly reveals his self-consciousness about conventions. He explains, for example, why he subtitled *Waverley* " 'Tis Sixty Years Since," rather than "A Tale of Other Days":

> Every novel reader [would] have anticipated for the latter title a castle scarce less than that of Udolpho, of which the eastern wing had long been uninhabited, and keys either lost or consigned to the care of some aged butler or housekeeper whose trembling steps, about the middle of the second volume, were doomed to guide the hero or heroine, to the ruinous precincts. [Ch. 1, pp. 31–32]

On the other hand, "A Romance from the German" would have evoked for the most obtuse reader "a profligate abbot, an oppressive duke, a sacred and mysterious association of Rosy crucians and Illuminati...," and so on. If we were to take the first chapter entirely seriously, we would have to read *Waverley* as an evasive action among competing romance conventions or at least as an attempt to define his kind of historical fiction against them.

Such a passage suggests that Scott, in his commitment to fact, was inching toward what would be called a more "realistic" literary form; and he was doing it with the self-conscious clumsiness we have noted in the first chapter in passages from George Eliot and Charlotte Brontë. Scott goes on longer, if less pointedly than they:

The reader may perhaps anticipate, in the following tale, an imitation of the romance of Cervantes. But he will do my prudence injustice in the supposition. My intention is not to follow the steps of that inimitable author, in describing such total perversion of intellect as misconstrues the objects actually present to the scene, but that more common aberration from sound judgment, which apprehends occurrences indeed in their reality, but communicates to them a tincture of its own romantic colouring. [Ch. 5, p. 56]

Even the madness Scott describes will be more "realistic" because less extreme. He is concerned with the "tincture" of the mind's coloring, recognizing in his protagonists that slight failure or distortion of perspective so crucial to realistic narrative.

Scott's kind of fiction was thus to be somewhere between "romance" and "novel." On his definition, a romance is "a fictitious narrative in prose or verse; the interest of which turns upon marvellous and uncommon incidents," as opposed to a novel, "a fictitious narrative, differing from the Romance, because the events are accommodated to the ordinary train of human events, and the modern state of society."[23] Romance, then, tends to be associated with the past, and with excess; the novel, on the other hand, is associated with the present, and the present with a higher degree of civility and prudence in which Scott seems imaginatively uninterested. Perhaps the clearest statement of the way Scott sought to balance the conflicting claims of realism and romance, past and present, excess and sound judgment appears in his introduction to *The Fortunes of Nigel*:

the most picturesque period of history is that when the ancient rough and wild manners of a barbarous age are just becoming innovated upon, and contrasted, by the illumination of increased or revived learning, and the instruction of renewed or reformed religion. The strong contrast produced by the opposition of ancient manners to those which are gradually subduing them, affords the lights and the shadows necessary to give effect to a fictitious narrative; and while such a period entitles the author to introduce incidents of a marvellous and improbable character, as arising out of the turbulence, independence and ferocity, belonging to old habits of violence, still influencing the manners of a people who had been so lately in a barbarous state; yet, on the other hand, the characters and sentiments of many of the actors may, with the utmost probability, be described with great variety of shading and delineation, which belongs to the newer and more improved period, of which the world has but lately received the light.[24]

But given Scott's sense of the conventions, and of the sharpness of the distinction between the factual and the imaginary, he actually felt free to play very casually with the world of the imaginary. Often, the play is allowed to extend into boredom or mere cuteness. The first chapter of *The Bride of Lammermoor*, for example, gives us Peter Pattieson, an unsuccessful artist, Dick Tinto, and an extraordinarily irrelevant narrative of Dick's career. All this is ostensibly to place the narrative in the "past," that is, in traditions of ballad and folktale. But the excess of the story of Dick Tinto can be accounted for only by Scott's unwillingness to take himself seriously. The playfulness is usually, in Scott, related to himself as author and his technique, and thus the sequence is obliquely about the kind of fiction that will follow. The discussion of Peter's excessive use of dialogue is both a defense of Scott's tendency to rely on dialogue and an occasion for suggesting that *The Bride of Lammermoor* is going to be a little different, more descriptive and gothic in mode. Yet one hardly needs Dick or Peter to make such points. In the attenuated tradition of Cervantes and Sterne, the early part of the chapter is devoted to Scott's own disguises as author of the novels, disguises that clearly gave him great pleasure: "Few have been in my secret while I was compiling these narratives," says Peter, smirking with Scott's features.

But because he is merely playing, Scott misses what later novelists would see as opportunities to make the problem of fiction itself one of the novel's major preoccupations. What Carlyle does seriously in *Sartor Resartus*, Scott tosses off casually. Peter, after all, is an editor, piecing together out of the fragments given him by Dick Tinto the narrative of *The Bride*. As the Editor constructs his narrative from the fragments of Teufelsdröckh's life, stuffed in six paper bags, so Peter works with "a parcel of loose scraps, partly scratched over with his pencil, partly with his pen, where outlines of caricatures, sketches of turrets, mills, old gables, dovecotes, disputed the ground with his written propaganda."[25] In Carlyle, of course, the act of constructing Teufelsdröckh's biography is as important as the narrative itself. In Scott, we never again hear of Peter's difficulties. Comfortable among narrative conventions, unalarmed by confusions between fiction and fact, Scott feels no need to push these games to their logical or illogical conclusions. Once we know that the narrative is fictitious, we need not seek revelatory truth behind the narrative, or explore (as in *Wuthering Heights* or *Under Western Eyes*) the complexities of narrative perspective for their influence on the substance of the story.

One of the most painful, self-deprecating intrusions of this kind comes at the end of *Old Mortality*, when Peter Pattieson calls upon Miss Martha Buskbody, who had "read through the whole stock of three circulating libraries," for advice about how to bring the story to a proper conclusion.[26] The sequence is actually funny at the expense of popular taste but it is also embarrassingly incongruous. It implies Scott's radical lack of interest in his own plot, and reminds us again of the severe disjunction between the imagined and the real that marks his narratives. What matters is the recovered past, the beautifully circumstantial realizations of moments both historically singular and humanly characteristic. But the conventions in which Miss Buskbody is interested belong to a different order of writing, an order in which Scott participates and Miss Buskbody delights, but no serious person can invest energies. Lovers must be matched, morals must be carefully educed, villains must be punished, and all loose ends must be carefully tied. The struggle to bring literary form and plausible content together was the task of realists who followed Scott, who took the "creative imagination" more seriously than he.

Scott's dualist attitude toward narrative is interestingly reflected in the attitudes of Macaulay, for whom the split between imagination and fact loomed so large that he had to choose between history and fiction. In that famous burst of youthful excess, Macaulay wrote that "as civilization advances, poetry almost necessarily declines."[27] The consonance of Macaulay's attitudes with Scott's is deliberate. Like Scott, he adored literature and poetry, even while he saw that they were primitive creations, to be displaced by modern sophistication. Fiction could not, then, be a genuine option for him, and he aspired rather to invest history itself with the excitement and the local realism of Scott's novels. Holding tightly to the difference between fiction and fact, he wrote his wonderfully novelistic history—a history that, ironically, is now usually seen as an impressive imaginative construction, rather too self-indulgent in its fictional ways, not entirely reliable as fact.

The self-consciousness about the real and the imagined drives a further wedge between plot and narrative. Scott cannot help being aware of the difference, as he puts it, between "what most frequently occurs in nature," and what must be done in the "artificial . . . province of romance." His historicism, which implied for him a steady progress in history to the present moment, also pointed to all kinds of unfinished stories, meaningless experiences, alternative possibilities, and a cultural relativism. The variousness of experience uncontainable within his chosen narrative forms made him highly conscious of the mere conventionality of the narrative devices he felt obliged to use. He might have agreed with Northrop Frye that "every inherited convention of plot in literature is more or less mad. The king's rash promise, the cuckold's jealousy, the 'lived happily ever after' tag to a concluding marriage, the manipulated happy endings of comedy in general . . . none of these was suggested by any observation of human life or behavior: all exist solely as story-telling devices."[28] Yet, in agreement with Whately, Scott would have some reservations.

History, he might have said, although it demonstrates the madness of these conventions in particular, validates them in general. The various manipulations by which Scott softens reality and, for example, gives Edward Waverley the right bride, the inheritance, the freedom from responsibility for his own rebellious actions, are, in Frye's sense, mad. But that is the very point of the disenchantment plot and of the critical ironic nature of realistic fiction. As the tricks reemerge from the romancer's bag, however, they begin to do the work of history itself. The tag, "they lived happily ever after," in Scott is likely to mean that the protagonist, having found the right side in large historical conflicts, is rewarded personally with the success of the winning party.[29] The good fortune that befalls the hero is absurd in particular but truthful in general.

The romance conventions, then, are forced into consonance with the "plausible content" of Scott's detailed and circumstantial description of people and places. Scott connects "romance," with all its associations of pastness and excess, with a historical vision: all characters are comprehensible only as part of a living society and of a time that determines the possibilities of their most private dreams. This constitutes Scott's great originality and importance, as it has been valued almost from the beginning. John Buchan provides a typical description of this quality of Scott's work: "He led the way in showing his figures in relation to their environment. No novelist has ever painted in more convincingly a social and historical background, for he anticipated Stendhal and Balzac in regarding each character as largely the product of certain material conditions."[30]

Thus, in Scott we find the primary insights upon which realism in the nineteenth century developed accompanied by a powerful distrust of fictions. His work provides the strongest evidence yet that realism was never naively deluded into believing itself a perfect mirror of reality. Certainly, later realists attempted to move toward a more "scientific" rendering of human experience, but Scott, who provided the impulse for this "science," knew he was merely inventing stories. The easy distinction, frequently invoked by modernist critics who focus on the self-reflexive literature of modern French and American writers, cannot hold.[31] Scott is confronted with the modern question, How is it possible to tell the truth in a form that is by its nature untrue? If he does not provide a fully "modern" answer, it is for no lack of sophistication about fictions. He engaged in the realist struggle to get "beyond words," fully conscious that it was impossible, and unwilling to assert the seriousness of his enterprise.

In the theme of disenchantment, as in the details of his narratives, Scott is putting language to the test. Peter Pattieson remarks, in *The Bride of Lammermoor*, that he, "like many others in this talking world, speak now and then a deal more than they act" (ch. 1, p. 26). The duality is at the heart of the Heir of Ravenswood's failure, of the failure of the Jacobites in *Redgauntlet*. As Scott moves closer to the subject and method of realism, he finds himself in a world of words from which action has been withdrawn. Talking without action is the condition of Peter Pattieson, Walter Scott, and the novelist writing for amusement. For Scott, the text takes the place of action: it *is* the novelist's action. Within the text, language and history confront each other, as dreamer and history do, and survival is dependent on not making the wrong commitment, not reaching for the power that history will deny. Language is the protection from the action Scott instinctively admires and will not risk. He notes in a letter how "my rogue always, in despite of me, turns out my hero."[32] But the rogue is one of Scott's lost causes, an exemplar of the threat of ambition. Thus the text, aspiring to a larger, more various, and hence more dangerous reality, circumscribes action, reveals the separation of language and action through language itself. Such a division is central to Scott, central to the realistic novel's tortured history, central to the historical novel. And it entails the demise of the very realistic fiction Scott was so influential in developing all over Europe during the nineteenth century.

II

Action, the "real" as opposed to the merely verbal, belongs in Scott's novels contradictorily to both history and plot. History in Scott is the great plot maker and yet also the redeeming province of fact rather than of his own creative imagination. Yet it manifests itself often in the conventions of romance. Like almost everything else in Scott, history leads a double life, emerging sometimes as the resolver of complexities through the dominance of rational force (in *Waverley*, *Redgauntlet*, or *Old Mortality*), sometimes as monstrous and uncontrollable (as in *The Bride of Lammermoor*). In "A Postscript That Should Have Been a Preface" to *Waverley*, Scott notes for the first time what was to become a convention of his novels: "The most romantic parts of this narrative are precisely those which have a foundation in fact" (p. 513). History releases Scott into romance because it anchors him firmly in fact. While reckless and perfunctory with the inherited materials of romance, Scott gave these same materials, in the shape of a meaningful history, the scrupulous care and engaged energy that seem incompatible with "light" literature.

History in Scott testifies to the *fact* of the marvelous and mysterious. Modern man, the sensible narrator, looks back on the fact and attempts to demystify it by making the extraordinary part of the ordinary. Such demystifying is analogous to what we have already seen in *Northanger Abbey*, but the effect is rather different. The realistic impulse is evident in the way Scott gives to antiquarian details precisely the energies of passion and desire that in romances are traditionally invested in the fates of the protagonists. As the fictional historian of lost causes, Scott finds the richest possibilities of human feeling invariably thwarted by history itself. The novel's tradition of cruelty to the ambitious hero seems confirmed by his histories. His novels thus become fascinated explorations of the rich possibilities of experience held within aesthetic frames. They both invoke excess and restrain it beneath the science and sanity of antiquarianism, conventions of narrative, protective layerings of time.

Edward, the typical Scott protagonist, establishes the model for what amounts to Scott's reconciliation of romantic and Enlightenment materials. In *Waverley*, Scott turns the romantic past into a comprehensible and humanly recognizable experience and yet sustains romance to the end. A consideration of that novel is thus an essential preliminary to any study of the development of realism in English fiction. *Waverley's* formula—its resolved and unresolved tensions—is the formula upon which almost every major English writer of the nineteenth century plays variations. As late as Conrad, we see the shadows of Scott, and as Razumov sits in his rooms with Haldin, we are reminded of Scott's belief that in reality "the schemes of the individual" are destroyed by larger national forces "as the casual touch of a more powerful being sweeps away the web of the spider."

In the postscript to *Waverley*, Scott establishes that critical dichotomy between past and present that embodies so many of the dualisms and self-divisions of his art. He looks back at the difference between Scotland in 1745 and Scotland at the time of the writing, and he is struck by the vast change and improvement:

> There is no European nation which, within the course of half a century or little more, has undergone so complete a change as this kingdom of Scotland. The effects of the insurrection of 1745—the destruction of the patriarchal power of the Highland Chiefs—the abolition of the heritable jurisdictions of the Lowland nobility and barons—the total eradication of the Jacobite party, which, averse to intermingle with the English, or adopt their customs, long continued to pride themselves upon maintaining ancient Scottish manners and customs—commenced this innovation. The gradual influx of wealth and extension of commerce have since united to

render the present people of Scotland a class of beings as different from their grandfathers as the existing English from those of Queen Elizabeth's time. [512–13]

The totality of the change in such a short time makes "sixty years since" conveniently separate the events in the novel from the possibilities of action in the present. Although Scott has been reported as saying that had he been alive in '45 he would have joined the Stuart cause, his Jacobitism in 1814 was a romantic dream. The passage, strictly re-portorial as it purports to be, implies approval of the general condition of the early nineteenth century, of a unified Scotland and England, against the almost tribal and uncivilized conditions that existed only a "half century" ago. There is pride here in the suddenness and com-pleteness of the improvement, although the novels testify to his prefer-ence for the past whose wildness has been properly "eradicated."

Waverley manages to indulge Scott's fascination with vast historic upheavals, large heroic action, irrationality and fanaticism, while finding a language that implies that such things are well gone from human experience. The form that Scott is inventing here—the historical novel—is one that tends to judge the past in terms of the present;[33] Scott the commentator finds the past wanting in all but the charm of ritual and story, and his narrator seems not to participate in the Romantics' antiindustrial nostalgia for the simple life.

But the distance of time allows him a dispassion that is both a mark of the enlightened gentleman and a characteristic for which Scott was honored—or condemned—throughout the nineteenth century. George Eliot, for example, reported that Scott helped her to reject the rigid evangelical piety of her youth because his novels revealed to her that goodness had little to do with belief in any particular religion. Scott's historical particularity, then, was for Eliot importantly ahistorical be-cause it allowed her to see beyond local events into the essence of human nature itself. Scott himself said, at the beginning of *Waverley*, that he had tried to make his true subject universal, not historically particular. He wanted "to throw the force of his narrative upon the characters and passions of the actors—those passions common to men in all stages of society, and which have alike agitated the human heart, whether it throbbed under the steel corselet of the fifteenth century, the brocaded coat of the eighteenth, or the blue frock and white dimity waistcoat of the present day" (ch. 1, p. 34).

But in Scott's language, echo though it may of the Enlightenment, permanence, if it can be imagined at all, is to be found only in history—in the continuities that a historical vision provides. Perma-nence is an aspect of change. Like Eliot, Scott finds his stabilities in those intimations of traditions and past cultures whose transformation he chronicles. The past is a means of explanation of the apparent discontinuities and excesses of experience. The comfort of his confidence that past and present are intelligible helped release him into the primary pleasure of his fiction—not that of explaining, or demystifying, the complications he creates or records, but of presenting the muddles, the contrasts, the variousness of the simple facts of everyday life. Modestly, and with no claims to be doing anything but "light" romances, Scott imagined the possibility of representation of the elusive truth of past reality. The antiquarian and the realist impulse merge.

Scott's confidence allows him not to take sides, and to treat with equal compassion Fergus and Colonel Talbot, Flora and Rose Bradwardine, Jacobite and Hanoverian. It also suggests, however, that the realist impulse makes an odd and only temporary bedfellow with the moral engagement that accompanied it in early and mid century. For any writer seeking a way to identify some meaningful authority, Scott's dispassion is sign of a failure of belief, of a disengaged literature. "One sees not," says Carlyle, "that he believed in anything: nay he did not even disbelieve; but quietly acquiesced, and made himself at home in a world of conventionalities; the false, the semi-false and the true were alike true in this, that they were there, and power in their hands more or less."[34] Belief in what was there—exactly what Carlyle did not really believe in—kept Scott free of the sage's burden of disentangling "the false, the semi-false, and the true." Yet, surely, Carlyle's own historical reconstructions, especially the wonderful Jocelin sections of *Past and Present*, depend at least in part on a very Scott-like awe of the simple reality—the "thereness'—of people of the past. Carlyle is right that Scott tends to write without intensity—"*in extenso*, . . . not *in* ˙*intenso*"—but casual toying with plot and prose is a condition of that risk-taking thrust at reality through which Scott recreated the past. He sees the past with a passion for the variety of reality, not with inhibiting judgment of moral placing.

Where Carlyle could insist on the intrinsic wonder of the most trivial object of experience, in a prose powerfully selective and symbolic, Scott wrote—even in his most conventionally stilted passages—in a relaxed narrative style that gives the appearance of a genuine democracy of observation. The details are there as what they are, objects that an antiquarian or student of human nature would know belong in the ordinary lives of his characters. Intensity gives way to an ideal of polite and decorous talk that assumes the audience's interest in the details for their own sake. In other words, the failures Carlyle notes in Scott, like the virtues George Eliot approves, are evidences of Scott's centrality to the tradition of realism.

If Scott had been a true "romancer," he would have attended more to his plots. That wedge between plot and narrative that becomes of greater importance later in the century begins with Scott.[35] His fascination with details, with character, with good things to hang on his plots[36] left him impatient with plot itself. He could not bear to work his plots out beforehand and wrote—as Carlyle noted—with unsystematic energy that seems regardless of large-scale development and coherence, and is unconcerned with the "ideal." *Waverley* thus unfolds, somewhere between novel and romance, between past and present, most interesting when the plot stands aside for the plausible and textured imagination of another time, another place.

Despite enthusiasts and heroes on both sides, Edward Waverley, the first of Scott's inadequate heroes, comes as close as any figure might to bearing the burden of the novel's moral ideal, for that ideal is as much aesthetic as moral. He is disengaged from the violence of history, while he becomes the vehicle through which Scott evokes that violence; and his own politics are entirely personal. He is no more partisan than the narrator. Midway in the novel, Waverley "contemplated the strangeness of a fortune, which seemed to delight in placing him at the disposal of others without the power of directing his own emotions" (ch. 39, p. 298). Such fortune happily keeps him from serious choice. He is, characteristically for a young Scott protagonist who has a lot to learn, swept away by energies and enthusiasms of the moment, but consequently not held responsible for his action by his narrative. The most powerful force, ultimately, will be the force of history, and thus the fortune that keeps Waverley from responsibility turns out to be great good luck. Others are more courageous, more clever, more devoted to political ideals, but none is so lucky.

That luck represents both the necessities of the form of disenchantment and its reconciliation with history and "fact." Scott merges his values with the romance form by seeing Waverley caught up in history in spite of himself, and then allowing him, as it were, to join history. Typically, the hero of a Scott novel moves with history (as does, for example, Roland Graeme in *The Abbot*). His "insipidity" allows him to acquiesce in the historical shift of power to join the winning side, since he has never made anything but a superficial commitment to either side. And thus, as in the beginning it is history that brings the burden of disenchantment to the romantic youth (the capture of the Jacobites ends Waverley's flirtation with them), so in the end it is history that frees the now sensible young man (a Whig once more, Waverley inherits the family lands and the affections of Colonel Talbot and the far more moderate Rose). The romance plot is awkwardly assimilated to the historical context, yet it makes sense by rewarding the disengaged. Of course, the literary luck that aligns the hero with history and gets him off free from his rebellious activities keeps Scott and his hero from having to face the full political, social, and literary implications of his story and of his form. The coincidence of history and romance is rather too convenient.

Scott rarely attempts to probe deeply into the problematic nature of the reality his novels create. His world is so changeable and so powerfully determining of the lives of individuals that its potentiality for tragedy or irony is very high, but his novels offer no ironic exploration of reality implying a critique of the conventions and values of his own time. Even in Scott realism is an ironic form, but the ironies seem invariably at the expense of a mistaken past, or of youth, or of dream. As the heroes acquiesce in the flow of history toward Scott's own times, the power of their stories to provide a critical perspective on the present diminishes. The humorous self-exposure that Pottle finds in the most serious of Scott's works is the ultimate protective irony. Like his heroes, Scott has acquiesced in the "sound judgment" of the modern world, and thus his art almost invariably lapses into the self-deprecation that can be the ultimate complacency: none of this really matters very much, after all. The fictions, in their casual and rapid movements, minimize themselves and refuse to attain distinction. Carlyle's remark here is appropriate: "No man has written as many volumes with so few sentences that can be quoted."[37]

In a sequence that might have been the dramatic center of *Waverley*, we can observe most of these qualities of Scott's art. It mixes irony and romance, lapses into an extraordinarily stilted abstract language— almost a parody of Enlightenment prose—and, while bringing the protagonist to a critical choice, attempts to control the enthusiasm that it is mimicking. Given the stilted nature of the language, it ought to be an absolute failure. Yet there are elements in it, emerging from Scott's mixed perceptions of the experience and his sense of its historical place, that redeem it. The key passage is introduced by the prince's invitation to Waverley to join the rebellion. The prince speaks in a wonderfully regal way, and yet with a touch of the familiar, alluding to Waverley's family and concluding with this touching and yet still formal appeal:

> If Mr. Waverley should, like his ancestor, Sir Nigel, determine to embrace a cause which has little to recommend it but its justice, and follow a prince who throws himself upon the affections of his people, to recover the throne of his ancestors or perish in the attempt, I can only say, that among these nobles and gentlemen he will find worthy associates in a gallant enterprise, and will follow a master who may be unfortunate, but, I trust, will never be ungrateful.

Prince Charles speaks like a figure in a romance, an ideal and embattled fighter for the just who is full of compassion for others and has retained his dignity despite injustice and dispossession. Yet we can see Scott understanding that it *is* idealizing, and self-idealizing, at that. Charles is using the conventions of romance to persuade a naive but important young man to join him. Thus, though the language is that of romance, the context is that of a novel in which the character and motive of the speaker and of the listener undercut the idealization. Scott is here attempting to give us his sense of how Charles managed to muster his forces and gain such popularity in 1745: he may be enjoying but he cannot possibly be taken in by the romance language.

The evidence of much else in the novel indicates that the narrator knows quite well that there is some doubt about the "justice" of the cause. It is not that Prince Charles is a hypocrite; rather, he is a politician. Since, on the whole, the prince is imagined entirely in his public guise, the novel will not allow us to speculate on his sincerity. Certainly, the rhetoric of the novel, here as elsewhere, allows the prince his public dignity, but requires that we understand that his enterprise is both foolhardy and illegal, if not unjust.

The entire rhetorical strategy of this and the crucial passage that it introduces are aimed at exonerating the hero of *Waverley* from the crime of acquiescence in the prince's request. Emphasis falls on the essential powerlessness of Waverley under the pressure of accumulated circumstances and the undisciplined enthusiasms and naiveté of his spirit. The next paragraph shifts away from the romance of the moment, explores the politics of the situation, and allows us to see it from the perspective of the naive Edward Waverley himself. Thus, when the passage concludes with another romance gesture, we can only have a double perspective on the scene:

> The politic Chieftain of the race of Ivor knew his advantage in introducing Waverley to this personal interview with the royal Adventurer. Unaccustomed to the address and manners of a polished court, in which Charles was eminently skilful, his words and his kindness penetrated the heart of our hero, and easily outweighed all prudential motives. To be thus personally solicited for assistance by a Prince, whose form and manners, as well as the spirit which he displayed in this singular enterprise, answered his ideas of a hero of romance; to be courted by him in the ancient halls of his paternal palace, recovered by the sword which he was already bending towards other conquests, gave Edward, in his own eyes, the dignity and importance which he had ceased to consider as his attributes. Rejected, slandered, and threatened upon the one side, he was irresistibly attracted to the cause which the prejudices of

education, and the political principles of his family, had already recommended as the most just. These thoughts rushed through his mind like a torrent, sweeping before them every considera- tion of an opposite tendency—the time, besides, admitted of no deliberation—and Waverley, kneeling to Charles Edward, devoted his heart and sword to the vindication of his rights! [Ch. 40, pp. 308–9]

Concentrated here, albeit in relatively simple form, are the essential patterns of the English nineteenth-century realistic novel, although not yet free from the storytelling romance traditions that Scott inherited and modified.

This, then, becomes the characteristic moment of choice of realistic fiction. Waverley looks to be an ancestor of Isabel Archer choosing Osmond. Stylistically, of course, the difference is immense; structurally, the difference is that Waverley is taken off the hook of his choice (or of his ignorance). But it is important to note how much Scott invests in the psychological elaboration of his protagonist's choices, for the new em- phasis inserts history into the details of the consciousness of the par- ticular people who live through it.

Such psychological elaboration means the end of romance, since the focus of romance remains primarily on action and plot. Scott is in the process of creating a fiction in which there is a radical disparity be- tween the external and the internal, or psychological, action. What ac- tually happens is of far less significance than the preparation for what happens. Waverley can be relieved of responsibility because the action has become only a stage in the development of character. The dazzling surfaces that led Scott and most of his audiences to regard him as ro- mancer are, of course, still there; but they are set within a frame of sensuously austere, abstract, and antiromantic perceptions and lan- guage.

The concreteness and precision of Scott's descriptions of costume and scenery are replaced in this passage by a redundance and circumlocu- tion that may reflect the dazzle in Waverley's mind, but also reflect a narrator straining to keep our attention. Fergus becomes "Chieftain of the race of Ivor," Charles, "the royal Adventurer," Edward, "our hero." Equally awkward, the meeting place becomes "the ancient halls of his paternal palace," and the prince's sword was "bending towards other conquests." All of this heavily stylized narration insists on the primary fact that it *is* narration, distanced from the immediate experience and reminding us not only that Edward is living in a storybook, but that we are reading one. Moreover the clichés—our hero, bending the sword, thoughts rushing like a torrent, kindness that penetrated the heart— suggest not simply that Waverley is responding in clichés, but that Scott is writing carelessly. The works send out conventional signals to the reader, but seem as divorced from the action they purport to describe as Waverley is from the reality of his own situation.

It is a matter, again, of Scott's incapacity to take his writing seriously enough. The materials here are remarkable and, I believe, innovative and the conception is carefully organized. But the full implications of the materials are unexplored in the language. The passage is effective in forcing us to see that any romantic investment Waverley makes in the moment is in excess of what the writer, his prose, and the book itself actually care about. That the "Chieftain" (romantic word) is "politic" is the first sign that the romance is contrived. That Charles is an "Adventurer" deprives him of some of the dignity his preceding speech seems to have justified, and undercuts Waverley's perception (inspired by words rather than action) that Charles answers the idea "of a hero of romance." Scott's weakness as a writer seems to result from the acquiescence of his own language in the weakness of the protagonist he is allowing us to see with some irony.

But of course it is misleading to talk as though the "materials" were different from the "language." Even this defensive, circumlocutory, cliché-ridden passage has genuine strengths. The accumulation of the possible causes of Waverley's conversion to the prince's party is convincing. And that distinction between Waverley's perception of romance and the narrator's is deeply embedded in the language. Even the clichés loaded into the last sentence, with Waverley devoting heart and sword to Charles, come at us with a rapidity that effectively emulates the movement of Waverley's enthusiasm, makes us feel the righteous pride of Edward in finally having a clear sense of right and wrong and a thing to do about it, and allows us to feel how the romantic ritual is a cliché that climaxes—pathetically—Fergus and the prince's manipulations. The entire strategy by which Scott moves us to sympathize with Waverley and reject his judgment, to see the romantic through his blurry and idealizing eyes, provides us with a striking example of Scott's characteristic dualities. He has been able to instill into his fiction a sense of the coming together of history and personality, of the grand and the particular, of the romantic and the mundane. Self-deprecation is built into the very texture of the prose, yet in spite of it (or perhaps because of it, and the disrespect for romantic conventions it implies) he builds a complex and serious drama in a way that breaks free from earlier traditions of the imagination of the individual in history and society.

The separation between language and action that this new way of seeing implies is reflected in another aspect of the passage and of the book as a whole. In the entire passage, there is no direct concern with the substance of the rebel cause. Waverley has inherited some attitudes, and the prince believes his cause is just, but the substantive issues are peripheral to the personal commitment. Scott's new self-consciousness about how history and society impinge on the private lives of his characters is accompanied by a new preoccupation with the personal desire to be oneself, to be defined not socially but privately. The characteristic realist's subject—the necessity to make one's peace with a determining society—is always, as in Scott, the other side of a powerful desire to withdraw from society altogether.[38] The romance conventions come in handy here in resolving the issues that realistic technique would make too painful. Thus Scott does not much engage us with the details of the dispute between the contending sides—that would entail the narrator's making a choice. The implicit moral ideal of the novel is one not of historical and social substance but of personal loyalties and private integrity.

As the narrative devises ways for Waverley to retreat from the engagement in revolution or repression, it gives to this passive hero the power of its world. Withdrawal can be achieved only through power. Waverley earns the peace of domesticity because he belongs to the privileged class of historical winners and fictional protagonists. Lurking quietly behind the passive hero is a destructive and assertive history, embodied in romance conventions, and implying the continuing assertiveness of those potent, even monstrous desires, from which the narrative of *Waverley* attempts to distance us.

The moral ideal of the civilization that Waverley joins is sanctioned by some seriously uncivilized exertions of force. Waverley never has to pay the price of violence or become an instrument of the progress he joins. His disenchantment is only with a false ideal of precivilized conditions, and that ideal is replaced with a new one, ostensibly outside history and politics: the ideal of propertied, domestic comfort, which allows the sort of ineffectual private romantic dreaming that Flora mocks. The narrative of disenchantment focuses on the personal rather than the social, while politics and the struggle for power remain part of the impressive historical narrative. To keep the two separate, Scott walks a tightrope.

We are thus prepared when Flora discovers that "the real disposition of Waverley . . . notwithstanding his dreams of tented fields and military honour, seemed exclusively domestic" (ch. 52, p. 386). Nor are we surprised, after the defeat of the rebels, to hear that Waverley had "acquired a more complete mastery of spirit tamed by adversity than his former experience had given him; and . . . he felt himself entitled to say firmly, though perhaps with a sigh, that the romance of his life was ended and its real history had now commenced" (ch. 40, p. 434). The

tone is characteristic: with a "sigh." Waverley becomes the potential
subject of the realism that followed, separated from the excesses he
dreamed of. He comes into the world afresh, reborn into history and out
of the lost cause of the past, into private integrity, into an acceptance of
what is there. The reborn Waverley can choose his past, and does not
have it thrust upon him.

This is the politics of the apolitical. The ideal is privacy which can be
achieved only when one is at truce with what is there. To stand against
what is there is to be a fanatic, and can be indulged by those in power
only as long as it is not a threat—as Jacobitism is not to post-1745
England. The special texture of the conclusion of *Waverley* depends on
these conditions. At the trial of the rebel Fergus and his faithful lieutenant, Evan Maccombich, Fergus accepts his sentence nobly and unafraid,
and Evan rises to offer his life if Fergus might be spared. It is a scene of
great romantic attractiveness in which the madness of fanaticism is
made to appear secondary to the loyalty it inspires. The judge's voice is,
in this context, the official voice of moderation, sound judgment, and
the mercy they make possible. After announcing that there will be no
mercy for Fergus, he turns to Evan:

> For you, poor ignorant man, . . . who, following the ideas in which
> you have been educated, have this day given us a striking example
> how the loyalty due to the king and state alone, is, from your
> unhappy ideas of clanship, transferred to some ambitious individ-
> ual, who ends by making you the tool of his crimes—for you, I say,
> I feel so much compassion that if you can make up your mind
> to petition for grace, I will endeavour to procure it for you.
> Otherwise— [Ch. 88, pp. 486–87]

Evan responds by offering to kill the judge.

Like the judge, the reader is lured into compassion for Evan; and like
the judge, the reader must recognize that Evan has to be killed. We are
invited to participate in the humanity available to power, and, at the
same time, to understand the necessity for the total destruction of the
clans as political and social as opposed to decorative entities. The political implications of the form of Scott's fictions become clear. In choosing
an insipid hero between forces guilty of excess on both sides, Scott
allows a sympathetic and relatively unprejudiced view of contending
historical forces. Since the hero cannot act responsibly (that is, so as
to be held responsible for his actions), he can achieve maturity and
happiness only by being absorbed into the winning side and, thus,
transforming his actions into nostalgia and dream.

It is interesting to note that the most active figure in the book, Fergus,
is a fatalist. So, too, is his sister. Although in several of his novels, Scott

portrays fatalists—particularly the Puritan Covenanters—as misguided, fanatic, and dangerous, the narrative here endorses the MacIvors' fatalistic reading of the experience. Flora tells Waverley, for example, "I do not regret his attempt because it was wrong—oh no! on that point I am armed—but because it was impossible it could end otherwise than thus" (ch. 68, p. 489). Even Scott's footnotes confirm this. History destroys Fergus as it awakens Edward from romance, and the narrative achieves its remarkable reverence for an inadequate past by showing the inevitability of its defeat. The substance of the rival ideologies and the justice of their contending positions is almost beside the fact of history's power, except that Scott's history is ultimately a benevolent one. The judge's voice, asking Evan to "petition for grace" (as the religious and the legal terminology fuzz together), is very much the voice of history, which in Scott almost replaces "fate" and God.

As Waverley is freed from the responsibility for his actions, he is allowed to slip into the romantic passivity Flora had envisioned for him; and he thus approximates the conditions of Scott himself. Though briefly in "stupefied misery" at the execution of Fergus, he emerges to acquire Scott's characteristic doubleness of vision. Looking back comfortably from a present marked by commercial success and civilized manners (he would have been about eighty when Scott began writing the novel in 1805), he can indulge a passionate retrospect on the dead past from which he is exempt. Edward even becomes an artist, of sorts, or at least a patron of the arts, by seeing to it that Tully-Veolan is meticulously restored for Baron Bradwardine and by setting a new large painting in the dining-parlor:

> There was one addition to this fine old apartment, however, which drew tears to the Baron's eyes. It was a large and spirited painting, representing Fergus MacIvor and Edward in their Highland dress; the scene a wild, rocky, and mountainous pass, down which the clan were descending in the background. . . . Raeburn himself (whose Highland chiefs do all but walk out of the canvas) could not have done more justice to the subject; and the ardent, fiery, and impetuous character of the unfortunate Chief of Glennaquoich was finely contrasted with the contemplative, fanciful, and enthusiastic expression of his happier friend. Beside this painting hung the arms which Waverley had borne in the unfortunate civil war. The whole piece was beheld with admiration and deeper feelings. [Ch. 62, p. 510]

The image presents Scott in all his duality and all his characteristic ambitions. The great historical experience just narrated becomes in the text itself a work of art, distanced and romantic, yet realistic. History is thus aestheticized. The fact is there, but the practical force of the fact is transformed in art. Action becomes image. But we must note that the description of the romantic picture is preceded by a detailed discussion of the rather unromantic legal matter of transference of property back to Baron Bradwardine, and is followed, neatly, by a paragraph beginning, "Men must, however, eat, in spite both of sentiment and virtue." Again, the voice of common sense provides a practical context that disarms the romance. Even the "admiration and deeper feelings" with which the company regards the painting (the baron weeps) are signs that the experience has been removed from practical reality into a past that can now be safely admired and that can bring satisfying feelings to the breast. But, then, business is business and dinner is dinner.

The historical distance turns out to be aesthetic distance. The burden of choice is off, and Waverley has learned not so much to put away childish things as to place them in the right relationship to practical matters. That relationship is not engaged but explanatory. As he approximates the condition of the narrator, Waverley needs to find ways to unite past with present without allowing the past to impinge on the present dangerously. The painting makes the relationship comfortable, and as we "read" the painting we come to understand the experience. There is Fergus's fiery, impetuous character; there is Waverley's comtemplative one. The novel as a whole embodies the full explanatory and demystifying force of the realistic tradition.

Scott's habit of referring "all incident that fails the test of common sense to some idiosyncrasy of time and place"[39] is his major explanatory mode, and it is of course an aspect of the historic distancing. Edward's mistakes are the result of a historical and factual blindness. The larger perspective of the narrator allows us to see and understand Edward's failures and the impossibility of the cause he joins. Even Fergus's special powers and plausibility are seen in the light of historical explanation: "Had Fergus MacIvor lived Sixty Years sooner than he did, he would, in all probability, have wanted the polished manner and knowledge of the world which he now possessed; and had he lived Sixty Years later, his ambition and love of rule would have lacked the fuel which his situation now afforded" (ch. 19, p. 166). History becomes fate as it becomes explanation. It also, surreptitiously, transforms and universalizes Fergus. For he is a victim of history; deluded by the prospect of fulfilling a dream, he is an exemplar of what it costs to attempt to fulfill it in history.

Waverley has read history more prudently and has earned the right to contemplate it, Scott-like, as an aesthetic object. He withdraws his desires from politics to focus them on Rose, on the Waverley estate, on the memory of desire and excitements of its risks. Waverley's narrative, therefore, acquiesces in the movement of history, and the mad romance devices that rescue him from the fate that befalls the risk-taking Fergus and his loyal lieutenant are only embodiments of the power of the court. Scott brings his narrative judgment into accord with the movement of history, as well. The dream of power and freedom, romantically embodied in the rebels, is compromised; Waverley, like Scott, is left with the freedom, not to act, but to dream of action.

5

Scott and the Death of the Hero

Their love of past time, their tales of bloody battles fought against romantic odds, were all dear to the imagination, and their idolatry of locks of hair, pictures, rings, ribbons, and other memorials of the time in which they still seemed to live, was an interesting enthusiasm; and although their political principles, had they existed in the relation of fathers, might have rendered them dangerous to the existing dynasty, yet as we now recollect them, there could not be on the earth supposed to exist persons better qualified to sustain the capacity of innocuous and respectable grandsires.

Sir Walter Scott, Introduction to *Redgauntlet*

Not all of Scott's protagonists are as bland and disengaged as Edward Waverley. Scott does not always offer them the rewards of history, and his admiration for the excess he denies is often more direct than it is in *Waverley*. In two of his most interesting novels, Scott points toward tragic conclusions. In *The Bride of Lammermoor*, the hero aspires to be like Waverley, but he is driven by inherited traditions of heroic revenge and the opposing force of love, traditions to which he is unequal. Both are genuine commitments, and the conflict between them leads to death. In *Redgauntlet*, with its three protagonists, the *Waverley* pattern is modified in another way. The dreamer there is a man of action who finds himself alone in a world he seems to have invented. The drama is the most moving enactment of the way language and action separate in Scott, for history will not even take the trouble to turn the dream into tragedy. The two novels reveal Scott following out the logic of the realist vision we have found in *Waverley*. But *The Bride* is steeped in the excess, the mystery, the uncontrollable energy whose price *Waverley* refuses to pay. It points toward romance or toward a later phase of realism in which the requirement of compromise had become intolerable. *Redgauntlet*, on the other hand, forces upon its protagonist the historical inevitability of the merely domestic and points toward the Victorian realism it does not itself quite achieve.

I

Superficially, at least, *The Bride of Lammermoor* belongs in the gothic tradition against which early-nineteenth-century realism was in reaction. Moreover, it is not, structurally, a novel of disenchantment, since Edgar Ravenswood does not enter the scene with illusions of the sort harbored by Edward Waverley. His naiveté and inexperience are emphatically asserted, but his story is connected not with the quixotic tradition of parody, but with the tragic patterns of ballad and folktale and, implicitly, with the high literary tradition of Shakespearean tragedy. The obvious parallels to *Romeo and Juliet* and *Hamlet* need no emphasis. Yet the impressive and unusual formal relevance of the details of the novel (in keeping with the manner of the highly structured romance)[1] and the constant narrative insistence on the doom that awaits all the major figures are not enough to keep the novel from a place in the tradition of realism. *The Bride of Lammermoor* is a drama of the death of the past, of the fate of romantic dream in its contest with history. In it, we can watch the transformation of the past into legend, into a tale sufficiently distant that its horror becomes attractive.

Francis Hart argues that in *The Bride* Scott cannot be seen simply as a comedist or as an "apologist for civil prudence,"[2] but he separates the book too completely from the mode of *Waverley*, *Guy Mannering*, and *The Antiquary*. The most important prudential figure in the book—Ashton—is a complicated sort of moral weakling, ultimately villainous in his prudence, and Hart is correct to argue that the "present," if it be embodied in the Ashtons, is hardly more satisfying than the past, embodied in Caleb Balderstone. But the Ashtons are also part of a narrative past, separated from the "present" of the narrator himself, who stands outside the story and allows us a vision of a future possibility beyond the emotional power and historic vision of the protagonists. Edgar Ravenswood, in his capacity to be the destroying avenger that tradition tells him he should be, partially represents that possibility. His failure to achieve this best ideal is rendered in novelistic rather than romance terms and makes a kind of reverse image of Waverley's tale.

With all its gothic trappings, its adoption of the gothic descriptive mode at the cost of the usually dominant dramatic dialogue, *The Bride of Lammermoor* still implies a world rational, comprehensible, explicable. The trappings, which include the legends of the Ravenswood motto, "I bide my time," and of the fated fountain, and the choral voices of Old Alice and the three witches, are all dramatically effective, but rendered in such a way as to keep them compatible with realistic technique. They form an appropriate symbolic commentary on the central action, which is deeply anchored in historical fact.[3] Moreover, they give a feeling of historic authenticity to the tale, set as it is meant to be in a moment of transition between a feudal culture and a newly unified, commercialized, and pacified England and Scotland. Through George Eliot and Hardy (who undoubtedly learned from Scott), we are used to choral commentaries at public rituals and even, for the most part, connect such choruses (however misguidedly) with realistic technique. We are also used to translating the omens out of the supernatural into literal phenomena that carry symbolic weight. The mysterious fatality that surrounds Edgar Ravenswood and Lucy Ashton is the embodiment in narrative of history not supernature, and of the disastrous confluence of history and individual character.

In any case, Scott is as usual meticulous about maintaining an enlightened stance toward the mysterious. Only the vision that comes to Edgar at the time of Alice's death is allowed to go unexplained. Scott himself wrote early in his career that "the Marvellous in poetry is ill-timed and disgusting when not managed with moderation & ingrafted upon some circumstance of popular tradition or belief which sometimes can give even to the improbable an air of something like probability."[4] Ravenswood's tragedy does not result from failure to read the omens. For the narrator seems unequivocal in supporting Ravenswood's anti-superstitious stance. It is not the supernatural that Ravenswood fails to read, but the natural—history itself. Even the mystery of the vision coinciding with Alice's death is set in a paragraph that reminds us of Scott's enlightenment and antiromantic tendencies:

> [Ravenswood] despised most of the ordinary prejudices about witchcraft, omens, and vaticination, to which the age and country still gave such implicit credit, that to express a doubt of them was accounted a crime equal to the unbelief of Jews and Saracens; he knew also that the prevailing belief concerning witches operating upon the hypochondriac habits of those whom age, infirmity, and poverty rendered liable to suspicion, and enforced by the fear of death, and the pangs of the most cruel tortures, often extorted those confessions which encumber and disgrace the criminal records of Scotland during the seventeenth century. But the vision of that morning, whether real or imaginary, had impressed his mind with a superstitious feeling which he in vain endeavoured to shake off. [Ch. 23, p. 242]

The material about superstition is presented here in so anthropological a way that it tends to undercut every instance of mystery in the book. The very power of this one instance over Edgar confirms the absurdity of most "superstition." Even here we are left with the possibility that the vision is imaginary; what matters is the effect. The vision fits in

neatly with the milieu of the entire story—the superstitious and preju-
diced culture that seems to be resisting the new civilization—and yet
turns out to have no real effect on the major action. Similarly, the
willow-wand episode in George Eliot's *Adam Bede* (yet another instance
of Eliot's use of Scott), the rapping at the Bedes' door at the time of the
father's death, fits; it is explained only in terms of the beliefs of the
country people at the time and thus, ironically, makes for greater credibility while it increases the dramatic tension.

Ravenswood's relation to the supernatural has to be juxtaposed with
that of Lucy. Lucy is passive, intense, and highly susceptible to
superstitious fantasy. Overwhelmed by the impression of meeting the
young Master of Ravenswood she

> was involved in those mazes of the imagination which are most
> dangerous to the young and the sensitive. Time, it is true, absence,
> change of scene and new faces, might probably have destroyed the
> illusion in her instance as it has done in many others; but her
> residence remained solitary, and her mind without those means of
> dissipating her pleasing visions. [Ch. 5, p. 63]

Scott's distrust of the imagination is evident here. Lucy is instinctively
attracted to and terrified by horror stories that agitate her undisciplined
imagination, and Lady Ashton deliberately exploits her sensitivity to
frighten her out of her engagement to Ravenswood. Indeed, one of the
indications of the place of the superstitious material in the novel is that
Lady Ashton tries to use it. She hires Ailsie, the most potent of the
choral witches at the end of the novel, and this witch is the occasion for
some very strong Enlightenment rhetoric on the narrator's part: "It
somewhat relieves the disgust with which we read, in the criminal
records, the convictions of these wretches, to be aware that many of
them merited, as poisoners, suborners, and diabolical agents in secret
domestic crimes, the severe fate to which they were condemned for the
imaginary guilt of witchcraft" (ch. 31, p. 298). We look back from an
Enlightenment standpoint that allows us to make rational discriminations, allies us with a higher level of humanity and compassion, and keeps us aloof from the mysteries that ensnare the protagonists. The book never endorses mystery. Instead, it translates the
mysterious into the errors of an earlier time. Mystery becomes literal,
comprehensible, social evil, and the strange visions and omens are
always seen to belong to that time.[5]

Placing the mysterious and the monstrous in the past is a major
strategy of the novel. One important instance comes near the very end
of the book, when Bucklaw is described as refusing ever to give a hint of
what occurred on his wedding night. The narrator, still sensitive to the

problem of the mysterious, interrupts: "By many readers this may be deemed overstrained, romantic, and composed by the wild imagination of an author, desirous of gratifying the popular appetite for the horrible; but those who are read in the private family history of Scotland during the period in which the scene is laid, will readily discover, through the disguise of borrowed names, and added incidents, the leading particulars of AN OWER TRUE TALE" (ch. 34, pp. 319–20). Again, the rhetoric allows Scott to have things both ways. The monstrous is placed back in time, but by being so placed it is made credible. At the same time, the implication is that in the modern world such things cannot happen. Beyond this, the strategy of excusing himself for "gratifying the popular appetite" allows him not only to do precisely that, but to give the indulgence a moral sanction—the sanction of truth and historical fact.

One last instance of the way Scott as narrator refuses to commit himself to the supernatural and romantic excess of his materials requires attention. Scott concludes the chapter describing the funeral of Edgar's father by invoking a present-day peasant who immediately signals the disastrous culmination of the narrative to follow:

> The peasant who shows the ruins of the tower, which still crown the beetling cliff and behold the war of the waves, though no more tenanted save by the sea-mew and cormorant, even yet affirms, that on this fatal night the Master of Ravenswood, by the bitter exclamations of his despair, evoked some evil fiend, under whose malignant influence the future tissue of incidents was woven. Alas! what fiend can suggest more desperate counsels, than those adopted under the guidance of our own violent and unresisted passions? [Ch. 2, pp. 35–36]

Here the inescapable monster of the gothic tradition is translated into the psychologically comprehensible evil of the realistic novel. As Scott gives us his ambivalent vision, we are allowed to have the monstrous in its traditional forms, and the monstrous as it is transformed by enlightened people. The mysterious needs no explanation but what common sense can tell us about our own irrational tendencies.

The intellectual position implied here is in the Johnsonian tradition of moral and psychological scrupulosity that will be central to the work of the great Victorians. Just as Dr. Johnson investigates each report of ghostly apparitions, so Scott assumes that every instance can be explained rationally and that in most cases there will be fraud. But he too recognizes the possibility of something beyond human comprehension, and hence remains open where rational explanations are not available.[6] Such openness and scrupulousness lead almost invariably to at least some rudimentary psychological analysis, a consideration of one's own susceptibility, one's motive for belief or disbelief. Consequently, what may be the real moral crisis of *The Bride* occurs in a quietly understated and infrequently noticed episode that anticipates again the method of George Eliot and reveals once more how Scott's literary modes are inevitably mixed.

The scene occurs after Ravenswood visits Old Alice and hears her warn against his remaining near Lucy. Alice has made plain not only that an alliance between Ravenswood and Lucy would entail constant humiliation for him in his life among the Ashtons, but that given his nature, Ravenswood would be driven to wreak revenge and cause disaster to Lucy and himself. In addition, to stay near Lucy while knowing that Lucy loves him would be villainous unless he married her, and disastrous if he did. The situation points forward to the scene in *Adam Bede*, when Arthur Donnithorne struggles against his growing passion for Hetty, or, more complexly, to the scene in *Middlemarch*, in which Lydgate attempts to resist the social and moral pressures—and his own instincts—to propose to Rosamond.

Arthur, it will be remembered, decides not to ride to meet Hetty, but quickly persuades himself that meeting her just to say good-bye would be harmless and kind. So, too, with Ravenswood:

> With one bitter pang he adopted this resolution, just as he came to where the paths parted; the one to the Mermaiden's Fountain, where he knew Lucy waited him, the other leading to the castle by another and more circuitous road. He paused an instant when about to take the latter path, thinking what apology he should make for conduct which must seem extraordinary. [Ch. 20, p. 196]

The pause, it turns out, is fatal, for suddenly Lucy's brother runs up, asking Ravenswood to accompany Lucy back to the castle:

> Betwixt two scales equally loaded, a feather's weight will turn the scale. "It is impossible for me to leave the young lady in the wood alone," said Ravenswood: "to see her once more can be of little consequence, for the frequent meeting we have had—I ought, too, in courtesy, to apprise her of my intention to quit the castle."

Without George Eliot's complex analysis of how feelings surprise and dominate the mind, Scott gives us precisely George Eliot's kind of moral casuistry.

The sequence of the following passage foreshadows that about Rosamond and Lydgage. Lydgate, loking into the eyes of a suddenly weeping Rosamond, melts with compassion, and proposes. The shifts are rapid, convincing, and catastrophic in their consequences. Similarly, as Ravenswood informs Lucy that he must leave, she begins to weep. But "each attempt which the Master made to explain his purpose of departure, only proved a new evidence of his desire to stay; until, at length, instead of bidding her farewell, he gave his faith to her forever, and received her troth in return" (ch. 20, p. 198). As the failure here is not in Ravenswood's understanding but in his power to cope with undisciplined desires, so the crisis is not evidence of Scott's rejection of the ideal of prudence but of his sense of its difficulty.

There is, however, one moment in this sequence when Ravenswood is described as failing to read omens. As he approaches, he sees Lucy sitting by the fateful fountain (the site of his initial rescue of her, and the site of legend):

> To a superstitious eye, Lucy Ashton, folded in her plaited mantle, with her long hair escaping partly from the snood and falling upon her silver neck, might have suggested the idea of the murdered Nymph of the Fountain. But Ravenswood only saw a female exquisitely beautiful, and rendered more so in his eyes—how could it be otherwise—by the consciousness that she had placed her affections on him. As he gazed on her, he felt his fixed resolution melt like wax in the sun. [Ch. 20, p. 197]

The "superstitious eye" might have been valuable here, but the rhetoric does not endorse superstition. The strategy of the passage is to remind the reader that the sheer attractiveness of the beautiful woman prevents the hero from remembering what he ought to be doing. The "omen" is simply a physical manifestation of the literal and explicable moral responsibility which, in the daze of Lucy's loveliness, Ravenswood forgets.[7]

The novel's success depends a great deal on the way the gothic moments become precise external equivalents of the moral states of the characters. Evil is present, but not in the omen. We can return to that overstrained question near the start: "Alas! what fiend can suggest more desperate counsels, than those adopted under the guidance of our own violent and unresisted passion?" The language is Frankensteinan; the materials, finally, are the materials of realistic moral and psychological analysis.

Ravenswood's story is told within a triple time scheme that explains historically why this admirable and well-intentioned young man is unequal to the crisis. The narrator's present is the time that provides the enlightened perspective from which the book is seen. The narrative past precedes the state of civilization implied, for example, in *Waverley*'s post-1745 conclusion. The modern characters of this time, particularly the Ashtons, are implicated in the disasters of the past and carry its burden with them. Finally, the remote past is the time of the

Ravenswood's power, the time of prerevolutionary England; and this past is the source of the curse upon the Ravenswood house and of the disasters in the narrative present.

Edgar Ravenswood, like his brother protagonists of other Scott novels, is between two worlds; but the decaying world in which he exists, while reflecting the past, will not release him—as Edward Waverley is released—into the present. As the narrator can look back and understand the limits of the times in which the story is set, Ravenswood tries unsuccessfully to separate himself from the past and, like Waverley, achieve the perspective of the narrator himself. Out of sympathy with the rituals and the demands of the past, Ravenswood curses the Ashtons—as is to be expected from a Ravenswood—only in instinctive response to the intrusion upon the funeral rites, during which "a numerous part of the assembly applauded this speech as the spirited expression of just resentment; but the more cool and judicious regretted that it had been uttered" (ch. 2, p. 34).

Left alone with dying rituals, Ravenswood is doomed to the past he (with the prudent narrator) rejects. Immediately after the funeral, "the mourners returned to the tower, there, according to a custom but recently abolished in Scotland, to carouse deep healths to the memory of the deceased, to make the house of sorrow ring with sounds of joviality and debauch, and to diminish, by the expense of a large and profuse entertainment, the limited revenues of the heir of him whose funeral they thus honoured" (ch. 2, pp. 34–35). The words, "according to a custom but recently abolished," help distinguish the narrator's present from the time of the action, and provide Scott's characteristic explanatory note. They put us in an enlightened present, but link Edgar's time with a more primitive past. They indicate, also, how he is out of temper with his time. As the crowd leaves, Ravenswood accepts "their adieus with an air of contempt which he could scarce conceal." He looks about at his "ruinous habitation," further diminished by these last absurd rituals. Out of the gloominess there, the memories of the "phantoms," the "tarnished honour and degraded fortunes" of the house, he constructs his curse, releases his "fiend."

Torn between past and present, Ravenswood feels a bond to the past and a need for vengeance; but he falls in love with the daughter of a new class, whose ancestry is Roundhead. He disbelieves in the shams of chivalry, refuses to fight Bucklaw, for instance, but is finally driven to duel anyway—and, of course, wins. He wishes not to keep up the sham sustained by Caleb Balderstone, whose fanatic loyalty to a feudal past we must discuss. Moreover, Ravenswood cannot ally himself with the exiled court at Saint Germain, despite his apparent intention to go there after a confrontation with Ashton.

His instincts are toward a mediator's role, one which would conserve the best of the past and present and transcend party politics. The chapter in which Ravenswood meets Bucklaw and Craigengelt at the inn for the first time nicely contrasts him with another and inferior young inheritor and allows him to distinguish himself from political opportunists and partisans. His voice, for a moment, becomes like that of the Scott narrator. He has, for instance, no illusions about the Stuarts; "When I recollect the times of the first and second Charles, and of the last James, truly I see little reason, that, as a man or a patriot, I should draw my sword for their descendants" (ch. 8, p. 98). Such a position disentangles Ravenswood's fate from that of the Stuarts, but it suggests vividly where his own self-divisions come from. As Hart says, in *The Bride*, "history as public panorama or epoch is coincidental; history as particular condition, as amoral force, is not only present, but uniquely domesticated."[8] The conflict between the Ravenswoods and the Ashtons may perhaps be seen as a contest between exiled Stuart and triumphant Whigs; but Edgar is no convinced Jacobite. His difficulty derives from his natural connection to an inadequate past that is being displaced. The politic and Whiggish Ashtons suffer because they try, in their new wealth, to emulate the worst qualities of the ousted traditional families.

In his best self, Ravenswood seeks a reconciliation that projects into the narrator's present. Hence, the romantic plot of love for the daughter of the opposing house has political and historic significance. When Bucklaw accuses Ravenswood of being concerned about the Roundheads, of mourning "over the crop-eared dogs, whom honest Clavr'se treated as they deserved," Ravenswood replies:

> "They first gave the dogs an ill name, and then hanged them . . . I hope to see the day when justice shall be open to Whig and Tory, when these nick-names shall only be used among coffee-house politicians, as slut and jade are among apple-women, as cant terms of spite and rancour."
>
> "That will not be in our days, Master—the iron has entered too deeply into our side and our souls."
>
> "It will be, however, one day," replied the Master; "men will not always start at these nick-names as at a trumpet-sound. As social life is better protected, its comforts will become too dear to be hazarded without some better reason than speculative politics."
> [Ch. 8, p. 98]

Such a passage, especially as it comes in the context of a contrast between the intelligence, sense, and bearing of Ravenswood, and the lightheadedness and thoughtless bigotry of Bucklaw, again implies a moral preference for the modern over the past. Ravenswood's dignity, despite his mistakes and his psychologically and historically comprehensible surrender to passion, is sustained by the vision of a future, which is the narrator's present: a time when "social life is better protected, its comforts . . . too dear to be hazarded without some better reason than speculative politics."

Ravenswood's attempt to disentangle himself from the past is a continuing thrust of the narrative. To Old Alice, who harbors a deep antagonism toward the Ashtons despite her very sensible readings of Ravenswood's character, he retorts: "You drive me to madness, Alice. . . . you are more silly and more superstitious than old Balderstone. Are you such a wretched Christian as to suppose I would in the present day levy war against the Ashton family, as was the sanguinary custom in elder times?" (ch. 19, p. 193). Alice, unwilling herself to take vengeance, offers the best advice. Since the antagonisms are real and the old options are not available to civilized people, Ravenswood should flee.

Unusually for Scott's novels, Ravenswood is an active figure, but he is almost reduced to passivity, after all. Most of his acts are defensive, or responses; rarely does he initiate anything. There is, indeed, nothing for him to initiate. He is a prisoner of his dying past and his social position, both of which are transformed into his personal psychology. He is driven by circumstances at the riotous funeral to curse the house of Ashton, as he is driven into love of Lucy. He fights Bucklaw because he is forced to do it. He shoots the charging bull (and of course we remember that the bull is the symbol of the avenging Ravenswoods) in instinctive response to danger and attack. He leaves the Ashton home as Lady Ashton requests, and his final bitter scene with Lucy is acted out under the force of the uncontrollable passions we have learned are more evil than "the fiend." Even in the crucial confrontation scene, when Ravenswood demands to see Lucy alone, he allows Lady Ashton to do all of Lucy's talking so that the entire point of his return is lost.

Ironically, toward the end of the novel, history turns in Ravenswood's favor, and the marquis manages to improve Ravenswood's family fortunes in a new Tory government, while William Ashton loses power. But by then, the commitment of the passions is irreversible, and the time is not ripe for the sort of "luck" usually available to Scott heroes. Lady Ashton is intractable, in part, as she says, because of the Ravenswood family's traditional resistance to "the freedom of the subject and the immunities of God's kirk" (ch. 27, p. 278). Her reversal of fortune allows Lady Ashton to readopt the Puritan language most appropriate when the Puritans were less successful politically. "Sir, it is not a flightering blink of prosperity which can change my constant opinion in this regard, seeing it has been my lot before now, like Holy David, to see the wicked great in power, and flourishing like a green bay tree." Despite, then, the Ashtons' alliance with the new Whig power, they are bound by historical animosities as brutally and backwardly as the old Ravenswood. But this whole shift of historical power—really unnecessary for the main plot—makes clear again that what is at stake is not the party or the partisan dogmas, but the inflexible adherence to historic divisions. This reduces Ravenswood to powerlessness, even before his own most loving and faithful servant. To act out in one's personal life the ideal of reconciliation requires the cooperation of history itself.

It would seem that the politic William Ashton might provide some of the historical force necessary for reconciliation. But the book implies a serious contrast between his sort of reconciliation and the sort that Ravenswood hopes for. Ashton is a mere opportunist, rather like Turntippet and other "waiters upon Providence" (ch. 27, p. 275). These "uniform adherents to the party who are uppermost" seem to be, like Ravenswood, between two worlds. Rather, they are between two parties. Ashton carefully works his way toward reconciliation because he is frightened of Ravenswood's power of vengeance and because he is wily enough to know that history may move against him (in the short term, at least). But Ravenswood's eye is on a personal conciliation, which, ironically, requires a longer term view of history. He cannot act—as lover, politician, or warrior—because there is no valid external sanction, nothing that history can give him.

It is not Ravenswood's effort of reconciliation that is morally catastrophic, for that, on the whole, is sanctioned by the narrative. He is, simply, too weak to anticipate history, not quite hero enough. Sir William's efforts at reconciliation, however, are catastrophic because they are merely politic and pursued regardless of their possible effects on his own daughter. He leaves Lucy and Ravenswood in a compromised position because he imagines a union between them as useful. But Ravenswood understands that his union with the Ashtons cannot be useful, for it would entail public disgrace and domestic humiliation. Hearing the sexton's comments on the marriage, Ravenswood exclaims, "And I have stooped to subject myself to these calumnies, and am rejected notwithstanding! Lucy, your faith must be true and perfect as the diamond, to compensate for the dishonour which men's opinions, and the conduct of your mother, attach to the heir of Ravenswood" (ch. 24, p. 250).

The relationship pushes Ravenswood to domesticity, and out of the historical battle for his family's property and dignity. He is willing to make the painful sacrifice that is a happy ending for Waverley—a marriage that removes him from the large actions of history into domestic romance. But this is Waverley's nature, not Ravenswood's. William Ashton, never having thought of reconciliation as anything but a political maneuver, always connects his private activities with larger political considerations. Ironically, Lady Ashton, with whom he is so much at odds, is engaged in precisely the same kind of merely pragmatic reconciliation. For in attempting to marry Lucy to Bucklaw she is also trying to bring together Tory and Whig, Episcopalian and Presbyterian. Her principled, Roundhead, rejection of Ravenswood is merely an expression of personal hostility against the traditional family she had directly displaced (and, of course, of her desire for more immediate wealth). Again, the Ashtons manifest no power of vision (Lady Ashton will die inflexibly believing in the correctness of her behavior all through); and there is no implicit rejection of reconciliation in the narrative. Rather, we have a narrative of the crossing of the personal and the historical. The "historic fatality" that bears down upon all is acted out in the private nature and choices of each character. The Ashtons, obsessed by history and politics, are destructive because they surrender the personal to the public. But Ravenswood's attempt to act without reference to political expedience and the demands of the past becomes destructive, too. Imagining that it is possible to resist the inherited pressures of family and society for the sake of a personal satisfaction, he is all the more vulnerable to those pressures. Old Alice and the sexton remind him of the larger implications of his family responsibility, of the cost to others of his family's failure, but he is without political power to change their conditions. He is personally unequal to the struggle to escape from the past and redeem its failures, which are his primary inheritance. The struggle to break free—as George Eliot, learning from Scott, will show—entails extraordinary self-discipline, and self-knowledge.

Remarkably, then, *The Bride of Lammermoor*, deliberately using traditional folk and ballad materials more centrally than most other Scott novels, and dwelling on the past with a special new descriptive fascination, implies the necessity of transcending the past. In the parrallel movement of the gothic elements with the main narrative stream, we find that the catastrophes of the book are carefully associated with traditional materials—the curses, dreams, and fantasies of ancient narratives and witches and blind seers. This story of the death of a family, of the destruction of the feudal past, implies an apparently absolute schism between fantasy and fiction, which belong to the past, and action and fact, which belong to the present. Scott seems to have made his dramatic subject here out of his own uneasy relation to the life of the imagination. Imaginatively, he banishes imagination from practical life. He sees, with the clarity of a figure from the Enlightenment, the worthlessness, the positive danger, of the imagination; and he dwells upon the dangers with an affection that almost belies the strictures of common sense. The narrative of *The Bride of Lammermoor* shows us the past in the act of self-destruction that will distance it sufficiently to make it an object of nostalgia.

The characteristically ambivalent attitude toward the past and its lost causes is perhaps most prominent in the treatment of Caleb Balderstone, Scott's most extensive and ironic treatment of the past's association with fantasy. Caleb is wonderfully comic (though better in smaller doses); he is highly imaginative and resourceful, a con artist; and he is, finally, totally consumed by his loyalty to a dying family. As the "absurd embodiment of the house's tragic degeneracy," Caleb is, as Hart argues, a symbol of "the degeneracy Edgar can never redeem and never escape."⁹ He is the perfect representative of the past as it functions in Edgar's lifetime, dominated by empty forms that impose impossible modes of action on those trapped by it. The narrative indulgence in Caleb's excesses, beyond what is necessary for the book's development, is further evidence that for Scott the past is fascinating and attractive precisely in its distance from the practical exigencies of action. Caleb is allowed his extravagances (that even anticipate Dickens) because he is dying, because the kinds of loyalties he lives are no longer conceivable in the narrator's present. His attachment to Edgar and his total loyalty to the family achieve, in spite of his lying and cheating, an ultimate pathos.

And "pathos" is precisely the word. For Scott's attachment to Caleb is as ambivalent as is his relation to, say, Jacobitism itself. His affection is sustained although he knows how destructive Caleb is. In Caleb's last days, the narrator tells us, he "ate without refreshment, and slumbered without repose; and with a fidelity sometimes displayed by the canine race, but seldom by human beings, he pined and died within a year after the catastrophe" (ch. 35, p. 333). The feudal loyalty is touching as a sad dog is touching, certainly worth writing about or inventing, but dehumanizing, and hardly a model for modern life. The past sustains its attractions in language, when the subject is dead, just as Caleb maintains the forms of the past amid the ruins of Wolf's Crag and the emptiness of its larder.

In the context of Caleb's lying to sustain the false dignity of a dying house, Edgar's moral and historic dilemma can be yet more sharply focused. Just as the old retainer is consumed by the Ravenswood house, so Edgar is consumed by the feudal demands of the old retainer. He is implicated in the lies and the decay, whether he will or no. Caleb assures Edgar, after the false fire that keeps the marquis from the castle, that "it fits an auld carle like me weel eneugh to tell lees for the credit of the family, but it wadna beseem the like o' your honour's sell" (ch. 26,

p. 268). But Edgar cannot escape the "lees": he cannot disclose Caleb's lie to the marquis, nor can he escape the ruins of Wolf's Crag. Although we are reminded, at an early dinner over which Caleb presides, "how little on such occasions can form, however anxiously and scrupulously observed, supply the lack of substantial fare" (ch. 7, p. 88), for Edgar there is only form.

In his life, the separation between language and action becomes almost absolute. As Edgar tries to speak the truth of what he feels and believes, he is invariably contradicted by his own actions. He cannot enact the vengeance he vows; he cannot redeem his father's lost estate; he cannot emulate William Ashton in manipulation and false conciliation; he cannot marry the woman to whom he is betrothed. He cannot, even in so trivial a business as a hunt, be in on the kill; he is too much of the "future" to be anything but appalled by the butchering of the prey, so lustily enjoyed by Bucklaw.

Though the form is different here, *The Bride of Lammermoor* gives us a version of the realist's dominant preoccupation—the disparity between dream and reality. But given Scott's own radical distrust of his creative imagination, he cannot comfortably resolve the problem. The past can safely hold fantasy because it is past. But all fiction, Scott believed, was rather like Caleb's dinner, form without substance. And *The Bride of Lammermoor*, like much of Scott's fiction, anticipates the later realists' increasing preoccupation with finding a fictional language that would also be true. The quest, of course, turns out to be as difficult as Ravenswood's for a way to reconcile his language with his actions. And Ravenswood dies according to a prophecy by one of those witches the narrator does not believe in.

There are other, less complicated ways, in which *The Bride* points toward later forms of realism. The book is a mixture of fictional modes, blending historical fatality with moral and psychological fatality, translating the mysterious and monstrous into entirely human terms. In resisting the mere gothic shock and attempting to base all these materials solidly in the historic and the credible, Scott reminds us again of the way the antiromantic and ironic mode of realism, committed to the explicability of all experience, invariably includes threatening elements that cannot quite be accounted for rationally or empirically. But as the inexplicable is a threat to the realist's form, so is it a threat to Scott's protagonists.

In *The Bride of Lammermoor*, as in the other Waverley novels, genuine entrance into history, into the narrator's present, is available only to protagonists who have mastered romantic excess. We observe here the failure of that mastery, and the logic of the disaster that follows. Lucy is destroyed by an undisciplined imagination. Edgar succumbs to the passions against which he has inadequately struggled through the narrative. The old seers and witches, it turns out, are correct, but in being so, they foresee the death of the culture that nourished them. And we come to understand that it is not Alice, or Ailsie, or the old legends (the formal gothic frame of the narrative) that determine Edgar's fate. In the central tradition of the realistic novel, Edgar is shaped by society—by his inherited losses, by public opinion, by his inherited and unstable values—by his past, by his passion. Without the discipline to control his feelings, without the power to resist the pressures of a dying past or of an unstable present, he is, unlike Waverley, held responsible by the narrative for choosing without really choosing, for choosing what he could not help but choose.

In Edgar's death, as he slips into "Kelpie's flow" on the way to the duel, *The Bride of Lammermoor* exorcises the traditional active hero. Ravenswood, driven to defend his ancient family's honor, achieves the dignity that the book could not allow (enlightened as the narrator is) to a mere victory or defeat in a fight. The new world to come will reject the family, will reject the past whose traditions and rituals Ravenswood was forced to stand for. In such a new world, the story of Ravenswood slips into gothic fantasy, in which heroic action is a dream, set amid mysteries and horrors that will survive as mere entertainment for a middle class public, as the dream of sentimental young gentlemen like Edward Waverley or of passionate young women like Maggie Tulliver.

II

The transformation of heroic action into dream, or into a past framed and made merely aesthetic, is, in a way, the primary subject of *Redgauntlet*. But the movement of *Redgauntlet* to one of Scott's most powerful and revelatory sequences[10] is foreshadowed as early as *The Antiquary*. *Redgauntlet* achieves its power by turning the death of heroism into the dramatic subject; but heroism dies at the outer limits of Scott's own time. *The Antiquary* merely gropes for a subject, set as it is in the years of Scott's young maturity, "the last ten years of the eighteenth century."[11] But it is consistent, at least, in creating a world from which even the dream of the heroic is banished, in which value seems to inhere in the aesthetic contemplation of the past or in the last vestigial signs—carried by Edie Ochiltree. The transformation of the past into dream is also, here, the transformation of romance into novel. Lovel's story has none of the strength required even to provide a frame for "good things."

The Antiquary is consistently antiromantic, but not genuinely parodic in style or structure—even in the Dousterswivel episode in which the charlatan performs some mock witchcraft. Yet it is self-conscious enough to allow the characters to provide the critique of romantic illusion one might have expected from the narrative style—as we find it in Austen, or at moments even in *Waverley*. The book's preoccupation with the past in the midst of contemporary life is not a formal but a substantive concern, a preoccupation of the characters themselves. The central figure, Jonathan Oldbuck, is an antiquarian, not an adventurer. He is no young man full of illusion, but a middle-aged misogynist, shrewd but obsessed with things past. Even his comic error in purchasing worthless land because he thought it was a Roman site, though it foreshadows Samuel Pickwick's attempt to decipher "BILL STUMP HIS MARK," does not undermine his role as a sensible and antiromantic figure.

As such a sensible man, he can laugh at his occasional attempt to read the past into the present and to turn his scholarship into genuine action. The key moment comes in the climactic sequence near the end of the novel. When he buckles on the sword "which my father wore in the year forty five," at the false alarm of the French attack, he "thrust the weapon through the cover of his breeches pocket" (vol. 2, p. 295). When he discovers that it was his burning of the materials bought from Dousterswivel that was taken as a signal of the attack, he sheepishly takes off the sword: "And here, take this what-d'ye-call-it. . . . I wonder what I would have said yesterday to any man that would have told me I was to stick such an appendage to my tail" (ch. 2, p. 300).

The self-conscious ironies in this sequence, pointing to bathos and the *absence* of need for heroic action while all are absurdly poised to perform it, are compounded by the fact that Dousterswivel's fake machinery has managed once again to produce a false romance. It is as though only inherited superstition can produce in our own time the equivalent of past excesses. A final irony, surely uncontemplated by Scott, results from his need to resolve what plot there is; the deliberately bathetic scene is concluded with one of the embarrassing moments in Scott when the young hero discovers who his parents are, and when the traditional madness of traditional plot imposes itself on the reluctant materials of antiromance: "Gracious Heaven! the child of my Evaline!" exclaims Lord Glenallan, as Lovel, alias Major Neville, alias the new Lord Glenallan, steps forward to complete his role in the novel.

David Daiches notes in *The Antiquary* the movement from romance to realism that I have been suggesting; "*The Antiquary* provides the most specific example of the movement from heroism to antiquarian study; the old heroic way of life is, by the latter part of the eighteenth century, only something to be argued over and written about. Scott himself—lawyer, antiquary, historian, novelist—is the perfect example of the shift from participation in the life of heroic adventure to nostalgic scholarship about it."[12] But what Daiches describes is not merely a phenomenon of Scott's novels. The movement from participation to nostalgia, like the fading of heroism into the past, is one of the major motifs of English fiction in the nineteenth century, where new Saint Theresas can find no vocation, can achieve no world historic acts. In *The Antiquary*, the past is transformed into tokens and fragments and texts to be read, while those like Dousterswivel, or Oldbuck's hotheaded nephew, Captain McIntyre, are mocked or defeated. Even Edie Ochiltree can sustain his relatively unusual position and his useful capacity to be everywhere at the same time only because he refuses to enter the present. Since he is free of the decorous restraints of the upper classes, he can be the instrument of comic vengeance on Dousterswivel, and of the resolution of the plot, settling issues in a way unavailable to the protagonists. Heroism disappears in a cloud of antiquarian fact, as the past recedes into objects of aesthetic or scholarly contemplation.

The Antiquary dismisses the past from the living present without, as it were, knowing that this dismissal is its central subject. The antiquarian, in his love of the past and his practical recognition of its impracticality, may stand as a perfect representative of Scott's own vision in the Waverley novels; but because antiquarianism is so much the book's subject, *The Antiquary* cannot dramatically make us experience the transformation and the act of distancing. This rich subject, hinted at again and again in the novels, becomes, self-consciously, the focus of *Redgauntlet*. There, at last, bathos becomes drama, the exploration not only of a past dying but of a present that might satisfactorily replace it; and there, the "present" had to be not only in the voice of the enlightened narrator but convincingly in the voices of the characters themselves. The subject, moreover, precluded the strategy of *The Bride*, which exorcised romance in the act of constructing one; the exorcism had to come without the assistance of gothic machinery, precisely because the process of history (as it is imagined in the fiction) had invalidated the romantic posture. Averting a tragic climax and averting bathos at the same time entailed a special difficulty. Most difficult task of all, perhaps, *Redgauntlet*, shaping itself into a nineteenth-century realistic novel, had to be about how it became that sort of book.

Not surprisingly, *Redgauntlet* is painfully casual about defining itself. The uncertainties and false starts are, however, instructive, because they allow us to watch Scott struggle toward the appropriate form and because the dead ends are, at last, formally to the point. The uncertainties of the narrative can be taken to reflect the problematic nature of the materials themselves. At the start, the form appears to be a variation on and a concentration of the form of disenchantment we have seen in *Waverley*. Yet we have two protagonists, Darsie and Alan, and their experiences are at first rendered in letters so that we are locked into their perceptions. When Scott clumsily discovers that those perceptions are inadequate and too slow in the unfolding, he shifts into a third person narrative and skips between Alan's and Darsie's story until they meet at the climax of the book. Moreover, we begin to notice that despite Darsie's apparent lack of discipline and Alan's perhaps excessive steadiness, it is not they who undergo the disenchantment or who are, finally, the focus of concern. In fact, the third protagonist, Hugh Redgauntlet (although he belongs in the tradition of Fergus MacIvor),[13] undergoes the most radical disenchantment in all of Scott's fiction. Mature as he is, his whole energies have been directed toward asserting the possibility of the past in the present.

Redgauntlet must learn painfully that there is no choice but acquiescence in history, a lesson that, ironically, he has been trying to teach Darsie. The problem is the perception of where history is. Redgauntlet finds it in his family past (where Ravenswood, to his sorrow, found his), in the commitments of generations before him, in the curse on the Redgauntlet house. Consequently, he assumes that Darsie, a biological Redgauntlet, must share in the past, that commitment, even that curse. But Darsie is far too sensible (which makes him a rather awkward *Bildungs* hero), and he has long since learned to acquiesce in history and to identify correctly where history lies, in the activity and power of the moment, not the dream of the past. Redgauntlet watches as great historical issues are consumed in trivia and gossip, and as genuine rebellion is replaced by mere nostalgia for an irretrievable past. Daiches, then, is correct in arguing that "*Redgauntlet* is the novel in which Scott found the most adequate 'objective correlative' for his feelings about Scottish history and for the complex attitude toward the relation between tradition and progress which explains so much of the workings of his mind and imagination."[14]

That attitude is best comprehended in the transformation of Hugh Redgauntlet himself. When we first perceive him through Darsie's eyes, he is a perfect embodiment of the "dark hero." Such heroes, having the energy that Scott's more insipid protagonists lack, usually are transformed into villains. But to turn Hugh into a villain would be to allow him the power that verifies a romantic reading of the experience, and therefore to turn *Redgauntlet* itself into a kind of romance. Though Hugh looms as a conspiratorial, obsessed, and almost superhumanly strong figure (he rescues Darsie twice and merely toys at fencing with Nanty Ewart), and although he appears dangerous to Darsie and Alan, he is finally powerless. The past and romantic-gothic elements cannot seriously influence the present of Darsie and Alan. The details of romance conspire to transform the past into nostalgia. (It is even worth noting that in Scott's careless and self-indulgent elaboration of Wandering Willie's role in the novel, Willie does not seriously assist Darsie, and the warning that "the Campbells are coming" is too late and irrelevant to the outcome of the narrative).

Finally, in one of the great moments of restraint in Scott's fiction, Redgauntlet becomes a figure of compassion. Informed that General Campbell will help escort the prince to the boat and that there is no threat of reprisal or punishment for conspiracy Hugh clasps his hands together "as the words burst from him, . . . 'Then, gentlemen, . . . the cause is lost forever.'"[15] The situation is precisely right in releasing Scott from the structure of romance. For Hugh can accept failure only when he recognizes that his Hanoverian opposition no longer takes him seriously enough to be threatened by him. Whereas in *Waverley*, the romance of the Jacobite dream is sustained when the judge pronounces his solemn judgment against fanaticism and condemns Fergus and Evan to death, here, twenty years later, General Campbell is all compassion and tolerance. Worse, perhaps, for the romantic dream, Hugh is reduced to tolerance himself, agreeing that the change of allegiance to the reigning monarch "sits more easy on honourable men than I could have anticipated" (II, p. 336).

The deflection from romance form is evidenced in almost every detail of *Redgauntlet*. As it finds its direction and builds to a climactic confrontation, it rejects the very literary concentration it was about to achieve. Just as *The Bride* builds to a remarkable operatic climax, so *Redgauntlet* moves to an operatic scene in which Hugh and Prince Charles Edward are to initiate a new rebellion. But despite the gathering of almost every major character at the inn, the climactic scene never happens. Earlier, the prince's interview with Alan had been interrupted by a domestic squabble with his unintimidated mistress. Now the gathered conspirators search desperately for an excuse not to become involved in an actual rebellion, and happily for their dignity light on the prince's unfortunate insistence on keeping his mistress. Hugh himself puts the crucial question of the whole novel to the conspirators: "I hope there is no gentleman here that is not ready to redeem, in his prince's presence, the pledge of fidelity which he offered in his absence" 'II, p. 291).

This question is about the connection between language and action. The Jacobites are being asked to turn their words into politics, the romance of their youth into the deliberate action of their maturity. But the scene implies precisely the novel's dramatic conclusion: the Jacobite romance is over. People's lives are governed by immediate needs, by considerations of prudence, by the banalities of ordinary experience.

Nevertheless, within the deliberate undercutting and slightly confused narrative frame, Scott gives us once again the materials of the past, the supernatural, in order to make us feel, in the early part of the novel, that Hugh's dream is not an isolated anachronism but representative of a large underground commitment waiting for some unifying action. There are at least four interludes out of romance: the famous Wandering Willie's Tale, with its supernatural machinery (a tale which prefigures the failure of the Redgauntlet cause and allows translation of the supernatural, as in *The Bride*); the story of Alberich Redgauntlet and the origin of the famous Redgauntlet horseshoe mark; the autobiographical narrations of Pate-in-Peril (to explain Darsie's heritage and continue the Redgauntlet legend); and Nanty Ewart's story. Each of these stories, fragments of the past thrown forward in anomalous contexts, implies the decadence of the Redgauntlet and Jacobite cause. The family is cursed to fight heroically on the losing side, in a way that parallels the fate of the Stuarts. Lord Glendale, learning that the prince will not consider the rebel request that he reject his mistress, speaks in a way applicable to Redgauntlet too:

> "My God, sire!" exclaimed Sir Richard, clasping his hands together, in impatience, "of what great and inexpiable crime can your Majesty's ancestors have been guilty, that they have been punished by the infliction of judicial blindness on their whole generation!" [II, p. 305]

Such language seems more appropriate to a book like *The Bride* than to *Redgauntlet*, but the full context and denouement imply no tragedy. The line of the Stuarts, like the planned conspiracy and rebellion, merely fizzles out in a rather sordid and unromantic affair.

Moreover, the supposed adventure of the early part of the book, the apparent dangers of Darsie and Alan, are rarely threatening. Mysteries are quickly dispelled. The two young men, in peculiarly unheroic and prudent strategies, weather each difficulty more or less comfortably by postponing resistance on the assumption that the worst will blow over. Hugh, who is a fatalist himself, writes to Darsie: "Beware... of struggling with a force sufficient to crush you, but abandon yourself to that train of events by which we are both swept along, and which it is impossible that either of us can resist" (I, p. 238). Darsie, Waverley-like, acquiesces, even to the point of putting up with the humiliation of being dressed in women's clothing. Alan, too, accepts the terms of his confinement, waiting for events that will be propitious. Toward the end, Darsie is relieved, as he enters the room full of reluctant rebels with Hugh, to see signs that the conspiracy will wear itself out without his active resistance. Although Scott again seems to be critical of fatalism, the narrative implies something of the "historic fatality" we have already seen in *The Bride*.

The young protagonists, all descended from Jacobites, have prudently and quietly learned to be Hanoverians. Darsie's father was killed, probably at trials in Carlisle like those that condemned Fergus in *Waverley;* Alan's father, modeled after Scott's own, was "out" in 1745. Lilias turns out to be Darsie's sister, but though under the control of Hugh for much of her childhood and though educated in a convent, she yet managed to reject the Jacobite cause. Implying an attitude central to most of Scott's work, the book, on the whole, loses interest in these young people, and shows that they inherit the earth—Darsie quite literally, Alan by virtue of remarkable application as a lawyer, and Lilias by marriage. They survive, credibly, by postponing resistance, as if they know what only the narrator of *Waverley* knows, that history will take care of the romantic dream and that chivalric heroism of the sort we might expect from, say, Bucklaw, or Seyton, or even Captain McIntyre, is not only immoral but absurd.

The true conclusion of the novel is the farewell to Prince Charles. *Redgauntlet* then moves us to the modern world, as Scott imagined it, a world in which hard work, prudence, rational discipline determine success and power. The protagonists from that world, including even the sympathetically drawn Quaker Joshua Geddes,[16] are ineffectual when in the power of plot—literary or conspiratorial. But against the apparent magical power of Redgauntlet and his dream, they are the survivors. Redgauntlet, like the past, once understood, is doomed to surrender his power. And as Prospero throws his book into the ocean to surrender his magical powers, so Redgauntlet will "sink [his sword] forty fathoms deep in the wide ocean" (II, p. 360). The spell of the past is gone, without tragedy without romance. Dryasdust takes over the last pages, acting (one might say) the role of a scholarly Miss Buskbody, but indicating with final clarity that Scott was not deeply engaged with his plot. Plot here is severed radically from narrative, and becomes merely a set of mad conventions: the happy ending, the inevitable marriage, the inheritance. The cost of history, the transformation of heroism into dream, the severing of the active life from the life of the imagination—these are the engaging subjects of *Redgauntlet* as, without parody, it makes the heroic figure an anachronism.

Insofar as Scott is identified with the forms and the times he both romanticized and rejected, he is himself an anachronism. His casual relation to the remarkable and complex materials he sporadically explored, his distrust of his own imagination, and his rather too simple commitment to fact kept him from achieving in any given work the sort of mastery we have learned to expect from his successors. But by rediscovering the past, by in effect inventing it, Scott established a precedent in form and substance for realistic fiction to follow him. The burden of discovery for protagonists depends after Scott not on some traditional moral and psychological scheme but on the complexity of their relationships to their own past and to society. Almost imprisoned in historic fatality, the young dreamers of later fiction—Dorothea Brooke, or Pip, or Isabel Archer, or Pendennis, or Richard Feverel, or Jane Eyre—must all in their own ways make their peace with the practical world they never made. The theme and form of the realist novel tend to be the quest for truth, for the fact, as opposed to the dream, and that "fact" threatens always to elude the conventions of plot and of literature itself. For there was the threat that the "fact" was itself a dream. This threat, latent in Scott, will come back to disturb those serious successors who dreamed of a language that would speak nothing but truth, that would deny its own nature. The realist drive for explanation will eventually confront the unnameable monster—the irrational and inexplicable that Scott had loved and exorcised in the form of heroism and romance.

Part Three

Mid-Victorian Realism

Conventions of the Real

6

Thackeray
"The Legitimate High Priest of Truth" and the Problematics of the Real

Hₒw do you like your novels? I like mine "hot with," and no mistake: no love-making: no observations about society: little dialogue, except where characters are bullying each other: plenty of fighting: and a villain in the cupboard, who is to suffer tortures just before Finis. I don't like your melancholy Finis.

W. M. Thackeray, *Roundabout Papers*

I

Thackeray loved Scott, but he disliked Ravenswood. I have never, he wrote "fetched [Ravenswood's] hat out of the water since he dropped it there when I last met him."[1] The sentence is characteristic of the parodic Thackeray. Every word deflates Scott's conclusion to *The Bride of Lammermoor*. "Fetched" and "dropped" seem to have little to do with Caleb Balderstone's melancholy retrieval of Ravenswood's "large sable feather" (rather than quotidian "hat"), which he "took . . . up, dried . . . , and placed . . . in his bosom" (ch. 35, p. 333). But the diminishment is part of Thackeray's self-mockery. For what he dislikes about *The Bride of Lammermoor* is certainly not its rhetorical inflations but its "melancholy Finis." Ravenswood's death in Kelpie's flow (not "water") is the death of romance. The childish pleasures of Scott, as Thackeray nostalgically talks of them, cannot be qualified by details, except of the pleasurable violences of romantic triumph and revenge. Ravenswood's death may have been too directly evocative of the sort of tragedy its abruptness averts, as George Eliot was to avert it in Maggie Tulliver's death by drowning—the realist's tragedy.

"I protest," says the narrator of *The Newcomes*—the compromised Arthur Pendennis himself—, "the great ills of life are nothing—the loss of your fortune is a mere flea-bite; the loss of your wife—how many men have supported it, and married comfortably afterwards? It is not what you lose, but what you have daily to bear, that is hard" (II, ch. 2,

131

p. 19). What you have daily to bear comes, rhetorically, not in the grandiloquent language of Scott's large romantic moments, but in the modern banalities of "fetched," "dropped," "last met him." And Thackeray's career begins in deflating every kind of social pretension, every sort of rhetorical falsification. He becomes a stylist of the ironic mode, comically asserting the pervasiveness of the ordinary, the vanity of self and society, writing fictions that wryly refuse to be "hot with." But he loved fictions and fantasies that relieved him of the burden of what we have daily to bear, and he loved Scott for the largeness of his scope, the distance of his action, the strength of his dark heroes.

Ironically, however, Scott's heritage for Thackeray was more in the novels he implied than in those he wrote. The popular Scott becomes an inevitable object of Thackeray's parody, as in *Rebecca and Rowena* he tries to imagine a yet more satisfying ending, in which Ivanhoe gets the vital, risk-taking, foreign-seeming, and dark-haired Rebecca, rather than the prim and prudish Rowena. But it is the skeptical Scott that informs Thackeray's fully developed fictional styles. This was the Scott Thackeray would not have liked very much: the self-deprecating Scott who deflated his own rhetoric, who substituted the pedestrian hero for the chivalric one, who disbelieved in the seriousness of fiction and unabashedly wrote for money: the Scott, in other words, who was too much like Thackeray.

Thackeray turned Scott's doubts into a pervasive self-consciousness that floods over from the framing devices of his fiction into the style and substance. Although one may find near the center of any Thackeray novel a Scott-like nostalgia for a lost and exciting past, Thackeray builds his career from a comic perception of that very past as it is embodied in the conventions of narrative.[2] Like Austen, almost like Scott himself, he begins with parody, but his art is always importantly parodic, seeking to displace the delightful absurdities of literary conventions with the truths that lay beyond literature. The complications and emotional losses of such displacement make his fictions diffusively unstable and self-conscious.

The most obvious examples of this manner occur when Thackeray steps back from his own effective satire, and from the "truth" implicit in his satirical dismissals. If Miss Buskbody can enter Scott's *Old Mortality* to impose upon it the most conventional possible conclusion, Thackeray can move, at the end of *The Newcomes*, from behind Pen's voice to remind us that his antiheroic, antiromantic fiction is, after all, only a fiction and hence subject to the controls of desire: "But for you, dear friend, it is as you like. You may settle your Fable-land in your own fashion. Anything you like happens in Fable-land" (II, ch. 42, p. 412).

Unlike Scott's casual dismissal of his own more romantic fiction, this sudden reversal, emerging from a context of plausible and recognizable details, is seriously discomfiting. Scott pokes fun at a certain kind of busybody novel reader but reflects no unease about giving the public what it wants. In Thackeray, it is not a joke, but a melancholy deprecation of the whole enterprise of fiction making and of novel reading. The apparently genial concession implies contemptuous rejection of the reader's unreflecting assumptions about narraitve, and of the writer's attempt to take writing more seriously than Scott did. The distance between the dreams so simply fulfilled in Fable-land, and the possibilities of experience outside the fictions—in the silences of the "real"—becomes unbridgeable. The easy freedom of doing as we like is perhaps the most powerful reminder that we have no such freedom beyond literature. The marriage becomes our responsibility, not Thackeray's, and we are consequently forced to reflect that our desires have been composing the fiction all along; its reality is only a "sentiment." After nine hundred pages, Thackeray reminds us that he has told us so from the start, and that as *The Newcomes* began with a peculiar melange of animal fables, so it must end: "The frog bursts with wicked rage, the fox is caught in his trap, the lamb is rescued from the wolf" (II, ch. 42, p. 412).

The last pages of *The Newcomes* constitute a disruptive gesture at some truth beyond fictions. The slow evolution of what felt like a realistic novel is suddenly denied. Thackeray casually confesses that he has made mistakes, as in his resurrection of Lord Farintosh's dead mother. We achieve the fullest realism in Thackeray when we see how it entails precisely the violation of illusion for which James criticized Trollope. If Thackeray's novels are in any way serious about the need for their protagonists to see beyond the fictions created by their own desires, they must be serious about their own fictionality as well. Thackeray's peculiar and unstabilizing self-consciousness leads to confusions in his art that cannot be explained away; but it is also intrinsic to what is most interesting in it.

Alexander Welsh calls the ending of *The Newcomes* a "failure" that is "something of an event in literary history." It is a moment when, says Welsh, Thackeray finds himself struggling with "the conventions of the novel."[3] Here, the latent split between the conventions of narrative and the impulse of realism, delayed by Austen's sense of a meaningful world, by Scott's uses of history, becomes manifest. Thackeray uneasily recognized realism as no more real than the romances he so gleefully parodied. To have struggled with the limits of the novel form as Thackeray did—however awkward and inconsistent the results—was to write with special intelligence and to belie Henry James, Sr.'s, delightfully malicious remark that Thackeray's mind was "merely a sounding board against which his experiences thump and resound."[4] In the course of the struggle, Thackeray helped not only to shape the conventions of the realistic novel, but to subvert them radically.

There is some irony in the reputation Thackeray developed. With the most complex sense of any of his generation of the untruth of fiction, he found his struggle to speak truth rewarded in relatively simple ways. His own formulations are less decisive than his critics': "The Art of Novels is to represent Nature: to convey as strongly as possible the sentiment of reality."[5] Yet Charlotte Brontë spoke of him as "the legitimate high priest of Truth." Elizabeth Rigby saw *Vanity Fair* as "a literal photograph of the manners and habits of the nineteenth century." David Masson, in his obituary tribute to Thackeray, called him a writer "sternly, ruthlessly real." "If the power of producing the impression of reality were the test of the highest creative power," said W. C. Roscoe, "Thackeray would perhaps rank higher than anyone who ever lived."[6]

This is the same Thackeray who, along wtih his very Victorian passion for truth and sincerity, felt the insincerity of the most sincere fictions and the attraction of fictions "hot with," which bend reality to the shape of desire. Reality, he believed, was no simple matter, and the price of pursuing it was likely to be great. He pursued it, like Jane Austen, from parody to novel, in the pattern described by Harry Levin: "from the imitation of art through parody to the imitation of nature."[7] And he pursued it further into self-parody and that striking consciousness of self and audience that seems invariably to accompany developments in realistic technique.

Unlike Austen, Thackeray could never get comfortable about incorporating the old conventions, which he admired as long as he did not have to believe in them. His novels become nostalgic commentaries on forms no longer possible. His comfort with serialization,[8] and with the rambling, bathetic style it encouraged accorded with his realist's resistance to Scott's kind of crystallization of form required by action, resolution, narrative convention, and a Whig reading of history. Every movement of plot is a violence done to the multiplicity and variousness of experience, to the elusiveness of reality. In the interests of truth, Thackeray felt impelled to mute the violence and to imply its incompatibility with the diffuseness and aimlessness of the ordinary. Yet Thackeray was not only attracted to the passionate excesses of traditional romance forms; he saw how what we had daily to bear concealed another, perhaps a more horrible violence. There was a Bertha Mason in his attic, a mad wife who filled him with guilt and sorrow. The strategy of the ordinary, of satire, and of the diffuseness of time, was both an ironic dismissal of the imposed happy endings of traditional comic forms, and a protected diversion from the quite monstrous irrational energies that lay beneath the surface of the ordinary. By averting the one, he averts the other. Yet the result, in his strangely compromised narratives, is often the quotidian tragedy, the melancholy survival of what we have daily to bear. The characteristic resolution of Thackeray's novels is the muted and not quite satisfactory happiness of, say, Dobbin and Amelia. In his work the strange conjunction of realism with comic form is threatened. Even where the comic form emerges, it is half-mocked as a manifestation of Fable-land.

II

In what follows, I do not want to minimize his culture's common sense that Thackeray was talking to them about reality. To read his novels as "representations" is inevitable and important. Certainly, he was concerned to imagine ways to navigate the perplexities of personal life in Victorian society, and his satire is pointed as directly at the insanities of social behavior as at the madness of art. But my concern here is to examine the enormous difficulties that underlay the Victorian ideal of representation and to emphasize the perplexities that manifested themselves not only in the period's self-tormented poetry and intricate nonfiction, but in the apparently stable forms of realistic fiction, where "massive confidence" is most striking only in its absence. The greatness of Scott's art lay primarily in its capacity to extend experience, to find foci not only in the great historical moments, but in the minutiae of domesticity and personal conflict. If anything, Thackeray's art, focus though it does on a relatively small range of Victorian society (and some Scott-ish eighteenth-century society as well), is more democratic than Scott's, more alert to an unmanageable multiplicity. Scott can frame that variousness only with history; Thackeray tries it through memory. But in the process, he reaches beyond the limits of the literature he knew to take the risks of a reality he could not finally know or frame. It is worth speculating on the implications for realistic fiction of his peculiarly embracing and exclusive method.

In a recent discussion of the way narrative dominates our imagination of the world, not only in fictions, but in all our modes of discourse, Leo Bersani talks of Flaubert's critique of narrative, and the terms he uses seem remarkably applicable to Thackeray. Flaubert's critique, says Bersani, was not merely of the "expectations imposed on life by literary romantics," but of "the expectations which those same romances raise concerning literature itself."[9] Narrative, he says, encourages us into an "orgasmic" mode of reading, in which "the mind

would excite itself out of consciousness." Since the explanations of
experience and sensation that narrative offers imply a time-connected,
causal set of relationships, they are, in effect, secondary elaborations of
a primary experience that comes to us—and to the writer—with
inexplicable immediacy. Narrative organizes those experiences and, in
Bersani's account, can become a satisfyingly climactic substitute—
masturbatory and orgasmic—for a dangerously unnameable experience.

There is no character in Thackeray quite as intent on such experience
as Emma Bovary, who succeeds, as Bersani says, in "producing ecstasy
from literary narration." But Fanny Bolton, particularly in her excitement over Pen's novel, *Walter Lorraine*, produces at least a faint echo of
Emma. And Thackeray's fiction, like Flaubert's, is preoccupied with the
mindless triviality of narrative, and in particular with anticipating and
thwarting "orgasmic" readings. His novels, says Jack Rawlins, in what
I read as a very useful exaggeration, "are dissertations on the novel,
with a novel provided for discussion."[10]

The parallels between the two novelists extend interestingly beyond
concern with characters who misapprehend both life and literature. As
Bersani's discussion suggests them, they help illuminate Thackeray's
position in the tradition of realism I have been tracing. In particular,
Bersani can help us see that realism has strong connections to the
modern tradition normally connected with an almost contemptuous
rejection of realism.[11] Realism, as we see it working in Thackeray's
novels, is an impulse to get beyond the very conventions of literature
modernists object to when they find them in nineteenth-century
novels. Moreover, the distrust of narrativity that Bersani takes as a clear
sign of Flaubert's modernity is evident in Thackeray's self-conscious
manipulations of his narratives and his narrative voice. Realists
themselves, in the very struggle to find a way to "represent," were
intensely aware of the limitations placed upon them by the singleness
of their vision, and the disparity between the verbal medium and the
world they were struggling to name.

Bouvard and Pécuchet provides an excellent controlled analogue to
the slovenliness of Thackeray's similarly pointless and meandering last
books. Bersani calls *Bouvard and Pécuchet* "an unqualified mockery of
any climactic significance at all."[12] One might say of a novel like *Philip*
that it is, at least, a qualified mockery of any climactic significance.
Rawlins, for example, notes "a horrible tautological propriety" to its
"badness."[13] He suggests that Thackeray's distrust of plots and
climactic scenes issued inevitably in fictions that could no longer create
such scenes (even in parody) to give narrative shape and meaning. It is

as though he had learned fully the lesson of the nonscene among the rebels at the end of *Redgauntlet,* taking it a step further by refusing the power even of anticlimax. Thackeray seems to have been engaged in a criticism of "orgasmic" fiction by means of the "gradual and finally radical denarrativizing of his own writing," of the sort Bersani attributes to Flaubert. It is precisely the enterprise implicit in Thackeray's earlier parodies, such as *Rebecca and Rowena,* where he builds to a union between Ivanhoe and Rebecca, only to settle it all in a paragraph. They were married, "of course," and the narrator does not think that they were "subsequently very boisterously happy."[14]

The refusal of climax is accompanied by promiscuity of attention to the multiplicity of experience. Both Flaubert's narrators and his characters, says Bersani, are ready to "swerve" their attention "to the sides of its objects and linger over insignificant, irrelevant, and yet sensually appealing digressive activities."[15] What is most striking is his characterization of Flaubert's tone; it is close to how one would be tempted to characterize the tone of some of Thackeray's most interesting narratives—*Pendennis, The Newcomes,* and (alas) *Philip.* The digressive enterprise, says Bersani,

> in Flaubert generally takes the form of a desultory discouragement, of a low-keyed but persistent and crippling bitterness about, precisely, the factitious nature of both the so-called big subjects of history and the essential feelings of individuals. Flaubert's famous sympathy for Emma Bovary can thus be re-defined as a longing for her longing for exciting stories, or as an envy of that naiveté which allows her to believe not only that life is novelistically serious but also that literature consists of serious and meaningful fictions.[16]

Thackeray's relation to his audience and to himself is rather more sentimental than such a description will allow. But there is a developing air of fatigue about his novels that suggests a comparable attitude. *Philip,* for instance, seems a novel that does not want to get written. Turning through it randomly one finds everywhere evidences of distractions, discontinuities and, more important, disbelief in its own seriousness. Describing Philip's love of Agnes, for instance, Pen, the narrator, does all he can to avert both the passion and the language required for it, and to cut short any narrative investment the reader might make in it:

> And yet, if a novelist may chronicle any passion, its flames, its raptures, its whispers, its assignations, its sonnets, its quarrels, sulks, reconciliations, and so on, the history of such a love as this

first of Phil's may be excusable in print, because I don't believe it was a real love at all, only a little brief delusion of the senses, from which I give you warning that our hero will recover before many chapters are over. [I, ch. 9, p. 185]

But Philip's true love receives similar treatmment: "Do gentle readers begin to tire of this spectacle of billing and cooing? I have tried to describe Mr. Philip's love-affairs with a few words and in as modest phrases as may be—omitting the raptures, the passionate vows, the reams of correspondence, and the usual commonplaces of his situation" (II, ch. 8, p. 105). Thackeray proceeds with his usual invocation of our memory of such passions and a kind of indulgence that seems inconsistent and ironic itself. Desire, in Thackeray, is distanced and diminished, trivialized by generalizing. Is it the passion or the writing which provides "the usual commonplaces"? Either way, the tone is more than disenchanted; it is so deflating that it implies a "desultory discouragement" about the possibilities of life and of literature. He cannot, at any rate, keep his eye on the object, but moves to speculating on his own feelings, on his readers' feelings, on what other people have done in similar situations. This paragraph ends, for example, with other imagined young people whose hearts are bent on marriage:

> There is the doctor's brougham driving away, and Imogene says to Alonzo, "What anguish I shall have if you are ill!" Then there is the carpenter putting up the hatchment. "Ah, my love, if you were to die, I think they might put up a hatchment for both of us," says Alonzo, with a killing sigh. Both sympathize with Mary and the baker's boy whispering over the railings. Go to, gentle baker's boy, we also know what it is to love!

This is funny, but self-indulgent, a cross between cynical parody and sentimentalism, but hardly a way to impel a narrative. It is Thackeray trapped in a narrative medium in which he no longer believes.

By this time, Pen, having been long married to Laura—providing Thackeray with occasions for long discussions which further forestall the narrative—has distanced passion so that at its most intense it will emerge as mere sentimental nostalgia. But Pen is himself a device by which Thackeray further distances passion and can refuse the strategies of narrative by which passion is reasserted. Pen, once a disenchanted protagonist, is a disenchanted narrator. Through him, Thackeray, un-like Flaubert, found strategies by which to sustain nostalgia (not merely bitterness) for the childish dreams he could no longer allow himself. The deflated Pen deflates experience, and protects Thackeray from the pain of his frustrated desires, from the risk of indulging them or believing them. Thackeray's realism becomes, in part, a way to protect dreams, as was Scott's antiquarianism; the way to sustain desire is *not* to satisfy it—"forever wilt thou love, and she be fair"—and in place of satisfaction we find ironic memories of desire.[17] The deflating and re-tarding narrative forms are a way to postpone the confrontation with narrative climax, the recognition of "the factitious nature of both the so-called big subjects of history and the essential feelings of individuals."

The exuberance of youth, in Thackeray, is reported in the language of memory—memory of the innocence that allowed a character, or the narrator, to desire the consummation intensely enough to stake his life on it. The intensity of Emma Bovary's passionate dreaming gives her a dignity that belies the sordidness of her life and the absurdity of her dream. Less powerfully, Arthur Pendennis's adolescent love of the Fotheringay is the primary evidence that he is worth his novel's nine hundred pages. Arthur's rescue from marrying her is a turn of plot that spares him the consummation required by plotting, and the banalities required by realism. Here already, but increasingly down through *Philip*, Thackeray's novels are the enacments of desires or dreams that can be articulated only by being thwarted. Formally, this entails the at-tenuation of plot in the frustration of the characters' desires—totally unlike the sharpness of plot necessary to satisfy Catherine Morland.

In Austen, as I have argued, a romance form is required to resolve the realistic materials. Romance is the form in which plotting projects upon the narrative screen the lineaments of desire. But in Thackeray, the imagined satisfactions constructed from the manipulations of narrative are normally so blatantly artificial and so laden with ironies that they are unequal to the intensities of desire that precede. Consider the ab-surd resolution of *Philip*, or the killing off of Rosie at the end of *The Newcomes*, so that Clive will be free to marry Ethel, or Blanche Amory's attempt to marry Foker in *Pendennis*, which frees Pen to marry Laura.

In another context, Bersani has defined desire as "a hallucinated satisfaction in the absence of the source of satisfaction."[18] Plot is, as it were, the hallucination. The refusal of satisfaction to the audience is a refusal of plot, a refusal to impose the conventions of romance on the developing conventions of realism. Ironically, however, the refusal of satisfaction is a way of sustaining both desire and narrative because it keeps the quest alive and denies any ending. In a sense desire un-satisfied is the driving force of realistic fictions as of the protagonists within them.

Thackeray's characters, who attempt to live romances, are frustrated by plots that do not develop, events that do not take place (except when it is too late for passion). The narratives carefully enfold passion in layers of irony and of time that diminish passion and transform it into self-consciousness. The obligatory nineteenth-century plot in which Thackeray was trapped normally ends by providing surrogates for the protagonists' first desires. In his four best novels, Dobbin gets Amelia only when he has discovered the vanity of her selfishness; Esmond gets not the beautiful and sexually vital Beatrix, but her mature mother; Pen gets neither Fotheringay, nor Blanche, but a saccharine Laura who looks suspiciously like Rowena; and we bestow Ethel on Clive only after she has outgrown her youthful energy, and he has gone through the embittering experience of a loveless marriage.

But however elaborately Thackeray's novels resist the entrapment of romance, they cannot entirely avoid it. At the points of crisis, he can withdraw from the "literary form" by blaming it on his narrator, or, as at the end of *The Newcomes*, by stepping out of narration completely and reminding us that he has made up both the story and the narrator. Such moments may even contribute to the effectiveness of his realistic technique, as Rawlins argues.[19] Thus realism, the modernist's scapegoat, the apparent superstition that literature can represent life, is in Thackeray a means beyond the limiting conventions required of any narrative form (and for which—especially in discussion of closure—realism is unjustly blamed), a stretching beyond literature, an elaborate and saving articulation of a modern consciousness of the fictionality of fiction.

Thackeray's realism thus provides us with strong evidence that the realism in mid-Victorian fiction bore within it elements of a fragmenting, unstable, and self-conscious art that radically challenged the terms of our common sense apprehension of reality and of the relation of language to that reality. Looking back on Victorian novelists, early modern writers detected a complacency, a moralism, an insistence on explaining everything and tying it neatly, a sentimental and self-indulgent impulse from which they had to free themselves. But fresh readings of Victorian fiction constantly turn up subversions of these qualities, and the discoveries are often not merely modish applications of current critical methods but readings of what the texts explicitly offer. The inconsistencies in realist art are part of the realist's exploratory enterprise; and the effort to find a containable, a nameable, order in reality was invariably compromised by the integrity that led writers like Thackeray and George Eliot to confront the disruptive energies and elusively nonverbal texture of the "real."

It is possible to reverse the Jamesian judgment of the Victorian "large loose baggy monster," and to find in the Victorian realist's mode—and, in particular, in Thackeray's—a viable alternative to the more rigorously formal Jamesian aesthetic by which much Victorian fiction has been condemned. Here, for example, is the passage from the Preface to *The Tragic Muse* in which the famous phrase occurs:

A picture without composition slights its most precious chance for beauty, and is moreover not composed at all unless the painter knows *how* that principle of health and safety, working as an absolutely premeditated art, has prevailed. There may in its absence be life, incontestably, as "The Newcomes" has life, as "Les Trois Mousquetaires," as Tolstoi's "Peace and War," have it; but what do such large loose baggy monsters, with their queer elements of the accidental and the arbitrary, artistically *mean?* We have heard it maintained, we will remember, that such things are "superior to art"; but we understand least of all what *that* may mean, and we look in vain for the artist, the divine explanatory genius, who will come to our aid and tell us. There is life and life, and as waste is only life sacrificed and thereby prevented from "counting," I delight in a deep-breathing economy and an organic form.[20]

Until recently, the assumptions about art implicit here have not required articulation because we have all, with modifications, tended to be Jamesians in our criticism of narrative.[21] "Organicism" now is a bit suspect, too easily identifiable as another kind of fiction. And there are other problems.

The leading assumption here is that satisfactory "composition" entails artistic premeditation, and that it requires not only "selection" but a hierarchical arrangement of materials, all ultimately "counting," to be sure, but nothing counting in its own right. Making things "count" and "mean" is what distinguishes art from life, as James sees it, and he has no tolerance for that more "democratic" energy of Victorian realism that aspires to make all reality count. The unaccountable, the "accidental," the "arbitrary" are in James's argument, waste, or life sacrificed. In Victorian realism, and particularly in Thackeray's uneven art, all meaning that will not allow for varieties of experience uncontainable within "premeditated art" must be recognized as itself merely arbitrary and far too selective.

For James, the inevitability of form in language is not a concern, nor is he interested in what Nietzsche has taught us to recognize as the Dionysian sources of art, the large, irrational energies that will not be teased into form and are, indeed, falsified by language. Composition in this Jamesian sense (and I am not, of course, attempting to deal with the shifts and complexities of James's entire theory or practice) can be seen not as an aesthetic virtue but as a fundamental distortion of the multifarious intensities of feeling and the resistant "wastes" of experience. Thackeray's art, like most Victorian fiction, was unquestionably anti-classical. While Arnold was seeking architectonics, novelists were finding the need to sacrifice architecture for particularities and to make their compromises with the "accidental and the arbitrary," compromises that for them reflected both the disruptive irrationality of experience and the convenience of prerealistic forms and conventions. Thackeray's usual refusal to premeditate, though it can be seen as a concession to his laziness, was a reasonable concommitant of his distrust of narrative and his uneasiness about making things "count."

James is insisting on the familiar distinction between art and life, and implying that recognition of it should lead to "art." We probably still find it easy to approve his rejection of the notion that the "life" in the large novels is somehow "superior to art." Yet James's terms imply his own acquiescence in the notion that there is, in novels, life without art, and one might well ask what *he* could mean by that. All "life" in art is artful, not merely selected, but created and shaped through the medium. Thackeray knew this well, and it filled him with misgivings about fiction writing. The Jamesian attempt to create illusion sufficiently powerful to make us forget we are reading a novel would have seemed to Thackeray misguided. His novels willfully remind us of the difference between art and life, and "the sentiment of reality" is not after all, "reality," but more like James's "verisimilitude," or Conrad's appeal to the "temperament."[22] Trollope, describing Thackeray's art, calls it "realistic . . . by which we mean that which shall seem to be real."[23] Such an awareness requires sophistication about the nature of the medium.

James talks as though the large loose monsters reflect no such awareness. He seems to be assuming that the art that places a Clive Newcome in a large and diverse context of other Newcomes, and that refuses to stay focused on a single Newcome and a single strand of relationships—that takes all Newcomes for its province—is somehow less an art than that which does a single thing fully. We will put aside here the question of the means by which a novelist, who is preoccupied with the pressures of community and society on individuals (in the tradition established by Scott) and aware of how diverse, arbitrary, and elusive such pressures may be, can manage an art with so intense a focus as that which James requires. Thackeray cannot and does not want to place all the action inside, and thus his composition is looser, but composition it is. In tightness of composition there is implicit a commitment to "literary form" that Frye's analysis places with plot. Even in James, that is, one can detect the violence of narrativity that Thackeray was so self-consciously avoiding.

James cannot cope with the "queer elements of the accidental and the arbitrary." He asks, what can they artistically mean? Precisely. Thackeray's art, though it will retreat from its full implications, risks the not-meaning, and the denigration of literature itself. From the start, realism, in its antiliterary preoccupation with the real as opposed to the art that has always deformed it, found itself threatened by nonmeaning. Thackeray's strategy in *The Newcomes* is to imagine a world that resists the falsely explanatory and clarifying controls of art. The distinction between what counts and what is waste becomes increasingly artificial and arbitrary. If the deluge of details represses the monster latent for Thackeray and other Victorians in undisciplined desire, it also reveals the monstrously shapeless and unattainable nature of ordinary reality. Arbitrary and disruptive material keeps emerging.

In James, the artist becomes "the divine explanatory genius," and it is precisely such heroic claims for the artist that the realist attempts to exclude from his art. Thackeray, simply, does not take his art as seriously as James takes his, although he takes his responsibility to the truth with perhaps greater seriousness. The democracy of truth outranks the elitism of art, and Thackeray is thus less able to distinguish between what "counts" and what is "waste." Any narrative, he understands, "wastes" a background that might as well have been a foreground. By invariably asking the readers to remember whether they have not had experiences similar to those of his novels, Thackeray, in effect transforms all into "waste." The ideal of his realism is to find its subject anywhere, amid the waste; and even when confined to a single narrative line, he swerves his attention to the infinite other novels that might be going on out there at the moment.

Obviously, Thackeray is no modernist, however susceptible his novels become to modernist readings. Yet it is important to complicate our ways of thinking about his work so that we can see in the midst of what has too often been taken as a Victorian "massive confidence" in the real, or a Victorian facility for boxing up experience into cubes of meaning, or a Victorian slovenliness about form, a viable, sophisticated realist art. His is a realist art that implies an aesthetic pluralism, a profound uncertainty about the nature of reality, a fine alertness to the complications of his medium and of his audience's expectations of the medium, and a persistent self-consciousness about the strategies by which desire imposes itself on narrative. In the midst of a genuinely experimental art form, Thackeray, like the other Victorians, normally exploited certain narrative conventions whose very conventionality is at odds with the realism. Moreover, in their explorations of "reality," beyond the literary conventions and against literature, Victorians were eager to disrupt complacencies of conventional order, to resist the irresistible conventionality of language, and to speak the truth. Thackeray belongs in the midst of this difficult aesthetic tangle. But if we step back from his work to locate the specific elements of the realist impulse evident there, we can identify an art that took large risks, anticipated modernism in many ways, and reflects what is, for me at least, a deeply moving effort to surprise the elusive fair maiden, even though, were she to turn around, she might show the face of the monster.

7

Thackeray
Some Elements of Realism

*N*o one can read Mr. Thackeray's writings without feeling that he is perpetually treading as close as he dare to the border-line that separates the world which may be described in books from the world which it is prohibited so to describe.

Walter Bagehot, *Estimations in Criticism*

One might extend Bagehot's meaning. It is not merely the moral (or immoral) world prohibited by Victorian culture that Thackeray intimates in his respectable novels. It is the world beyond books, beyond words. The conventions of realism that Thackeray develops, even though they *are* conventions and, at best, mediations of experience, all point toward the elusive truth that realists could not capture. E. S. Dallas, praising the "truth" of fiction, registers the Victorian intellectual's awareness of the prevasiveness of fictions in our experience:

> Behold, it is a world of fictions in which we live, and history itself, that prides itself above all else on its adherence to fact—history has not without a show of reason been pronounced to be false in everything but the names and the dates. Amid all these fictions of the senses, of the heart, of reason and of revelations; amid fictions of history, fictions of law, fictions of philosophy, fictions of mathematics, fictions of language, fictions that are all more or less short of the truth, but still are charged with truth and mean truth—shall we be told that in art alone fiction is not allowable, and can only mean falsehood?[1]

Dallas brings to bear on the problem of fictions a mind steeped in Victorian science and philosophy, but what he articulates here is a view central to the Victorian experience and one accessible to the thinking public at large. The problem of the relation between fictions and truth had accounted for much of the pious resistance to novel reading already noted; but certainly for the novelists, the disparity between what language could say, and the truth the words were written to mime, was a

continuing concern without constituting a subversion of their enterprise. The self-consciousness we have already noted in Thackeray
makes clear that he understood, as Dallas did, the difficulties in imitating nature, the radical fictionality of his own fictions. Yet his enterprise
as novelist was to reconcile "fiction" and "truth" in terms consistent
with Dallas's, and the realistic methods he developed are all means to
that end, as well (Dallas would be sure to insist) as the means to "pleasure."

I want here to isolate, rather artificially, four elements of Thackeray's
method essential to his realism and to that of most realists of the century, and directed to the reconciliation of "truth" and "fiction" that
Dallas's argument implies. Each of these elements implies the others,
and each has traditional associations with realism, as it developed from
Defoe on.[2] As Thackeray developed them, moreover, they intensify
the self-contradictions in realism I discussed in the first chapter, and
point forward to modernist developments in an art self-consciously
"fictitious."

I

Plot and Character

As I have suggested, Thackeray's attitudes toward plot were shared by
writers like George Eliot and Trollope who, in their different ways,
were perhaps more bound by the conventions than he. The traditional
notion of the primacy of plot in narrative, dating back to Aristotle's
Poetics, was being displaced by emphasis on "character." The nineteenth-century realist ideally began with intensely imagined characters,
and found a plot for them only in working out the inevitable developments of their "characters." "A novel," says Trollope,

> should give a picture of common life enlivened by humour and
> sweetened by pathos. To make that picture worthy of attention, the
> canvas should be crowded with real portraits, not of individuals
> known to the world or to the author, but of created personages
> impregnated with traits of character which are known. To my
> thinking, the plot is but a vehicle for all this. . . . There must, how-
> ever, be a story.[3]

The formulation suggests that "plot" is a mere inconvenient necessity
(the implicit contrast to "portrait" was a special, Jamesian, interest).
Plot, that is to say, is not an essential element for realism, especially if
one uses E. M. Forster's definition of it as a "story" whose causal
explantations are made clear,[4] or Thackeray's (implicit in his parodies),
as a narrative full of striking incidents, inorganically and conventionally

imposed upon the materials. The latter is also what Trollope meant by "plot," but neither he nor Thackeray, even in their mutual abjuring of "surprises," could be exempt from it. One does not have to look far among the realists to find "plot" awkwardly asserting itself: the last-minute rescue of Hetty Sorrel, the garroting of Mr. Bonteen in *Phineas Redux*, Jane Eyre's discovery of the light at her cousin's door, or the return of Dr. John to Lucy Snowe's story, Warrington's convenient tragedy in *Pendennis*, or Philip's good fortune in his last pages.

But the ideal required that plot exist only in *organic* relation to character, so that character becomes fate: the motto out of Novalis is Hardy's, and George Eliot's. It implies, once again, a meaningful universe, although not now in such strict moralist terms as we have seen in Whately. Rather, characters must be seen not so much to get what they deserve, as to create or place themselves in the conditions that correspond to their natures. Like Frankenstein, they cast the shadow of themselves on external reality. The narrative merely makes objective in experience what a character *is*. Technically, this means that the protagonist's imagined nature is once again the determiner of plot or, better, inseparable from it, evoking the flood from the Floss, or Elizabeth-Jane's real father (in *The Mayor of Casterbridge*) from the sea. Yet it also means that fiction must avoid merely contriving fates by external manipulation of plots: if a long lost relative returns, there must be an explanation in keeping with plausibility and a world recognizable to the reader. Realist plotting begins to break down the simple distinction between self and other at the same time as it thematically asserts, in the form of disenchantment, the necessity to understand the difference between self and other.

Kenneth Grahame notes that "as the melodrama of earlier Victorian fiction is superseded by the greater psychological realism of George Eliot and Trollope [both of whom recognized Thackeray as the greatest English novelist writing in the 'fifties], critics come to identify 'plot' with the particular incidents and conventions used by older writers."[5] The inevitable association (encouraged, of course, by the example of Scott) of plot with the past—both literary and cultural—tended to place "character" in the here and now as a displacement of the artificial and unreal from the center of narrative. Plot, as the bearer of desire, is the means by which the extreme—or the "orgasmic"—enters narrative, and in the quest both for truth and for the civilizing morality which the novel was attempting to affirm, the extreme was banished with plot. The monstrous, domesticated by Austen, exorcised by Scott, is, in Thackeray, transformed into banality (which occasionally, as in the story of Colonel Newcome, achieves an almost tragic intensity again). If Becky Sharp is occasionally perceived as a mermaid with skulls wound within her submerged tail, she is more often a clever social climber, an occasion for minor scandal, as she is seen, glancingly, even in *The Newcomes*.

The mid-century realist's exclusion of extremes (detectable even in the range of their images)[6] reflects not only a cultural attitude toward the advance of civilization, and the responsibilities of fiction, but a new secular science, of which Dallas's aesthetic is only one manifestation. Technically, sharply plotted fiction can be seen as a narrative analogue to a pre-Darwinian catastrophism, a view that the world and its species are permanently what they are, unless a catastrophic change takes place. The self-conscious shift away from "plot" to "character" is, I would argue, the beginning of a shift to a vision of the world that is in constant flux and inaccessible to human orders of naming. It is a shift away from the Whatelyan realist's confidence to a more compromised secular vision of a world slowly transforming, absolute in nothing, not even—it will turn out—in the solidity of "character," which allows the possibility of a fixed "portrait." If species change—as Whewell and Tennyson knew before Darwin—then certainly character must inevitably change, too. Thackeray, certainly, writes with some faith in "character," yet there are evidences already in his art (as I will suggest in a reading of *Pendennis*) that character is as much a falsification of truth as plot.

We can detect a moment in the transition to this vision in the work of Thackeray's most apocalyptic contemporary, Carlyle, and in that inescapable reference point, *Sartor Resartus*. Carlyle's extravagant style, continuing preoccupation with revolution, and attempt to reconstruct a viable religion of absolutes are invariably put to the service of a *thematic* antirevolutionary cause. He asserts a world from which the miraculous and the extreme have been banished by humanity's incurable pursuit of secular knowledge. Yet the monstrous is always there, ready to explode even out of the forms of empiricism and rationalism, as it did in the French Revolution. The miraculous is visible, for those who have eyes to see, precisely in the details of ordinary life that the scientists and secularists are trying to explain rationally. The battle between transcendental and descendental, spirit and matter, idea and thing, continues secretly, at the risk, if the materialists win, of being left with a meaningless and violently inexplicable universe.

With external authority withdrawn, all things dissolve into a meaningless Flux, an intense Inane; redemption begins for Teufelsdröckh with the assertion of Selfhood. The quintessential Victorian statement in the famous "Everlasting No" chapter of *Sartor Resartus* helps explain the priority of character over plot in Victorian fiction: "Alas, the fearful Unbelief is unbelief in yourself." It is the self, finally, not some externally ordered Providence slipped into narrative through plot, that makes the world meaningful. The new wisdom of selfhood allows Teufelsdröckh to see through the mere surfaces of things, through the old clothes, and to a certain extent it allows him to be a satirist like Thackeray. But he moves beyond satire to the mystery that underlies the ordinary. This is not plot-action, but introspection and the projection of the imagined self on an apparently valueless world.

However far Thackeray moved from the extremes of mysticism and rhetoric of Carlyle's *Sartor Resartus,* his novels depend, for what form and meaning they can find, on the establishment of a definable self. The difficulties his narratives encounter suggest that the definition is far more difficult than it seems. Teufelsdröckh, for example, knew that the "belief" in the self depends on our discovery of its reflection in "Our Works . . . the mirror wherein the spirit first sees its natural lineaments" (p. 162). For Pendennis, as for Thackeray himself, his works were his fictions, and the novels normally depend heavily on a narrator constructing a self by talking to his audience. The Vanity that Thackeray preaches about in *Vanity Fair* is the other side of a solipsism so complete that there threatens to be *no* reflection from the outside world to confirm the self. "Ah sir—" sighs the sometimes tediously digressive narrator of *Pendennis* (who sounds supiciously like Pen himself), "a distinct universe walks about under your hat and under mine—all things in nature are different to each—the woman we look at has not the same features, the dish we eat has not the same taste to the one and the other—you and I are but a pair of infinite isolations, with some fellow-islands a little more or less near to us" (I, ch. 16, p. 149). Yet the narrator is a gesture at community, a means of constructing self by invoking, even in the hopeless and untouchable separateness of other isolations, a community of private feelings. We are at least alike in our separateness.

The self Thackeray constructs to make his fictions possible is a self that has forsaken "plot," in the sense that it knows all plots to be mere attractive illusions. "Character," in the sense of a personality shaped from recognizable characteristics, is, for Pendennis, a creation of youthful energy or of the sustained illusions of ambition and desire. Pen encloses action and ideals in youth and in a knowing monologue with his audience about the charm of illusion. "There was once a time," he begins the actual narrative of *The Newcomes,* "when the sun used to shine brighter than it appears to do in this latter half of the nineteenth century; when the zest of life was certainly keener; when tavern wines seemed to be delicious, and tavern dinners the perfection of cookery; when the perusal of novels was productive of immense delight" (I, ch.1, p. 6), and so on. But this "time" is less a historical fact than an imagination of youth, and this is implicit in the very tone of the passage. Out of that past, the narrative evokes Colonel Newcome who, even in his age, is a child and hence a "character." He has a firm selfhood against which everything in the novel is tested, and yet, as the narrative unfolds, it is clear that the price of the colonel's selfhood is disaster. His firmly defined self is seen always from the admiring perspective of the narrator, Pen, and yet the colonel's insistence on the ideal inflexibility of virtue and manners, the reflex of a powerful loving energy, is a sharp contrast to the worldly-wise pragmatism of the sentimental-cynical Pen. The serious "plot" of *The Newcomes* is very much a matter of "character," as well. But, as we have already seen, the self surviving the plot, Pen the chatty narrator, is dismissed in the last pages, with a description of the colonel's death that evokes both the colonel's childhood and his own at Grey Friars: "He lifted up his head a little, and quickly said 'Adsum!' and fell back. It was the word we used at school, when names were called; and lo, he, whose heart was as that of a little child, had answered to his name, and stood in the presence of The Master" (II, ch. 62, p. 411). Here Thackeray manages to indulge the pleasures of character and of plot while sentimentally registering their disastrous consequences.

The self constructed to impose meaning on experience in Thackeray's novels tends then to be one whose essential being is in the memory of feeling, rather than in feeling itself. As narrator, he is recognizable, that is to say, as a figure who envies the innocence that makes feeling possible, and who finds that feeling representable within the discredited conventions of plot and character that he carefully places in the past. It is not so much the self as the remembered self that creates meaning and value. As against the firmly defined self, however, there is a digressive and fluid world that seems to resist plot for the pleasures of its own multiplicity and variousness.

The distancing of desire and of violence that the narrative strategies accomplish cannot be complete. Although Thackeray tries to stay with the minute while Carlyle deals with vastnesses, he is only partly successful in banishing the extreme to the past and to its forms. The largeness and looseness of his novels can indeed become monstrous, even as they attempt to articulate a vision in which the extreme is an aberration in the texture of life. The novels tend to imply—whatever arbitrarily invented closures there may be—that there are no beginnings or endings, only continuities, repetitions, minutely incremental changes. Everything is compromised, complicated, multiplied, and the inability to recognize this leads to a disastrous inflexibility. But the ordinary suddenly flares up into aggressive selfhood: Mrs. MacKenzie, the old campaigner, merely a greedy and otherwise pleasant dowager, becomes, in effect, a killer; Blanche Amory almost traps the already compromised Pen into a life of continuing misery.

Finally in Thackeray's fiction, the false romance has its analogue in the true. In the defensive tones of the narrators, in the slightly frightened distancing of desire, we can detect a violent reality which is also a guarantee of community with audience. Nobody is exempt from the ultimate violence, which is the deprivation of redeeming memory of life and desire by the slow grating of time toward death. This is not so much plot as a mere chronology of the drying up of desire and, hence, of value. In Thackeray, at least, the strategy of realism, in its constant refusal of plot, catastrophe, and the absolute, is the strategy of defense against violence through the moderation of desire. The real becomes a substitute for passion. Says the narrator of *Pendennis*, "Grey hairs have come on like daylight streaming in—daylight and a headache with it. Pleasure has gone to bed with the rouge on her cheeks. Well, friend, let us walk through the day, sober and sad, but friendly" (I, ch. 29, p. 304). Yet Thackeray is better than this. The very self-conscious surrender is, to reverse the reading, a way to reintroduce the passion and face a world beyond words. The integrity of the realist seeker who has found the incompatibility between language and reality pushes him beyond the literature in which he can no longer believe to the sad, but wonderful and difficult, tangle of a densely particular world.

II
Particularity

From Defoe on, realistic narratives have depended on circumstantial particularity to establish verisimilitude. Thackeray belongs in that tradition, for his prose is frequently thick with minutely perceived details, with accumulations of named objects, with nuances of gesture and of voice—all suggesting an intimate and extensive acquaintance with the texture of real life. His eyes swerve with digressive fascination from the narrative focus to a world jammed with things and differences, and the effect is to evoke from readers nods of recognition and confidence that they are at home in that fictional world. Of course, there is also in Thackeray's prose a great deal of generalizing and speculation. But the context, as at his famous fictional dinners, is a very detailed and descriptive menu.

The realist's rejection of plot is normally accompanied by a preoccupation with particulars that can become digressive, whether unintentionally as even in the businesslike *Robinson Crusoe*, or intentionally as in *Bouvard and Pécuchet* and *Philip*. The nonstructural detail, apparently thematically irrelevant, provides the primary evidence of the antiliterary thrust of realism, and ironically, the case for its trustworthiness. Such details normally can serve as a parodic reminder of the artificiality of the materials of nonrealistic narrative. Particulars can, thus, allow Thackeray to assimilate certain traditional literary forms into his narrative without succumbing to them; the verisimilitude calls those traditions into question and is itself put to question by the traditions. Ethel Newcome, for example, is judged against the Diana-ideal,[7] which can find no place in the meticulously registered amorality of the marriage market. Yet the unrealized and unrealizable ideal provides the energy for her narrative growth and keeps her sympathetic in spite of her compromised plausibility. While partly mocking the Diana-ideal, Ethel's story also uses that ideal to mock the too credible story of her sale to the highest bidder.

Deflation of the ideal is the work of sharply perceived particulars. We can see how this works in simplest form in a parody like *Rebecca and Rowena*. Ivanhoe, stifled by marriage to the rigid and puritanical Rowena, tries to find a way to escape, and wants to tell Rowena that he is going to join King Richard in the battle at Chalus. At breakfast, he adopts "a *degagé* air, as he sipped his tea." The language, of course, is of a bad modern domestic comedy, not of a medieval romance. Who could think of Ivanhoe as "sipping" his tea? How did "tea," not introduced into Europe until the sixteenth century, get on the table in the first place? "My love," Ivanhoe uxoriously begins, "I was thinking of going over to pay his Majesty a visit." Rowena, too, participates in this domestication of romance, for she lays "down her muffin" before answering. And she proceeds, with domestic casualness and an alacrity suggesting modern comedy once more, to mend "his linen," and pack his "carpet-bag." Self-evidently parodic and light-hearted, *Rebecca and Rowena* works because of Thackeray's capacity to evoke, through carefully selected particulars, the texture of a bourgeois domestic scene (and of a trivial literary form). All depends on a fine notation of tones of voice, and of things normal in the domestic context.

Of course, what is "particular" in this passage might well be quite general in another. There is nothing very particular for example, about the word "tea." We do not find out what kind of tea, or how it smelled. But here it is enough to violate our literary expectation of Scott-like romances. The degree of particularity—especially given the inescapable generality of language—must be determined by context; but the more a piece of prose discriminates particularities, subdivides exactly the classes language must imply, the more it averts the ideal, and stretches toward the infinitely receding reality beyond words. Unless the writer, like Hopkins in his poetry, is constructing an ethics or aesthetics in which the fullest individuation becomes the fullest articulation of the essence of a thing, and thus an ultimate transcendence of worldly limits through worldly forms, if he insists on particulars extensively he is

working, prima facie, in an ironic mode. Irony and transcendence, in
this mode of nineteenth-century realism, turn out, indeed, to be closely
related.[8] For each writer, the force of the particular is dependent on the
larger context in which it is imagined. So Ruskin's gorgeously precise
prose, obsessed with the finest striations of the smallest blades of grass,
evokes romantic intensities and feelings of the sublime; but he insists
that when he "sees," he detects an ultimately harmonious form,
sanctioned by the divine. Un-Arnoldian as he is, Ruskin yet is even
more frightened by fragmentation.

Normally, particulars contribute effectively to a comic-ironic mode,
for even if they are cumulatively serious, they tend to imply the failure
of some previously imagined—literary—mode of ordering. Particulars
are the instruments of disenchantment. When Newman, in his superb
and breathless catalogue near the beginning of the fifth chapter of the
Apologia pro vita sua, looks at the world in its secular reality—that is,
without a supporting metaphysical context—it becomes terrifying to
him, and meaningless.[9] The particular, without ideal sanction, is
equivalent to the deprivation of self, and Newman describes the condition as what it would be like to see no reflection in the mirror. Only
when he begins looking at the particular by assuming a God can he
cope with reality, or even believe in it.

Thackeray's novels often read like Newman's particulars without a
prior assumption of God. The complication of reality by means of increasingly detailed particulars violates both the clarity of the real, as
Whately saw it, and traditional generic distinctions.[10] Within most
secular fiction, it increasingly subverts clear patterns of meaning, ideal
imaginations of relationships or society, and the shaping energies of
romance plotting. The disenchanted protagonists of Thackeray's novels,
as of most nineteenth-century realistic ones, must face a world so densely
particular that it will not take the shape the imaginations and wills
impose. Against the shaping dreams of the characters, particularities
imply a multitudinous external world that stands as a permanent irony
at the expense of all dreams and wishes—and, ultimately, ideas. For
Thackeray, at least, the world does not offer itself in Whateleyan forms,
and the forms of romance consequently come to him as merely absurd
and artificial constructs.

The secular vision of particularity is also one of multitudinous-
ness, and to such a vision any single narrative focus will seem narrow
and provincial. The external fact may be falsely used, as in the pathetic
fallacy, and thus falsely assimilated to merely literary structures; but in
profusion, facts get uncontrollably beyond the assimilating powers of
characters or even narrators. Thackeray's novels, with their constant
allusions to and introductions of characters from other novels, imply

both the artificial closure of any single narrative, and the proximity of other equally important novels while any particular narrative is going on. Their implied reality, ironically, implies the unreality of the one actually being read. The ultimate discovery of the novelist, as Thackeray's self-deprecating narrators may be implying, is that to take seriously any set of particulars is to falsify; yet the particulars imply a stretching toward the unattainable truth, which is the stamp of integrity.

In *Pendennis*, there is a simple and explicit example of this. As Pen is convalescing in his chambers, Laura occupies the chambers on the second floor temporarily vacated by P. Sibwright, Esq.:

> With Sibwright in Chambers was Mr. Bangham. Mr. Bangham was a sporting man, married to a rich widow. Mr. Bangham had no practice—did not come to chambers thrice in a term: went a circuit for those mysterious reasons which make men go to circuit—and his room served as a great convenience to Sibwright when that young gentleman gave his little dinners. It must be confessed that these two gentlemen have nothing to do with our history, will never appear in it again probably, but we cannot help glancing through their doors as they happen to be open to us, and we pass to Pen's rooms; as in the pursuit of our own business in life through the Strand, at the Club, nay at Church itself, we cannot help peeping at the shops on the way, or at our neighbour's dinner, or at the faces under the bonnets in the next pew. [II, ch. 52, pp. 140–41]

Here, starkly, is that swerving of attention Bersani finds in Flaubert. The rooms are first known as Sibwrights, but we must learn, too, about Bangham. The narrator, however, to justify the swerving, swerves further, to himself and to the various ways he, like us, peeps in on business not his own. Since we are at what might be taken as a crisis in Pen's narrative, when he is deathly ill, the swerving has a comically deflating effect.

The particulars, however, appear more fully in a previous paragraph, in which the peeping narrator has given us an extensive catalogue of the contents of the room—the pomatum, the bear's grease, the bed's chintz curtains with pink trim, the bad romantic pictures that barely disguise a young man's prurience, and so on. The details have a function, or at least a frame, in that they imply the vanity and silliness of the absent Sibwright. But it is hardly a useful point since, as the narrator takes pains to say, he will never appear in the novel again. Ironically, the very silliness of Sibwright suggests that he, and his equally vain friend, Bangham, are as worthy of a novel as Pen. The Sibwright digression is a very pleasant diversion from Pen's narrative. It takes on its own fragmentary and independent fictional life.

There is, in *Pendennis,* an unpleasant novelist happily named Wagg. The rhetoric places him unkindly, but it also demonstrates that he is indeed a novelist, with a novelist's compulsion to peep at things: "Mr. Wagg noted everything that he saw; the barometer and the letter-bag, the umbrellas and the ladies' clogs, Pen's hats and tartan wrapper, and old John opening the drawing-room door, to introduce the newcomers. Such minutiae attracted Wagg instinctively; he seized them in spite of himself" (I, ch. 25, p. 251). When Wagg tells his story of his visit to Pen's mother, he tells it "with wonderful accuracy of observation"(I, ch. 25, p. 253). Although the narrator treats Wagg as a mere wag, and as a mean-spirited (and lower class) snob, he obviously admires his novelist's skill, and his capacity to read into details whole ways of life. Wagg's is a rather Thackerayan mode of acerbic satire, and he is almost a parody of the early parodic Thackeray. He seizes details, almost in spite of himself; he "cannot help peeping." The result is a delighted perception of the disparity between the fact and the pretense, between, for instance, Pen's pretensions to aristocratic style and the reality of his domestic situation. As Barbara Hardy notes, Thackeray's "world of expressive objects is part of his satire and moral preaching."[11]

But the objects have more (or other) than such expressive function. In life as in narration, Thackeray unembarrassedly, although sometimes half apologetically, relishes the particulars for their own sake. If all "the objects emerge tainted," as Barbara Hardy says,[12] so do all the characters. This is, after all, vanity fair, but without the transcendent judgment implicit in that label. Unlike Bunyan, Thackeray describes vanity fair not to make us choose against it, but to shake our complacent moralisms and to elicit indulgence of the vanities that mark us all. Stern moralism—though Thackeray certainly saw himself as a moralist—is made questionable by our peripheral vision of multitudes of irresistible details suggesting that for every Pen there is a Sibwright, and a Bangham, for every lovesick Pen there is a lovesick Mirobolant or Smirke.

"He devoted himself in his fiction," says Gordon Ray, "to accumulating countless concrete details,"[13] and the practical wisdom of Thackeray's narrator invariably includes a pragmatic acceptance of the attraction of things of this world. Pen, Clive Newcome, and Philip Firmin are sufficiently spoiled by "things" to be kept from fulfilling their work as artists; and they are all forgiven by their novels. Ethel Newcome, recognizing herself as an object for sale with a "green ticket" pinned to her, nevertheless wants what her purchase price will bring. In the place of the romantic ideals or the passions of adolescence, fantasies that become valuable only in retrospect, when they are beyond reach, there are the practical claims of a good dinner—carefully described —handsome clothing, and a great deal more than nothing a year.

This is another way that the objects work to deflate the literary forms that affirm the power of desire. For they make us see that who characters are is contingent upon the facts of their physical and social world. Almost everything in a Thackeray novel is contingent. It is true, especially in the later novels, that Thackeray's treatment of narrative can be extremely undramatic, or panoramic. This is another apsect of his deflation of narrative. Yet the concreteness remains. Barbara Hardy, again, notes how Thackeray's concreteness brings "people into relation with the world of objects," or shows "that their relations to each other, and sometimes even their solitary passions, are inseparable from the environment of objects."[14] Inevitably, then, Thackeray's subject is most often the central subject of realistic fictions, the relation between the dreaming self and the indifferent other. But Thackeray's self-conscious dispersion of focus disallows the sorts of catastrophic shapes we find in *Madame Bovary* or *The Mill on the Floss;* no narrator can take the contrast between dream and fact so seriously as the protagonists. The dispersion of narratives into details that make ironic commentaries on the romantic passions of young protagonists almost by virtue of their irrelevance to them helps turn Thackeray's novels into James's large loose baggy monsters. The desire that transforms—as in George Warrington's history—into a monstrous deformation of life is filtered through almost intractable particularities. Thackeray's realist imagination of a contingent and ironic world is a deliberate rejection of Newman's kind of assumption of transcendence and a strategy of resistance to the monstrous implications of a world without God or, perhaps, even self.

III
Heroism and the Ordinary

In Thackeray, the realist tradition of the unheroic hero is pushed further than we have as yet seen. *Vanity Fair* is genuinely, after all "A Novel without a Hero," and even his titular heroes are questionable. Scott's heroes, we have noted, seem bland and domesticated, but they are given, if only by accident, some of the accoutrements of heroism: firm military bearing, generosity, genuine love of a heroine. Austen's less than perfect heroines achieve a kind of alternative heroism, even though in their awkward positions as women dependent on marriage, they are never, even in Emma's case, unequivocally privileged. But the characteristic Thackeray hero—Pen, or Clive Newcome, or Philip Firmin—has at best only a kind of good nature to engage us. Although they become underdogs for a while, their narratives trace the falseness of their expectations, the vanity of their dreams, the awkward discovery of their own compromises. They are all more or less compromised by their distinctly unheroic relish of cigars, good clothing, fine wines. In his treatment of heroes, Thackeray makes evident how the realist apotheosis of character can have moved to the destabilizing of character. Like George Eliot after him, Thackeray insisted on the mixed, even inconsistent, nature of character, especially in moral matters. If the "old stable ego" of character remains (it is almost all, in vanity fair, that gives character consistency), the idea that it may not be stable is already latent.

Thackeray, we know, lamented in *Pendennis* that since Fielding's day, "no writer of fiction among us has been permitted to depict to his utmost power a MAN" (I, p. 16). Yet, despite Thackeray's own youthful sexual energy, it is hard to imagine what such a MAN might have looked like in his fiction. Pen, we see, might have gone through with his seduction of Fanny; the protagonist's moral failings might have been less primly delineated. What is missing from Thackeray is not merely what society precluded from fiction, but the Tom Jonesian energy and exuberance. Even if he could have confronted sexuality honestly the likelihood is that sexual vagaries would have been treated much as he treated the primmer romantic fantasies—as pleasant but dangerous youthful exercises of desire, quickly gone and not very important. In place of that sexuality, his heroes are allowed passions for wine and cigars.

Against the rigor of Victorian moralism and, perhaps, his own desires, Thackeray created worlds not ordered by the standards of Christian virtue but, rather, mixed, compromised, contingent, unfair—though on the whole, not too unfair. His sentimentality and his moralism merge in commentary on the fact; but they do not alter the fact. The world Thackeray creates, though resistant to the dreams of the young (dreams too much in the shape of literature), and askew from the desires of the virtuous, is yet not impossible. Here, as in all other respects, Thackeray eschews extremes, which belong to the young. His characteristic note (in harmony with the antiromantic passages I quote in the first chapter) is struck at the conclusion of *Pendennis*, when Pen is compared with his better friend, George Warrington:

> If Mr. Pen's works have procured him more reputation than has been acquired by his abler friend, whom no one knows, George lives contented without the fame. If the best men do not draw the great prizes in life, we know it has been so settled by the Ordainer of the lottery. We own, and see daily, how the false and worthless live and prosper, while the good are called away, and the dear and young perish untimely,—we perceive in every man's life the

maimed happiness, the frequent falling, the bootless endeavour, the struggle of Right and Wrong, in which the strong often succumb and the swift fall: we see flowers of good blooming in foul places, as, in the most lofty and splendid fortunes, flaws of vice and meanness, and stains of evil; and knowing how mean the best of us is, let us give a hand of charity to Arthur Pendennis, with all his faults and shortcomings, who does not claim to be a hero, but only a man and a brother. [II, ch. 75, p. 394]

The biblical allusiveness here, and the language of right and wrong, in no way provide the transcendent context that would make the injustices comprehensible. The strategy of moralism here is different. The universality of injustice is invoked to make us accept it, and the hero who is implicated in it.

The injustice invoked is characteristically moderate, for Pen is not so bad, only ordinary, or second-rate. As the realist excludes extremes from narratives, so he must exclude them from character. The landscape of Pen's world is suburban and urban. He moves in a world of mock pastoral, mock silver-fork. His potential duel is with a French chef; his most violent confrontation is with his mother. The test of characters, in Victorian realism, is not some Conradian test—a typhoon, an assassination, a voyage to the heart of darkest Africa—but the daily life of muffins and teas and bank accounts and the temptations of good cigars and large investments. "Here or nowhere is America"; every drawing room is a crossroads of infinity. Our history, says Pen, as narrator of *The Newcomes*, "is of the world, and things pertaining to it. Things beyond it, as the writer imagines, scarcely belong to the novelist's province" (I, ch. 37, p. 394).

The world, as Thackeray imagines it, is, in its very ordinariness, perilously close to another kind of monstrousness, to the very materials that become the object of his mockery in gothic and romantic literature. The test of character in the drawing room is not so much an exclusion of the monstrous as another translation of it. The ordinary threatens to expand beyond itself at any moment, and must be not only represented, but controlled. Here is the well-known excursus, in *The Newcomes*, on the fact that all of us have a skeleton in the closet. The defensiveness implicit in Thackeray's narrative techniques and his diversion into irrelevant details are treated with comic rhetoric here; but the implications are not comic:

Have we not all such closets . . . ? Who, in showing his house to the closest and dearest, doesn't keep back the key of a closet or two? I think of a lovely reader laying down the page and looking over at her unconscious husband, asleep, perhaps, after dinner. Yes, madam, a closet he hath: and you, who pry into everything, shall never have the key of it. I think of some honest Othello pausing over this very sentence in a railroad carriage, and stealthily gazing at Desdemona opposite to him, innocently administering sand-wiches to their little boy—I am trying to turn the sentence with a joke, you see—I feel it is growing too dreadful, too serious. [I, ch. 11, p. 121]

Which, of course, is true. The passage is subversive in ways only Victorian realism at its most self-conscious can be, for it places the reader in railroad carriage or drawing room, holding the book in hand, inside the book. And in so doing it transforms—or threatens to transform—characters in the reader's real world. Thackeray's ultimate seriousness extends beyond the reach of the realistic techniques he adopts into an impenetrable mystery which he cannot know or name. The un-remittingly faithless secularity of the drama—pious digressions aside—implies the inadequacy of realistic imaginations of the ordinary to satisfy or console.

Usually, when Thackeray approaches this kind of seriousness, he tries to turn it with a joke. Even the passage in *Pendennis* that concludes with "you and I are but a pair of infinite isolations, with some fellow islands a little more or less near to us" (I, ch. 16, p. 149) is introduced with a deliberately banal rhetoric. But it is, after all, a romantic vision, only the rhetoric refusing the seriousness the words imply. Matthew Arnold's "To Marguerite—Continued" written in 1849, after *Pendennis* had begun in monthly parts, reverberates with the language; but for Arnold, of course, the subject requires the deepest lyrical intensity: "We mortal millions live *alone*." In the face of infinite isolation, Arnold struggles to find language and image sufficiently intense to convey the magnitude of the pain. He stridently italicizes *"alone,"* and finds the same island images that Thackeray so casually uses: "The islands feel the enclasping flow, / And then their endless bounds they know."[15]

In Thackeray, the isolation is not allowed to become a matter of despair, but remains a sad recognition of the universality of both solitude and egoism. One does not, as a consequence, begin a pursuit of Arnoldian perfection or a quest for the best and hidden self which makes all things one; rather one makes the best of things, loves as one can, forgives where one can, and reaches by means of narrative to some sort of community, at least of privacies. The vain protagonists of Thackeray's novels embark on no heroic pursuit. There is no point in making a fuss about an inevitable fact; better work to minimize the pain, and to find pleasure in that lonely self. Those most fully aware of the fact, like George Warrington, are those most fully excluded from the pleasures; yet they find pleasure anyway, in part because they have learned not to expect too much, in part because they are, like the narrators, indulgent of those who have not yet learned. The novelist, as we have seen, is rather like Warrington, taking pleasure in the desire to be capable of the desire of another character. Warrington is to Pen as Bersani says Flaubert is to Emma.

The protagonists must make peace with what they have daily to bear (even when they are rescued into happiness by devices in which the narratives really do not believe). The characteristic pattern of realistic fiction emerges everywhere, in the disenchantment of Pen, Ethel, Clive, Philip, Dobbin, Henry. In the process, the materials that had been the early subjects of Thackeray's almost venomous irony are humanized. Major Pendennis, the quintessential "snob," becomes a minor hero, and the absurd social climbers are seen as comically sad rather than as evil. Even the villainous Barnes Newcome (who, characteristically, survives his humiliations) is described at the end as having married again. Pen can only conclude by hoping that Barnes's wife "bullies" him. Disenchantment in Thackeray is not, then, embittering, but almost the reverse. To recognize one's weakness and separateness from the external "other," to see that one's dreams of passion cannot be made to fit the world as it is, relieves one of the responsibility of self-assertion and rebellion, and of the pain of having to face over and over again the disparity between ideal and illusion. Thackeray's realism, with all its ironies, yet makes its peace with the world. The monsters in the closet are riskily invoked and then locked in; the worst the narrator does, as he resists the artificiality of literary structures and reaches forward to some value laden truth, is quietly and comically to remind us that there are monsters, after all.

IV
Perspective and the Narrator's Stance

The tendency is to think of nineteenth-century realism as bound up with the convention of the intrusive author or with the omniscient author convention and to associate early modernism with the break from those conventions, either as in Flaubert's "objectivity" and "impersonality"—the withdrawal of the author from the scene—or as in James's deliberate narrowing of narrative perspective to the vision of particular characters within the fictions. Both of these conventions, however, are directly continuous with the realist's aspiration for both truth and verisimilitude, and both are fully anticipated in the work of the great Victorians. The difficulties with omniscience were fully understood by Thackeray, whose sense of the limitations of human power and knowledge was, as we have been seeing, intense. Although Thackeray tries to give to his narrators a kind of worldly wisdom that allows them to look with compassion on the dreams of the protagonists, he does not exempt them from the limitations his fictions impose on the actors; indeed, he most often makes the narrator some kind of actor in the narrative proper. Moreover, his choice to be intrusive is both a strategy consistent with his sense of the limitations of the perspective of the narrator, and a deliberate effort to establish—within the central Victorian conventions of the author's responsibility to the audience— some kind of community to avoid the full potential anguish of our infinite isolation. What I am suggesting, again, is that the Victorians' conventions were not failures of aesthetic sophistication but coherent imaginations of possible ways to cope with the incertitudes and difficulties of their imagination of reality.

One of the clearest signs that "naive realism" is itself largely a fiction created by critics is that the dominance of realism in Victorian fiction corresponded to the development of concern with the limitations of point of view. Even the much-abused intrusive narrator is a mediator between the experience and the reader, certainly often a guide, but certainly also dramatically fallible. The narrator's stance, indeed, depends for its authority on the narrator's close kinship—in weaknesses and strengths—with the reader. The various devices by which Thackeray suggests the limitations of his own narratives—the invented narrators, the implication that the life of the characters continues outside the focus of any particular narrative, the deliberate refusal of extremes of action and of sharp plotting, the suggestions that the story might be told from entirely different perspectives—all suggest his awareness of the limitations of any single vision.

To argue, however, that the source of Thackeray's "realist illusion" is his admission that the novel is "a lie" is to overstate and distort an important point. I have been trying to suggest how Thackeray participates in (perhaps, more accurately, develops the model for) certain basic conventions of Victorian realism. The accumulated felt authenticity of these conventions, along with the invoked participation of the audience, creates the sense that, for example, the narrator's description of himself as a puppet master is a concession only to the literal fact that the fiction is fiction, but not an important denial of the fiction's "truth." Certainly, nineteenth-century critical discussion seems not to have been put off by the assertion of fictionality from discussing Becky, Dobbin, Amelia, and all the dramatis personae as though they were real. There is no escaping (nor is there any need to want to escape) the way the novels appear to be making direct and plausible commentaries on how people lived in specific times and places, how they talked, how their lives were filled with the sorts of minutiae that clog and characterize our own.

Simply, Thackeray's narrations are not consistent, nor, given their self-consciousness about being narrations, do they take much responsibility to be so. Thackeray talks as though his narrative were true, and then reminds us it is a novel. The "puppet" frame of *Vanity Fair* was not intrinsic to his imagination of the narrative proper. In the later works, he becomes less able to keep his eye on the narrative, or to see it without also watching himself writing it. *Philip* ought to be a great premodernist fiction, self-referential, convoluted about the nature of its own reality, self-parodic, even stopping to consider how much the narrator earns for each word, including the words with which he asks the question (II, ch. 35, p. 148). Yet *Philip* is still primarily about Philip, although it is also about how Pen perceives him.[16] Its ending is as unsatisfactory as that of *The Newcomes*, but even more perfunctory.

Such an abruptly quasi-parodic happy ending is a point at which Thackeray refuses the full implications of his discovered method. If we say, as Rawlins does, that these events do not matter in the novel because the real issues have been worked out before, we are partly accepting Thackeray's own antiplot arguments, and that separation of plot from narrative we have considered elsewhere, even in Scott. "I disdain, for the most part," says Pen/Thackeray in *The Newcomes*, "the tricks and surprises of the novelist's art" (II, ch. 32, p. 324). But realism's insistence on what we have daily to bear cannot coexist even with the parodic use of romance conventions. For even if they imply the opposite of the romance resolution of discovered treasures or identities, they avert in the narrative itself the full working out of the potentially monstrous banality of experience, its secular pointlessness. They avert the irremediable anguish of the ordinary.

What remains consistent in Thackeray's art, however, is his awareness of the limits of perception. If we are all—characters, audience, and novelist—citizens of vanity fair, we are all, in our infinite isolation, blinded by the self that limits and desires. Narrative strategy and substance become one, as Thackeray's readers learn to suspect the imagination of the narrator himself, and even to suspect their own impositions of expectations and desires on the narratives and on their own lives. The gesture beyond words that Thackeray's art makes is an attempt to assimilate the limitations of his narrative world to the limitations of his audience's lives. The constant dialogue between narrator and reader in Thackeray is in part the same sort of extension of the narrative we get in George Eliot, in which the reader's world is invoked to confirm the truth of the fiction.[17] We have seen this strategy already in the passage about the skeleton in everybody's closet from *The Newcomes*, or in the passage invoking "JONES" at his club from *Vanity Fair*.

But the elaborately constructed and elusive narrator of *Vanity Fair* is replaced in Thackeray's later fictions by narrators perhaps less complex, but less trustworthy also.[18] The narrator of *Vanity Fair*, as he manipulates us into recognizing limits and engaging ourselves in the fiction, is at least firm in his intentions if not in his attitudes toward his materials, and although either puppet master or reporter, he is not quite a participant in the story he creates. Pendennis, the surrogate novelist, is a participant in the world of his characters; his judgments are challenged by equally trustworthy characters (especially the tedious Laura); his presence as mediator between the experience and the audience allows the novels to take the process of narration itself as an important focus. Although Pen calls himself a novelist, he is writing "biographies" of his friends. The confusions are more absolute than in *Vanity Fair*, in which the narrator can, at times, be taken as a creator. In any case, the quasi-omniscience of *Vanity Fair* pretty much disappears.

This entails an even more radical short-circuiting of plot because the sorts of questioning of narrative we already find in *Vanity Fair* become a subject, *almost* a substitute for the plot itself. Thackeray must begin inventing excuses for inconsistency of point of view, the most famous of which comes in the middle of *The Newcomes*:

> All this story is told by one, who, if he was not actually present at the circumstances here narrated, yet had information concerning them, and could supply such a narrative of facts and conversations as is, indeed, not less authentic than the details we have of other histories. How can I tell the feelings in a young lady's mind; the thoughts in a young gentleman's bosom?—As Professor Owen or Professor Agassiz takes a fragment of a bone, and builds an enormous forgotten monster out of it, wallowing in primaeval quagmires, tearing down leaves and branches of plants that flourished thousands of years ago, and perhaps may be coal by this time—so the novelist puts this and that together: from the footprint finds the foot; from the foot, the brute who trod on it; from the brute the plant he browsed on, the marsh in which he swam—and thus, in his humble way a physiologist too, depicts the habits, size, appearance of the beings whereof he has to treat;—traces this slimy reptile through the mud, and describes his habits filthy and rapacious; prods down this butterfly with a pin, and depicts his beautiful coat and embroidered waistcoat; points out the singular structure of yonder more important animal, the megatherium of his history. [II, ch. 9, p. 90]

More is at stake here than the problem of point of view. The passage implies much about the underpinnings of nineteenth-century realism, the culture's dominant epistemology, and the inklings of realities not observable on the surfaces of experience, but frighteningly latent. It is inappropriate here to dwell long on problems of epistemology, but the importance of the empiricist induction to Thackeray's art should not be underestimated.

In establishing verisimilitude, a writer who uses narrative omniscience can only falsify if it be understood that all human knowledge is limited to what is directly available to the senses. It is a problem that will plague writers throughout the century. The "feelings in a young lady's mind" are accessible only to that young lady, perhaps the "Desdemona" of the railway carriage. The method that Thackeray half-mockingly invokes to help explain how Pen knows so much is inductive. Like a "physiologist," the novelist must work from fragments of knowledge, and with scrupulous care piece together what is not immediately observable. But induction, we know, is a risky business; and the knowledge it yields cannot be absolute.

Both novelist and scientist are engaged in constructions of a world. Their processes are the means of breaking out of the limitations of the self, establishing both a community of experience and knowledge, and a social community. Thackeray's narrators speak to their readers as mutual participants in the creation of such a community; yet behind them is the implied author—equally seeking community—who creates novels that reenforce the confusions empiricism and induction invariably create. The novelist must see that even the need to create the world this way is an acknowledgment of a primary solipsism. The self, which is the ambiguous theme of *The Book of Snobs* and of *Vanity Fair*, is finally trapped in its separateness. As Pater was to put it, the self is a personality through whose thick walls no human voice can ever penetrate. In Thackeray, however, such a melodramatic formulation is premature, for there is no occasion for aestheticism, or for a rejection of conventional moral standards, or for an art directed only to the needs of the self and the few like-minded sensitives who might just hear. There is, for example, a marveling excitement about Thackeray's invocation of the famous professors, Owen and Agassiz. The evidence of novels and science was clear, that something might in fact be learned.

There is, of course, the interesting ambiguity of his phrase, "not less authentic than the details we have of other histories." How authentic is that? we might ask. And there is the uncomfortable implication that what the studious novelist will discover, in piecing his fragments together, is something quite monstrous. The observable facts of the real become, to the scientific mind as to the religious mind that preceded it, delusive. The innocent-looking remains allow us to infer the whole context of the brute—the plant he browsed on, the marsh in which he swam. Man is an animal that, brute as he may ultimately be, survives by participating in a larger world that leaves its evidences upon him, upon which he is dependent. By focusing empirically on the observable manifestations, Thackeray can, however, avoid the monstrousness that, as inductive scientist, he detects.

In the construction of his world, Pen, as Thackeray's narrator, has at least the virtue of reminding us that he is not quite trustworthy and that his guesses are, indeed, personal. The realism here depends not so much on the admission that the novel is a lie but on the likelihood that its reality might well be described another way. In a passage also from *The Newcomes*, but less revealingly metaphorical than the one just quoted, Pen gets more explicit:

> in the present volumes, where dialogues are written down, which the reporter could by no possibility have heard, and where motives are detected which the persons actuated by them certainly never confided to the writer, the public must once for all be warned that the author's individual fancy very likely supplies much of the narrative; and that he forms it as best he may, out of stray papers, conversations reported to him, and his knowledge, right or wrong, of the characters of the persons engaged. And, as is the case with the most orthodox histories, the writers own guesses or conjectures are printed in exactly the same type as the most ascertained patent facts [I, ch. 24, pp. 239–40]

The tone is distinctively Thackeray's: one makes the best of a situation which, if pursued with philosophic passion, might explode horrifically.

One might attribute such a passage to a certain novelistic clumsiness in handling first-person narration; it was, after all, a difficulty that threatened fictions from *Pamela* to *Jane Eyre*. But Thackeray needed the narrator and, in his integrity as a writer, had to pay the price. The distortion is inevitable. Thackeray tries to minimize it by something analogous to scientific detachment, that is, by withdrawal from the stream of experience. The most trustworthy narrator speaks in retrospect, on the basis of much experience, after he has grown beyond the risks of desire that the immature and passionate self must undergo. He speaks with the voice of disenchantment, seeing things in the cold light of day, aware that they are not malleable to dreams and wishes, and incapable of the passionate energy required to believe in dreams. He believes in the fact of having once believed, and he becomes a scientist of dead passions, of the extinct brute.

This distinctive Thackerayan style emerged early, after his most painful personal crisis, in 1840–41, with the mental breakdown of his wife. Then, as Gordon Ray has shown, Thackeray seems to have deliberately used his new pain to reimagine himself. It was only then that he began naturally and easily to take his readers into his confidence, to alleviate his loneliness by talking to them as he would to the intimates who were no longer at hand. And though he was not yet thirty, he fell into the habit of presenting himself as a man fifteen or twenty years older, who had become an observer of the battle of life, rather than a participant in it. He began to look back, to compare, to reflect in the manner of advanced middle age, as if the past were more important to him than the present.[19]

Scientific empiricism blends curiously here with an antiromantic attitude, a belief that all experience must be mediated by knowledge. The realist tradition of disenchantment pervades this new way of seeing for Thackeray, and his disenchanted narrators regularly interpose themselves between himself and the narration. Thackeray removes himself, becomes a spectator of other spectators, who allow the passions against which the accumulation of ironies and details, diversions and speculations, asserts itself. The fictions move ideally toward disengagement and rest, yet allow themselves that last desire for the capacity to desire. Even Michelangelo Titmarsh, as Juliet McMaster points out, is imagined as a "spectator," looking into the world of action and thinking about participating, yet at the same time clinging desperately to his position beyond the pale when it seems he will get drawn into the world.[20]

Thackeray's handling of perspective makes him central to the tradition of realism's self-consciousness about limits—of power, knowledge, and desire. The risks he takes are framed by the protections of limited narrators, limited knowledge. He at once reaches out to a reality from which knowledge and the pain of loss have excluded him, and holds back from the possibility of touching it. His flawed and inconsistent art allows him the pleasure of the surfaces he fears to penetrate and opens new possibilities of narration which he himself does not consistently achieve.

8

Pendennis
The Virtue of the Dilettante's Unbelief

*T*he *misfortune of dogmatic belief is that the first principle granted that the Book called the Bible is written under the direct dictation of God for instance—that the Catholic Church is under the direct dictation of God and solely communicated with him—that Quashimaboo is the direct appointed priest of God and so forth— pain, cruelty, persecution, separation of dear relatives, follow as a matter of course. . . . Every one of us in every fact, book, circumstance of life sees a different meaning and moral and so it must be about religion.*

W. M. Thackeray, Letter to His Mother

Despite their resistance to the threats of passion and their ironic and disenchanted acquiescence in things as they are, Thackeray's novels reimagine both literature and reality subversively. We have seen that his strategies of representation are elaborate, inconsistent, and perilous. The seductive world of things (which the Thackerayan narrator indulges cozily) disguises a latent hostility to human ideals; the digressive plots deflate all energies directed toward the extreme, the violent, or the ideal yet imply the impossibility of narrative control; the narrator himself cautiously encapsulates the romance of the past in the language of disenchantment or of a slightly sour sentimentality, as though the energies there have no further life. The multiplicity and disorder of Thackeray's worlds, finally, leave only the smallest space for belief; for the order belief might impose entails the violent obliteration of all that does not conform to it. While Thackeray resists his own suppressed energies of desire, which might manifest themselves in narratives that manipulate experience through the constrictions of plot, he strains at the limits the novel form imposes in his effort to honor the variousness of a reality that will not submit to human shaping. "Every one of us in every fact, book, circumstance of life sees a different meaning and moral." Belief in the objective reality of that "meaning and moral" is more deadly than the aimless wanderings of disbelief.

Of course, even in the disruptiveness of form in his later novels,

Thackeray never allowed himself fully to imagine a literature built from a world so chaotically solipsistic. He consistently wrote comedy, and if he risked in his casualness the fragmentation and pluralism his anti-dogmatism implied, he always tried to draw back. He took his fictions to the edges of a world that threatened always to dissolve into pointless and amoral multiplicity. His baggy monsters did indeed become monstrous in the solidity and density of their resistance to idealizing literary energies.

To sustain the possibilities of realistic comedy in a world so threateningly amorphous, Thackeray was forced to invent a new kind of protagonist. Arthur Pendennis belongs in the antiheroic tradition of Catherine Morland and even Edward Waverley; but he is not merely *not* a hero. He is a figure who is invented to avert the fanatic's catastrophe of defeated idealism (as, say, that of Scott's Balfour of Burley) and the moral catastrophe of aimlessness into which the rejection of the ideal might thrust him. Pen has no genuine alternative ideal, nor does his world. He is not only unheroic, then, but ironically disengaged from his own ambitions and imaginations of a self requiring satisfaction, and from the ordering norms of his society. His maneuverings for survival through the constrictions of narrative form and the exclusiveness of moral beliefs threaten to exclude him from any recognizable conventions of narrative form or social ordering. He is a protagonist whose self tends to flow with the flow of experience itself, without a fixed point, without even a morality.

This is obviously an extreme formulation for such an apparently banal, egocentric, and worldly figure as Pen, but it suggests how Thackeray's art points forward toward a modernist skepticism about self and narrative such as we find developing in James and Conrad. The extreme is only an exaggeration, not, I think, a falsification of the sort of figure Pen tends to be. In Thackeray, certainly, dogmatic morality is as dangerous as immorality, while selfishness is the norm in a world so solipsistically structured. The pure character is always suspect, threatening to become a wimpy and parasitical Amelia or a compliantly aggressive and dangerous Helen Pendennis (rather like Thackeray's own mother, Mrs. Carmichael-Smith, to whom he wrote often about the dangers of her piety and dogmatism). *Pendennis,* of course, in keeping with realism's need for compromise, attempts to place Pen somewhere between this extreme piety and the immorality of those late-Romantic sufferers from ennui and cynicism like Dickens's James Harthouse or George Eliot's more impressive Grandcourt.

Thackeray's novels are novels of defeat, of ambitions unfulfilled, of frustrations and losses in loving, desiring, idealizing. They can remain comedies only if they can locate protagonists who risk little in defeat because they have no assertive, dogmatic selves that require satisfaction. Contrast Mr. Bows, the loving, loveable, and defeated musician, with the successful novelist Pen. Pen is Thackeray's survivor, not the heroic figure, or the loving dreamer, or the idealist, but the one who resists commitment as long as possible, who understands, in the midst of commitment, the absurdity of it, who dallies with the most possibilities, and who makes the best terms with his own inevitable weaknesses and irrational desires. He can believe nothing intensely enough to attempt to impose it on others and is therefore no revolutionary against prevailing beliefs. After all, although these are as absurd as their alternatives, they at least provide convenient modes of ordering, and antagonism to them would simply cause unnecessary pain. The great art becomes knowing the conventions and using them.

In *Pendennis* Thackeray invents himself as this kind of dilettante, and finds that he does not altogether like what he creates. The novel tests and challenges Pen's education as it weans him from the ideal, and in another surrogate (whose life dramatizes the heavy price of *not* being like Pen), George Warrington, Thackeray lovingly articulates what he does not like about his Pen-self. He allows George to love Pen and to be very hard on him as well, suggesting once again his desire for the kind of innocence that might make belief in the heroic and ideal possible. George, we should remember, comes to like Pen when Pen is fresh from college and still innocent, still full of the energies of desire that his sophistication will shortly subvert. In any case, George knows the dangers of those energies and the necessity for compromise, which is embodied in his very relation to Pen and, one might conjecture, in Thackeray's relation to himself.

As Pen develops, he finds that what seemed to him of ultimate importance turns quickly into a joke, and he loses much of his capacity to take himself seriously. The narrative implies that something of his boyhood generosity of impulse remains with him into his most cynical moments, and he is allowed some relatively disinterested acts, which rescue him from marriage to Blanche Amory. The rescue gives the novel the happy ending the form requires, yet it leaves behind a world of lonely people. And the rescue itself is curiously, one would almost think, deliberately, unsatisfactory. The resolution is long prepared for, but once more, plot seems out of harmony with the narrative as a whole. For one thing, the narrative has made it clear that Pen does not really deserve Laura and that the proper marraige would have been between Laura and George. For another, Laura is perilously close to an ideal figure; only her vitality when she finds herself popular and attractive in the middle of the book suggests the possibilities of life beyond self-denial. Finally, Pen treats Laura's beliefs in justice, morality, truth, and the moral life with condescending affection and admiration. He knows that they do not match the knowledge of the world he has acquired from the major and through his own disenchantments.

Women provide that small space in his novels where Thackeray can locate the ideal and save his fictions from the sort of modernist dissolution such disenchanted awareness might entail. In this Thackeray reflects certain dominant conventions of Victorian culture, for despite his obvious sexual attraction to women and his tendency to idealize them, his is a misogynistic world. Women, in Thackeray, are capable of believing, but we can see—as do his characters—that this is because they are barred from the knowledge available to men. When, in fact, they are educated about the world, they rather quickly become threatening or villainous—like Becky, or Beatrix, or Blanche. Women are, or ought to be, the repository of feeling and purity, virtues men are too busy and practical to sustain, and they thus become a kind of escape, both for Pen and Thackeray. In women, they can indulge the sentimentality they cannot otherwise afford. For Pen, Laura becomes the substitute for the romance and ideals of his youth, in which he can no longer believe (she is, in fact, his mother's childhood gift to him, as Elizabeth is a gift to Victor Frankenstein). The "rescue" of Pen is only part of a narrative fantasy of the ideal that the full narrative does not endorse.

In creating himself in *Pendennis*, then, Thackeray is writing an ironic myth of a new kind of hero. Pen, of course, has the obligatory "mixed" nature of realistic protagonists. But he challenges, in his conception, not only the absurd excesses of romance and pastoral, but the ideals of domestic fiction itself. It goes almost without saying that "there are men better than he" (II, ch. 75, p. 394). It follows that people distrust his marriage to Laura and have rather grim expectations of it. Innocuous as Pen may seem to be, Thackeray does recognize the morally dangerous implications of his way of life. We can understand more clearly where the danger lies if we see Pen as the first in a series of problematic figures in nineteenth-century narratives who acquire increasing importance through the century. Pen's combination of detachment, cynicism, laziness, self-indulgence, and aestheticism, along with his single real commitment to an almost ideal woman, is characteristic. Although they are all very different, such figures as Will Ladislaw, Ralph Touchett, and Martin Decoud can be seen as descendants of Pen (in a later chapter I will be discussing Ladislaw and Decoud in some detail). Each of them is a dilettante; each is importantly severed from his community and undefined. In their more or less ironic attentiveness to details of the life that moves past them, they see things differently and threateningly and like Pen tend to flow with the flow of experience, to be satisfied with the ironies and objects that life throws their way, except when they are attracted to women who might be seen as ideal.

But in mid-Victorian fiction it is surprising to find so detached, cynical, and compromised a figure as Pen so gently treated. One need think only of the immorality attributed to his cousins Henry Gowan in *Little Dorrit*, or Bertie Stanhope in *Barchester Towers*, to realize how subversive a conception Pen might be. Bertie and Henry are, after all, rather Pen-like figures seen from a more firmly moral perspective. Thackeray sees the potentialities of a Bertie in Pen but needs to judge him differently, for what might be thought of as a shameless laxity and selfishness might also be understood as a more honest and honorable way to deal with an experience that refuses to succumb to the ideal. Even Conrad has difficulty avoiding overt hostility to the dilettante figure, and his rhetoric about Decoud is contemptuous and angry. Thackeray, in keeping with his antidogmatism, is more merciful.

Pen's development as dilettante is connected with the novel's preoccupation with the problem of the presentation or re-presentation of feeling. The problem even becomes the central subject of a series of important dialogues between Thackeray's two surrogates—Pen and George Warrington. The novel is full of other people's writing, of real theatrical performances, and of the theatrics required by society. We have Blanche Amory's "Mes Larmes" and Pen's *Walter Lorraine*, and passionate and morally righteous editorials written in jail. We have the major's letters and performances. At the start we have the performances of the Fotheringay. Pen's second affair results from the performances of Blanche Amory. Amid all these performances, Pen must learn to distinguish good fictions from bad. Presumably, he must find also whatever direct, unmediated feeling may exist in his world, apparently located with Laura and Helen, who do not perform. Pen must learn to break through the layers of inauthentic, merely literary and social, representations of feeling. But the narrative as a whole ultimately makes it difficult to imagine that there is any such thing as unmediated feeling. Even Pen's most authentic passions seem to be shaped by literary conventions.

Pen's progress through the novel is marked by his developing capacity to distance or transform feeling through language. The major's brilliant early strategies lead the way, but Pen's first independent movement in that direction is not quite self-conscious. It comes early in the novel, after his affair with Emily is disrupted by the worldly-wise major. In a wonderful piece of false pastoral, Thackeray shows us a Pen already, if not quite consciously, acting the role of feeling. He fishes; he sits by a pond under a tree and composes "a number of poems suitable in his circumstances—over which verses he blushed in after days, wondering how he could ever have invented such rubbish" (I, ch. 15, p. 136). Here is an early example of the Thackerayan narrator's refusal to allow the intensity of immediate experience to escape the ironies of retrospect or worldly-wise distancing. The whole affair immediately becomes comedy. But this "rubbish" serves other purposes later. He shows the poems to his contemporaries at college as a badge of his manhood, and they all pronounce him a "tremendous fellow" (I, ch. 18, p. 177). The tree under which the rubbish is written is invoked for future use. "Under that very tree," the narrator warns us, Pen would shortly be carrying on another love-correspondence with his second flame, Blanche. But he does not say so, interrupting himself to note, "but we are advancing matters." All romance turns into slightly spurious literature.

More interestingly, the narrator treats Pen's writing of poetry as clear evidence that he is already himself rather separate from the experience of love:

> Suffice it to say, he wrote poems and relieved himself very much. When a man's grief or passion is at this point, it may be loud, but it is not very severe. When a gentleman is cudgeling his brain to find any rhyme for sorrow, besides borrow and to-morrow, his woes are nearer at an end than he thinks for. [I, ch. 15, p. 136]

The medium is itself a way to distance writer from feeling, and the primary relation becomes not that between lover and beloved, but between lover and poem. The writing of poetry is a kind of narcissism; the focus becomes the writer's power to convince his audience and himself that he feels intensely and loves deeply. When Pen achieves the sophistication of the narrator, he will begin (as Thackeray's later novels testify) to write self-conscious and self-deprecating novels that are insistently aware of the falsifications of language and the vanity of writing. Both Thackeray and Pen know that writing is a defense against what it purports to describe, or an ironic substitute for it.

In the debate between Pen and Warrington, the moral questions related to these problems of writing are paramount. To write is to stand outside of exeprience. Yet the moral energy of the Victorian tradition and Thackeray's own sense of himself as moralist (manifested in some degree in Warrington) require of the writer a fuller engagement than Pen could give. The narrator, whose own detachment has been manifest, puts the question this way: "Which is most reasonable, and does his duty best: he who stands aloof from the struggle of life, calmly contemplating it, or he who descends to the ground and takes his part in the contest?" (II, ch. 54, p. 66). Thackeray's position here is difficult to locate, for both Pen and Warrington speak with authority and, in all likelihood, for him. The writer must stand apart from the experience in order to write about it; yet the writer needs the experience before he *can* write about it. At one point, Warrington mocks Pen and poets in general, rather accurately describing the Pen we have just seen. "Poets," he says, "fall in love, jilt, or are jilted: they suffer and cry out that they suffer more than any other mortals: and when they have experienced feelings enough they note them down in a book" (II, ch. 41, p. 24). At this stage, Pen wants to argue that poets can have more sensibility than most and still, like Shakespeare, write for money, but the question of the authenticity of the writer's experience will recur.

Later, convalescent from his illness after his affair with Fanny, Pen begins to transform that affair by subjecting it to distancing Thackerayan irony. The process already undergone with the Fotheringay now becomes more self-conscious: "He laughed at himself as he lay on his pillow, thinking of the second cure which has been effected upon him. He did not care the least about Fanny now: he wondered how he ever should have cared: and according to his custom made an autopsy of that dead passion, and anatomised his own defunct sensation for his poor little nurse" (II, ch. 57, p. 144). Fanny becomes part of a usable past, a story to tell; ironically, it will be Warrington who tells it. For Warrington had led a Pen-like life until he married beneath his class, a Fanny-like girl, as Pen just escapes doing twice. In the inversions and doublings that mark Thackeray's unsystematic working out of his materials (Warrington himself says that "there was no one to save me as Major Pendennis saved Pen" [II, ch. 57, p. 195]), Warrington is forced, because he is tied to an impossible wife, to choose the disengagement into which Pen drifts. Wishing not to be "out of the stream," Warrington can yet only *argue* for the value of being in it.

Warrington's story, as I have already suggested, reveals the other side of Pen's way of choosing: being "in the stream," acting on one's passions, is so dangerous that it can lead to a permanent paralysis. Pen survives because he is intrinsically less serious than Warrington and is therefore a quick pupil of the worldly major. Withdrawal from engagement—as Warrington's life dramatizes—leaves only the joys of vicarious feeling: Warrington eagerly tells Pen to go out and play the game. But Pen's sort of pleasure in the game derives from a kind of disenchanted detachment, a bemused and playful recognition that the actors make fools of themselves and that the stakes are really lower than they seem. The comic substance of the novel is in its indulgent play with the tokens—the dinners, the wines, the clothing, the titillations, the social maneuvering. For Warrington, however, even these things risk pain: "What was he about dancing attendance here? drinking in sweet pleasure at a risk he knows not of what after sadness, and regret, and lonely longing?" (II, ch. 56, p. 182).

As the dialogues between Pen and Warrington suggest, Thackeray was divided about himself and about his art. In a late chapter he puts the divisions about dilettantish disengagement with clarity and force. Both characters speak in Thackeray's voice. Pen, in rejecting dogmatic belief, pleads for toleration, even of the decadent aristocrats Thackeray had so acerbically parodied earlier in his career and of the outmoded and narrow-minded institutions of the Church:

> I would have toleration for these, as I would ask it for my own opinions; and if they are to die, I would rather they had a decent and natural than an abrupt and violent death. . . . I will not perse-cute. Make a faith or a dogma absolute, and persecution becomes a logical consequence. . . . Make dogma absolute, and to inflict or to suffer death becomes easy and necessary. [II, ch. 61, p. 247]

It is a conventional liberal argument, of course, but it is consistent with the thrust of Thackeray's realism. The ideal and the attempt to enact belief threaten a terrible violence. The narrative forms that embody the ideal, that enforce the demands of Number One, are violations of the very possibilities of human knowledge. Pen's politics and morality here seem to Warrington, as they would have seemed to many in Thack-eray's audience, merely amoral. The profoundly skeptical realist vision moves inexorably in this direction, but Pen is articulating another sort of morality, an almost Arnoldian one of refusing action. It is akin to the conservative-reforming politics of George Eliot, the commitment to free expression of John Stuart Mill, the Victorian secular faith in the possi-bility of discovering the truth by reason, and averting premature action until then.

But the other Thackeray, as we find him in Warrington, has affinities with Carlyle, and to that very un-Arnoldian faith that the end of man is action. Warrington recognizes the difference between his enforced dis-engagement and Pen's deliberate choice of it. More important, he finds Pen's tolerance merely the reverse side of a radical skepticism:

> A little while since, young one . . . you asked me why I remained out of the strife of the world, and looked on at the great labour of my neighbour without taking any part in the struggle. Why, what a mere *dilettante* you own yourself to be, in this confession of general scepticism, and what a listless spectator yourself! you are six-and-twenty years old, and as *blasé* as a rake of sixty. You neither hope much, nor care much, nor believe much. You doubt about other men as much as about yourself. Were it made of such *pococuranti* as you, the world would be intolerable; and I had rather

live in a wilderness of monkeys and listen to their chatter, than in a company of men who denied everything. [II, ch. 61, p. 248]

Warrington not only urges engagement, but speaks in Carlyle's language, reflecting Thackeray's early enthusiasm for Carlyle, and the conscience with which he judged himself. His tirade here echoes the chapter "Gospel of Dilettantism" in *Past and Present*. For Carlyle, one of the marks of dilettantism is "insincere speech," that is, speech that dissolves action rather than points directly to it or precedes it. Carlyle's chapter concludes with a parable that dramatizes the effect of such speech, the story of Moses and the dwellers by the Dead Sea. These dwellers found "the whole universe now a most indisputable humbug," and they disregarded Moses's Heaven-sent words. The result is that the dwellers were turned into apes, and "sit and chatter to this hour."[1] The wilderness of dilettantish monkeys Warrington prefers to the world of men who deny everything is merely the true image of that world. From Carlylean perspective, Pen's plea for tolerance is the refusal to distinguish God's words from chatter. The problem is that in novels like Thackeray's God's words are indistinguishable.

The whole dialogue (although like everything else in the novel, it is not allowed to be as serious as the substance of it would seem to require) points to the divisions not only in Thackeray's art, but in realism itself. The condition for writing novels, it would seem, is the condition of the disengaged spectator. The moral price of Warrington's plea for authority, choice, and engagement is, as we have seen, very heavy. Pen for his part, sees himself only as a realist: "I do not condemn the men who killed Socrates and damned Galileo, I say that they damned Galileo and killed Socrates" (II, ch. 61, p. 249). Here is at least one Victorian writer whose ideal of truth turns out to be at odds with Carlylean moral firmness; to Carlyle it would seem very much like chattering. Yet when the narrator intrudes shortly after, he justifies the presentation of Pen's amoral view obliquely, by writing in a very Pen-like way. He will not endorse Pen's arguments, but in effect he uses them. He is merely trying, he says, "to follow out in its progress the development of the mind of a worldly and selfish, but not ungenerous or truth-avoiding man" (II, ch. 61, p. 250). As Thackeray knows, Pen might well have been consigned to the chapter on the Dandaical Body in *Sartor Resartus*. The narrator, however, pleads for tolerance of this "man and brother," a tolerance that might be merely a disguise of not much caring.

But Pen cannot presume to judge since he does not presume to know, and it may be that the pain of discovering ignorance leads to a retreat from a dangerous caring. Like a young and cynical John Stuart Mill, Pen recognizes that all views are partial, but all views have a right to be presented. The function of his novel is then to record reality as truthfully as possible, incorporating as part of the reality the recognition of the limits of this possibility, and to withold firm unqualified judgments. Thackeray attempts to resist, and through Warrington he does resist, the effects of what he ungenerously calls Pen's "general scepticism and sneering acquiescence." But the skepticism is ultimately endorsed by the very shape of the novel.

Pendennis seems to want to suggest that Pen's progress *is* a progress, that he grows and changes, so that his cynical arguments with Warrington are described as a "stage." But later on, the same narrator will argue that there are no real changes in character. In the midst of the argument with Warrington, the narrator intrudes in a very Warringtonian-Carlylean voice. He talks of Pen as being in a "lamentable stage." "To what," he asks, "does this scepticism lead?"

> It leads a man to a shameful loneliness and selfishness, so to speak—the more shameful, because it is so good-humoured and conscienceless and serene. Conscience! What is conscience? Why accept remorse? What is public or private faith? Mythuses alike enveloped in enormous tradition. If seeing and acknowledging the lies of the world, Arthur, as see them you can with only too fatal a clearness, you submit to them without any protest further than a laugh: if, plunged yourself in easy sensuality, you allow the whole wretched world to pass groaning by you unmoved: if the fight for the truth is taking place, and all men of honour are on the ground armed on the one side or the other, and you alone are to lie on your balcony and smoke your pipe out of the noise and the danger, you had better have died, or never have been at all, than such a sensual coward. [II, ch. 61, p. 250]

The rhetoric is inflated and uncharacteristic. It lacks the self-consciousness about rhetoric that Pen has been developing, and it is, finally, unconvincing: first, because Thackeray as satirist was precisely the figure who made no further protest than a laugh; second, because the act of writing is an act of withdrawal from any engagement but that of seeing clearly. Moreover, the growth of Pen beyond the position denounced here is dubious.

Indeed, even here, in answer to both Warrington and, one must presume, the narrator (the distinction breaks awkwardly down in the passage), Pen speaks with more authentic Thackerayan substance, if still in too inflated a style: "The truth, friend... where is the truth? Show it me?" The lesson of his own self-consciousness and of his own limitations is here: "I see the truth in that man, as I do in his brother, whose logic drives him to quite a different conclusion, and who, after having passed a life in vain endeavours to reconcile an irreconcilable book, flings it at last down in despair, and declares, with tearful eyes, and hands up to Heaven, his revolt and recantation. If the truth is with all these, why should I take side with any one of them" (p. 251). There is, of course, some casuistry here. But if Thackeray really (at least probably) agrees with Pen, he wants to break from the complications of knowledge to the authenticity of feeling. Pen's discovery of inauthenticity everywhere, of a world full of bad literature, has led him to this point. The very structure of the book, even to the point of the division implied by the two convincing protagonists, George and Pen, leaves Pen and Thackeray with no satisfying place to locate authenticity. If there be authentic feeling in the book and not merely literary and dramatic constructions, it is among the losers, and it can be destructive. Mr. Bows, like the gruffer and more important Warrington, loves and longs for love, moves through the novel with a sad integrity and is betrayed by both Emily and Fanny. He makes a private music to sustain him. Like Warrington he is excluded from the "stream," and as a result he is not so much compromised as defeated. He cannot turn his feelings into a public art, except as he teaches Emily Costigan to mime it. Yet Pen manages to create a successful art (though not, on the narrator's account, very good art) because the authentic feelings he had are transformed into the materials of his writing and in the very act of transforming them, he enacts their absence.

Still, the narrator writes as though authentic feeling were somewhere to be found, and his strongest hostility is consequently reserved for Blanche, the purest feigner: "For this young lady was not able to carry out any emotion to the full; but had a sham enthusiasm, a sham hatred, a sham love, a sham taste, a sham grief, each of which flared and shone very vehemently for an instant, but subsided and gave place to the next sham emotion" (II, ch. 73, p. 364). Thackeray's hostility to Blanche implies a longing for the feeling he cannot represent. The quest for the authenticity of feeling that will justify the engagement Warrington insists on (but cannot himself undertake) is almost universally frustrated in the book. Its negative structure short-circuits every action that has claims to authenticity, as well as many that do not. Pen does not marry Emily or Blanche; Bows does not marry Emily or Fanny; Warrington does not marry Laura; Pen's mother does not marry the man she loves. Finally, despite the narrator's insistence that Pen, in his moral paralysis, is going through a stage, Pen does not really change either. The narrator makes a point of pausing to remind us, with a *vanitas vanitatum*, that we are always what we were, but older (II, ch. 59, p. 222).

In Pen, at least, this is confirmed, for his general skepticism remains with him until the end. There is, for example, his well-known excursus on "But":

"But will come in spite of us. But is reflection. But is the sceptic's familiar, with whom he has made a compact; and if he forgets it, and indulges in happy day-dreams, or building of air-castles, or listens to sweet music let us say, or to the bells ringing to church, But taps at the door and says, Master, I am here. You are my master; but I am yours. Go where you will you can't travel without me. I will whisper to you when you are on your knees at church. I will be at your marriage pillow. I will sit down at your table with your children. I will be behind your death-bed curtain. That is what But is," Pen said.

"Pen, you frighten me," cried Laura. [II, ch. 71, p. 343]

"But" is a monster that will be with Pen on his wedding night, and it is the monster that pervades this book of compromises and retreats. Pen's vision has taken him through the traditional forms of representation, has allowed him to become a successful writer, and to marry the rare "ideal" figure in the novel. But "But" persists, and undercuts the ideal in the act of marriage and, we presume, of love. For Pen it is a saving But. For Laura it is understandably frightening. For Thackeray, it is a burden he could not shake.

Pen survives his dilettantism without the sort of banishment and alienation that characterizes the dilettante figure in much later fiction. He neither learns to work hard and reject the clever superficiality of his earlier days, as we are to believe Will Ladislaw does in *Middlemarch*, nor allows his cynicism to become suicidal, as it does for Decoud. Like Will, he is apparently redeemed by the idealist woman he loves. His cynicism and his sentimentality exist side by side (as they apparently did for Thackeray himself), and he accepts the limits of the world because, despite his self-consciousness about the absurdity of it all, he enjoys it. Thackeray, finally, though he gives Pen a certain integrity, never quite allows him to be serious enough either to feel the full bitterness of his acquiescence (as Warrington has expressed it in his invocation of the wilderness of monkeys) or to attempt to impose some kind of ideal meaning on experience. His strategy is the strategy of toleration.

The more intense issues of Pen's life are carefully disguised by the narrative, which sticks with remarkable consistency to the rambling diffuseness, deflation, and density of particulars that characterize the realistic mode. The episode with Fanny, for example, might have provided the materials for naturalistic treatment, and the critical illness that Thackeray allows Pen (echoing, as we know, the critical illness into which he fell while writing the novel) suggests the intensity of the issue and the eagerness with which Thackeray wanted to avert its extreme implications. During the illness, like so many of those passive heroes, as we have observed them in Scott, or *Frankenstein*, Pendennis loses the power to make determining choices. His decision to avoid Fanny, which provokes the illness, makes little difference until Helen and Fanny finally battle it out.

The novel is even more devious in avoiding extremes in the sequence relating to Helen's banishment of Fanny, for there Pen comes as close as he is allowed to do to the sources of his anger. The loving Helen, sentimentalized down to her last breath, is shown to be dangerously protective and exclusive, as idealists must be in Thackeray's compromised world. Pen's hostility can have no outlet, but when it is about to explode, Laura warns him that the confrontation he seeks with his mother will kill her. The book does not make much of it, and of course she dies in a new loving embrace with Pen; but beneath the sentiment and the respectability there is an intense and violent hostility. Neither Pen nor the narrative can find a place for so aggressively loving a figure. In effect, Pen does kill her, but in doing so he repurchases his past and cloaks and distances the intensities he could not entirely avert.

It is worth reminding ourselves that *Pendennis* was written in the midst of Thackeray's deep and thwarted love of Jane Brookfield. His relation to her may remind us of that of Warrington to Laura, but in any case he could not fully confront the feeling either in life or in the novel. The expression of the feeling would be the occasion of its death, and Thackeray could not have escaped recognizing the ironies implicit in his passion though, certainly, he did not want to subject it to irony. As John Dodds remarks about Thackeray's later letters to Jane, he wrote "as if he were maintaining at some cost the rather delicate poise of his ecstasy and were fearful lest the dream be broken."[2] *Pendennis* might be taken as a means to preserve the dream. The heart-whole Warrington survives the heartbreak: our self-conscious narrator reminds us that the "malady is never fatal to a sound organ." And the not quite deserving Pen, the more completely autobiographical figure, gets the woman. In his precarious teetering between romance and cynicism, Pen thus embodies for Thackeray the nostalgia that sustains and protects the dream while never threatening it with engagement.

He can be allowed the victory, precisely because he does not quite care enough. He is in the middling dilettantish state that newly embodies the realist's compromise—the quietly dishonest assumption that the real world is not rife with extremes of action and feeling. The parody of literary forms that take extremes as the norm leads directly to *Pendennis*, for Pen's education seems to teach him, first, that nobody ever dies of heartbreak; second, that taking oneself seriously is always at least mildly absurd; third, that everyone is out for number one—except Laura (while Thackeray knows that she is, too). He learns, too, that the world does not really make much sense and is entirely unmalleable under the pressures of dreams or desires, but that there is no necessity, simply because it is unjust, not to take pleasure in what is.

The self-consciousness and disenchantment that we see growing in Pen, in a novel full of realism's surfaces, digressions, and compromises, grow more and more deadly to Thackeray's art as Pen takes greater control of it. The mask of the prematurely old and thwarted wise man who prefers the memory of passion to passion itself, and thus can enjoy retrospectively the risks and the ludicrousness, will increasingly dismantle narrative. Though this reflects Thackeray's idiosyncratic preoccupation with the thwarting and the necessity of passion, it is also absolutely right for the mode of realism, a form in which time, not human choice, is likely to be decisive, in which all things clamor for their significance and, thus, in which anything can be a subject and must be deflated as a consequence.

If we think of Victorian realism as an exuberant clearing of the house of fiction of its absurdities and obsolete conventions in the interests of a clear-eyed and forceful assertion of the truth, we must remember how much it is also a literature of compromise. Its characteristic morality is implicit not so much in Dickensian exposures of the violence and brutality of which our society is capable, as in a George Eliot-like dissolution of easy moral categories, a recognition of our own ordinary and compromised natures, a toleration of the failures and fallings-away of others. From what seemed to be a scathing and cynical judge of mankind's cruelty and pretensions, Thackeray becomes a saddened man who is content to observe others fail as he has done and find his pleasures in the variousness and disorder of exeprience. The characteristic tone toward which we see young Pen moving is registered in a letter of Thackeray's quoted by John Dodds:

> As I go this journey, I remember other thoughts scattered along the journey 3 years ago: and griefs which used to make me wild and fierce, and which are now sweet and bearable. We get out of the stormy region of longing passion unfulfilled—we don't love any the less—please God—let the young folks step in and play the game of tears and hearts. We have played our game: and we have lost. And at 45 we smoke our pipes and clear the drawing room for the sports of the young ones.[3]

This is the novel Thackeray wrote for himself. The protection of his dream of passion is the comfort of knowing that it is too late to fight for it. He makes himself the novelist of memory.

9

Trollope

Reality and the Rules of the Game

*A*s the writer of the leading article picks up his ideas of politics among those
which he finds floating about the world, thinking out but little for himself
and creating but little, so does the novelist find his ideas of conduct, and then create
a picture of that excellence which he has appreciated. . . . He collects the floating
ideas of the world around him as to what is right and wrong in conduct, and
reproduces them with his own colouring. At different periods in our history, the
preacher, the dramatist, the essayist, and the poet have been efficacious over
others. . . . Now it is the novelist. There are reasons why we would wish it were
otherwise. The reading of novels can hardly strengthen the intelligence. But we have
to deal with the fact as it exists, deprecating the evil as far as it is an evil, but
acknowledging the good if there be good.

Anthony Trollope, "Novel Reading"

I

Trollope shares with Thackeray the tendency to minimize the significance of novel writing, but he has none of Thackeray's disturbing yet
creative ambivalence about the act of writing itself.[1] With some satirical
elements, Trollope's novels are nevertheless rarely satirical in Thackeray's vein and yet more rarely parodic of other narrative forms. The
difficulties and ambiguities of the realist mode, so forcefully evident in
Thackeray's work, sit rather comfortably in Trollope's. Thackeray's art,
which Trollope greatly admired, extended the theme of disenchantment
beyond the characters within the narratives to the narrator and narrative itself, for in his works, the passionate quests of ingenuous characters are no more chimerical than the passionate quests of their creators
for an adequate representation of reality. We can watch, in Thackeray,
the painful acquiescence in a world of melancholy compromise, sustained by a memory of the impossibilities of youth. But Trollope's fiction shows few of the strains of such quests. His art begins in the
compromises to which Thackeray's seems to have been driven.

The antiromantic realist, enthusiastically rejecting the falsifications of

181

earlier narrative forms, cannot very long remain true to the elements of the realistic. Thackeray's self-deprecating defensive strategies are only extreme versions of the refusal to take art seriously that realism requires if it is to sustain its vision of a compromised world full of mixed natures in which the extremes of passion—even the passion for the parodic truth—are aberrations. Trollope had no trouble with the refusal. The dreams he allowed himself were themselves moderate. His career and its implications, therefore, are in contrast not only to Thackeray's, but, for example, to Charlotte Brontë's, as well. We can see how incompatible with the realist effort to be tough-minded, disenchanted, and faithful to the textures of experience was her commitment to the life of feeling. In her antiromantic rejection of the world of Angria in her first novel, *The Professor*, Brontë has her hero-narrator speak for realism:

> Novelists should never allow themselves to weary of the study of real life. If they observed this duty conscientiously, they would give us fewer pictures chequered with vivid contrasts of light and shade, they would seldom elevate their heroes and heroines to the heights of rapture, still seldomer sink them to the depths of despair; for if we rarely taste the fulness of joy in this life, we yet more rarely savour the acrid bitterness of hopeless anguish.[2]

But for the solemnity of the voice, we might detect here something of Thackeray's way of imagining the world, and especially of his ironies at the expense of his characters' most intense passions. In her late Preface to *The Professor*, Brontë describes how she required of her hero that he "work his way through life as I had seen real living men work theirs— . . . that no sudden turns should lift him in a moment to wealth and high station." In what seems a deliberate statement of a central part of the realist's creed, she argues that "as Adam's son," the hero "should share Adam's doom, and drain throughout life a mixed and moderate cup of enjoyment."[3] Yet if Jane Eyre, for example, drinks only a "moderate cup" because she returns to a maimed Rochester, she certainly inherits from the conventions of fiction several "turns" that make her both wealthy and happy, where the logic of her life seemed to point in a very different direction. In *Villette*, Lucy Snowe does not receive such a "turn," but her life is "chequered" despite her efforts to diminish the violent contrasts of rapture and despair. Charlotte Brontë's imagination, despite her longing after the study of "real life," felt experience with too much unironic intensity to allow her to settle for the moderate cup. There is a Providential structure to her reality that requires the devices of formal and narrative ordering of the very modes realism begins by parodying.

In Dickens, however much he insisted on the literal reality of the worlds he created, and in George Eliot, perhaps the most self-consciously realistic of all the great Victorians, we find similar incongruities. A special case for Dickens's realism can be made,[4] and certainly despite the highly "chequered" nature of his narratives and his unabashed use of romance conventions, much of his work is in the main line of Victorian realism. But we find in it no minimizing of the novelist's art and none of the ironies at the expense of feeling that dip realism so regularly to moderation and the portrayal of thoroughly mixed natures. George Eliot's art, too, though it is marked by ironies and mixed natures and a thematic preoccupation with disenchantment, grows more not less serious about itself. She moves from the characters with "dull grey eyes," like the Rev. Amos Barton, to idealized if highly complex figures like Romola, Dorothea Brooke, and Daniel Deronda. Indeed, in her last novel she gives us her first pure villain—Grandcourt. Reality itself, having lost its Whatelyan meanings, had become too deeply obscure and complex, too dangerous, to hold still for a portrait of the ordinary.

But Trollope with a consistency astonishing for a writer who could range so freely through so many different types of "reality," remained always the realist, sacrificing the "chequered" intensities of romance fiction for the faithful portrayal of recognizable characters. Though his novels may flirt with the tragic, they tend to remain in realism's central comic tradition, in which his first responsibility as writer was to his audience. He chose to value his art entirely as it amused while it kept the moral faith: "I do believe," he wrote, "that no girl has risen from the reading of my pages less modest than she was before."[5] Without Thackeray's hesitations, he yet wished "to vindicate my own profession as a novelist," but the vindication was of a "profession" not an art, and it was against the charge of immorality. The "high nature" of the novelist's work, he wrote in the *Autobiography*, consists primarily in teaching "lessons of virtue," while yet making himself "a delight to his readers" (pp. 185, 186, 190).

Ironically, Trollope's argument for the high nature of the profession struck later writers as a denial of the novel's claim to be a high art. Trollope talks in his *Autobiography* as though novel writing were indistinguishable from any honorable craft. Indeed, the *Autobiography*, which Michael Sadleir claims did Trollope's reputation so much damage,[6] might be taken as a surreptitious attempt to be witty and *épater les intellectuels*. It has a texture of aggressive modesty, of the bluff commonsense arrogance of a Bounderby, although without Bounderby's self-righteousness and inhumanity. The Trollope of the *Autobiography* is not ashamed of his own limitations and feels the falseness of large romantic presumption. Unlike Thackeray, Trollope shows no slightest indication of indecision or apology. The writer is a professional, doing his job as responsibly as he can—no more, no less. The nonfictional prose, like the fictional, thus never lapses into the kind of sentimentality we can find sporadically in Thackeray; and the novels, although they may be loosely built, never reveal disturbances of sturcture like those we find in *The Newcomes* or in *Philip*. Trollope tells his stories and his life with relentless clarity and directness. His novels multiply plots, refuse strong climaxes, and show remarkable and un-Thackerayan restraint from asserting their artificiality or fictionality.

Such direct confidence makes it particularly ironic that Henry James's most damaging attack on Trollope was for the habit of reminding readers that they are, after all, only reading a novel. Surely, Thackeray was far more a culprit in this respect. Trollope, moreover, had some Jamesian ideas about fiction, believing for example, in verisimilitude—"that which shall seem to be real"—rather than in the possibility of naive representation. Of Thackeray's characters, Trollope says: "They talk not as they would have talked probably, of which I am no judge—but as we feel that they might have talked. We find ourselves willing to take it as proved because it is there, which is the strongest possible evidence of the realistic capacity of the writer."[7] With the realist's traditional self-consciousness about his medium and his audience, Trollope is aesthetically satisfied with realism of coherence rather than with realism of reference.

James's harshness, in the light of Trollope's relative innocence of the charge, is worth some further consideration. Trollope, James says,

> took a suicidal satisfaction in reminding the reader that the story he was telling was only, after all, a make-believe. He habitually referred to the work in hand (in the course of that work) as a novel, and to himself as a novelist, and was fond of letting the reader know that this novelist could direct the course of events according to his pleasure.... These little slaps at credulity ... are very discouraging, but they are even more inexplicable; for they are deliberately inartistic, even judged from the point of view of that rather vague consideration of form which is the only canon we have a right to impose upon Trollope. It is impossible to imagine what a novelist takes himself to be unless he regard himself as an historian and his narrative as a history. It is only as an historian that he has the smallest *locus standi*. As a narrator of fictitious events he is nowhere; to insert into his attempt a backbone of logic, he must relate events that are assumed to be real.[8]

Looked at afresh, this passage displays a strange lack of faith in fiction and naiveté about the relation of readers to novels. Surely, no Victorian audience ever thought it was reading anything but a novel when it picked up a work of Trollope's or Dickens's. Yet notoriously, much weeping and laughter greeted each new monthly number of Dickens's novels, and people pleaded with the author not to kill little Paul Dombey or Nell. No readers seemed to be disturbed in their engagements with great novels by the acknowledged fact that they were novels. The illusion, after all, depends not on authorial commentary but on dramatic vividness and on the conventions of narrative that the audience might be expected to understand.

Choose randomly any Trollope novel, and one will hear an unobtrusive voice, telling its story without fanfare and without drawing attention to itself. The audience, Trollope knows, seeks to have a story told and assumes not its reality but its fictionality. Although the audience will accept a great deal of authorial commentary, Trollope is, on the whole, sparing with it. The audience assumes that the novelist will guide judgment and take care of the fundamental business of storytelling, and this Trollope does. The "backbone of logic" that James demands is unnecessary because there is a previously established logic in the very narrative conventions Trollope adopts so cozily. It depends on no artificial assumption that the novelist is a genuine historian. Integrity in the business of storytelling is all that is required, and the Trollopian voice is designed to induce trust.

The narratives often begin very directly: "When young Mark Robarts was leaving college . . . *(Framley Parsonage)*, or "When Louis Trevelyan was twenty-four years old . . ." *(He Knew He Was Right)*. Sometimes, Trollope will speak in his own voice because there are special narrative problems intruding on direct narration, and he feels obliged to explain them: "I would that it were possible so to tell a story that a reader should beforehand know every detail of it up to a certain point" *(Is He Popenjoy?)*. He faces a similar problem at the start of *Mr. Scarborough's Family*: "It will be necessary for the purpose of my story, that I shall go back more than once from the point at which it begins, so that I may explain with the least amount of awkwardness the things as they occurred which led up to the incidents I am about to tell." There is no nonsense about Illusion, here, but at the same time there is no gratuitous reminder that this is only a novel. The professional storyteller is at work. To be sure, there is nothing here that implies the pressure of great art. The tone is casually conciliatory to the audience in a way that James would have found unfortunate. There is no evidence of a struggle to find new ways to get stories told. Technically, despite thematic coherence and parallel plotting,[9] Trollope is profoundly uninteresting; his work, unlike Thackeray's and George Eliot's, points to no changes in fictional art. Yet the casually inherited conventions of storytelling, and the muted voice they allow him, release him to deal with materials that, if handled at a higher pitch, would have caused him great difficulty.[10] The shattering of illusion, in any case, is not a serious problem.

Given the long history of self-reference in narrative,[11] it is not clear why Trollope's self-reference should seem "deliberately inartistic." Which, after all, implies a fuller faith in the novel—Trollope's frank but undemonstrative acceptance of the storyteller's role, or James's curious assertion that the novelist has no place to stand except as "an historian"? Why, as a narrator of fictitious events, should the novelist be "nowhere"? What else *is* a novelist but a narrator of fictitious events? In the only sense of "assume" that might describe a reader's normal relation to fiction, does Trollope "assume" any less than James the reality of the related events? Both write their fictions with an invisible prefatory "as if." They conduct their narratives as if their subjects were real; both restrict their power to manipulate events for the sake of strict accountability to the realism of coherence. Trollope's fundamental lack of interest in plot as a formal device and his primary concern with making his characters credible suggest what might be taken as an even larger commitment to their reality than James, with his scrupulously contrived structures, could make. In the long run, James is arguing not for a historian's fidelity but for an artist's power. He felt in Trollope as in many of the great Victorians the tendency of realistic art to sprawl beyond the artist's control. While he seems to be arguing for a greater realism, James is ultimately arguing—as the direction of his own career suggests—for the priority of the artist making over the historian describing.

"As an artist," says James, "[Trollope] never took himself seriously." This, not the technical flaws or intrusions, to which he was really responding only as symptoms, is the primary source of James's discomfort with Trollope's novels. And here James's ground would be firmer. In my discussion of Thackeray, I suggested that the realist's program tended to preclude commitment to the conventions of narrative ordering and even to the capacity of language—however faithful—to do justice to the complexity and movement of reality. For Trollope, as well, reality failed to correspond to the sorts of resolutions and shapings that narrative conventions required. Truthfulness, if it did not require the subversion of fiction, entailed a frank if not aggressive recognition that a story was a story. In his deliberately compromising way Trollope did, of course, accept and use the conventions. No writer was more concerned with narratives about legacies, inheritance, and marriage, and no writer, in the long run, more frequently or casually acquiesced in the convention of somehow bringing together inheritance and love. Yet, as in *Is He Poppenjoy?*, there is often something a bit askew about the ultimate connection. Though the marquis and young Popenjoy die conveniently enough for the heroine, Mary, and her husband, Lord George, theirs is a compromised relation to begin with. The inheritance itself seems almost beside the point of the novel's primary concerns. As James Kincaid puts it in his excellent study of Trollope, "We are urged, on one hand, to find full meaning in pattern suggested by action, but there is a concurrent sense of artificiality, even falseness of that pattern, a sense that genuine life is to be found only outside all pattern."[12] It is as though Trollope is always writing the end of *The Newcomes,* but more quietly than Thackeray, with less obvious subversive impact.

Trollope is a great Victorian realist largely because he unwaveringly lived out the implication of realism, pronounced early in its origins in parody, that "genuine life is to be found only outside all pattern." It is surely partly for this reason that Trollope, as James unhappily noted, developed so elaborately the practice, "which he may be said to have inherited from Thackeray . . . of carrying certain actors from one story to another."[13] James points out that the practice adds "illusion" to the imagined world, but it does so in the same way as Thackeray's practice—by implicitly denying the closed nature of any narrative, by recognizing every stop not as a terminus but as an arbitrary point in a continuing process. In this way and in many others, Trollope's fictions sprawl toward the realist formlessness that none of the conventions of narrative or language can sustain and that James, in the interests of art, sought to contain. Thus Trollope accepts casually the conventions of resolution that surely seemed to James—quite justly—merely conventional, in part because he understood his professional responsibilities to his audience, but in part because he wrote in such a way that the resolutions, when they came, mattered far less than they seemed to. Characteristically, instead of struggling toward a new form—or formlessness—consonant with his realist vision, Trollope accepted the conventions and limits of art quite comfortably.

Of course, the novels, by their very nature, cannot achieve such formlessness—and this is one of the central contradictions in the realist mode with which this study has been concerned. In one sense, Alexander Welsh is correct when he notes that the classic English novels "always pretend to give the crucial period of the hero's life, the whole of his life that matters, and therefore close when the event that is morally decisive in life has occurred."[14] But if each Trollope novel conforms to this view, together the novels suggest that the "closing" is deceptive and arbitrary. Like Thackeray's, Trollope's instincts were at least half toward the openness that the form itself denied.

His refusal to write with Jamesian seriousness is one of the running

motifs of Trollope's narratives. Art, as Kincaid points out, is often perceived as dangerous in Trollope's novels because it requires too rigid a
patterning of experience. Josiah Crawley is a less lovable version of
Thackeray's Colonel Newcome, too rigidly adhering to a code of conduct and too strenuously imagining himself in a special role. Crawley,
says Kincaid, "constructs for himself a grand tragic drama in which he
takes the leading part."[15] Against even the just and moral ideologue,
Thackeray built the defenses of a Pendennis-like dilettantism, which
remains flexible and responsive to experience if aesthetically and morally somewhat irresponsible. Trollope, for his part, forces compromises
on all those who attempt to resist the casual irrationality, injustice, and
disorder of his world. Thackeray's distrust of dogma and of pattern
reemerges in Trollope as a continuing distrust of any absolute commitment or ideal, any preimagined structure. As he confessed in his *Autobiography*, he wrote almost more casually than Thackeray: "I have
indeed for many years almost abandoned the effort to think, trusting
myself, with the narrowest thread of a plot, to work the matter out when
the pen is in my hand" (p. 134).

The price of imposing an inflexible ideal on later experience is
dramatized frequently. Two obvious although very different examples
are Lily Dale and Louis Trevelyan, both doomed by their inflexibility.
Alternatively, Ayala's "angel" is diminished into the practical and
homely figure of Jonathan Stubbs, and Ayala's becomes a realistic "romance" because of her flexibility. And as an alternative to the obsessed
Louis Trevelyan, married by an almost equally inflexible Emily Rowley,
Trollope gives Hugh Stanbury, "undoubtedly an awkward-mannered
man," to Emily's sister, Nora, in *He Knew He Was Right*.[16] The resolutions in the novels are compromises with ideals—both of the characters
and of the novel form itself. Compromise, that central condition and
subject of Victorian realistic fiction, does not, of course, imply the absence of seriousness. The staggering energy evinced in Trollope's work,
both in the post office and as a novelist, implies how much was at stake
in compromise. As his artists and other characters maneuver successfully through experience only by rejecting their inclinations for the
ideal, so Trollope himself probably could not have survived his grotesque childhood or his early failures as a novelist had he been given to
romantic intensities and large demands. Ultimately, then, James is right
about Trollope's unwillingness to take art seriously (at least in a Jamesian
way). Yet the refusal to do so may have been his primary enabling act.

II

It was, in a sense, the realist's refusal of extremes that allowed Trollope
to become an artist. He chose the novel form, as he said in his *Autobiog-*

raphy, because although poetry was not "within my grasp," and drama was "above me," "I thought it possible that I might write a novel" (p. 45). Here hard work and common sense, not genius, were the requisites. The Carlylean strategy of reducing one's demands to zero so that *any* satisfaction becomes infinite makes an appropriate analogue to Trollope's self-protective maneuverings. He could not, then, on the strength of his early failures with the novel imagine himself as an alienated and suffering artist: "The idea that I was the unfortunate owner of unappreciated genius never troubled me" (p. 73). He chose, instead, to keep at it until, with *Barchester Towers*, he achieved the success he had sought. But the artist, at least the Trollopian artist, is not special. He is like other people in this compromised world, and his major responsibility is not to an ideal of art but to life itself. In his description of Ayala Dormer's father—a painter with all the surface qualities of the hypersensitive artist—he implies the relation to art that he could consciously allow himself:

> Where is the painter who shall paint a picture after his soul's long-ing though he shall not get a penny for it,—though he shall starve as he put his last touch to it, when he knows that by drawing some duchess of the day he shall in a fortnight earn a ducal price? Shall a wife and child be less dear to him than to a lawyer,—or to a shoemaker; or the very craving of his hunger less obdurate? A man's self, and what he has within him and his belongings, with his outlook for this and other worlds,—let that be the first, and work, noble or otherwise, be the second. To be honest is greater than to have painted the San Sisto, or to have chiselled the Apollo; to have assisted in making others honest,—infinitely greater. All of which were discussed at great length at the bijou, and the bijouites always sided with the master. To an artist, said Dormer, let his art be everything,—above wife and children, above money, above health, above even character. Then he would put out his hand with his jewelled finger and stretch forth his velvet clad arm and soon after lead his friend away to the little dinner at which no luxury had been spared.[17]

Dormer, who "could not have touched his brush if one of his girls had been suffering," is forgiven his affectation in the ironies that demonstrate his compromises with the high ideals of art. In Trollope, these ideals tend to be affectation, and this passage echoes one of those outrageously practical and decent sequences in the *Autobiography*. There Trollope happily risks offending artists who claim not to be concerned with money, but only their art, when they know that "the more a man earns the more useful he is to his fellow-men" (p. 93).

Trollope, then, offers himself as a model for writers without genius. In his *Autobiography*, he accepts Hawthorne's praise of him as a writer whose books are as "real as if some giant had hewn a giant lump out of the earth and put it under a glass case, with all its inhabitants going about their daily business, and not suspecting that they were being made a show of" (p. 125). The realist mode is, implicitly, precisely right for Trollope's sort of skill, for "a man devoting himself to literature with industry, perseverance, certain necessary aptitudes, and fair average talents"; by example, it is clear that such a man "may succeed in gaining a livelihood" (p. 92).

Obviously, Trollope is leaving out a good deal here. There is something of John Stuart Mill's avoidance, in his own *Autobiography*, of the intensities and complexities of family relationships and personal feeling. Trollope, like Mill, is almost disingenuous in suggesting that anybody could, with the same sort of application, do what he did. Preoccupied, like his novels, with literal surfaces that remind us of the ordinariness of the most extraordinary things and with rejecting the extremes of experience, Trollope's *Autobiography* carefully keeps the monstrous possibilities of so irrational and disordered a world under control. His reminiscences of childhood are symptomatic. If we remember Dickens's secretiveness about the blacking factory episode, we must be struck by Trollope's bold assertion: "Something of the disgrace of my school days has clung to me all through life. Not that I have ever shunned to speak of them as openly as I am writing now, but that when I have been claimed as school-fellow by some of those many hundreds who were with me either at Harrow or Winchester, I have felt that I had no right to talk of things from which I was kept in estrangement" (p. 14). The difference from Dickens is almost complete, but the strategy of openness is almost as effective as the strategy of secrecy.

I would suggest that Trollope's "disgrace" played almost as important a part in his writing career as Dickens's did in his, not only in the obvious significance of literary success for a boy perceived as oafish and stupid by the young elite of his country, but in the very anti-romantic texture of his novels. In Dickens, who wrote no autobiography but that fragment shown to John Forster and incorporated into *David Copperfield* as a fiction, the imagined world is one of extremes, suggestive of demonic energies and mysterious and providential or dangerous possibilities. Fictionally, the disgrace emerges in the purgative self-pity of *Oliver Twist*, or the increasing though disguised frankness and self-knowledge in *David Copperfield*, or in the vigorous yet salutary guilt of *Great Expectations*. There the submerged monstrous comes almost to the surface when Pip, having heard Magwitch's narrative upon the convict's return from Australia, thinks: "The imaginary student pursued by the misshapen creature he had impiously made, was not more wretched than I, pursued by the creature who had made me, and recoiling from him with a strong repulsion the more he admired me and the fonder he was of me."[18] But such psychic and moral doubling in the extreme situations, whether metaphoric or literal, rarely emerges in Trollope. He too, of course, has his madness, murders, crimes, and aberrations, but there is nothing mysterious about them. Trollope's openness allows him to confront a great deal of very unconventional behavior in ways perilously close to unconventional, but he manages this because, like a good realist, he deprives the unconventional of its mystery and shows, indeed, that it is strikingly like the conventional.

The conventional, finally, matters a great deal to Trollope, although he is consistently sympathetic with those who for good reasons are driven to violate many of the social conventions. He requires of them, however, if they are to become part of the happy endings his novels contrive, that they respect the very conventions they break, and that, in the long run, they adhere to them. This is a consistent narrative pattern in his novels, and it reflects, I believe, the way in which Trollope coped with his disgrace. *Is He Popenjoy?* is a particularly good example of Trollope's handling of conventions, and in the character of Dean Lovelace we surely have some muted autobiographical reflections. The dean does indeed have a tincture of that vulgarity that in an exaggerated form the Germains attribute to him as a man having been brought up in a stable. He behaves with unclerical aggression and ambition, despite his overall gentlemanly—and "manly"—bearing. He is, then, one of Trollope's typically mixed natures. In his manliness he is forced to defy conventions occasionally, as when he violently thrashes the marquis of Brotherton for calling Mary Lovelace a "————"! Trollope's summary of the dean's failings, however, suggests Trollope's conscious relation to his own career and implies the possible range of legitimate action within the limits of social conventions: "But he had been subject to one weakness, which had marred a manliness which would otherwise have been great. He, who should have been proud of the lowliness of his birth, and have known that the brightest feather in his cap was the fact that, having been humbly born, he had made himself what he was—he had never ceased to be ashamed of the stable yard."[19] Trollope admires the aristocratic tradition embodied in the Germains (and particularly in the sisters), but admires more the power of talent to rise into that class from out of the stables. In his own life and in the dean's, he sought to violate traditions of inherited dignity by assimilating to them. Rebellion, guilt, or shame has no place.

The extreme, in any case, rarely takes center stage with Dickensian energy. Half admiring Dickens, Trollope objected in his *Autobiography* that it was "the peculiarity and marvel of this man's power, that he has invested his puppets with a charm that has enabled him to dispense with human nature" (pp. 214–15). Rather, one might say, he perceived Dickens's "human nature" as charged with too much energy and mystery to be absorbed without strangeness into the conventions of the ordinary that make the dominant strategy of his own realism. Trollope's human nature depends on its recognizably mixed and compromised motives. Examining the extreme in the clear light of day, Trollope gives us the realist's disenchanted vision and domesticates the monstrous. No man, Trollope agrees with Thackeray, ever died of a broken heart. The most intense moments of our lives are absorbed by time and the ordinary inexorable flow of life. If there is some loss of visionary intensity, there is the gain that comes from absorption into a larger community of shared social experience and from avoidance of the alternative to Dickens's visionary affirmation—romantic despair. Unlike Thackeray, Trollope does not move from disenchantment into melancholy nostalgia. He takes the risk of experience and finds life not in the lost romantic past, but in the moderate and satisfying present.[20] Not having dreamed great dreams, Trollope is free to accept the disenchantment that dispels ideals for reality.

It is worth pausing for some more detailed analysis of the way Trollope mitigates the intensities of extreme feeling and thus averts the worst by facing it with unimpassioned directness. The strategy is characteristic, but we can take as an example an extended passage in which Trollope uses the realistic mode to deal with a special case of the frustration of romantic desire. The passage, from *The Vicar of Bullhampton*, describes Harry Gilmore's response to his realization that he can never marry Mary Lowther, with whom he is hopelessly in love.

> At last he cut the letter open, and stood for some moments looking for courage to read it. He did read it, and then sat himself down in his chair, telling himself that the thing was over, and that he would bear it as a man. He took up his newspaper, and began to study it. It was the time of the year when newspapers are not very interesting, but he made a rush at the leading articles, and went through two of them. Then he turned over to the police reports. He sat there for an hour, and read hard during the whole time. Then he got up and shook himself, and knew that he was a crippled man, with every function out of order, disabled in every limb. He walked from the library into the hall, and thence to the dining room, and so, backwards and forwards, for a quarter of an hour. At last he could walk no longer, and, closing the door of the library behind him, he threw himself on a sofa and cried like a woman.
>
> What was it that he wanted, and why did he want it? Were there not other women whom the world would say were as good? Was it ever known that a man had died, or become irretrievably broken and destroyed by disappointed love? Was it not one of those things

that a man should shake off from him and have done with it? He asked himself these, and many such-like questions, and tried to philosophise with himself on the matter. Had he no will of his own, by which he might conquer this enemy? No; he had no will of his own, and the enemy would not be conquered. He had to tell himself that he was so poor a thing that he could not stand up against the evil that had fallen on him.

He walked out round his shrubberies and paddocks, and tried to take an interest in the bullocks and the horses. He knew that if every bullock and horse about the place had been struck dead it would not enhance his misery. He had not much hope before, but now he would have seen the house of Hampton Privets in flames, just for the chance that had been his yesterday. It was not only that he wanted her, or that he regretted the absence of some recognized joys which she would have brought to him; but that the final decision on her part seemed to take from him all vitality, all power of enjoyment, all that inward elasticity which is necessary for an interest in worldly affairs.

He had as yet hardly thought of anything but himself;—had hardly observed the name of his successful rival, or paid any attention to aught but the fact that she had told him that it was all over. He had not attempted to make up his mind whether anything could still be done, whether he might yet have a chance, whether it would be well for him to quarrel with the man; whether he should be indignant with her, or remonstrate once again in regard to her cruelty. He had thought only of the blow, and of his inability to support it. Would it not be best that he should go forth, and blow out his brains, and have done with it?[21]

Typically, the very length and elaboration of the passage diminishes the intensity of the feeling so forcefully captured in "and knew that he was a crippled man." Gilmore's loss is absorbed in a matter-of-fact and simple descriptive prose. The passage goes on for several pages; but it can be taken only within the full context of Gilmore's later actions. It depends very heavily on notations of time, the whole first paragraph, for example, developing through a series of time phrases: "at last," "then," "for a quarter of an hour," "at last." Calendar time also matters: it is mid-October, Parliament is not in session, society is still on vacation, and it is thus "the time of the year when newspapers are not very interesting." What Gilmore does is more important, for the moment, than what he feels—or perhaps the description of surfaces is an implicit description of feeling. The feeling itself is described in the same plain style as is the reading of the police report and settles easily within the time sequence: "Then he got up and shook himself, and knew that he was a crippled man, with every function out of order, disabled in every limb."

By insisting on a fairly external description of time and objects, and by resisting the perhaps natural tendency to heighten his style, Trollope avoids both irony and parody. Gilmore's own matter-of-factness here implies the intensity of his feeling by its very refusal of romantic hyperbole; it also keeps him from Thackerayan mockery. Gilmore is allowed his despair without condescension or passionate commiseration, and only within the context of the details of his ordinary life.

Gilmore's thoughts, in the succeeding paragraphs, are treated as matter-of-factly as his actions. Like a Thackerayan narrator, Gilmore attempts to minimize the importance of his feelings and provides the very judgment that Fenwick, the vicar of Bullhampton himself, will later make. He recognizes the reactions appropriate to "a man," but sees himself as a "poor thing," and succumbs to the feeling. Even this, however, is handled without narrative judgment. The uninsistent sympathy of the patient recording of feeling is characteristic of Trollope. What the passage makes us feel most forcefully is not so much Gilmore's loss as the contrast between what he knows is right and what he can feel. In Trollope feeling is taken seriously; but at the same time it is seen in a larger context that makes us recognize it as only one fact among many and that requires of us great discipline. Gilmore's behavior is not quite up to the rules of the social game, to his responsibility as squire and gentleman, despite his warmth, generosity, and genuine dismay.

The whole passage and its context serve to remind us that Trollope's regular subversions of conventional moral judgments,[22] and his sometimes remarkable complication of moral issues, are dependent upon a firmly conservative way of seeing. Trollope's world is defined and its narrative judgments guided—though not altogether restricted—by clearly understood if not always explicitly defined rules of social behavior.[23] The ideal of the gentleman is a constant presence throughout his fiction although, as an ideal, it has Trollope's characteristic flexibility. The "real" world Trollope depicts, having sacrificed a Whatelyan Providential shape, has a social substitute. In accepting things as they are, Trollope does not quite surrender to the absurd and meaningless universe of late-century novelists. It is clear, for example, that for him civilization is "better" than savagery, that the rich are on the whole more interesting than the poor, that inherited wealth is superior to earned wealth (though here the discriminations become subtler), and that established conventions of behavior and value are superior to ideals. The rules, of course, are there for the breaking, and they very frequently come in conflict with normal human instincts, most particularly the instinct of love, which figures so importantly in all social relations as well. "There are," as the narrator of the *Vicar of Bullhampton* notes, when Mary Lowther declares her love to Walter Marrable, "moments in one's life in which not to be imprudent, not to be utterly, childishly forgetful of all worldly wisdom, would be to be brutal, inhuman, and devilish" (p. 142). Such moments as this test the dominant rules and complicate the morality of Trollope's novels, yet, as in the scene when Gilmore reads Mary's letter, they rarely provide an unequivocal valuing of the experience. Gilmore behaves humanly, feelingly, sympathetically; he is in the grip of a feeling that cannot succumb to worldly wisdom. Nevertheless, he is not quite acting up to the gentlemanly ideal. There are situations in Trollope where, though the rules remain in force, they cannot be obeyed.

Fenwick enunciates the view that seems to be endorsed by the novel as a whole when Gilmore has been rejected by Mary a second time. The forlorn and suicidal lover is one who

> "throws his head down on the roadside, and does not care who may bear it, or who may suffer because he is too poor a creature to struggle on! Have you no feeling that, though it may be hard with you here,"—and the Vicar, as he spoke, struck his breast,—"you should so carry your outer self, that the eyes of those around you should see nothing of the sorrow within? That is my idea of manliness, and I have ever taken you to be a man." [p. 490]

Trollope has, by this time, already shown some of the consequences to Gilmore's tenants of his leaving and indulging his sadness. But when Gilmore fails to respond to the rule, he slips out of the novel—quietly and undramatically bearing his sorrow with him, and perhaps a bit less of a man. He is allowed to return to Trollope's world, with the typical Trollopian implication that no crisis is an ultimate one, when, in the last line of the novel, it is reported that after years of wandering, "he was expected home" (p. 527).

In the first passage quoted, we are asked to watch Gilmore walk out into his property and to realize himself indifferent to his fate. The moment of intense personal feeling is immediately bound up in something larger and loses the passionate edge it would have in a more deliberately romantic narrative. As an excellent squire, worthy of the respect of everyone in the novel, Gilmore had been entirely wrapped up in the responsibilities of his estate, but the thwarted love so unbalances him that he rejects those very social connections that have given him his character and his purpose in life. The threat of such a personal disaster is frequently present in Trollope, but it would be difficult to say that there are any figures—even the mad ones like Kennedy and Louis Trevelyan—who lose their identity in this way. In the last of the quoted paragraphs here, Gilmore does begin to shake himself into consideration of what can be done, which is the first sign of reviving reality for

Trollope. The notion of suicide comes, and will recur later, but the matter-of-factness with which the thought is treated diminishes its power and implies that it is not a real option. Although it is an option open to the alien Lopez, in *The Prime Minister*, it is not really available to a gentleman.

In any case, Gilmore's responses here encompass by and large the limits of Trollope's world. The narrative is thick with surfaces, registering behavior and talk more than feelings, and it implies for every character limitations and responsibilities, virtues and vices, and the social identity of private selves. It implies a not quite sharply defined hierarchy of values, and points toward perhaps irremediable and almost blameless conflicts between private need and social rule; but in that conflict the social rule, built out of a wider and longer range of experience, tends to have primacy. Action, as implied in the last quoted paragraph, is a way to integrate self and society; without action there is the fruitless paralysis in self-contemplation. And whatever the conflicts and recognitions, time moves with irrevocable coercive force through Trollope's narratives, connecting all things, diminishing the intensity of the pain in moments when the irrational and perhaps nonhuman structure of the world shows through.

The disorder implicit in Gilmore's story in *The Vicar of Bullhampton*, a characteristic Trollopian story of a good person whose love is unrequited, is muted by the other stories—by Mary's happiness and Carry Brattle's redemption and the vicar's triumph over the marquis of Trowbridge. Yet it is one of those inevitable loose threads in Trollope's world, a skein never woven in either by the conventions of narrative closure that Trollope so often used (Walter Marrable, for example, gets the inheritance after all; the marquis has no right over the land on which the Dissenting chapel is built), or by more elaborately artful designs, such as James might have approved. The story is, as it were, dissolved in several other stories, none of which is, in Jamesian terms, quite "done." But it is essential to Trollope's compromised vision of the complexities and disorders of experience that things not be "done."

III

As I have already suggested, Trollope's realism depends not on a Whatelyan faith in the ultimate order and significance of experience, but on an almost cynical acceptance of the necessity for arbitrary and traditional rules to sustain what order civilization has been able to construct. There are losses, of course, as Harry Gilmore is at least a temporary loss. But the loss is not tragic. Trollope is everywhere committed to acceptance of social traditions while his narratives regularly demonstrate that the traditions are arbitrary and incoherent and that even the most virtuous characters are incapable of observing them consistently—and would be inhuman if they could. With no Providential structure, his world and his novels would be meaningless but for the meaning that society itself creates. But while such a view, stated in the abstract, sounds almost Conradian, Trollope's novels show no inclination to gesture toward some ineffable heart of darkness. He explores with equanimity the incoherences, confident that by virtue of the realist's refusal of abstract systems or ideal aspirations, he can maneuver his characters, as he maneuvered himself, though to some kind of mature compromise.

In Trollope selfishness is never transformed into demonic evil, and he shows no unease with its pervasiveness. It is not at all a metaphysical problem and it holds no mystery. At worst it is a social problem, and one which, as many economists agreed, could be enlisted in the cause of the good, as he explained in his *Autobiography*, "All material progress has come from man's desire to do the best he can for himself and those about him, and civilization and Christianity itself have been made possible by such progress" (p. 91). What Trollope says of Burgo Fitzgerald, the charming wastrel Glencora McCluskie loves, seems to apply to everyone: "Every man to himself is the centre of the whole world;—the axle on which it all turns. All knowledge is but his own perception of the things around him. All love, and care for others, and solicitude for the world's welfare, are but his own feelings as to the world's wants and the world's merits."[24] Such a perception leads George Eliot to the extraordinary manipulations of point of view we find in *Middlemarch,* and to a quest for transcendence of the ego. Trollope's art, on the other hand, moves easily toward disorder, proliferation; it takes what might look like solipsism for granted but at the same time takes for granted the shareability of language and of the social rules. The traditions of civilization are normally sufficient to deal with the monstrous possibilities caused by the imposition of the self on the world.

There are, however, extreme instances, especially in the later Trollope, when the contest between the self and traditional social ordering becomes both more explicit and more problematic. More subversively than figures like Melmotte or Lopez, who are outsiders to begin with, Dr. Wortle and Mr. Scarborough, insiders of good will, but strong will also, challenge the conventions. Mr. Scarborough explicitly asserts his own will against the traditional power of society and, in fact, wins, outsmarting and defeating that almost ideal figure, the attorney Mr. Grey. Both *Dr. Wortle's School* and *Mr. Scarborough's Family* make gestures at conventional resolutions, both narrative and social, but they are not ultimately resolved. Neither, however, are the challenges to order endorsed. Such fictions take us to the edge of the Victorian realist vision, yet they step back from the horrific visions they might have implied.

In *Dr. Wortle's School*, the Peacockes are, formally, the violators of the social rules. When Dr. Wortle learns that the unexceptionable Mr. Peacocke is not legally married to his ostensible wife because her first husband—a thorough scoundrel—is not actually dead, he defends the Peacockes against universal public disapprobation and almost loses his school as a consequence. The defense is based on traditional moral grounds; the Peacockes not only acted with a consciousness of right (having investigated to discover that the first husband was dead), but, in protecting Mrs. Peacocke when she would otherwise have been stranded and helpless, Peacocke did what Wortle himself would have done in the same position. The precise moral issue is here, again with characteristic Trollopian subversion, formulated against the convention. Peacocke has decided to risk defying the convention for the sake of a higher moral good as he personally understands it.

Wortle adheres as closely to the convention as he can without rejecting the Peacockes. He requires that the two live apart until more evidence be found, and he sends Peacocke on an extended trip across America. Although he is full of sympathy for Mrs. Peacocke, he discontinues her connection with the school; nevertheless, he allows her to live in the same house. Finally, in the character of Mr. Puddicombe—a steady, just, and moral clergyman—Trollope embodies a convincing and acceptable rejection of Wortle's compassion. Puddicombe is neither so interesting nor so attractive as Wortle, but the narrative requires that we admire him as he gives renewed force to the apparently arbitrary and inadequate conventions of society's morality. All of this, combined with Wortle's notorious stubbornness and tyrannical control, as he insists on his own will at all times, calls into question the correctness of his risking all for people who have violated three of the cardinal rules of society: that a man and a woman who are not married must not live together, and that one should neither keep a mystery nor act under false pretenses.

Yet the evidence is clear that the novel asks us for approval of Wortle's actions. Mrs. Wortle, after standing out a long time and refusing to get to know Mrs. Peacocke, succumbs to the latter's dignity and warmth. Mrs. Wortle's compassion grows from the kind of imaginative sympathy with another human being that is Trollope's means of finding "an equivalent center of self":

> Mrs. Wortle had been made to doubt whether, after all, the sin had been so very sinful. She did endeavour to ask herself whether she would not have done the same in the same circumstances. . . . Mrs.

Wortle,—who found it indeed extremely difficult to imagine herself to be in such a position,—did at least acknowledge that, in such circumstances, she certainly would have done whatever Wortle had told her. She could not bring it nearer to herself than that. She could not suggest to herself two men as her own husbands. . . . It was terrible to think of,—so terrible that she could not quite think of it; but struggling to think of it her heart was softened toward this other woman. [p. 212]

The "softened heart" implies the tension, usual in Trollope, between the personal and the social; but the softened heart does not suggest the superiority of the personal to the social. There is nothing in *Dr. Wortle's School* to equal the intensity of difference we find between Maggie and the town of St. Ogg's in *The Mill on the Floss*. There the rhetoric of the narrative comes down hard against the "men of maxims" who cannot adjust a general morality to particular circumstances. Trollope, whose morality is also largely governed by a sense of particular conditions, cannot, however, condemn a moral stupidity that is in conformity with social norms.

Surely, whatever else the novel is doing, it is not being very hard on society's hardness to the Peacockes. Even Mrs. Peacocke agrees that it is natural for society to regard her as a sinner. The rule is essentially right (in a way the narrative redeems the Peacockes because they believe this); and it is indispensable for the operations of society. The character who is most venomously treated, both by Wortle and the narrative, is Mrs. Stantiloup, who is spiteful and has a grudge against Wortle. She exploits the trouble with the Peacockes, but cannot be taken as representative of society's own views.

In *Dr. Wortle's School*, as in *Phineas Finn, The Claverings*, and *Orley Farm* (where Lady Mason is guilty of forgery), Trollope is free to treat violators of the rules with compassion because the rules have for him not a divine but only a social sanction and are thus, like everything else, rather a mixed, rough and ready business. Michael Sadleir comments on Trollope's skill in "rousing pity even for a deserved misfortune";[25] but this skill works safely within a framework of general acceptance of the necessity for the rules and the adequacy of the existing ones. One misses in Trollope the partly stifled energy for change and moral progress we find in George Eliot, whose respect for established conventions grew with her conception of the "truth of feeling" and of the slow evolutionary process of change. Trollope sees all such energy, beyond the very limited personal conditions of his protagonists, as chimerical, and outside the range of realism. Such energy promotes the ideal conception of things that promises to intensify the pain of actual experience, and open the pathway for the monstrous as well. An unwillingness to compromise and to find compromise satisfying is the beginning of the quest for order, for Promethean overreaching, for the creation of monsters that realism, in its happy disorders, ironically represses.

One of the most interesting and overt instances in Trollope of the contest between self and society occurs in *Mr. Scarborough's Family*. At the center of that novel is a figure like George Eliot's Peter Featherstone, a sick and dying old man who insists to the end on doing as he likes. The story—of romances thwarted or fulfilled and of inheritances and wills, and families grasping for the old man's wealth—seems conventional in many ways. Yet Mr. Scarborough, unlike Peter Featherstone, is an unconventionally attractive and good-natured man, and the story is really far less about who will inherit the Scarborough estate than about the relation between justice in the inheritance and social rules. The true struggle is between Mr. Scarborough, who wants to be able to control the inheritance in accordance with the deserts of his two sons, and Mr. Grey, his lawyer, who is committed to upholding social law as it exists, and who acts throughout his life with perfect integrity. It is a novel that seems to have the obligatory happy ending, in which the better son inherits the fortune, in which the hero and heroine of subplot inherit and marry. And yet, at the very center of the novel is a disquieting irresolution.

For Mr. Scarborough succeds, and his success implies a radical subversion of society: "To run counter to the law! That had ever been the chief object of the squire's ambition. To arrange everything so that it should be seen that he had set all laws at defiance! That had been his great pride!"[26] What is startling about the conception of Mr. Scarborough is that in him Trollope's consistent refusal to portray any but "mixed natures" makes sympathetic a figure whose utter disregard of conventions threatens the very texture of society. In effect, Scarborough drives the humane and gentlemanly Grey out of society by actually outwitting society without breaking any laws. Mr. Grey gives way to the sharp-practicing Mr. Barry, whose way of doing law is conformable with Mr. Scarborough's way of circumventing it. Indeed, the loose ends of the whole novel imply a general disintegration of social institutions that makes Mr. Scarborough's story something more than a particular one about a specially clever old man. Mr. Grey is displaced; his daughter Dolly does not marry; Mountjoy, who inherits the estate, does not get his love and is destined to squander what Mr. Scarborough has so laboriously won for him; the incorrigible Carroll family remains incorrigible to the end. As Mr. Grey says, "as things go now a man has to be accounted a fool if he attempts to run straight" (p. 390).

Yet the book has no touch of the apocalyptic about it. It refuses to end on the note of moral decline, but instead focuses on the one completed romance in the novel, between Harry Annesly and Florence Mountjoy.

Florence, in her comic, pragmatic voice, announces that "one has to risk dangers in the world, but one makes the risk as little as possible" (p. 408). Even this is antiromantic in its translation of her affair with Harry into a calculated gamble. It is, however, a happy compromise. And despite all the moral deterioration with which the book confronts us, its note is still that of the happy compromise. Trollope will not quite let us see Mr. Scarborough as satanic, and the notion that the book's rhetoric asks us to judge him severely seems to me to result from too abstract a conception of Trollope's commitment to the rules.[27]

Scarborough does violate all the rules, and Mr. Grey's appalled reaction has about it the right moral texture. Yet his withdrawal from so compromised a society is no more worthy—however high-minded—than Scarborough's exploitation of it. Mr. Merton's judgment of Scarborough seems to carry the novel's own authority, for Merton has almost a Jamesian role. He is not implicated in the action but remains a dispassionate observer. The very mixed nature of his judgment gives it the authenticity of Trollopian vision and is entirely consistent with the movement of the novel itself. Mr. Scarborough, he says, is not "an honest man." But, he tells Mountjoy Scarborough,

> I think he has within him a capacity for love, and an unselfishness, which almost atones for his dishonesty. And there is about him a strange dislike to conventionality and to law which is so interesting as to make up the balance. I have always regarded your father as a most excellent man; but thoroughly dishonest. He would rob anyone,—but always to eke out his own gifts to other people. He has therefore to my eyes been most romantic. [p. 335]

The word "romantic" here is, as Robert Tracy points out, a crucial one. The desire to order experience according to one's own will, even if that will is loving and unselfish, is romantic and hence dangerous. Following out Scarborough's way of dealing with society might well release those corrupting energies that Trollope's whole literary strategy is designed to minimize. Yet to judge Scarborough with unqualified harshness, as though he were not a clever old man but some kind of Nietzschean overreacher, is equally romantic. In *Mr. Scarborough's Family*, Trollope once again averts the demonic, or what I have been calling the monstrous, by assimilating it within a narrative that reduces it to life size and that, at least in the pragmatic romance of Harry and Florence, implies an alternative. The fragility of social order is, indeed, implicit in the novel, but the fragile purity of Mr. Grey is inadequate. Mr. Scarborough, at least, is interesting, and he has astonishing powers of life, which, however compromised, is superior to any ideal.

It might be possible to locate a Trollopian ideal, after all, but that

would have to be in one of Trollope's favorite characters, Plantaganet
Palliser, a figure thoroughly compromised in his own way. With all his
nobility and generosity, with his willingness to forgive Glencora and
even allow her to escape the need for forgiveness, Palliser is himself
something of a hypocrite and a cynic. While telling Glencora what is
proper in *Can You Forgive Her?*, he omits to tell her of his own bumbling
attempt at adultery (recorded in *The Small House at Allington*). The
novels in which Palliser figures importantly invariably show him
struggling to avoid the compromising pressures of his wife and of politics. He sustains his dignity by accepting what compromises he must
but also by maintaining a demeanor remote from the reality of his
personal feeling. His strength as prime minister is his willingness to
accept his usefulness as a politician who makes sure that nothing happens. In Dickens, such behavior would have earned him not respect but
a position in the Circumlocution Office.

At their best, Trollope's novels imply a morality far more interesting
than anything he had to say about it in his nonfiction. His ideals are
compromised; the rules of society he respects are seen as arbitrary; each
character must, at some point, act counter to some leading principle.
Trollope seems to become bitter in his novels only when characters
violate the rules of trust—and not always even then. His is a morality of
surfaces, not ideals, because realism is a mode of surfaces. What people
are can never be disentangled from what they wear, where they live,
whom they know. Trollope acts out the trust he requires by abjuring
surprises and mysteries in a prose which faithfully, clearly, ploddingly
records objects and events, with no flourishes or pretenses. His is an art
of acceptance.

In this sense, it would be fair to say of Trollope's realism that it
confirms things as they are and is thus subject to the modernist's
ideological critique of all realism. Nevertheless, Trollope's realism also
reveals the arbitrariness of the system upon which its narratives are
built, and it is healthily regardless of conventions of closure and resolution as often as it employs those conventions. The unsystematic disorder of the inherited conventions keeps them alive for Trollope even
against Mr. Scarborough's brilliant mechinations; and the muddiness
of Trollope's thinking is almost a condition of the sort of world he
imagines in his novels. His creed is rather like the one he attributed to
Palliser in *The Prime Minister*.[28] Experience requires qualification of the
ideal, so that both Palliser and Trollope place themselves comfortably
with the antidemocratic biases of their culture; yet they both imagine
themselves as, in some sense, liberal as well. What is really in the
liberal's mind, says Trollope in his *Autobiography*,

is,—I will not say equality, for the word is offensive and presents to the imaginations of man ideas of communism, of ruin, of insane democracy,—but a tendency towards equality. In following that, however, he knows that he must be hemmed in by safeguards, lest he be tempted to travel too quickly; and therefore he is glad to be accompanied on his way by the repressive action of Conservative opponent. Holding such views, I think I am guilty of no absurdity in calling myself an advanced conservative liberal. [P. 253]

The man with an ideal cannot be trusted unless he accepts the inhibiting pull of convention. In *The Prime Minister*, Palliser's ideal "is so distant that we need not even think it possible" (II, p. 321), and in his own term in power the ideal takes the shape of an administration whose only real virtue is that it succeeds in doing nothing. Politically (even, perhaps, morally), Trollope's world is half-cynical, half-mad; his own political creed he understands to seem absurd. The strategies of realism entail precisely such a world, moving toward a disorder from which it is preserved by arbitrary and unsystematic conventions—both social and literary.

Trollope's realism is, then, no more than any other literary method, a precise description of a "real" world. It is rigorous only in its exclusion of extremes, or in its assimilation of them into the multiplicities and diffusions of the continuing flow of surfaces. Mystery is transformed into the quotidian. Bluebeards, he writes in *Is He Popenjoy?*, though they "have no chamber of horrors, . . . interfere dreadfully with the comfort of a household" (II, p. 81). Romantic heights—the rocks and mountains—must be balanced by "bread and cheese." Realism becomes the myth of the ordinary,[29] and in the solidity and complacency of its narrative movement through time it quietly resists the very radical questioning that some of its elements may seem to provoke. All kinds of extremes enter on the periphery of the Trollopian vision, but all are contained within the possibilities of sheer plod, which will assert the primacy of conventional and arbitrary order against the rebellious energies that provoke admiration at times, but must be absorbed. Mr. Scarborough wins the battle, but in the long run his way of doing things will lead to the destruction of what he chooses to preserve. The monster is always quietly at work destroying its creator.

10

The Landscape of Reality

*W*hen I would account to myself for the birth of that passion, which afterwards ruled my destiny, I find it arise, like a mountain river, from ignoble and
almost forgotten sources; but, swelling as it proceeded, it became the torrent
which, in its course, has swept away all my hopes and joys.

Victor Frankenstein

I

In *Frankenstein*, as we have seen, Alps and Arctic wastes are the normal
geography: these suggest lives violently checkered. Conversely, in
Victorian realism, such as Trollope's, country villages, gently sloping
hills, fertile lands and, occasionally, urban clutter are the norms. The
English countryside figures forth the life of moderate expectations that
Charlotte Brontë originally sought to represent in *The Professor*, where
an industrial town and a foreign city intimated more than was narrated.
In a world whose reality is defined—as we have seen it in Trollope—
according to inherited traditions of social order, no "inhuman" landscape can occupy much space. Victorian realism's attempts to exclude
extremes extend not only to heroism, psychic intensity, or violent behavior, but to geography as well. When the monstrous is "translated,"
the gothic castle is remodeled or altogether displaced by the cottage or
the modernized estate. The stage of dramatic confrontation is not some
Alpine waste but the club in London, or the drawing room.

Romanticized and yet threateningly divorced from divine meaning
and order, only when it has been domesticated can Nature in its massive energies be even partly trusted, although it can be endlessly sentimentalized and admired.[1] Outside the drawing room or the cultivated
fields or the gardens, mystery lurks dangerously. Even in them, there
may be sudden threats or storms. The setting for ideal aspirations remains, as it was in *Frankenstein*, outside the geography of ordinary
England (or an aberration within it). It is, for example, falsely con-

ventionalized in Pendennis's pastoral affair with Blanche Amory, ominously secluded in Maggie Tulliver's meetings with Philip Wakem in the Red Deeps, spuriously inspiring for Nevil Beauchamp alone for the first time in Venice with Renee: "Such happiness belonged to the avenue of wishes leading to golden mists beyond imagination and seemed, coming to him suddenly, miraculous."[2]

The realist's landscape, like the community and traditions it embodies, and like the particularizing strategies of realism itself, affirms what may be the only intelligible reality—the humanly ordered world. It is intelligible because it has human scope, implies no absolute but only mixed conditions, bringing together nature's mysterious energies and the human capacity for using and ordering those energies, in farms, and gardens, and parks. The equivalent of unrestrained nature is the Frankensteinian idealist, whose ambition points beyond the compromises of the social order tcward illimitable social or personal satisfactions. The problem with the idealists is that, like great mountains or vast seas, they release energies too large to be controlled and thus threaten to destroy, as Frankenstein's monster destroys, all human relations and creations. Like the powers behind Carlyle's French Revolution, seeking to right the terrible injustices of the French monarchy, the idealists, even in their purest rational ideas of order, become irrational forces of nature. Seeking to impose an idea on the multifariousness of history and experience, they lose control of self and of others. The mountain stream accelerating from its source works as a metaphor here. The forces rush like a river over the falls and flood violently the gardens and the cultivated peace of the valley. For admission to the realist novel, the monstrous energies must be damned. Disenchantment is the restraint of the ideal, the idea seen from the perspective of a complicating experience.

Of course, when the monstrous is translated it can manifest itself in the most ordinary places; no realist can quite ignore it. The strategies of disenchantment place the dream in the clear light of the sun, as George Eliot regularly does with her protagonists. But people with "dull grey eyes" are capable of remarkable depths of feeling, of dangerous actions, and of martyrlike selflessness, and novels need to find appropriate space for such realities unassimilable to the conventions of realism. Truthfulness required not only the diminution of great expectations, but the admission of violence and mystery beyond realistic explanation. Thus Victorian novels tend to establish geographical pockets of excess, "natural" or "foreign" places in which community is no longer implicit. The city frequently becomes such an alien place, with energies too large to be contained within inherited conventions. The view from Todgers propels us beyond the quotidian and ordinary, and it gives us an exotic landscape. The foreignness of the city is felt even in so firmly realistic a novel as Mrs. Gaskell's *North and South,* and obviously in its demonic counterpart, *Hard Times.* At least as often, the place of excess is literally a foreign country. When Dickens seeks a place for the young Martin Chuzzlewit's radical moral conversion, he sends Martin into the swamps of the American South. From America, too, comes Mrs. Hurdle, the husband-slayer, in Trollope's *The Way We Live Now.* France is where Edith Dombey and Carker have their violent assignation. Italy is where Daniel Deronda meets his mother, and where Grandcourt drowns. George Osborne is killed on the battlefields of Waterloo. Monsieur Paul Emanuel goes to the West Indies and is drowned in a storm on the way back.

That drowning, like Beauchamp's, like Maggie Tulliver's, like Steerforth's, like Grandcourt's, suggests another "place" in the realist landscape for the monstrous possibilities that society and the English countryside would seem to exclude. On the one hand, there is the sea. On the other, there are the mountains. The notorious prominence of the sea and drownings in Victorian literature merely emphasizes the inescapability of the extremes realism tries to deny. Water, surely, is a more accessible and consequently a more natural "place" in and around the English landscape. But both water and mountains carry with them the suggestion of primal realities beyond the reach of social restraint. Life begins, as it does metaphorically and literally in *Frankenstein,* in the mountains, from "forgotten sources." Life ends, whispering in Paul Dombey's ears, in the sea. Yet out of the sea comes resurrection—as with Walter Gay or Romola. And David Copperfield goes to the Alps to recover from his deadly fever. It is, in any case, difficult for Victorian realism to follow its characters to these mythic reaches.

In what follows, my focus will be on mountains, or, at least, on heights, as they are imagined to be part of the landscape of the real. They may be taken as representative of all those spaces suggestive of extremity in that landscape. The mythic intensity (or at least the mythic resonances) of their appearances suggests something of the conventionality required of writers as they aspired to truths that seemed beyond the reach of language. Realism, in its quest for plausibility, had developed a language for the ordinary. Beyond the ordinary it was driven to the shaping conventions of myth, and seemed at times absurdly melodramatic or falsely heightened (one thinks of Dickens's frequent lapses into blank verse in his early novels). Mountains, after all, were where the Tablets were received, where the Ark came to rest, where the Sermon was delivered, where Christ was crucified. On mountains, too, the muses dwelled. To mountains a whole culture looked for its fullest conception of the sublime, where the realist's particularity became mere intrusion and the poet's symbolic and metaphoric instincts were required. Moreover, Victorian mountains were fortunate in having a spokesman in John Ruskin, whose passion for them contrasts interestingly with the feelings of the novelists themselves. Ruskin's struggle to accommodate them to his typical realist's engagement with things human suggests something not only of the novelists' ambivalence about idealism and ambition, but of the Victorian novel's continuity with traditions of Romantic literature. In a way, mountains are a substitute for the missing God, and in novels they often become the imagined secular counterpart of the religious vision. In Alpine landscape, Victorian novels are driven outside of themselves and their own conventions; in those landscapes they are confronted with energies too powerful for the moderation Charlotte Brontë wanted to believe was the human norm, too vast to find articulation in the literal and accessible and matter-of-fact language whose transparency apparently puts us in touch with the realist's world of things.

II

When Trollope wants to suggest a reckless flouting of the social rules and an ambition for personal freedom, he sends his protagonists on vacation into the Alps, where Kate Vavasor and later Glencora Palliser imagine themselves as swimming in the rushing currents of the mountain river. It is a dream, of course, that neither can fulfill. In an interesting discussion of "places" in Trollope's novels, Juliet McMaster notes that "where water flows swiftly passions run high, and great changes are contemplated."[3] The swiftness of water and the "heights" of passion have their sources in quite literal heights. But one does not, in Victorian novels, need mountains; lesser heights will do. Above the stolid unimpassioned natures of the community, Lucy Snowe confronts the mysterious "nun" in the attic of the pensionnat; in the attic Bertha Mason haunts *Jane Eyre*. Literal heights easily become metaphorical.

Yet on the whole, Victorian fiction breathes only at low altitudes. Air is thin among the huge and terrifying reaches of Shelley's Mont Blanc, whose river violently establishes the mysterious metaphors that underlie the mundane geography of realism. Even Wordsworth's Snowden suggests a supernatural inspiration, a more than human awe. On Mont Blanc, ice forms—"a city of death," or "a flood of ruin." It rushes destructively down, but becomes in the vale a "majestic River, the breath and blood of distant lands." The mysterious energy of death creates life and flows at last back into the ocean.[4] Wordsworth believed that the mind and nature could marry, even at the heights. Victorian romantics—novelists in the realist tradition—were interested in less lonely, more literal marriages.

In novels, the heights are not for marriage, but for dreams or disasters. They are where Frankenstein meets his monster and hears its narrative. In Scott's highlands, outlaws rebel and conspire, their romantic excesses ultimately to be destroyed by the civilization of the lowlands. Even on Box Hill, the highest and most "natural" point in *Emma,* the laws of civilization are violated as Emma cruelly insults Miss Bates. The world of nature, absurdly romanticized by Mrs. Elton, is antisocial. The heights, as the extreme expression of nature, are where society is not. From the beginning of "Mont Blanc" to the end of D. H. Lawrence's *Women in Love,* the heights are wild and seductive and incompatible with ordinary life. In their cold and brilliant whiteness, they become the landscape of the wild living intellect, strangely abstract and passionate. They invite us to the ideal unstained world of spirit that makes the mixed condition of the bourgeois world below seem petty and contemptible; yet the cold passion of the hills is outside the range of ordinary human feeling.

Thus, the typical landscapes of Victorian fiction are places like Loamshire or Hayslope, the river Floss, Dingley Dell, suburban London (or the city itself), Barsetshire, the Belgian lowlands. Notoriously, the pictorial analogue most frequently implied by the Victorians is not the sublime of Claude, Poussin, or even Turner, but Dutch realism: landscapes barely varied by the slightest rise, flatlands and cows and peasants and northern skies whose sun throws its sharpest lights indoors, on the fustian colors of work and domesticity.

Ruskin, of course, was not a great admirer of the Dutch school, and he was correspondingly unsympathetic to the best fiction written in his lifetime—even when it was written in what the authors might well have felt was a Ruskinian spirit. *The Mill on the Floss,* that splendid Wordsworthian and Ruskinian venture, he called a "striking instance" of the study of "cutaneous disease," the "blotches, burrs and pimples" of trivial people. *Bleak House,* almost a dramatization of many of Ruskin's views about organic connections and moral responsibility, was taken by him as a symptom of the disease it is fighting.[5] But the judgment makes sense. Ruskin's love of Turner and mountains implies an aspiration to the ideal of purity and nobility that is incompatible with the realist's world, where good and bad, noble and ignoble, are hopelessly mixed. A topographical translation of George Eliot's program for fiction would be that the novel must come down from the mountains into the vale of tears, the "valley of humiliation." In the name of truth and realism, she and Ruskin moved in opposite directions: *because* this is the valley of humiliation, Ruskin climbed the Alps.

But the geography is more complicated. There are valleys in Ruskin, some mountains, or hills, in George Eliot. The river cannot flow in the valley if it has not come down from the hills. And the great mythic seat of innocence is the garden, not the craggy mountain. Ruskin knew this and struggled through two volumes of *Modern Painters* to prove that the ostensibly amoral and nonsocial implications of mountain landscape are superseded by an ultimate morality. The argument is complex, idiosyncratic, moving, and yet importantly symptomatic of the way the novelists themselves had to struggle both with their own romantic passion for the ideal and with the disappearance of Whately's kind of metaphysical sanction of nature and experience. The novel could not acquiesce in Ruskin's solution: it needed not only to end with the social, but to begin with it.

If writers like Trollope seem instinctively comfortable in worlds of blotches, pimples, and cutaneous diseases, the passion for the ideal remains alive among the compromising realists. We can see it in Thackeray's nostalgia, in the consistency with which Trollope views his characters from the perspective of the ideal of the gentleman, in the repressed passion of Charlotte Brontë's heroines, in the aspirations of George Eliot's. I have all along been suggesting that monstrous energies are active in Victorian fiction, akin I think to the powerful Turnerian landscapes that so enraptured Ruskin, struggling to be released from contingency, compromise, and the social order. Ruskin points out that mountains are a relatively new thing in art, and that every Homeric landscape "intended to be beautiful, is composed of a fountain, a meadow, and a shady grove."[6] Rocks and crags are dangerous and ugly. Ironically, the cultivated landscapes of the very unclassical Victorian novel tend to point back to the classical tradition in which happiness is possible only within bounded human landscapes: salvation for heroes and heroines must return them to fields, farms, towns, the hearth; it comes most often in such places or, with Lizzie Hexam, beside rivers that intimate the possibilities of both life and death. "Salvation" is itself too radical a word for the moral recuperation of Victorian protagonists. But when transformation comes, it does intimate something beyond the narrative explanatory powers of realism. It has something of the quality of dream, as in Pen's recuperation from his fever, or Lucy Snowe's, or Pip's, or Eugene Wrayburn's. The landscape of such returns has the quality of dream and is accompanied, as for Oliver Twist in the Maylies' garden, by a passivity not much different from death.

Analogously, as happiness in novels is often without aesthetic energy or interest, it is often true that rocks and crags are imagined with enthusiasm. Indeed, there is a universal Victorian tendency to find them seductive. Mrs. Greenow of *Can You Forgive Her?* wants her "rocks and mountains" once she is assured of "her bread and cheese." But the dualism of attitude is often more serious than this. Empedocles' advice to Pausanius is almost a novelist's: insisting on social responsibility, self-denial, compromise, the importance of work in the community below. But Empedocles does not take the advice. Nor do Cathy and Heathcliff when Nelly Dean urges it. The two examples are indicative of the normal stance of realism, for there, unrestrained admiration of wild nature is an invitation to suicide.

For the true novelist, the world of mountains is judged against the standards of the human community below. The value of the landscape is determined by how conducive it is to life. Prostration before sublimity is, simply, a mistake—an irresponsible tourism. It is the equivalent of the dogmatism Thackeray despised, reckless of the needs of most of the human community. In Dickens, passionate religion is almost always a sham. Similarly, in his reports on his travels in Italy, Dickens does have some conventional praise of mountain landscape, but he gives us much more in this vein: "Looking out . . . upon the marble mountains, all red and glowing in the decline of day, but stern and solemn to the last, I thought, my God! how many quarries of human hearts and souls, capable of far more beautiful results, are left shut-up and mouldering away: while pleasure-travellers through life avert their faces, as they pass, and shudder at the gloom and ruggedness that conceal them."[7] One needs not so much a new way of seeing as a railroad to transport the marble from the quarries, and compassion. Almost anticipating Ruskin's chapter "Mountain Gloom," he notes that "much of the romance of the beautiful towns and villages on this beautiful road [in the hills from San Remo to Genoa], disappears when they are entered, for many of them are very miserable."[8]

The novelist could be neither view-hunter nor tourist nor, indeed, mystic. Dickens's resistance to the sublime and the nonhuman ("My God" is merely an exclamation, and "quarries" are human hearts) suggests something of the difficulty Ruskin had in convincing himself and his audience that the primacy of landscape painting was not merely an aesthetic but a moral truth. No doubt Ruskin felt its primacy, but as he became more aware of human suffering, especially after the success of *Modern Painters I*,[9] he increasingly felt the urgency of Dickens's kind of moral directness. Like a good Victorian he pursued "Truth," and rejected the picturesque as a touristic falsification of nature. But the new truth he found, of the innocent eye, still seems a long way off from the truth of the pain and separation of the mountain people themselves.

The Victorian romantics offer us at least two possible ways of dealing with separation. One—Wordsworth and Ruskin's—is especially dangerous and risks an ultimate separation. This is the attempt to see nature as a healthy antidote to the corruption of community, as an essentially divine expression of a more than human power in harmony with the human. As we have seen, such a nature makes realistic fidelity, of the kind Whately saw in Austen, safe and enspiriting. Despite tooth and claw and the dirty streets of Alpine villages, nature is kind. This attempt reaches "higher" than the other and in forcing a wedding between mind and nature risks the separation of mind from itself, sometimes called science, sometimes schizophrenia. The other way, we might characterize as George Eliot's (although it is akin to the whole method of the realistic novel): the explicit rejection of divinity and of the possibility of community among mountains. The "other" is not to be an object for whom we care as much as for people, but the people themselves, who, by virtue of their place in family and society, are bound each to each. The focus must be on the ordinary, the mixed, the drab lowlands, at whatever cost in beauty. The wedding that finally takes place comes by the effort not to *see* the other, but to feel what the other feels.

In fact, these two ways of struggling against separation mix. So George Eliot thinks of her work as Wordsworthian and praises Ruskin for teaching the great lesson of realism. Ruskin, for his part, could admire the Pre-Raphaelites almost as much as he could the great landscape painters and spoke as earnestly in support of the detailed representation of the quotidian in their painting as George Eliot might have wished. The landscape painter must begin by lying on the ground and learning to draw a blade of grass accurately. Although Ruskin does instinctively follow the way of transcendence, George Eliot the way of accommodation, they both sought some embodiment of the ideal in the real as Thackeray and Trollope, on the whole, did not.

To the end of *Modern Painters*, Ruskin was unresolved in attempting to reconcile his aspiration to the beautiful and the ideal and his very Victorian (almost novelistic) sense of his responsibility both to the audience and to the banal and quotidian and manifestly corrupted world. In the last pages, he speaks of a "far deeper reverence for Turner's art than I felt when this task of his defence was undertaken" almost twenty years before. But, he says in *Modern Painters*, "I am more in doubt respecting the real use to mankind of that, or any other transcendent art" (ch. 5, p. 441). "Peace," the title of the last chapter of the original edition, is the fading dream. One of the last images of the book is of a mountain, but high on it "full descried, sits throned the tempter, with his old promise—the kingdoms of this world, and glory of them" (ch. 5, p. 460). To defy the devil it was necessary to come down from the mountain. The struggle within Ruskin himself, labor without peace, continued to the end. Is it the devil or God up there? Love of the beautiful, passion for the ideal seem forever at odds with love of people with dull grey eyes and of a community thoroughly compromised.

That responsibility is the primary surface concern of the realists, for whom the figure on the mountain, ambiguously beautiful, is deadly and demonic even in its possible purity. His seductiveness, and the novelists' repressed Alpine longings, quietly energize the very literature which keeps its back to the mountains; and Ruskin's idealism of the heights gives distinctive shape to the realism of the valleys.

III

The simplest explanation for the absence of the sublime in English fiction is the absence of the sublime in English landscape. But the mind is its own place, and the landscape of fiction, as I have been trying to suggest, is no literal transcription of the world as the novelists could see it. Mimetic language is always compromised by its own nature, and Victorian realism was no less so. Northrop Frye has argued that "the total form of art, so to speak, is a world whose content is nature but whose form is human; hence when it 'imitates' nature it assimilates nature to human forms."[10] Much of the energy of Victorian fiction was consciously directed by translating the extreme and potentially monstrous energies of a previously religious and now Romantic tradition so that the lowlands would be endowed with feelings, however restrained, that Ruskin, for example, had projected on the Alps.

In terms of the mountain-valley metaphor, George Eliot's famous excursus in chapter 17 of *Adam Bede* can be read like this: most people live in the lowlands, in "the dusty streets and the common green fields," and the attempt to portray only the heights, the world of "cloud-borne angels," unfits us for the experience of the lowlands; we are left with visions suited only to "a world of extremes." Ironically, however, the landscape of the lowlands must, if it is to evoke the reverence of the mountains, contain those larger energies associated with mountain landscape. The landscape and the human form coincide. "Yes!" George Eliot says, "thank God; human feeling is like the mighty rivers that bless the earth: it does not wait for beauty—it flows with resistless force and brings beauty with it."[11] Shelley's Arve is slightly domesticated and tamed, but it is still resistless.

Here is yet another variation on the problem of separation. In the argument it is understood that the experience of extremes is a cause of human separation—"Close thy Byron; open thy Goethe." But connection is possible only through extreme energy, and the power of the mountains is brought down into the landscape of connection: rivers, like human feeling, bring people together (yet they also bring some of the dangers of the mountains into the valley). Although rivers contain energy from "forgotten sources" they also seem, running broadly and quietly, a part of the human and quotidian rather than the sublime.

In another famous passage, from the chapter "A Variation of Protestantism Unknown to Bossuet" in *The Mill on the Floss*, George Eliot invokes two contrasting un-English landscapes—one on the Rhine, "with its green and rocky steeps," the other on the Rhone, with its dreary "ruined villages" which "in their best days were but the sign of a sordid life."[12] The Rhine landscape, where castles harmonize with the mountainsides, suggests a race "who had inherited from their mighty parent a sublime instinct of form. And that was a day of romance!" For a moment sounding like Wordsworth wishing he were a pagan suckled on a creed outworn, George Eliot looks at the Rhine and thinks of the enthusiasms implicit in the structures and the hills. The Rhine castles "thrill me with a sense of poetry; they belong to the grand historic life of humanity, and raise up for me visions of an epoch" (p. 238). But the Rhone's is like the life of her own Floss. The vision is so oppressive that "even sorrow hardly suffices to lift above the level of the tragi-comic" (p. 238). The dullness and unimaginativeness of her characters are stifling "for want of an outlet toward something beautiful, great, or noble" (p. 238). The people here are "out of keeping with the earth on which they live—with this rich plain where the great river flows for ever onward and links the small pulse of the old English town with the beating of the world's mighty heart." Here is a complete separation, and here also we can see how the energy of mountains has been transferred to the plains in the language, not in the life described. The mighty flood embodies a more than human energy (as the conclusion of the novel makes clear), and embodies, too, that mystery that Ruskin found in mountains.

But even the new force of idealization entails the metaphor of high and low (as in Maggie and Tom's death it entails the ambivalence about extremes). If the metaphor of the flood focuses on flowing to the larger sea and is appropriate because rivers do end division, still, a paragraph later, George Eliot urges us to put up with the "oppressive narrowness" of this lowland life, to "feel it," in order that we may understand how it acts "on young natures in many generations, that in the onward tendency of human things have risen above the mental level of the generation before them" (p. 239).

The way George Eliot's novelistic imagination overlaps with and differs from Ruskin's "extreme" imagination can be illustrated clearly through the way they use a similar image—the vision of the roadside cross. In volume 4 of *Modern Painters*, Ruskin sees the cross in a context of mountain splendor:

Far up the glen, as we pause beside the cross, the sky is seen through the openings in the pines, thin with excess of light; and in its clear, consuming flame of white space, the summits of the rocky mountains are gathered into solemn crowns and circlets, all flushed in that strange, faint silence of possession by the sunshine which has in it so deep a melancholy; full of power, yet as frail as shadows; lifeless, like the walls of a sepulchre, yet beautiful in tender fall of crimson folds, like the veil of some sea spirit, that lives and dies as the foam flashes; fixed on a perpetual throne, stern against all strength, lifted above all sorrow, and yet effaced and melted utterly in the air by that last sunbeam that crosses to them from between the two golden clouds. [P. 387]

It is a Turneresque painting, the mountains blurring in an excess of light into the air and sun, and it is a Ruskinian reading of Turner. The mountains are lifted above all sorrow, but the awesome (and religious) crowns and circlets participate in a deep and contradictory melancholy. In those high reaches the cross is belied by the glory of its sublime setting; its sadness is not sublime. Yet everything in that Turneresque wash of color, movement, transience, bespeaks a deep Ruskinian sadness for which the "cross of roughhewn pine, iron-bound to its parapet," is an alien and inadequate symbol.

In *Adam Bede*, when Hetty sets off on her "journey," it is a beautiful day:

What a glad world this looks like, as one drives or rides along the valleys and over the hills! I have often thought so when, in foreign countries, where the fields and woods have looked to me just like our English Loamshire—the rich land tilled with just as much care, the woods rolling down the gentle slopes to the green meadows—I have come on something that has reminded me that I am not in Loamshire: an image of a great agony—the agony of the Cross. It has stood perhaps by the clustering apple-blossoms, or in the broad sunshine by the cornfield, or at a turning by the wood where a clear brook was gurgling below; and sure, if there came a traveler to this world who knew nothing of the story of man's life upon it, this image of agony would seem strangely out of place in the midst of this joyous nature. He would not know that hidden behind the apple-blossoms, or among the golden corn, or under the shrouding boughs of the wood, there might be a human heart beating heavily with anguish. . . . No wonder man's religion has much sorrow in it: no wonder he needs a Suffering God. [Ch. 35, p. 371]

For Ruskin, the deep sadness of human life is in the landscape itself; for George Eliot, it is hidden by the landscape. Loamshire contains the lessons of Ruskin's Alps, but the mystery is not projected into the scene. Consequently, Ruskin's prose is marvelously precise, evocative, and sensitive in the notation of the physical scene while George Eliot gives us a wholly conventionalized landscape in which brooks gurgle and apple blossoms cluster and corn is golden. The particularity of her prose is saved for human life. Strangely, the only stable thing in Ruskin's shimmering landscape is the rough outline of the cross, and it is ugly—a terrible, crude expression of Ruskin's discovery of the presence of evil in nature. But for George Eliot, the quality of the visual cross is not important: it serves as the true expression of what she cannot see in nature itself. The extremes of experience are shifted from the Alps to the heart; *there* is the peril of the sublime, and there its idealization.

The programmatic object of this new sublime is accommodation to the actual and a relation to life that is not touristic. The problem is, as Thackeray, Trollope, George Eliot, and Hardy all knew, that the actual is harsh and unaccommodating, that accommodation sometimes means little more than weakness or insipidity, often little less than self-annihilation. The novelists' instinctive sympathy with the rebel is reflected in the landscape, in Ruskin's passions for mountains, in George Eliot's preference of the Rhine to the Rhone, in Thackeray's attraction to Becky Sharp or to Beatrix. In the novel, nevertheless, rebellion and ambition continue to be seen with some more or less sympathetic irony—as with Pendennis, Pip, Phineas Finn, Emma Woodhouse. Even in the romantic fiction which most fully indulges the ambivalence— both in landscape and in narrative form—much depends on the realist's sense of the dangers of energies that lie outside the social norms. *Wuthering Heights* is one of the few Victorian novels that treat such energies not in strictly social terms, but as a force of nature. In a sense, that novel speaks what realism knows but has been trained not to tell. Heathcliff's energy is both enormously attractive and deadly, and it is contained, finally, only by its own natural exhaustion. He dwells at the austere yet beautiful Heights, where strangely obsessive and yet curiously asexual passions are set against the domesticity of Thrushcross Grange, below. Heathcliff is almost a Trollopian idealist—seeking purity in love and absolute justice, he turns, like the monster, into a blind destructive force. He is the threat disenchantment abolishes and the techniques of detailed registration of particulars disguise. The space Emily Brontë finds for him is on the heights, and its accommodation to the realist's "actual" comes only in a later generation with a tamer and more sexual sort of love.

The options in Victorian fiction are rarely so extreme. *Frankenstein* suggested both the sublimity and the deadliness of great heights and gave us correspondingly extremes of nobility and evil. *Wuthering Heights* juxtaposes high lands and low, the attractive and dangerous

energies of Heathcliff and the generous moderation (or insipidity) of
Edgar. But in most Victorian novels, the contrasts are subtler, the dangers less visible. And while it is probably true that most Victorian
novelists shared with their culture the tourist's pleasure in mountains
and particularly in Alpine scenery, as artists they instinctively felt the
impropriety of the Alpine extremes for their own landscapes. Leslie
Stephen, as a member of the Alpine Club, could celebrate the glories of
the Alps, but he understood how recent the sense of their beauty was in
the history of Western culture; he too saw them as places outside of
society, particularly attractive *because* they offer sanctuary from the ordinary, from the compromised. He quotes "Matthew Arnold's friend
Obermann" admiringly: "Là, l'homme . . . respire l'air sauvage loin des
émanations sociales; son être est à lui comme á l'univers."[13] And even
Dickens once contemplated retiring to the Alps despite his tough-
minded awareness of the sordidness of much life there. Yet with all this
by now almost conventional admiration, with all this touristic awe of
the sublime, Victorian novels remain more conspicuous for the absence
of true heights than for their presence. *Frankenstein* and *Wuthering
Heights,* though they partake of much that belongs in the realistic tradition and project in large much that is only quietly implicit in realistic
fiction, are after all aberrations—more romance than realism.

IV

Since, in keeping with the compromises realism entails, the landscape
of the real is consistently rather flat, or at best rolling, a topographical
survey of the Victorian novel would produce a large and unilluminating
catalogue. It is worth pausing, however, for a glance at a characteristically low and domesticated landscape in order to gather some sense of
the way such a landscape at once denies and imitates more absolute and
more frightening realities, and accommodates itself to the more subtle
shades, the less checkered patterns of the novelist's reality. A convenient place to look for such a landscape—although it is also the
landscape of George Eliot's midlands, of Hardy's Wessex, of Trollope's
Barsetshire—would be in the works of Elizabeth Gaskell, a writer who
stands with Trollope as one of Victorian realism's most consistent practitioners. In Gaskell, as in Trollope, there are moments of violence and
suggestions of extremes; but few writers stay more firmly within the
limits Charlotte Brontë advocated but could not herself accept.

In her short novel *Cousin Phillis,* Gaskell confines her narrative to a
sharply imagined place that has the virtue, for my purposes, of neatly
focusing the dominant landscapes of the Victorian realistic tradition.
Hope Farm seems to imply all the qualities that led early modern writers

to reject Victorian realism as prudish and sentimental. The very name contains a suggestion of allegory which might seem inconsistent with the most rigorous realistic techniques, but is in fact consistent with its practice. (Think of Trollope's Mrs. Proudie, or the Duke of Omnium, of George Eliot's Middlemarch and Lowick, of Thackeray's Newcomes or, for that matter, Pen; it is not by any means only Dickens who uses names in this way.) Mr. Holman (again allegorical, of course) is both farmer and minister, an apparently complete man of learning and of physical power. But what Gaskell is giving us here is something very precisely individualized while also typical. Hope Farm seems almost the ideal of the old English countryside, showing evidence of its history and of an earlier grandeur ("two great gates between pillars crowned with stone balls for a state entrance"),[14] but now entirely functional and unpretentious. "It's an old place," we learn early, "though Holman keeps it in good order" (p. 224).

All the action occurs at the farm, in the widely interspersed visits of the narrator, Paul Manning, and, in effect, very little happens, for the narrative is marked by the absence of finality. The farm is governed by the rhythms of the seasons, in a characteristic mid-nineteenth-century fashion; and with quietly mythic implications "there was a garden between the house and the shady, grassy lane" (p. 225). Almost everything is understated or deflected, and the expected romance between Paul and Cousin Phillis is dismissed very shortly, for Paul finds it uncomfortable to imagine a wife in a beautiful young woman "half a head taller" than he, who reads books "I had never heard of" and talks about them too, "as of far more interest than any mere personal subjects" (p. 244). One senses, of course, that something dangerous enters the garden and threatens the carefully cultivated paradise; but it is difficult to find a clear villain. It has as much to do with the inevitable rhythms of natural growth and change—which are assimilated to the growth and change going on in society as a whole—as with "plot" in any ordinary sense.

The critical scenes in the narrative are all imagined very carefully in the landscapes, which are conceived subtly as both highly cultivated and vulnerable to natural violence. Holdsworth, the railroad engineer Paul introduces into the family, is the alien element in the garden that finally disrupts its peace, and he is the subject of the only abrupt intrusion into the narrative's direct movement through time that Paul (or Gaskell) chooses to make. Before the crisis comes, Paul writes, "It is many years since I have seen thee, Edward Holdsworth, but thou wast a delightful fellow! Ay, and a good one too; though much sorrow was caused by thee" (p. 266). The effect, of course, is to disallow any absolute imagination of evil—Holdsworth is no snake in the garden—before we have a chance to feel his behavior as such. But the critical scene in which Holdsworth evokes Phillis's love has about it the ominousness of evil's inobtrusive entrance into the garden. Interestingly, although the landscape is low, it is at least a bit higher than its surroundings. Paul goes to find his friends

> out on to a broad upland common, full of red sand-banks, and sweeps and hollows; bordered by dark firs, purple in the coming shadows, but near at hand all ablaze with flowering gorse, or, as we call it in the south, furze-bushes, which, seen against the belt of distant trees, appeared brilliantly golden. On this heath, a little way from the field-gate, I saw the three. I counted their heads, joined together in an eager group over Holdsworth's theodolite. [P. 269]

The scene is ominously pretty, quietly suggestive of disruption, and that disruption comes physically in a violent electric storm. Of course, Holdsworth himself is the disruption, and in several ways. First, we have already learned that there is something "foreign" about him. "He cuts his hair in a foreign fashion," Paul had told Phillis earlier, and she had answered with, "I like an Englishman to look like an Englishman" (p. 260). But the foreignness of Holdsworth has not merely to do with Italian haircuts. He brings the machine to the garden for he is learned both in languages and in the technology of the railways. Mr. Holman suggests that "there is a want of seriousness in his talk at times," but, Holman goes on to say, "it is like dram-drinking. I listen to him till I forget my duties, and am carried off my feet. Last Sabbath evening he led us away into talk on profane subjects ill befitting the day" (p. 266). Not accidentally, Holdsworth's first act with Phillis is to help her translate Dante's *Inferno*! The obviously symbolic collocation of facts is so muted in the text that it is easy to read over them and miss it, and in a way it is important that one do so. Holdsworth is not, we are early warned, a devil, but a "delightful fellow." The scene in the heath, in any case, wonderfully and subtly enacts the complexities and shadings Gaskell seeks.

While Holdsworth satisfies Holman's thirst for knowledge, they all fail to notice the upcoming storm—the rain came "sooner than they had looked for." Holman, who keeps his lands "in order" and is learning from Holdsworth how to "survey" it, opens himself to the disorder and violence of nature itself when it is not comfortably regulated in relation to home and garden. And it is here, after Phillis rushes to rescue Holdsworth's "apparatus," that we are allowed to see Phillis's own potentiality for sexual energy. "She came running back, her long lovely hair floating and dripping, her eyes glad and bright, and her colour freshened to a glow of health by the exercise and the rain." Holdsworth then, in a spirit of badinage that Phillis does not quite understand, calls her "Willful" and "Unchristian" (p. 270). The misunderstanding provokes Holdsworth to say "something gravely" to her, "and in too low a tone for me to hear." The snake has entered the Holmans' garden, and it has done so in an exposed geography, where forces beyond the control of cultivation are released. At the same time, it is important to note that the release of those forces is very much Holman's responsibility, intoxicated as he is with knowledge. It is equally important to see that on this only slightly raised elevation Holman's failure is barely evil at all. Through most of the novel, knowledge is not sinful; and, indeed, until the end a rigorously antiintellectual and puritanical reading is disallowed in the cold comfortings of Brother Hodgson and Robinson. They ask Holman, with a subtle significance for the text, whether "this world's learning has not puffed you up to vain conceit and neglect of the things of God" (p. 313). Holman's answer is, I think, decisive, and central to our experience of realism and of the natural landscape. "I hold with Christ that afflictions are not sent by God in wrath as penalties for sin" (p. 313).

The other crucial scene is also set deliberately out-of-doors where nature can do its worst; once again, however, it is not a place of wilderness and desolation but a great stack of wood in the orchard. There Phillis sits on a log in the snow on a "bitter cold day," and there Paul hears her "making a low moan, like an animal in pain, or perhaps more like the sobbing of the wind" (p. 283). Her pain and her direct assimilation to wild nature are the result of Holdsworth's departure. Significantly for our sense of realism's landscape, he has gone to foreign places—to Canada—there to help build a railway, that powerful emblem of the new knowledge and the new culture. Paul, to relieve Phillis's pain, then tells her that Holdsworth, before his departure, had said that he loved Phillis and wished to marry her. Again, the new knowledge has ambiguous value. It suddenly rescues Phillis from the anguish of her simple animality, allows her to resist the deadly cold and to return to the warmth of the hearth. Yet it also implicates the "innocent" narrator, for when Holdsworth, inevitably in that foreign place, falls in love with another Lucy (Paul had noted how Phillis reminded him of Wordsworth's poem) and marries her, the effect on Phillis is even more deadly. It finally saps her of all energy. The literal cold returns as a spiritual cold.

But what is perhaps most striking about Cousin Phillis is that its obvious mythic structure, which gives it a stunningly un-Trollopian shapeliness and coherence, finally undercuts itself. The violence of the weather that threatens with each critical access of knowledge in the novel's rarely exposed geography is ultimately understood to be both significant and random. Holman's humane faith that afflictions are not sent as penalties disorders the universe which was, apparently, so firmly and mythically ordered by the novel's garden, by Dante's Inferno, by Holman's and Phillis's acquiescence in Holdsworth's seductive attractiveness. In its quiet way the novel abstains from moral judgment—of Holdsworth, or Holman, or Paul, or Phillis. What happens is felt to be quite natural and unforced despite Gaskell's wonderful shaping art. At the same time, in the storm on the heath, in the cold at the woodpile, in the depths of Canada, there are energies beyond the control of either characters or author. When Phillis recovers at the end, we are reminded that in the ordinary world tragedy is never absolute; and we understand that she does so by force of will. Everyone has done for her what is possible. The servent, Betty, tells her: "Now Phillis! ... we ha' done a' we can for you, and th' doctors has done a' they can for you, and I think the Lord has done a' He can for you, and more than you deserve too, if you don't do something for yourself." Finally, there is nothing but individual human will in a world where the natural, however securely domesticated, moves inevitably to disruption. When Phillis concludes by asking for a "change of scene," we know that the mythic expulsion from the garden is completed. "Only for a short time," she says, "Then—we will go back to the peace of the old days. I know we shall; I can, and I will!" (p. 317).

The will is all that can do it; but it cannot do it. Paradise, surely, will not be regained. Moreover, as we examine the energies of nature quietly manifest in the book, and as we consider how implicated in them are the very figures whose force of will has brought order to the countryside, we recognize that it was no paradise in the first place—attractive though it may have been. The powerful father is less competent than the ignorant mother, and his interests are absolutely different. He had tried artificially to keep the family knit together—almost as the Frankenstein family did in its domestic haven in Geneva. The inevitable intrusion finds him unprepared. Only in Gaskell's quietly confident muting of the extremes does she avert the full implications of Mary Shelley's romance. Holdsworth, after all, is a "delightful fellow," and Phillis, as Thackeray and Trollope both would have known, does not die of a broken heart. The monster is in the garden, but Gaskell's realism dulls his ferocity sufficiently to make a life of quiet, wary compromise possible.

Gaskell, in demythifying the landscape and her narrative, implies that experience is an endless and disenchanting process, but avoids dissolution into sheer multiplicity. She stays within one sharply delimited narrative, and contains the monstrous energies figured by wilder landscapes. The effect is achieved in part by the continuities among the personal, social, and natural worlds; the precisely located place in which the action evolves implies the nature of the characters who live there, of the culture they represent (as opposed to that of the railroad people who visit them), and of the natural world that encroaches on its borders. But that place is clearly not the Alps. Its gentler outlines metaphorically imply a quiet Wordsworthian world of feeling. If the very prettiness implicitly hides the symbol of suffering that George Eliot places in the landscape of *Adam Bede*, we are not allowed to see the symbol. It is a sad domestic story, not a romantic tragedy.

The heights in *Cousin Phillis* turn out to be no more than an upland heath. And such is the landscape of most realist Victorian novels that imagine life more as a natural process than as mythic or tragic. In Hardy's first published novel, *Under the Greenwood Tree*, subtitled significantly *A Rural Painting of the Dutch School*, the movement of the seasons is also central to the narrative progress. And in this early work, before Hardy moves confidently through his landscape into narratives that deliberately confront the monstrous nonhumanity of the universe in ironic and carefully structured plots, the landscape has the muted quality we have seen in Gaskell. The highest point in the novel is "a ridge which rose keenly against the western sky." And on it, just as Dick Dewy is about to recognize the frivolity of Fancy Day, and free himself of her, "was now visible an irregular outline, which at first he conceived to be a bush."[15] It is, of course, Fancy, and her presence banishes all of Dick's doubts and settles his fate. Here, too, as in *Cousin Phillis*, there is little plot: the focus is realism's on character in context. The characters move with the rhythms of nature itself, as Fancy is mistaken for a bush, and the Mellstock choir goes the way of the peace of Hope Farm. Like *Cousin Phillis*, the novel reveals a nature potentially dangerous, yet on the whole not unkind.

In Hardy, the latent violence of experience will later become central, but in this more characteristically realist Victorian novel, there is only one moment when the terror emerges blatantly. It is an odd intrusion into the comic narrative, and it seems to have no function but as a premonition of the Hardy we know best. When Dick first goes to ask Fancy's father for permission to marry her, the early silence and stillness between them "was disturbed only by some small bird that was being killed by an owl in the adjoining copse, whose cry passed into the silence without mingling with it" (p. 183). The landscape is not at all mountainous. Fancy's father stands at the threshold "looking out at the pale mist creeping up from the gloom of the valley" (p. 183). The life of

Under the Greenwood Tree is primarily in the valley, and what is potentially tragic and latent with violence becomes merely an ironic comedy.
The tradition of realism is sustained, but only briefly.

V

But just as Hardy became the chronicler of "chequered" lives, so,
among the earlier Victorians, there were novelists who instinctively
imagined reality as more violent and extreme than we find it in *Under
the Greenwood Tree,* or in Gaskell or Trollope or Thackeray, and who,
unlike them, risked the ideal.

Dickens, of them all, is the most reckless with passions, and they
inhere for him in the minutiae of the most trivial experience, of a sort
that in the hands of a Thackeray or Trollope would work as an ironic
commentary on the passions. Though he needs no metaphorical
mountains or even rivers, he has quite a few, and he will often use
nature at its wildest (as, for instance, in the death of Steerforth) to act
out passions not legitimate within society. No Victorian novelist contrasts domesticity and personal separation so insistently; none cele-
brates the hearth with such exuberance or chastises ambition and separation so aggressively. It is therefore appropriate to conclude by looking at his most striking use of Alpine scenery. It appears in *Little Dorrit*
and begins where Ruskin, in the same year, was ending volume 4 of
Modern Painters, in "Mountain Gloom." Of course, Dickens did not
need Ruskin's book and probably did not even read volume 4 of *Modern
Painters.* [16] But the closeness of their visions in these two works suggests
why Ruskin had, at least metaphorically, to give up mountains, and
why the novelists could not have much to do with them.

The shock in volume 4 comes as Ruskin contrasts the expectation of
"the traveller on his happy journey" with what he actually will find:

> Here it may well seem to him, if there be sometimes hardship,
> there must be at least innocence and peace, and fellowship of the
> human soul with nature. It is not so. The wild goats that leap along
> these rocks have as much passion of joy in all that fair work of God
> as the men that toil among them. Perhaps more. Enter the street of
> one of those villages, and you will find it foul with that gloomy
> foulness that is suffered only by torpor, or by anguish of soul.
> Here, it is torpor—not absolute suffering—not starvation or dis-
> ease, but darkness of calm enduring; the spring known only as the
> time of the scythe, and the autumn as the time of the sickle, and the
> sun only as a warmth, the wind as a chill, and the mountains as a
> danger. They do not understand so much as the name of beauty, or
> of knowledge. [P. 388]

It is nature despiritualized, de-Ruskinized, hiding, as for George Eliot, human misery. The hearth triumphs over the sublime as Ruskin's theories of the necessity of mountains even for important artistic creation are challenged. The very houses of the Savoyards are ugly.

> No contrast can be more painful than that between the dwelling of any well-conducted English cottager, and that of the equally honest Savoyard. The one, set in the midst of its dull flat fields and uninteresting hedgerows, shows in itself the love of brightness and beauty . . . and happiness in the simple course and simple possessions of daily life. The other cottage, in the midst of an inconceivable, inexpressible beauty, set on some sloping bank of golden sward . . . is itself a dark and plague-like stain. . . . All testifies that to its inhabitant the world is labour and vanity; that for him neither flowers bloom, nor birds sing, nor fountains glisten; and that his soul hardly differs from the grey cloud that coils and dies upon his hills, except in having no fold of it touched by sunbeam. [PP. 389–90]

To compensate for the loss of the mountain spirit, Ruskin must look down to the humble English cottage—that staple of Victorian virtue and fiction.[17] For Ruskin here as for the realist novelists everywhere, the quotidian, the merely human, must fill up the space of the sublime. Ruskin's darkening vision takes notice of the way good and evil must exist together: "Where the beauty and wisdom of the Divine working are most manifested, there also are manifested most clearly the terror of God's wrath, and inevitableness of His power" (p. 416). The mountaineer, according to Ruskin, is being punished for placing his cross on the hillside, for his "Romanticism," and the metaphor Ruskin uses is directly to the point here: the mountaineer, "instead of raising his eyes to the hills, from whence comes his help, he does his idol sacrifice 'upon every high hill and under every green tree.'" The roughhewn cross among the glorious foam of sun, mountain, and sky bespeaks a false worship, attests to a genuine evil.

These and other extraordinary explanations of the Savoyards' failures help Ruskin swerve away, one final time, from the novelists' life in the lowlands. And "Mountain Glory" attests to the overwhelming power of mountains over Ruskin's imagination. Speaking now quite personally, with no scientific pretensions, he says that for him, mountains are "the beginning and end":

> If there can be *no* hope or association of this kind, and if I cannot deceive myself into fancying that perhaps at the next rise of the road there may be seen the film of a blue hill in the gleam of sky at the horizon, the landscape, however beautiful, produces in me even a

kind of sickness and pain; and the whole view from Richmond Hill
or Windsor Terrace—nay, the gardens of Alcinous, with their perpetual summer,—or of the Hesperides (if they were flat, and not
close to Atlas), golden apples and all—I would give away in an
instant, for one mossy granite stone a foot broad, and two leaves of
lady-fern. [PP. 428–29]

Not a novelist yet. And from there Ruskin proceeds to show that
mountains account for almost everything good, including Leonardo and
Dante. The gloom is, for a moment, left behind in "these pure white
hills, near to the heaven, and sources of all the good to the earth" (p.
466).

But as Ruskin sees man's love of natural scenery growing from an
attempt to escape from the city, so Dickens makes the Alps the place to
which William Dorrit escapes from his city prison. And as Ruskin
understands that the love of landscape is a sign of moral disease, so
Dickens shows William Dorrit carrying his moral disease with him into
the Alps. Unlike Ruskin, however, Dickens does not let us see the Alps
as a new kind of transcendence; rather, they are a bad dream, an unreality that makes a worse prison than the one below. The Alps do not
cure the disease; they make it worse. The Dorrit party climbs the
metaphorical mountain into an unreal world, the peaks silently receding, like romantic dreams, "like spectres who were going to vanish."[18]
And when they get to the top, the red of the sunset "faded out of them
and left them coldly white," with the deadly chill of death and isolation
upon them; and night left the convent of the Great Saint Bernard "as if
that weather-beaten structure were another Ark, and floated on the
shadowy waves."

The sequence seems to confirm all of Ruskin's worst fears about his
beloved mountains: they are all gloom or, in their visionary aspects,
unreality. Dramatically and metaphorically it is right that the mountains
should be unreal for Little Dorrit. They become an image of separation
from society, a reminder of the littleness of people, "reduced to miniatures by the immensity around" (II, ch., 3, p. 504). The Dorrit party and
their acquaintances are, after all, quintessential tourists. They have no
part in the life of the place they visit, and they see, through the clouds
into which everything on the mountain seems to be dissolving (the mark
of modern landscape, according to Ruskin), only their own lives, their
own pasts. Only Amy is selfless enough to see at all, but what she sees *is*
the old reality, and she distrusts the tourist experience: "It seemed to her
as if those visions of mountains and picturesque country might melt
away at any moment, and the carriage, turning some abrupt corner,
bring up with a jolt at the old Marshalsea" (II, ch. 3, p. 516). Yet she sees
the mountain gloom clearly enough, and the Manichaean battle Ruskin

described, "misery and magnificence wrestling with each other upon every rood of ground in the prospect, no matter how widely diversified, and misery throwing magnificence with the strength of fate" (II, ch. 3, p. 517). Things are "lovely without, but frightful in their dirt and poverty within" (II, ch. 3, p. 518).

The devil who presides over Ruskin's last mountainscape in volume 4 of *Modern Painters* also presides over Amy's mountain. Not only does the Convent of Saint Bernard invoke that dead and deadly faith that Ruskin blamed for the mountain gloom, but it is at the convent that the Dorrits meet Blandois-Rigaud-The Devil. As darkness, whiteness and then cloud dominate the approach to the mountain, so Rigaud dominates—in Amy's vision—the departure:

> she more than once looked round, and descried Mr. Blandois backed by the convent smoke which rose straight and high from the chimneys in a golden film, always standing on one jutting point looking down after them. Long after he was a mere black stick in the snow, she felt as though she could yet see that smile of his, that high nose, and those eyes that were too near it. And even after that, when the convent was gone and some light morning clouds veiled the pass below it, the ghastly skeleton arms by the wayside seemed to be all pointing up at him. [II, ch. 3 p. 509]

In this Ruskinian world where every good has its evil counterpart, Blandois is Amy's counterpart—"more treacherous than the snow, perhaps colder at heart, and harder to melt." Blandois is the perfect image of the Victorian mountain, where the ice does not melt and the stream of human compassion does not flow.

In the disenchanted world of Victorian fiction, a world without the Ruskinian spirit reasserted in "Mountain Glory," where the mountains can be only an escape and therefore an illusion, they must also be treacherous, seductively beautiful in their whiteness and coldness. Dickens gives us here none of Ruskin's color but an image in blacks and whites and greys, less color than we get in the Marshalsea itself, more totally imprisoning than the reality below. Whereas Wordsworth and Ruskin went to the hills to find community and tradition, William Dorrit goes to them to seek separation from his past, from his society, and from himself. Amy, the person of the dusty streets to whom the idealizing energy of the mountains has been transferred, therefore must see the mountains as unreal, or as the source of misery, the devil's seat.

It is significant that Dickens sends the Dorrit party to the Great Saint Bernard in the first place. He was greatly attracted to Switzerland because of the clean, hard-working, freedom-loving people he thought he found there and, too, because it allowed him to indulge a fantasy of getting away from it all. He had even thought, more or less seriously, that he would retreat to the Great Saint Bernard. This makes Mr. Dorrit's inability to escape his London troubles in the Alps all the more important in a reading both of the novel and of Dickens's attitude toward mountains.[19] He must certainly have understood that the mind was its own place and that the mountains themselves, in his state of mind, would become a hell.

It is appropriate, then, that the famous and wonderful last paragraph of *Little Dorrit* begins with the phrase, "went down"—"went down into a modest life of usefulness and happiness." Amy's home, like the home of the Victorian novel is in the streets, and it is in the streets that she and Clennam are "inseparable and blessed." It is a paragraph of disenchantment, but also of a new and "modest" kind of enchantment, away from the world of extremes, in a world where connection is possible and, therefore, also blessed. If we are to be blessed it will not be in the white, perilous, beautiful Alps where Ruskin first looked and Victor meets his monster, but down among the chartered streets, among the arrogant and the froward and the vain, near where the chartered Thames does flow.

Part Four

Transformations of Reality

11

Thomas Hardy's The Mayor of Casterbridge
Reversing the Real

I like a story with a bad moral. My sonnies, all true stories have a coarseness or a bad moral, depend upon't. If the story tellers could have got decency and good morals from true stories, who'd ha' troubled to invent parables?

Reuben Dewy, in *Under the Greenwood Tree*

I

Reuben Dewy seems a comic apologist for the later Hardy, in whose novels we find stunning reversals of the emphases and assumptions that guided realists through the first half of the nineteenth century. For Hardy, whose reserved hostility to the arbitrariness and cruelty of most social conventions is well known, the fullest truth inheres not in the moral ideals of modern civilization but in the essential passions and energies of human nature. These may be detected most convincingly in the unself-conscious traditions of societies, close, in their rhythms and morals, to the processes of nature, in which sporadic violence is a norm, and only barely touched by the movements of history. Or, more interestingly, the energies are most vividly present in those characters who have, for whatever reason, been touched into at least a primitive consciousness of the constrictions imposed by tradition, by social expectations, by moral ideals. The emphasis in Hardy shifts, not so much from the "ordinary," as from the realist's conception of ordinariness. His protagonists, from Dick Dewy to Michael Henchard, are all, in some respects, quite ordinary; yet they increasingly become focuses of tragic intensity. Their desires are not the romantic dreams to be mocked and minimized by wise or ironic narrators, but the stuff of nature and of tragedy.

In Hardy's fiction the realist's acceptance of compromise becomes itself a social convention, or an ideal either deadening when it is pursued without consciousness of the pain of experience, or almost

229

unattainable but by hard discipline. The disenchanted acceptance of the ordinary and decent in the sharp sunlight that banishes the fantasies of romance; the recognition of the needs of others and of the limitations of the self; the revelation like Gwendolen Harleth's, that "her horizon was but a dipping onward of an existence with which her own was revolving";[1] the discovery of one's own mixed nature, of the flaws in one's lover, of the insuperable pressures of society—all of these normal consequences of the realities of Victorian fiction become in Hardy not less inevitable, but less a means to moral growth, and less adequate as a summary of reality. They become, rather, almost unendurable occasions for the tragic. Hardy's fiction gives the impression that, although the narrator does what he can to minimize them, the stakes have been raised, not only far beyond the Trollopian norm, but to the level of the absolute. There are, to be sure, characters in his novels who make the compromise, but the focus is on a prior reality. Hardy's protagonists seem to echo the experience of Victor Frankenstein, whose history is a sequence of waverings between an absolute ideal and a domestic compromise. One feels, retrospectively, a Hardyesque quality to Frankenstein's last uncompromising recovery of his dream amid the vision of failures and compromises: "Yet another may succeed."

Indeed, in Hardy, the compromise with the dream of large romantic aspiration has itself something of the quality of romantic dream about it. That is, such compromise is intrinsically unavailable to the instinctively aspiring protagonists who, like Frankenstein, are impelled not by any moral consideration it may at any moment rationally offer, but by a longing for the absolute and for the pure power of the self triumphant. If *Under the Greenwood Tree* ends with one of those ironically imagined compromises, as a comedy, it nevertheless has within it the elements that will later make for tragedy. And it points forward, beyond its own pages, with a pleasant and satisfying humor that belies the seriousness of the possibilities: "'O, 'tis the nightingale,' murmured she, and thought of a secret she should never tell" (ch. 5, p. 237).

In later work, the attempt to limit aspiration is clearly a dream. When, in *The Woodlanders*, Dr. Edred Fitzpiers, in his Lydgatian retreat to a country practice, contemplates marrying Grace Melbury and settling in Little Hintock, he asks himself: "Why should he go further into the world than where he was? The secret of happiness lay in limiting the aspirations; these men's thoughts were coterminous with the margin of the Hintock woodlands, and why should not his be likewise limited—a small practice among the people around him being the bound of his desires"[2] What might in an earlier novel have been the disenchanted revelation of the inevitability and virtue of limits is for Fitzpiers an untenable dream. Immediately after he does in fact marry Grace, he falls in love with the richer and more "modern" Mrs. Charmond. The men whose thoughts were "coterminous" with the woods are themselves a dying breed, and the volatile and unstable Fitzpiers, who simply cannot internalize the limits he almost chooses, though he is an anomaly at Hintock represents a majority of the culture at large. The strangely distant narrator knows this, although none of his characters does. Fitzpiers, to be sure, is too shallow to be regarded as Promethean; yet the very compromises he is forced to make at the end of the novel in returning to Grace diminish him, as Grace's return to him leaves us only with the dignity of Marty South, who has been able to remain true to her impossible ideal. The novel implies no growth in compromise, only loss of the little dignity Fitzpiers had in the authenticity of his passion.

Thus if Hardy endorses the notion that the "secret of happiness lay in limiting the aspiration," it does not mean that he found the idea attractive or even practicable. Happiness is not a normal or safe human condition. The characters who aspire absurdly and beyond the control of their own will have about them a quality of heroism that distinguishes them impressively from those less ambitious and more controlled, those who have not tested the limits of social constriction or aspired beyond the security of their station. Hardy's narrative voice keeps him aloofly distant from the passions it describes;[3] he remains almost archaeologically disengaged from the action, protected from it so thoroughly that he can afford to release within his narratives precisely those energies that earlier realists, in their compassionate focus on the details and surfaces of ordinary experience, kept submerged. The self-effacement of the "Everlasting Yea," which might be taken as the ideology of the Victorian realist's world, is not in Hardy a tough-minded acceptance of a limiting reality. Rather, it is an act of self-protection, felt in the narrator's own refusal to engage himself, and yet largely and tragically inaccessible to the actors in his dramas. It is unnatural in life, requiring extraordinary discipline of will and feeling, and probably unsustainable. Self-denial is itself a romantic dream, and its consequences can be as destructive.

The primary reality among Hardy's characters is their uncontrollable, irrational desire in an imperfect world. The large aspirations that mark the romantic hero, that are manifested in Victor Frankenstein with catastrophic and Tertius Lydgate with pathetic results are not, for Hardy, rare exceptions to the human norm. They can manifest themselves anywhere; they can be felt, in small, in Dick Dewy's love of Fancy Day, as well as in Giles Winterborne's love of Grace. Whereas realism gets much of its originating thrust from a comic and ironic view of romantic aspiration and, through parody or Thackerayan satire, denigrates it as hypocritical or silly, Hardy treats aspiration neither as an aberration nor as a falsification, but as representatively, critically, tragically human. The qualities that distinguish the human from the merely natural are intelligence and language and the capacity to imagine and desire beyond the limits of nature. The human is the only element in nature incompatible with it.

Essentially, then, Hardy saw a world that was at once continuous with yet in almost every major respect the reverse of the world projected with such moral rigor, sincerity, and toughmindedness by the Victorian realists. If his landscape, for example, excludes the Alpine peaks, for an almost loving but careful registration of the local scene, it does not exclude the intensities that normally accompany them. The violence of the natural world intrudes into the flattest landscapes; and the upland stretches of Egdon Heath, "a vast tract of unenclosed wild,"[4] the hill above Weydon-Priors where Henchard sells his wife, the height from which Jude spies the distant lights of Christminster—all these release uncontrollable energies that destroy with the force of an Alpine torrent. With the realist's particularity and with a movingly precise vision of the details and energies of the natural world, Hardy yet creates a universe that stands in almost parodic antithesis to such landscapes as those of Barchester or Loamshire, although they might be taken as literally almost identical.

It is antithetical, for one thing, in respect to the rules of civilized living, according to which Trollope so carefully organizes his world, and to the notion that civilization is both more interesting and more important than the more primitive worlds it has displaced.[5] Civilization, his narratives demonstrate, is an arbitrarily acquired and extremely thin veneer over what is quintessentially human. The human, moreover, is both "natural" and hostile to nature, is both material and ideal. The rules of society, which govern Trollope's novels and largely determine both the texture and values of characters' lives, do not, even in Trollope, adequately cover the variety and complexity of experience; but in Hardy, those rules are powerful forces in the imagination of his characters and utterly powerless to control their actual behavior, while irrelevant to the shape of the narrative. That is, they serve as deadly obstacles to what is most valuable and interesting about humans and their fictions—the strength of desire. Notoriously, it is social convention that dooms Tess's relation to Angel Clare; it is social convention that keeps Jude from fulfilling his early ambition. Yet those conventions, mere "ideas" by which society organizes itself, are powerless to keep Jude or Tess safe from the instincts that so often govern their behavior. The conventions in Hardy exist not as a general ideal on which variations must be played but as a human fiction that is both necessary for society and destructive of its most interesting members. In effect, Hardy replaces Whately with Freud (and the Schopenhauer that lay behind Freud). The world does not correspond to human need, bringing individual and social together. But human need is divided and self-destructive, requiring both the protection of society and freedom from its restraints.

The antithesis implicit in Hardy's attitude to the rules manifests itself as well in his choice of subjects. There is, of course, a long tradition in realistic fiction of the comic use of peasants and rustics. Their lives are imagined as light echoes of the dominant narratives, which relate to less rustic, more literate protagonists. In Scott we find a world of rustics who bear with them the vitality and the authenticity of unself-consciously transmitted tradition and who frequently have a fictional life richer than that of the aristocratic heroes and heroines. In George Eliot, rustics often appear to comment shrewdly on the blindnesses of the protagonists and to invoke traditional wisdom with choric force, so as to impose a traditional pattern on the realist's potential disaster. In Hardy, however, although the tradition of both Scott and George Eliot is at work, the focus is distributed so that rustics and protagonists often blend into each other; rustics might well be protagonists. Clym Yeo-bright and Grace Melbury are only two who are educated beyond their class and are variously pulled back into it. To Trollope, a focus on a Dick Dewy or a Giles Winterbourne might have seemed misguided or wasteful. Where Trollope had argued that educated classes are on the whole morally and intellectually superior, and everywhere in his fiction implied the need for and the power of civilization to repress or outstrip savagery, Hardy opposed such a view, and novels of manners, of the drawing room and of the club:

> All persons who have thoughtfully compared class with class—and the wider their experience the more pronounced their opinion—are convinced that education has as yet but little broken or modified the waves of human impulse on which deeds and words depend. So that in the portraiture of scenes in any way emotional or climactic—the highest province of fiction—the peer and peasant stand on much the same level; the woman who makes the satin train and the woman who wears it. In the lapse of countless ages, no doubt, improved systems of moral education will considerably and appreciably elevate even the involuntary instincts of human nature; but at present culture has only affected the surface of those lives with which it has come in contact, bending down the passions of those predisposed to turmoil as by a silken thread only, which

the first ebullition suffices to break. With regard to what may be termed the minor key of action and speech—the unemotional every-day doings of men—social refinement operates upon character in a way which is oftener than not prejudicial to vigorous portraiture, by making the exterior of their screen rather than their index, as with untutored mankind.[6]

On this account, realism, in its preoccupation with social rules and material surfaces, misses entirely the primary realities of human experience. Civilization is a veneer, and reality lies primarily in what realists would have thought of as extreme—in the very checkering they attempted to eschew: the emotional or climactic is the highest province of fiction.

This sort of emphasis leads away from the realist's concentration on character toward a more traditional (or romantic) emphasis on plot. Hardy's finding in tragedy a model for his narratives is a logical consequence of the new preoccupation with narrative structure. And in his own writing about fiction, he talks about the importance of structure with a seriousness exceeded only by George Eliot among the novelists who immediately preceded him. Symptomatically, as he looks back for models of satisfactorily structured novels, he singles out Scott's *Bride of Lammermoor*—"an almost perfect specimen of form." Thackeray's disapproval of that novel, as I earlier suggested, had to do with its very singularity among Scott's works. All of Hardy's critical and narrative instincts opposed Thackeray's casualness about narrative form. Like George Eliot, instead, he asks that the work of art have the structure of an "organism," and that everything in it be related to everything else.[7]

In some well-known notes on fiction Hardy laid out several propositions that help clarify how, in his peculiar relation to realism, he had moved to a more "modern" preoccupation with structure. He is realism's continuator and adversary:

> The real, if unavowed, purpose of fiction is to give pleasure by gratifying the love of the uncommon in human experience, mental or corporeal.
>
> This is done all the more perfectly in proportion as the reader is illuded to believe the personages true and real like himself.
>
> Solely to this latter end a work of fiction should be a precise transcript of ordinary life: but,
>
> The uncommon would be absent and the interest lost. Hence,
>
> The writer's problem is, how to strike the balance between the uncommon and the ordinary so as on the one hand to give interest, on the other to give reality.
>
> In working out this problem, human nature must never be made abnormal, which is introducing incredibility. The uncommonness

must be in the events, not in the characters; and the writer's art lies in shaping that uncommonness while disguising its unlikelihood, if it be unlikely.[8]

The "uncommon," the "ordinary," "transcript," "illusion"—these are by now all familiar terms or concepts, but Hardy has somehow rearranged them. He argues for the risk of incredibility in plot in order to insure credibility in character. His actual practice seems to correspond to this argument, and *The Mayor of Casterbridge*, in a mere recital of its events, would seem absurd; yet from it Henchard emerges with overwhelming conviction. The love of the "uncommon" that Hardy attributes to his readers is, surely, his own love; and the "ordinary" world as he imagines it is a world of intensities and extremes. "Romanticism," he had written a few months earlier, "will exist in human nature as long as human nature itself exists."[9]

These notes indicate what is evident in the fictions, that as a self-conscious artist, Hardy was profoundly aware of the fact that art was—and ought to be—something other than reality. He seeks for organism and relevance in his fictions, for the symmetry of plot, for the imposition of consciousness upon experience. And in this respect, he is radically, at least in intention, at odds with all the realists who preceded him. He develops to an extreme their sense that experience and history may, in the long run, be without meaning or value. That sense allowed Thackeray to risk the near dissolution of many of his later narratives. It forced George Eliot to a new imagination of narrative (which I shall be discussing in the next chapter). But for Hardy it is precisely the disorder of experience that requires the order of art. Value is human; it does not inhere in nature. If as Henry James and J. Hillis Miller have argued, the novelist's model is the historian, Hardy's model is self-consciously the artist. For, he says, "History is rather a stream than a tree. There is nothing organic in its shape, nothing systematic in its development. It flows on like a thunderstorm-rill by the road side; now a straw turns it this way, now a tiny barrier of sand that."[10] Hardy's is the world of Huxley's *Evolution and Ethics*, a world in which not following nature but building human structures against it is the way to survival. For Hardy, art is the place where structures can be created against the disorders and irrelevances of history. For art unabashedly projects consciousness upon raw experience, upon "crass casualty." Art, indeed, names that.

It is this special aesthetic quality that we find in all of his great novels; an unembarrassed symmetry of action and reaction imposed upon the inorganic streaming of experience. The novelist hides behind his language and peeks out into the wilderness, even the savagery, that contends in human nature with the constructed ideals of society. Hardy shares with Thackeray the realist's sense of how every climax becomes only a moment in a process; and thus of how the dream of a stable achievement, of closure, is misguided in all respects but that of death. "It is the on-going—*i.e.* the 'becoming' of the world that produces its sadness," says Hardy. "If the world stood still at a felicitous moment there would be no sadness in it."[11] Yet unlike Thackeray, who retreats into the guise of the sage old disenchanted figure whose narrative strategy is to deflate each climactic moment as it comes, Hardy moves even further from the action in his distinctively labored and distant voice and yet produces dramas of desire and will, focusing on moments of passion with tragic clarity and intensity.

Thus realism, as practiced by Trollope or advocated by the early George Eliot, seemed to Hardy merely conventional—as conventional, at least, as Austen perceived the gothic novel to be. "Representations" of reality were of necessity merely conventions of ways to imagine reality. The disparity between art (organic) and life (merely streaming) assured that Hardy's own carefully outlined structures were no less "true" than the large loose monsters of the other Victorians. In the curious progress of realism's self-contradictory impulses, Hardy can be taken as the perfect exemplar. His fiction almost defines itself as being what Trollope's and Thackeray's is not, and all in the name of a faithful and sincere registration of the way things are. The way things are had changed, so that Hardy might have subscribed to the credos of realism I quoted in the first chapter although he constantly violated its conventions. The world had been transformed, and what the "dull grey eyes," the "cold lentils" actually indicated could not be contained within the dominant modes of mid-century realism. Hardy was essentially concerned with the artist's responsibility to this new imagination of the world:

> By a sincere school of Fiction we may understand a Fiction that expresses truly the views of life prevalent in its time, by means of a selected chain of action best suited for their exhibition. What are the prevalent views of life just now is a question upon which it is not necessary to enter further than to suggest that the most natural method of presenting them, the method most in accordance with the views themselves, seems to be by a procedure mainly impassive in its tone and tragic in its developments.[12]

The special pleading here is obvious. Yet it is true that the dominant comic mode of the realist tradition, evident from Jane Austen to mid-century, was shifting even in Trollope, but certainly in George Eliot. Comic endings had become more questionable—not only in Thackeray's *Newcomes*, or in *Little Dorrit*, but even in such Trollopian

comedies as *Mr. Scarborough's Family*, or in *Middlemarch*; and catastrophe became a possible conclusion—in *The Mill on the Floss*, or
Beauchamp's Career. The "impassivity" Hardy advocates suggests
something of the defensive maneuvering required of his narrators,
whose voices imply the discovery that the limiting of aspirations is not
a morally healthy repression of precivilized human energy, but directly
contrary to the human condition. Such repression can not end in comic
compromise, but only in violent explosions of unaccountable and
catastrophic energy.

But advancing secularism and an exciting yet disruptive new science
had in fact radically transformed "the view of life prevalent" in Hardy's
time. I will be discussing this transformation in the following chapters
on George Eliot and Conrad, whose response to it seems, finally, even
more radical than Hardy's. In every case, however, this transformation
had vast consequences for fiction. It entailed the final dissolution of the
kind of vision that allowed Whately to endorse Austen's realism by in
effect endorsing reality, and that, in various ways, lay behind almost all
Victorian realism to mid-century. Yet more important (since all the
writers we have looked at had already been undercutting traditional
faith in the meaning and order of the world), the transformation would
ultimately disrupt the process of realism by which it moved through
parody to new imaginations of the real requiring yet newer parody.

Hardy's kind of tragic and shapely—"geometric," he would call
it—fiction does not follow out the full disruptive consequences of the
new world view. Instead, it rebounds almost parodically away from
earlier conventions of realism, while sustaining much of its mood. He
had a deep commitment to the conventions of art itself rather different
in kind from that of the realists, for whom art required attention more
to the implications for living than to the medium itself. Thus, with all
his self-consciousness about the indifference of the universe, Hardy
could never imagine an antiart which, in its own dissolutions of
traditional forms, mimicked the dissolution of meaning in the universe.
"Good fiction," he wrote, "may be defined as the kind of imaginative
writing which lies nearest to the epic, dramatic, or narrative master-
pieces of the past."[13] In addition, Hardy's realism is distinctly
continuous with Wordsworth's. Experience must, in Hardy, be made
meaningful, even if the "meaning" is that the world has none, or is
inimical to human consciousness. Beyond the disastrous failures of a
nature ever completing itself, never complete, of a world incompatible
with human intelligence, there remains the power and dignity of the
human itself. Such power can *make* the world relevant by imposing on
it human intelligence.[14] Michael Henchard has more than a nominal
connection to Wordsworth's Michael. In seeing through the veneer of

civilization, Hardy finds a Wordsworthian universality even in the peculiarities of his peasants. As he noted in his diary, apparently in 1881: "Consider the Wordsworthian dictum (the more perfectly the natural object is reproduced, the more truly poetic the picture). This reproduction is achieved by seeing into the *heart of a thing . . .*, and is realism, in fact, though through being pursued by means of the imagination it is confounded with invention."[15] He could not drop at least this aspect of the realist's program although all his emphasis is on imagination, enthusiasm, passion. Realism defends him from the charge of mere invention. He is, rather, seeing with Ruskinian and Wordsworthian clarity.

But in Hardy, too, the ultimate severance of art from representation is already more than latent in his primary belief in the incompatibility of consciousness with the entirely material world from which it aberrantly emerged. As at last in *The Well-Beloved*, Hardy is continuously aware of the disparity between the human imagination of the real and the possibilities of the real itself. At its worst, this issues in what was often called Hardy's fashionable pessimism. But in the drama of the novels themselves, it points directly back to the sort of world implied in *Frankenstein*, one in which inexplicable destructive forces issued inevitably out of what might have seemed the most ideal conditions of civilization. The unnameable nonhuman reality burst forth, as he puts it, at "the first ebullition," over the impossibly tenuous restraints of civilization. In Hardy, the monster stalks freely and visibly again, bringing with him an art strikingly akin to that which the early great realist practitioners of realism, in their imagination of an uncheckered world of compromise and disenchantment, had laughed away through their parodies and satires.

II

The Mayor of Casterbridge is the novel that most precisely and powerfully focuses the relation of Hardy's new vision both to the realistic tradition out of which, and against which, it is imagined, and to the tradition of romance. It is a novel that belongs centrally in the nineteenth century, echoing with its naturalistic fidelity, with its preoccupation with "character," with its thematic concern about the relation of the individual to society, about the relation between past and present; yet it is also a novel that embodies a distinctly "modern" vision and that points forward, as Albert Guerard has noted, to the work of Conrad and the early modernists. Henchard, Guerard explains, traces a career remarkably similar to that of Conrad's Lord Jim, whose life is determined by a single instinctive act which he is doomed to redeem and repeat to the end. But I consider Hardy's novel here, rather than at the end of this study, because "modern" as Hardy's fiction may seem to be, it does not follow out in its narrative method the full implications of its vision. Reversal is not a rejection of order. *The Mayor of Casterbridge* evidences in a moving and satisfying way Hardy's fundamental unwillingness to surrender to the disorder he sees. It is a final assertion of the possibility of human control, however monstrous, against the ultimate horror of a world inimical to intelligence, casually destructive, and inaccessible to the very language by which humanity designates it. It risks the "violence" Bersani attributes to narrativity in order to affirm the power of imagination and the necessity for order.

In the preceding chapters, I have been concerned to examine the way realism moved toward an increasing multiplication and fragmentation of narrative as writers attempted to come to terms with their developing sense of the disorder of experience itself, and of the violence to reality done by dogma, ideals, and selfish desire. In Trollope and Thackeray, the contrivances of fictional ordering are postponed or diluted or, in subplots, qualified by alternatives. The large loose baggy monster had come to represent not so much an aesthetic slovenliness as one valid aesthetic consequence of the realistic vision, requiring us to see any narrative line as only one possibility. The rigorous shaping hand of the novelist, which in a different sort of art was to be hidden under the pressure of a Flaubertian aesthetic ideal, was for the Victorians to be restrained in the interest of the most honest possible registration of reality. The artist, among the Victorians, might comment and judge, but not control.

The Mayor of Casterbridge is an aggressively manipulated narrative. It belongs, in this respect, to a narrative tradition governed not by the criterion of plausibility but by that of coherence of feeling. It is one of those remarkable Hardyesque achievements that manage to carry overwhelming conviction while, at every instance, inviting us to dismiss them as incredible. From the perspective of realism, this represents a falsifying tradition of romance; but in *The Mayor of Casterbridge* it is brought into uneasy but effective conjunction with the traditions of realism. The organizing pressure of feeling that gives to romance its distinctive form and makes both *Frankenstein* and *Wuthering Heights* so remarkably symmetrical has an interesting and honorable life among the Victorians. Even among them, where the three-decker novel predominated, and serial publication encouraged the very disorder the realist instinctively found authentic, there are fictions that focus intensely around a single consciousness and absorb the world into that consciousness's needs. We have seen that even *Northanger Abbey* is controlled by the desires (however long delayed and uncertainly understood) of the heroine. Catherine Morland, in her consumption of the world about her, bespeaks those monstrous energies that Austen, in creating her, was mocking. *Jane Eyre*, too, reflects the shaping of experience to personal need. And even *Great Expectations* is ultimately constructed so that almost everything in the world reflects Pip or refers to him.

These narratives, all directed—within the conventions of realism—to demonstrate the folly of great expectations and the moral disaster of imposing the self on experience, nevertheless blur the distinction between the self and other. The special strength of the narratives depends largely on the sense, beyond reason or the power of the mimetic method to record, that the protagonist's fate is somehow entirely created by the self. It is not at all simply wish fulfillment, not at all simply that Jane Eyre gets Rochester but, rather, that she gets the conditions in which she actually lives by virtue of qualities intrinsic to herself. The figure that keeps her from Rochester, "Bertha Mason," is an element of herself that she consciously restrains but cannot eliminate, so that the figure that gives her Rochester is also Bertha Mason, who literally purges Rochester of those qualities that make him unfit for Jane. The landscape of *Jane Eyre* is a romantic one in that it is the self projected, with all its irrationalities and inconsistencies. One can talk and must talk about a literal landscape and about other characters, but *Jane Eyre* is also most powerfully a novel of the self coming to terms with itself. Similarly, as Julian Moynahan brilliantly showed many years ago, the landscape of *Great Expectations* is Pip projected outward. The realist's lesson of disenchantment is there not simply a new recognition of the incompatibility of selfish aspiration with a contingent and varied universe, full of other selves, but a discovery of personal responsibility and, indeed, of personal power. Pip, in a sense, wills the destruction of his sister, of Miss Havisham, and almost of himself. Such novels, like *Frankenstein* gothically before them, reflect the power of consciousness even as they dramatize the powerlessness of the self apart from the community. Each of them projects some monster into the world as Maggie Tulliver evokes the flood, and Victor creates his hideous progeny.

In such novels, plot bears the burden of uncommonness, and in *The Mayor of Casterbridge*, Hardy is consistent with his own dictum that the unreality should be in plot rather than in "character." But plot is not merely—if it is also—a vehicle for the display of "character." It is the means through which Hardy imposes a structure on the world and animates it. One feels in the plot of *The Mayor of Casterbridge* a mysterious but irresistible power lying behind the beautifully observed quotidian and asserting itself against the will of the protagonist in such a way as to imply a dramatic if uneven contest. One feels it despite the simple and abstract assertion of Hardy's pessimism, as in the narrator's invocation of the "ingenious machinery contrived by the Gods for reducing human possibilities of amelioration to a minimum."[17] However much Hardy will imply or, as in later novels, overtly argue the indifference of the world to human concerns, the plot of *The Mayor of Casterbridge*, the many twists, the curious and convincing hostility of the elements, of the landscape itself, so resonant with life, imply a meaningful—if perverse—world. And if this "plot" is further complicated by a richly subtle scene of the way the "external" animosity is inherent in the human will itself, that insight does not diminish the force with which the structure of the novel resists the disorder and meaninglessness toward which, we have seen, realism has been moving. The effect is achieved particularly by Hardy's relish for the "uncommon," his insistence on facing up to the most extreme possibilities.

In the almost numbing sequence of catastrophes that befall Henchard, none is diminished or minimized. They exist not in an aura of nostalgia for intensities no longer available to the disenchanted narrator in the grey modern world, but as continuing realities that no wisdom can efface. Henchard, the "man of character" whose story the subtitle announces, is imagined as precisely the sort of character who would find the realist's disenchantment unendurable. His story is, in a way, about Victorian realism and possible alternatives. Henchard moves in a landscape of ancient ruins, cornfields, Egdon Heath, all governed by the inexorable repetitions and transformations of time, all threatening to absorb him: yet in this landscape Henchard asserts his specialness, refusing to acquiesce in or compromise with the forces that require that he diminish his claims and make his peace. But he outwits both society and nature by anticipating the worst they can do, and he leaves his "will" to assert his final contradictory power.

Against the extravagance of Henchard's plot, there is a realist's subplot—plausible, moderate, compromised. Farfrae is a character from a mid-Victorian novel whose moderate demands, quiet self-interest, refusal of excess, and emotional shallowness all operate within the text as a commentary on Henchard's way of being. Farfrae's amiable shallowness is first observed in his moving rendition of "It's hame, and it's hame, hame fain would I be, O hame, hame, hame to my ain countree" (p. 43). This is followed by his announcement that he is going to America, and echoes with a developing realist preoccupation with dilettantism. Hardy seems to be taking up the tradition that had led Thackeray to focus on a protagonist like Pendennis, capable of surviving and of resisting the worst excesses of moral enthusiasm, by virtue of a fundamental shallowness; and in a voice reverberating with the awareness that the secret of happiness lay in the limiting of aspiration, he tests the mixed and compromised realist hero, Farfrae, against the overreacher, Henchard. When, at the end, Elizabeth-Jane attempts to enlist Farfrae in a search for the wandering Henchard, Farfrae has no objections: "Although Farfrae had never so passionately liked Henchard as Henchard had liked him, he had, on the other hand, never so passionately hated in the same direction as his former friend had done; and he was therefore not the least indisposed to assist Elizabeth-Jane in her laudable plan" (p. 285). It is part of the astonishing achievement of the novel that we feel in Farfrae's generosity less that is admirable than we would if, Henchard-like, he had been vengeful and adamant. Farfrae achieves the life of compromise and stands finally in the landscape of Casterbridge humanly diminished before Henchard's grand disasters. Henchard's story and Farfrae's comment almost parodically on each other. Henchard's reverses the comic pattern, which informed the earlier realistic fiction, and in its reversal averts the ultimate inconsequence of the middling life Farfrae enacts, the realist's casual disorder of experience and the inhuman indifference of Hardy's nature.

Ironically, Hardy's violation of the conventions of realism does not free his narrative for the creative unions of romance but leads to the very defeat from which, one might have thought, the rejection of realism would have protected it. Even here, Hardy plays with realism's conventions; for it was certainly a part—if an "impure" part—of the conventions of Victorian realism that manipulations of plot (Dickensian coincidences are only the extreme examples) enact for the protagonists the desires hindered by the particularities and complexities of experience. We have seen such enactment in *Northanger Abbey;* but Thackeray uses it as well, if almost cynically, and Trollope, too, with casual ease. The comic tradition of the novel relied very heavily on the coincidence, as it is used so conventionally and effectively in *Tom Jones.* But in the happy ending for Farfrae and Elizabeth-Jane, that tradition is implicitly criticized. If the realist must use coincidence to resolve narratives, the most "realistic" use of such coincidence, Hardy implies, is not comic conjunction but tragic disruption. Coincidence must become the chance that explodes the fantasy of happiness. If Elizabeth-Jane goes on to a life of "unbroken tranquility," she continues to wonder "at the persistence of the unforseen" (p. 290). Everything in the novel points to the exceptional nature, not of disaster, but of that "tranquility"; what predominates in life is the "unforeseen," and injustice. Elizabeth-Jane, whose relation to the narrative is of major importance, must renounce the enthusiasm that made Henchard so much a man of character. In Elizabeth-Jane it is not shallowness, as it is with Farfrae, that makes for survival. Although she is one of the lucky ones, she *knows* she is lucky. And having had more passion to begin with, she knows the price of tranquility, as Farfrae does not.

Thus, despite Elizabeth-Jane's concluding voice, *The Mayor of Casterbridge* is almost a celebration of disaster. The disaster, or at least the willingness to confront it, is Henchard's dignity. He chooses his own disaster, down to his last moments when, with the possibility of a new beginning before him, we learn that "he had no desire." Henchard becomes an inverted romantic hero: he makes his own fate. The novel, while asserting man's contingent and compromised nature, imagines the possibility of something freer. It pushes beyond the "small solicitation of circumstance" to a celebration of demonic human energies that realism had, at least since Frankenstein, been struggling to repress.

III

Critics have long recognized that Henchard, in one way or another, *is* the world of *The Mayor of Casterbridge*. Like Frankenstein before him, he absorbs all external reality into his dream of the self. Technically, this means not only that every character and event in the novel relates directly to Henchard, but that the more intensely one examines the novel, the more evident it is that every character in it reflects aspects of his enormous selfhood. As Victor Frankenstein is his monster's double, but also Clerval's, his mother's, his brother's, Walton's,[18] so Henchard is the double of Farfrae and Elizabeth-Jane, Jopp and Abel Whittle, Newson and Lucetta. As Victor moves with erratic repetitiveness from act to reaction, from aspiration to repentance, so Henchard enacts his self-division and Hardy projects that division on the landscape of his narrative. It is all done with the recklessness of conventional plausibility that marks gothic conventions, and yet it achieves a new sort of plausibility. For the large techniques of romance are incorporated here into the texture of a realism that allows every monstrous quirk its credible place in a social, historical, and geographical context belonging importantly to the conventions of realism. The landscape of the self in this novel, almost displaces the landscape of that hard, unaccommodating actual to the representation of which the realist has always been dedicated. But self and other exist here in a delicate balance, and it is probably more appropriate to say that in *The Mayor of Casterbridge* Hardy makes overt the continuing and inevitable presence of romance in all realistic fiction.

We may take the remarkable first scene, in which Henchard sells his wife, as a perfect example of the way Hardy's narrative embodies the tensions between the conventions of realism and that of romance in style and substance, and the way it daringly asserts the presence of the uncommon in the common. The whole sequence confronts directly the problem of inventing satisfying ways to cope with the limiting pressures of the realist's contingent world on large human energies and aspiration. Exploiting the conventions of realism to free itself from the conventional real, and at the risk both of alienating its readers by claiming kinship with great tragedy or mere sensationalism and of disrupting the life of its protagonists, Hardy's narrative implies both a new freedom of imagination and a new conception of human dignity. The freedom and the dignity are precisely in the willingness to take the risk—of uncommon art, of large hopes for renewal.

Strikingly, the human action begins in more than disenchantment, in utter fatigue with the Victorian realist's happy ending—marriage. By the time we meet the still young Henchard, he has been married for some time, and there is no romance in it. The ideal of the hearth, of the limited but satisfying life to which Dickens led his protagonists, in which Adam Bede resolves his career, has turned bitter. The married couple are not at home and content, but on the road and wearily out of touch with each other. We are here beyond the point to which George Eliot takes us when she begins *Middlemarch* with the fated marriage of Dorothea and Casaubon. For Hardy is not engaged in exploring the process by which marital ideals dissolve into sullen separateness and bitter disappointment. That is part of the progress of realism, to be sure. But Hardy begins with the given—with the assumption that marriage is bitterly disappointing and imprisoning. And that assumption, one might note, casts a suspicious shadow over the happy marriage between Farfrae and Elizabeth-Jane, with which the novel concludes.

Yet the scene is narrated with a realist's tender care for precision, an almost awkward quest for authenticity, which seduces us into trusting the narrator. Henchard, for example, is described as a man of "fine figure, swarthy, and stern in aspect; and he showed in profile a facial angle so slightly inclined as to be almost perpendicular" (p. 1). The language struggles to place the characters and define them against recognizable nonliterary categories, and implies that the narrator has a wide familiarity with the ways of agrarian laborers. He notes a typical "sullen silence," apparently bred of familiarity, between man and the woman. He describes Henchard's "measured, springless walk," which distinguishes him as a "skilled country man" rather than as a "general laborer" (p. 1). Later, he describes the furmity tent with the particularity customary to the realist: "At the upper end stood a stove, containing a charcoal fire, over which hung a large three-legged crock, sufficiently polished round the rim to show that it was made of bell metal" (p. 4). The narrator's omniscience is restrained: without entering the minds of his characters he implies a wise familiarity with their ways of thought and feeling: "But there was more in that tent than met the cursory glance; and the man, with the instinct of a perverse character, scented it quickly" (p. 5). Later, we are told that the "conversation took a high turn, as it often does on such occasions" (p. 5). Everything implies a quiet, worldly-wise narration of a story growing out of and repeating a thousand such untold stories buried in history, and whose connections with life outside the fiction will be constantly suggested. Peasant wisdom and bluntness mix with the larger historically saddened intelligence of the narrator. Yet within moments we discover that these devices have been working to force our acceptance of Henchard's sale of Susan: "It has been done elsewhere," says Henchard, "and why not here?" (p. 9).

Just as the scene begins to burst the limits of the conventions of realism, and daringly requires comparison to the abrupt beginning of *King Lear*, so Henchard attempts to free himself from the limiting conditions of his life. Everything noted in the densely particular style suggests that he has been diminished by his context; the sullenness of his relation to a wife who has herself been ground down by "civilization" (p. 2); the "stale familiarity" (p. 2) of their relationship; the "dogged and cynical indifference" (p. 1) manifest in every movement and feature of the man. As we meet him plodding beside his wife, Henchard is (significantly) reading a ballad sheet, turning from the reality of his intimacy with her to a poet's dream of the uncommon. As he drinks, this partly defeated man is transformed, rising to "serenity," then becoming "jovial," then "argumentative," and finally "the qualities signified by the shape of his face, the occasional clench of his mouth, and the fiery spark of his dark eye, begin to tell in his conduct; he was overbearing—even brilliantly quarrelsome" (p. 5). The latent Henchard, released from the restrictions of convention and responsibility, becomes realized. He asserts the sense of his own power and is longing to be free to exercise it: "I'd challenge England to beat me in the fodder business; and if I were a free man again, I'd be worth a thousand pound before I'd done 't" (p. 6).

In George Eliot, this boast would be deflated immediately, but here the larger wish becomes father to the fact, and the realistically created scene slides into romance in which Henchard is hero. Within a few pages, by a process we are not allowed to observe, Henchard has become mayor of Casterbridge. But he is clearly a man who, however firmly his will keeps him under control (as it keeps him from drinking for twenty-one years), acts outside the limits that confine ordinary people. He seems able to withstand the pressures that impinge on other lives, yet all of his life in reality curls around the monstrous secret of the sale of his wife. As Frankenstein hides from his monster, attempts to rejoin the community and conceal his great dream and his great mistake, so Henchard hides from the reality so vividly and abruptly rendered in the first scene. All of the novel grows—as all of *Frankenstein* grows—from the narrative of the inevitable reemergence of that hidden fact, that illicit thrust at freedom, into the community in which Henchard seeks to find his peace. And as with Frankenstein, but more richly and complexly, we find that the protagonist in the community is ultimately only reenacting his forbidden scene. In Casterbridge Henchard seeks with respectability to assert the absolute power of his self over a constricting and contingent world. The pressures he denied at the start avenge themselves on him with a completeness far beyond what the logic of his situation would require. But once set in a world carefully defined in the language of social analysis and historical tradition, once seen in the context of delicate financial and human transactions, Henchard must be destroyed. The man of large feeling and deep need—the hero of romance—cannot survive in the context of a carefully particularized society. Henchard is incapable of compromise. Neither success nor failure can be ordinary for him. And since the conventions the novel adopts make failure the only possibility for the largely aspiring man, it must be an extraordinary failure. The novel concentrates on his losses, juxtaposes his large ambitions to the moderate ones of Farfrae, and conspires to keep him from the comforts of the real. Henchard is his fate; and the narrative line transcends the limits of realism by cooperating with Henchard's refusal to compromise. All coincidences conspire to make things worse than the compromising conditions of realism would demand.

In retrospect, one feels, they are not quite coincidences, but Henchard writ large. His domination of the book, uncharacteristic of Hardy's work as a whole, forces us to see his hand—or spirit— everywhere. He evokes all the characters whose coincidental appearances play so important a part in the novel; and with each of these, at some point, he reverses roles. In the third chapter, for example, we learn of Susan and Elizabeth-Jane's search for Henchard, which brings them to Casterbridge and reopens his past; not long before we heard of Henchard's search for them, itself significantly cut short by "a certain shyness of revealing his conduct" (p. 15). Again, Henchard is responsible for persuading Farfrae, who will end the novel as the new mayor of Casterbridge, to remain in the town. Later, Lucetta, who had nursed him in an illness, arrives in order to marry Henchard, and he must repay her kindness and reverse their early relationship. The furmity woman comes to town to expose him and, in the powerful scene in which she is brought to trial before him, she argues: "he's no better than I, and has no right to sit there in judgment upon me." Henchard agrees, "I'm no better than she" (pp. 174–75). Even Jopp, who is responsible for the information leading to the skimmity ride, arrives in town just after Farfrae to take the job that Henchard has offered to Farfrae; by the end, Henchard is living where Jopp lives. Henchard creates the world which is to destroy him—even becomes that world.

The remarkable force of the idea that, as Hardy quotes Novalis, "character is fate" (p. 98) is worked out with a minuteness that seems to translate the whole world of the novel into a psychic landscape. Farfrae's dramatic entrance into the novel, for example, corresponds precisely to the moment when Henchard, defending himself against the demand that he replace the bad wheat he has sold, says "If anybody will tell me how to turn grown wheat into wholesome wheat, I'll take it back with pleasure. But it can't be done" (p. 31). Farfrae arrives and does it; and he stays because of Henchard's overwhelming emotional demands on him: "It's providence!" Farfrae says, "should anyone go against it?" (p. 55). Henchard makes "providence."

More important for a full sense of the daring of Hardy's achievement in his challenge of realist conventions is the way he takes pains to call attention to the creaking mechanics of his novel. It is as though, if we had not noticed how remarkable, unlikely or chancy an event has been, Hardy wants to make sure that we do not find it plausible or commonplace. When Farfrae turns up, the narrator remarks, "He might possibly have passed without stopping at all, or at most for half a minute to glance in at the scene, had not his advent coincided with the discussion on corn and bread; in which event this history had never been enacted" (p. 32). Here Hardy turns what might very well have been taken as a donnée of the plot into a coincidence upon which the whole plot must turn. As the story unfolds, Henchard's impulsive energy can be seen to be responsible for every stage of his eventual self-obliteration. He too impulsively reveals his past to Farfrae; he too intensely punishes Abel Whittle; he too ambitiously tries to outdo Farfrae in setting up a fair for the holidays; he too hastily dismisses Farfrae and too angrily responds to Farfrae's determination to set up his own business; he cuts off the courtship between Farfrae and Elizabeth-Jane though, as the narrator remarks, "one would almost have supposed Henchard to have had policy to see that no better *modus vivendi* could be arrived at with Farfrae than by encouraging him to become his son-in-law" (p. 97). Later he too hastily buys corn and then far too hastily sells it. He opens Susan's letter about Elizabeth-Jane at precisely that moment when being recognized as Elizabeth-Jane's father, "the act he had prefigured for weeks with a thrill of pleasure," was to become "no less than a miserable insipidity. . . . His reinstation of her mother had been chiefly for the girl's sake, and the fruition of the whole scheme was such dust and ashes as this" (p. 110).

The novel even implies that it is Henchard's responsibility that Susan dies. After reading a letter from Lucetta, Henchard says, "Upon my heart and soul, if ever I should be left in a position to carry out that marriage with thee, I *ought* to do it—I *ought* to do it, indeed!" The narrator comments, "The contingency he had in mind was, of course, the death of Mrs. Henchard" (p. 101). And the narrative immediately records the death of Mrs. Henchard. It is this kind of thing—possibly to be described as simple coincidence, possibly to be explained in naturalistic terms—which finally gives to *The Mayor of Casterbridge* its distinctive shape and power. Every detail of the action seems to feed into Henchard's being, and every detail of the text requires that we accept it only if we are willing to accept the extravagant with the plausible, or as part of it.

George Eliot had tried, by subtle allusion and careful elaboration of plot, to make the ordinary reverberate with mythic force. But in Hardy, sometimes with, sometimes without mythic allusions, the plot itself makes the real mythic. Henchard, the tragic king, responsible both for his kingdom and the sin that blights its wheat and him, must move with ironic absoluteness to death. And the movement toward death is prefigured early. "Why the deuce did I come here!" Henchard asks himself as he finds himself in the place of public execution after he has discovered, because of his refusal to heed the instructions on the envelope, that Elizabeth-Jane is not his daughter (p. 109). "The momentum of his character knew no patience," the narrator later remarks (p. 164). That momentum moves him, past all possibility of compromise, to disaster. He is saved from suicide after the skimmity ride only by the magical appearance of his effigy in the water. When the furmity woman returns, Henchard has no instinct toward the deception which would keep his long-held secret quiet. By attempting to kill Farfrae he not only finally alienates the last man who can save him, but makes it impossible for Farfrae to believe him when he attempts to inform Farfrae of Lucetta's illness. Again, his relation to Farfrae is rather like Oedipus' relation to the careful Creon. Thus, since he carelessly gave Jopp Lucetta's letters he is responsible for Lucetta's death in two ways.

Finally, his last two self-assertive acts complete his self-annihilation. He breaks into the royal visit, demanding the recognition which he had lost and forcing another scuffle with Farfrae. And when Newson returns to claim Elizabeth-Jane, Henchard unhesitatingly (driven by those same impulses which led him to sell his wife) asserts that she is dead; his final act of deceit loses for him his last possibility of ordinary survival.

His last acts have about them the quality, not of a modern novel, but of a pagan, religious ritual of self-annihilation. He refuses to plead for himself to Elizabeth-Jane: "Among the many hindrances to such a pleading not the least was this, that he did not sufficiently value himself to lessen his sufferings by strenuous appeal or elaborate argument" (p. 283). Elizabeth-Jane discovers that "it was part of his nature to extenuate nothing, and I live on as one of his own worst accusers" (p. 285). She then goes out to look for Henchard. We find that, to the last, the power of his being draws people after him. Elizabeth-Jane and Farfrae seek him; Abel Whittle against Henchard's command, follows him, and aids him as he can. Henchard walks until he can walk no more and ends in a hovel (the whole scene deliberately and daringly constructed to recall King Lear and Edgar in the storm) by writing his will—and the will wills his total obliteration:

"MICHAEL HENCHARD'S WILL.
"That Elizabeth-Jane Farfrae be not told of my death, or made to
   grieve on account of me.
"& that I be not bury'd in consecrated ground.
"& that no sexton be asked to toll the bell.
"& that nobody is wished to see my dead body.
"& that no murners walk behind me at my funeral.
"& no flours be planted on my grave.
"& that no man remember me.
"to this I put my name. MICHAEL HENCHARD." [P. 289]

The irony of "willing" his self-obliteration is powerful, complex, and inescapable. Even the putting of his name in upper-case letters becomes an important part of the effect. For Henchard's last written words are the name he is asking to obliterate—and boldly imprinted. The annihilation he asks is in excess of the possible, and so by a wonderful and moving irony, Henchard effects in death what he always fell short of in life—the dominance of his name. It is as though Henchard has stumbled onto the modernist criticism that reminds us of the peculiar status of language. It cannot quite name what it names; it speaks only of itself. It is a fact in the world, but not a representation of it. Henchard becomes here the absolute self of the fiction he created of his life and of the world. He ends, like the late-century writers who had, in effect, given up on the ideals of the Victorian writers speaking to their audiences and attempting to move the world. Since he cannot transform the ideal into the real, he transforms the real into the ideal.

In death, Henchard takes us as far as this novel can to the self-annihilating consequences of the contradictions and failures of the realist ideal. But in the last chapters, the narrator finally extends to Farfrae, that mixed sort of protagonist of realistic fiction, the kind of irony to which he could have been vulnerable throughout the novel. Everywhere, of course, Farfrae acts so as to represent a practical alternative to Henchard's egoist passion for the absolute. The final complex of alternatives and doublings comes when Henchard arrives at the wedding feast, like the ancient mariner, an uninvited guest with a monstrous, Frankensteinian tale he might tell. But he is mute, and hears instead Donald's voice "giving strong expression to a song of his dear native country that he loved so well as never to have revisited" (p. 281). And yet here is Henchard, actually "revisiting" his home, although he had intended to flee it forever. It is Henchard, not Farfrae, who sentimentally leaves the canary; and it is at this point that Farfrae is described as "not the least indisposed" to try to find Henchard, but largely because he has never cared enough either to hate or to love him. For a moment, that is, we can almost say that romance is parodying realism, that it is, through Hardy, having its revenge on an art that has attempted to drain all excess from experience and to subject human nature to the rules of common sense and the inevitable contingencies of ordinary life.

But the last word in the novel belongs to Elizabeth-Jane, a figure who does not fit easily into any of the patterns I have been suggesting apply to the novel, and one who seems rather at home in the world of realistic conventions that Henchard's narrative implicitly mocks. Elizabeth-Jane provides the only other perspective from which we see a large part of the experience, and despite her obvious littleness in relation to Henchard, she is a character more impressively drawn and more important than she is generally given credit for. Although she never surrenders to her impulses or to her needs, she is not, as I have already suggested, simply a Farfrae. If Farfrae, in supplanting Henchard in every detail of his life, in fact continues the life of the Henchard who is excessively sensitive to the demands of respectability, Elizabeth-Jane, herself entangled in respectability, becomes the most authentic commentator on Henchard's experience. Her heart remains always in hiding. It stirs momentarily for Henchard's grand misguided attempts at mastery. But in her quiet submission to the movements of the novel's narrative, she becomes an expression of the way in which "happiness was but the occasional episode in a general drama of pain" (p. 290). By accepting this view, staying protected within the limits of respectability and not rejoicing too much when good fortune comes, she survives to find "tranquility" and to forget the Henchard whose death brought her vision. She is the best sort of realistic audience to a tragic drama.

Her preoccupation with respectability indicates her acceptance of the limits society imposes on action and on dreams, but with her, clearly, the acceptance is an act of self-protection. There is something in Elizabeth-Jane of Hardy's own tentativeness, for while, in Henchard, Hardy ambitiously projects the passions of a large ego beyond the limits of conventional fiction, as, one imagines, he himself would have liked to do, the narrative voice in which he tells the story has something of

Elizabeth-Jane's own reserve, and of the wisdom Elizabeth-Jane has achieved by the end of the novel. Henchard is Hardy's monstrous fantasy: but he must, like the monster, be destroyed. Thus, it is through Elizabeth-Jane that Hardy allows us to return to the conventions of realism with a new understanding of their importance and of their tenuousness. Elizabeth-Jane makes us aware that it is not possible any longer to imagine the world as fundamentally accessible to the commonsense structures and language of earlier realists, that behind the veneer of society and quiet movement of ordinary life, there lies the "unforeseen," the continuing pain, the irrational intensities of nature and human nature.

Elizabeth-Jane's ultimate vision is a consequence of the experience of disaster. It embodies the wish in art that Hardy seems to have feared to enact in life. The only way to overcome the "worst" that lies beneath all human experience is to confront it intensely. Ironically, what Elizabeth-Jane arrives at is, in effect, the ideology of realism. She has learned and she teaches "the secret . . . of making limited opportunities endurable; which she deemed to consist in the cunning enlargement, by a species of microscopic treatment, of those minute forms of satisfaction that offer themselves to everybody not in positive pain" (p. 290). We emerge from the world of The Mayor of Casterbridge, in which the balances of fictional reality have all been reversed and in which, by the sheer force of narrative intensity, the conventions of realism are found wanting weighed against the monstrous energies of human nature, with a sense that the compromises of realism are after all essential. They do not, we see, adequately describe reality; they are modern disguises of realities that, ironically, belong to far more conventional literature; but they are conditions for our survival. Elizabeth-Jane does not allow herself to feel the pressure of Henchard's selfhood as we feel it in his bold concluding signature. Instead, she sensibly (and realistically) follows Henchard's literal instructions on the grounds "that the man who wrote them meant what he said" (p. 289). But in his life, he had rarely done what he "meant."

Realism survives in Hardy, not as a program for writing fiction, but as a discipline to be learned in the containment of the monstrous and the self-divided energies that make of mankind such an anomaly in a hostile universe.

12

George Eliot, Conrad, and the Invisible World

"Here am I," he said, "endeavoring to carry on simultaneously the study of physiology and transcendental philosophy, the material world and the ideal, so as to discover if possible a point of contact between them; and your finer sense is quite offended"

Edred Fitzpiers to Grace Melbury, in *The Woodlanders*

Science is penetrating everywhere, and slowly changing man's conception of the world and of man's destiny.

G. H. Lewes, *Problems of Life and Mind*

I

Having failed to acquire Grammer Oliver's brain, Fitzpiers is examining a fragment of John South's. Grace Melbury's revulsion recalls the horror of Victor Frankenstein's filthy studies, and, later, the Middlemarchers' superstitious anxiety about Lydgate's work with human bodies. But Lydgate and Fitzpiers are not engaged in unhallowed arts. They are, in fact, despite their deliberate isolation from large intellectual communities and their significant weakness for sexual activity, engaged in the centrally important quest of the post-Darwinian Victorian intellectual—the reconciliation of human ideals to material fact. We have already encountered in Hardy some of the consequences of the post-Darwinian world view that the world is all matter, and matter in motion, that consciousness is nothing but an accident of that motion, that the ideal and the material are antithetical. But it is not only Hardy whose sense of reality is transformed by the new science. The reversal of the Victorian realist's assumptions about the nature of the "real" is only one possible response. In transforming reality, the late Victorians were self-consciously engaged in a Frankensteinian enterprise which, begun aggressively and optimistically, in life threatened to be as disruptive and self-destructive as Frankenstein's, and which in literature did eventually lead to precisely the kinds of disruptions that Victorians like Hardy and George Eliot—and even Joseph Conrad— were attempting with more than Fitzpiersian seriousness to avert.

In this chapter, I want to consider the pressures toward the transformation of realism that we have already seen at work in *The Mayor of Casterbridge,* that are implicit in *Middlemarch,* and that manifest themselves in less directly philosophic and more overtly aesthetic ways in *Nostromo,* where the transformation seems almost complete. It will be necessary to move in and out of the novels to the context of late-Victorian scientific thought, which, with the continuing social transformations through reform, the economic restructuring, and the colonial expansion and wars, was confirming the impossibility of that unchecked life of compromise so central to the traditions of mid-century realism. The widening disparity between the conventions and the culture's modernizing experience, implicit in all those faintly "modern" figures in Hardy, was intensified by the way science, in the pursuit of common sense, was creating a reality not available to common sense, to be intimated perhaps through paradox or the language of fiction, but not directly presentable through language. Hardy's tragic sense of the disparity between the ideal and the real is a reflection of the late-century philosophical imperative, that one understand the difference between the laws governing language and the laws governing nature.

Once one begins to look, it is remarkable how pervasive the language of science was in what might have seemed merely bellelettristic or popular literature. The Victorians were learning a whole new vocabulary—one that we, with our atoms, molecules, neutrons, and so on, have unself-consciously accepted and expanded—and, consequently, a whole new reality. And although it may be risky to attempt to establish "any connection at all" between scientific theory and literary practice at the time, it is not difficult to do with George Eliot, whose awareness of contemporary science and philosophy was both broad and acute. She knew well many of the exceptional writers who made careers of spreading the scientific gospel, and who were, in lectures and published papers, daily transforming nature for the entire literate population of England. There was, of course, T. H. Huxley, a major scientist in his own right; there was John Tyndall, a wonderfully lucid writer and also a scientist of some importance; there was, for all too brief a time, the remarkable mathematician and philosopher W. K. Clifford. And of course, there was G. H. Lewes himself. The *Fortnightly Review,* with which Lewes was so intimately connected, became a focal point for the convergence of scientific and literary thought; other reputable journals read by lay people also published major scientific arguments. Indeed, the explanation of scientific texts was replacing the sermon as the most popular nonfictional form.

By the time Conrad began writing fiction, the sermons had been absorbed into the consciousness of the culture, and some of them were even changing their tone. From the exhilaration and optimism of discovery and the beating back of the frontiers of superstitious darkness, through the struggles to reconcile some of that dark superstition with some of that luminous brightness, there emerged some rather nervous, even gloomy visions. If science was promising at last to make the world comprehensible and subject to human ordering, it was also demonstrating with almost relentless Frankensteinian inevitability that the laws of entropy were inviolable, that nature was indeed red in tooth and claw, that mankind might itself be implicated with the ape and the tiger, that the free man's worship was rather like whistling in the dark. That the bulldog Huxley could move to the antinatural moral stance of *Ethics and Evolution* suggests something of the dangers of the transformations of the real in which scientists were engaged.

These transformations entered George Eliot's art early and Conrad's later and provide links between the two that help us to see his fictions as continuous with hers while being, at the same time, radical departures from them. The juxtaposition of the two provides an excellent point of comparison between the realism for which George Eliot was perhaps the most eloquent apologist, and the modernism that displaced it for serious writers.

In Conrad's art, the disruptions that in Eliot are repressed become overt and dominant; the fears against which popularizers of science were sermonizing, and from which Eliot's structures partly protected her, become the direct material and even govern the form of Conrad's narratives. In *Middlemarch*, Eliot's remarkable shaping vision takes the already scattered materials of a little world, and struggles to imagine structures of coherence, or to point to the possibility of such structures; in *Nostromo*, Conrad takes an equally wide range of perhaps more scattered materials—another self-consciously created little world—and seems to refuse to submit them to the unifying intelligence of a coordinating perspective. Yet both writers seek some kind of moral focus and significance in life and action that might begin to weave together both the social fabric and the fabric of self. To achieve this sort of focus, it was necessary for both of them, for Conrad in a more extreme way than for Eliot, to break out of the conventions of realism which, at one time, served precisely the function of making the world "meaningful." The "real" was the ostensible lesson of Catherine Morland or Edward Waverley or Pendennis. But the real, in which man's kinship with the animals was not merely an intellectual hypothesis or a moral judgment, but an observable fact of human behavior, and in which chance—not order—determined the possibilities and consequences of action: such a real could hardly be made "meaningful" in a way that could conform to nineteenth-century moral ideals. Eliot's religion of humanity must have seemed by Conrad's time, or with Conradian vision, a worship of rapacious monsters. And even in Eliot's last novel, the humanity ultimately to be revered lived in some other country that the novelist's hand—bound by the demands of realistic representation—could not describe. Perhaps the Promised Land to which Daniel Deronda migrates is, in the dream world of fiction, rather like the Sulaco that Mr. Gould's inorganic silver and Decoud's cynical dream create.

My allusion to the descent of man was, of course, not casual. T. H. Huxley, in his essay "The Progress of Science," notes "three achievements in physical science of greater moment than any other [epoch] has to show." They are the doctrines of the "molecular... constitution of matter," of "the conservation of energy," and of "evolution."[1] All of these figure prominently in *Middlemarch*, although the most violent contemporary discussions of the new science obviously had to do with "evolution." Yet even a most cursory reading of the scientific essays at the time reveals that all three of these "achievements" become inextricably related where antagonists and defenders address the problem of consciousness. Consciousness is the crux, that obscure something that seems not to be governed by the rules applicable to matter (though in this world it exists only in relation to matter), that distinguishes humanity from inorganic nature and even—though more problematically—from the beasts. The relation of consciousness to matter and to other consciousnesses is the subtext of many late-nineteenth-century works; it lives in the very texture of *Middlemarch* and *Nostromo*.

II

The scientific texture of *Middlemarch* is even denser than the usual recognition of its many scientific metaphors might suggest. Henry James's general objection to Eliot that she worked too consistently from an idea to dramatic embodiment might seem, on the basis of *Middlemarch*, quite reasonable. The novel's most intense dramatic moments are recognizable as articulations of the same scientific vision that impelled G. H. Lewes's astonishingly ambitious, and uneven, *Problems of Life and Mind*, the first two volumes of which were being written at the same time. Yet to criticize George Eliot for such sweepingly intellectual structure is to miss the point of *Middlemarch*, almost to fail to read its subtexts. For among other things, that book, with *Daniel Deronda* after it, is a demonstration of the human and moral necessity of the scientific vision. Dorothea's recognition of her participation in the "involuntary, palpitating life"[2] of mankind is dramatically powerful; but it is comprehensible in terms of the Victorian debate over evolution and the place of consciousness in nature. The ideas are dramatically central to Eliot's imagined universe, for her novels participate in a program like that of many writers on science: by virtue of rigorous secularity they attempt, in a way comparable to that of Feuerbach, to resacralize a world from which God has been dismissed.

Science stands to the text of *Middlemarch* as religion stands to that of *Paradise Lost*. It makes sense of an experience that threatens, to the perceptions of common sense, to disintegrate into meaninglessness. In his remarkable review of *Middlemarch* in 1873, Sidney Colvin sensitively noted the great ambition of the book and the integral part played in it by science. But he did not find the book "harmonious." The massive attempt to encompass everything was a grand failure. "Is it," he asks, "that a literature, which confronts all the problems of life and the world, and recognises all the springs of action, and all that clogs the springs, and all that comes from their smooth or impeded working, and all the importance of one life for the mass,—is it that such a literature must be like life itself, to leave us sad and hungry!"[3] Colvin finds the consolation of mere meaning, as opposed to more direct satisfaction, inadequate. The tough-minded disenchantment implicit in much of the narrative, corresponding, of course, to George Eliot's belief in the "externality of fact," and as Lewes was to call it, the "physical basis of mind," provides the wrong *kind* of meaning.

By detecting so well the way science works in the book, Colvin demonstrates, however, that there is an "ideal" shape to the narrative of *Middlemarch*. We are now perfectly comfortable with criticism that shows us how intricately and minutely Eliot makes everything connect (as everything in science was believed to connect). It is worth briefly noting here the unprovable assumptions Huxley says underlie Victorian science: the "objective existence of a material world," the "universality of the law of causation," and the truth "for all time" of "any of the rules or so-called 'laws of Nature,' by which the relation of phenomena is truly defined."[4] *Middlemarch*, through many devices that imply the coherence "assumed" by science, makes sense. But even these assumptions were under attack, and it was part of the enterprise of Lewes's intended magnum opus to provide a metaphysical ground for the assumptions of coherence on which science is based. In any case, Eliot gives us, in Dorothea's central act, the experience writ large of every human being. Dorothea chooses to do what is required of us all—not by God but by the evolution of our species. In the abstract, her absorption into an "involuntary, palpitating" life is grim and without warmth; in the dramatic experience, its incarnation, it is a remarkable and bracing moment.

Huxleyan science becomes a fully human, not merely an intellectual, possibility, and the novel here, the "nearest thing to life," or Lawrence's "one bright book of life," resists the abstraction for the incarnation. And the incarnation confirms the idea. Without the idea, ironically, the flesh would disintegrate, the real would become that corrupting horror that, as we shall see, Lewes observed in the world available to common sense, that Newman saw in the world without God, that Conrad's Kurtz was to see lurking in the mystery beyond the idea, beyond the Victorian faith that the mystery might be benign.

Of course it is not merely contemporary science that informs *Middlemarch*. That novel seems, encyclopedically, to participate in a vast range of intellectual activity. But George Eliot does attempt to make that activity ultimately consonant with the scientific vision. Her preoccupation throughout the novel with the problem of perception, for example, belongs in the whole tradition of Victorian concern with what it means to "see," and, once again, reminds us of the connection between Victorian realism and Ruskin. Ruskin may have sought the "innocent eye,"[5] but he knew that we had to be taught how to see. His recognition that one must "learn" to see as Turner saw, his attempt to see the noble and the grand in life and art—all make impossible for him the notion that the great artist simply records what is there. Among the earliest passages in *Modern Painters* are discussions of what it is possible to "see" and how what is seen may be "represented": "Thus nature is never distinct and never vacant, she is always mysterious, but always abundant; you always see something, but you never see all."[6]

Although the argument is offered only as an early step in an extensive justification of Turner's later style, and although the language echoes a more traditional sense of the world as an ordered plenum, the direction here is toward the position of scientific empiricists of the second half of the century. Like Ruskin, they were forced to explore certain crucial epistemological problems involved in the attempt to represent reality truthfully. Since all empirical data comes through our senses, how do we know what is really out there? Do we not have evidence for the existence of physical phenomena not detectable by the sense? How do we know whether the sensations of phenomena we receive are not "supplied by ourselves"?[7] In a brilliant essay, "The Unseen Universe," William K. Clifford demonstrated as a starting point that "innocent" perception is no part of experience: "However we express it, the fact to be remembered is that not the whole of a sensation is immediate experience...; but that this experience is supplemented by something else that is not in it."[8]

George Eliot was aware of such complication while she tried to sustain the ideal of realistic representation by supplying multiple perceptions and helping to make us understand what is "not in" the immediate experience. While modifying her actual practice and leaning toward the relativism that was shortly to dominate scientific thought itself, and toward the idea of complementarity already implied by her friend Clifford, she was attempting to avoid implication in the whole cultural movement to blur the distinction between the inner and the outer. That movement was incipient in Ruskin, who dogmatically denied it, but was developed self-consciously by Walter Pater, whose sensitivity to the new knowledge of science was profoundly informing his aestheticism. If Ruskin talked, as Arnold wished to talk, of the object as in itself it really is, Pater could talk of *that*, through a method consistent with developments in science, only by registering the object as it seemed to him to be. Ironically, that is, empiricism was making objectivity impossible. Matter comes to us only through sensation. If we are honest and "realistic," we must talk not of matter but of our own sensations.

While during the late century the intellectual avant-garde was moving toward an ultimate confrontation with subjectivism, or pluralism, in the years before *The Origin of Species* George Eliot could be an unambiguously enthusiastic "realist." It was, indeed, only in those years just before Darwin that the word "realism" began to come into common usage in England.[9] And in 1856, Eliot could say in her review of volume 3 of *Modern Painters:* "The truth of infinite value that he teaches is *realism*, the doctrine that all truth and beauty are to be attained by a humble and faithful study of nature, and not by substituting vague forms, bred by imagination on the mists of feeling, in place of definite, substantial reality."[10] Even then, Marian Evans knew that the reality of "substance" was not so easily attainable, but on the whole she seemed to believe that by strenuous effort she could establish the distinction between "vague forms" produced by one's own desires, and "definite" reality.

Yet, of course, almost every term in this passage would require alteration in the progress of realism through the century and in her art. Imagination, disentangled, one would hope, from the "mists of feeling" was important to science as well as to poetry. Lewes argued that imagination was essential to valid scientific exploration. So too did Tyndall, Huxley, and all serious propagandists for science.[11] In his well-known essay "The Use and Limit of the Imagination," for example, Tyndall almost echoes Lydgate: "Philosophers may be right in affirming that we can not transcend experience. But we can, at all events, carry it a long way from its origins. . . . We are gifted with the power of Imagination. . . . and by this power we can lighten the darkness which surrounds the world of the senses."[12] Lewes put the point more extravagantly in *Problems of Life and Mind:* "No speculation, however wide of actual experience, can be valueless, if, in any way, it enlarge our vision of the Real." (I, p. 173). "Doubtless," says the narrator of *Middlemarch*, "a vigorous error vigorously pursued has kept the embryo of truth a-breathing" (p. 351). The "definite substantial reality" George Eliot sought was becoming anything but substantial. Rather, by the time of *Middlemarch*, it had become microscopically attenuated, or so densely implicated in process and relationship that it seemed at times indistinguishable from the ideal.

Some of the latent problems might be inferred from another of Marian Evans's early statements about the necessity for precise study of nature. In her 1851 review of R. W. Mackay's *The Progress of the Intellect*, she wrote:

> The master key of this revelation [the "divine revelation" that is coextensive with the history of human development], is the recognition of the presence of undeviating law in the material and moral world—of that invariability of sequence which is acknowledged to be the basis of physical science, but which is still perversely ignored in our social organization, our ethics and our religion. It is this invariability of sequence which can alone give value to experience and render education in the true sense possible. The divine yea and nay, the seal of prohibition and of sanction, are effectually impressed on human deeds and aspirations, not by means of Greek and Hebrew, but by that inexorable law of consequences, whose evidence is confirmed instead of weakened as the ages advance; and human duty is comprised in the earnest study of this law and patient obedience to its teaching.[13]

Marian Evans was here putting her faith in the assumption that T. H. Huxley would be describing thirty-five years later, and that led him to argue that a "rational order . . . pervades the universe"[14] That rational order, for George Eliot, was not Providential, but scientific, explicable in terms of the mechanics that govern the relations of matter, and essential in the arguments of scientists defending their mechanical explanations of inorganic and organic nature. For Tyndall, the insistence on miracles, on discontinuities in the order of nature, releases the monster of irrationality in society.[15] W. K. Clifford makes a similar point, seeing the idea of "discontinuity" as monstrous and immoral, undermining our acceptance of responsibility for our actions, and introducing a deadly fatalism for the manipulation of "the fanatic or the adventurer . . . conspiring

against society"[16] All of this, however, effectually turns traditional notions on their head, for it associated determinism not with moral bondage and fatalism but with freedom, education, and responsibility. Eliot
could reconcile her early epistemology with this scientific insistence on
"law and order."

The law and order revealed by science were not, however, easily
available to the consciousness of the ordinary person (nor, as Lewes was
discovering, could the laws be rationally explained). In the close range of
personal relations, scientific law must have seemed as much like "faith"
as religion itself, as much to be learned as Turner's "nature." The consolation of law and order was, moreover, very different from the consolation of immortality. For though both consoled by making sense of the
world, explanation is *all* that scientific law offers. George Eliot, like Tyndall and Clifford, rejected the religious insistence on immortality as mere
selfishness, a bribe of ultimate satisfaction in a world whose moral being
depends on human ability to renounce personal satisfaction and thus the
immediate link with ape and tiger. "Invariability of sequence" makes
learning possible, but what one must learn—in keeping with the dominant traditions of realistic fiction through the century—is the necessity to
accommodate personal need and desire to the requirements of the "material and moral world."

The adjustment of desire to external fact requires, in George Eliot's
fiction, and in Victorian moral thought, the finest discernment, and is
further complicated by the possibility that "external fact" does not deserve accommodation—as seems true in *Daniel Deronda*. One's own
sensations complicated the "earnest study" Marian Evans sought, for
disentangling objective reality from individual perception required
nothing less than scientific rigor and seemed increasingly difficult the
more science revealed about nature. Victorian astronomers, for example,
had taken account of the fact that the reaction time of different observers
varied by fractions of seconds, but sufficiently to throw off astronomical
calculations vastly. There was introduced then into the earnest study of
the heavens what was called the "personal equation," which would help
correct for human differences. George Eliot's famous statement in *Adam
Bede* already notes how the narrator will attempt to "give a faithful
account of men and things as they have mirrored themselves in my
mind." But the narrator knows that the mirror is "defective" and that
"the outlines will sometimes be disturbed, the reflection faint or confused."

The deficiency of the mirror, the growing awareness of the possibility
of pluralism, increasing dissatisfaction with any modes of dogmatism,
lead directly to the preoccupation with perspective in *Middlemarch*, and
to the possibility of reading that book either as a subtle deconstruction of

objectivist narratives or as an inadequately self-conscious assertion of objectivity in the face of its own awareness of the inadequacy of any single perspective. The problem of Eliot's epistemology in *Middlemarch* is treated exhaustively by K. K. Collins,[17] but here it is important to insist that Eliot's enterprise was that of reconstruction. *Middlemarch* begins with a sense of the world in fragments; it demonstrates the way conventional modes of narration and perception lead inevitably to fragmentation and division. And its story focuses on the attempt to find a new kind of order by discovering the true—and scientifically imaginable—orders of reality that lie beyond the reach of simple common sense, of simple chronological progress, of single structures of language and statement. The subtle adjustment of perspectives in the book is a movement toward a new reality not quite available even to the narrator, whose wisdom can mislead us into thinking she knows all the answers. The structure of language does not correspond to the structure of nature. By honoring the complexities of the new reality and the new epistemology, George Eliot breaks out of the literary modes to which she was committed at the start of her career and evolves from them new forms, which changed from *Middlemarch* to *Daniel Deronda,* and obviously would have kept on changing had she lived longer.

The trustworthy narrator of *Adam Bede* describes a culture whose stable values provide a defining frame for each of the characters; expulsion is a kind of death. But by *Daniel Deronda,* Eliot was writing novels in which the stable values were merely ossified and inorganic conventions, and in which expulsion was a kind of life. It is not only that the "stable society" George Eliot describes in *Adam Bede* was a retrospective creation, but that the "earnest study" entailed in Eliot's moral-realist program required a pervasive skepticism, an openness to alternative possibilities, and an experimental freedom that would reveal as it enacted the evolving nature of reality.

"The improver of natural knowledge," wrote T. H. Huxley, "refuses to acknowledge authority, as such. For him scepticism is the highest of duties."[18] Skepticism, with all of its negative implications, would never, it seems, have been a very powerful virtue for George Eliot. Yet skepticism before the unverifiable—"the man of science," continues Huxley, "has learned to believe in justification, not by faith, but by verification"—was essential. "The men of maxims," the unreflecting dogmatics of our culture, fail to understand "that the mysterious complexity of our life is not to be embraced by maxims, and that to lace ourselves up in formulas of that sort is to repress all the divine promptings and inspirations that spring from growing insight and sympathy."[19] It is the mysterious complexity with which Eliot grapples, and which is the condition for her fictions as it is for life itself as she imagines it. Skepticism and a more sensitively registered morality are aspects of the scientific-empiricist world view she struggles to sustain. From Mill to Bertrand Russell skepticism is indeed both an intellectual and a moral virtue. As Russell was to put it in 1928: "I wish to propose for the reader's favorable consideration a doctrine which may, I fear, appear widely paradoxical and subversive. The docrine in question is this: that it is undesirable to believe a proposition when there is no ground whatever for supposing it true. I must of course admit that if such an opinion became common it would completely transform our social life and our political system."[20]

The association of a higher morality and a greater sensitivity with a world view condemned by contemporary clergymen as atheistic and materialistic was, in fact, fairly common. Note for example the uplifting tone with which Tyndall confronts the limits of human knowledge: "Meanwhile the mystery is not without its uses. It certainly may be made a power in the human soul; but it is a power which has feelings, not knowledge, for its base. It may be, and will be, and we hope is turned to account, both in steadying and strengthening the intellect and in rescuing man from that littleness to which, in the struggle for existence, or for precedence in the world, he is continually prone."[21] From the displaced religion, the new voices for science obviously appropriated the highest moral ideals, and a spirituality differing from the religious only in that its source was not God but Matter. The opening of Walter Pater's essay "Coleridge," for example, echoes in almost all its details the ideals of George Eliot:

> The moral world is ever in contact with the physical, and the relative spirit has invaded moral philosophy from the ground of the inductive sciences. There it has started a new analysis of the relations of body and mind, good and evil, freedom and necessity. Hard and abstract moralities are yielding to a more exact estimate of the subtlety and complexity of our life. Always, as an organism increased in perfection, the conditions of its life become more complex. Man is the most complex of the products of nature.[22]

Pater, we know, takes an altogether different direction from that of Eliot, yet his starting point is strikingly similar, and the connections among the matter, complexity, and morality are the same. The sense that dogmas are obsolete and that a new and universal quest for a fully coherent vision, in which body and soul, matter and morality, coalesce predominates here.

That quest for unity (and the belief that empiricism can provide it) is central to Eliot's work. Her narrators labor—with the same commitment to truth as if they "were in the witness box narrating [their] experience on oath"—to speak the truth of what they see. They labor equally to present a world ultimately explicable, coherent, pushed as little askew as possible by the personal equation, and finally consistent with the framework of the empiricist and positivist philosophy she shared with G. H. Lewes (though in her integrity as a "witness" she risked violating the frame).

III

Feeling inevitably issues in action; but it is limited to the direct relations and needs the guidance of a vision of relations that are not directly felt. Knowledge is simply virtual Feeling, the stored-up accumulation of previous experiences, our own and those of others: it is a vision of the unapparent relations which will be apparent when the objects are present to sense.

G. H. Lewes, *Problems of Life and Mind*

In the course of the Victorian debates on science and religion, a great many distinctions were blurred. Huxley, for example, claimed to be neither atheist nor materialist, while John Tyndall claimed to be both, although it would be difficult to distinguish their actual positions.[23] John Stuart Mill attempted to reconcile empiricism to rationalism and ended his career inching toward belief in a deity. And Darwin, of course, tried assiduously to withdraw from the field of combat. Even the positivists were divided among themselves on key issues. The blurring, however, was the condition of developing both a new language and a new reality, and it was characteristic of a movement that was turning the world upside down, making matter ideal and the ideal material, and implying a secular world as mysterious as the religious.

For the sake of convenience, in spite of important subtleties, it is reasonable to talk of George Eliot and G. H. Lewes as empiricists and materialists, although they would have rejected the latter label. Lewes specifically rejected materialism as a full explanation of life, as completely as he did spiritualism.[24] Their complications of these positions will be part of the subject of what follows, but both of them believed in the "physical basis of mind," and both of them demanded "positive" knowledge, assertions that might be verified experimentally. Neither of them, however, was an enthusiastic propagandist for science, although Lewes had propagandized for Comtism for a while. Rather they were among the skeptics R. H. Hutton described as possessing "those many fine chords of sympathy with [their] fellow-men which . . . securing for them a certain community of sentiment with their fellows, long after the sympathy of conviction necessary originally to agitate them to their full extent, has vanished."[25]

It was not, however, only George Eliot's famous commitment to the truth of feeling that gave to her empiricist commitments a push toward the values of religion. Feeling, in empiricist thought, is unquestionable fact; it is, indeed, knowledge itself. The question running from Hume through Newman and George Eliot herself is about the nature of that knowledge, the kinds of inferences to be built on it. Moreover, empiricism, while seeming to imply a commitment to the primacy of direct experience in the quest for knowledge, has invariably led to confrontation with the mysterious and unknowable. No serious scientist, Lewes comments in *Problems of Life and Mind,* could believe that science articulates what is available to common sense:

> It appears, then, that the search in all Science is never for the Visible which Sense reveals, but for the Invisible which Sense obscures. If, therefore, Truth is the conformity of Inferences with Sensation, all Science must be false. And yet we declare Science to be true; and moreover declare that its truth is only reached through the ministration of Sense. A paradox. . . . The truth of Science is the truth of ideal construction; and because its abstractions are formed out of sensible concretes, its truths are applicable to reality *in the precise degree to which the ideal constructions express the real facts.* [I, p. 348]

Philosophically, Lewes chose to write of the limitations of knowledge with a confidence and clarity that diminished their mystery, but his *Problems of Life and Mind,* like George Eliot's last novels, verges, at times, on the mystical. Certainly, the book implies a world of mystery—if not of the inexplicable, then of the unexplained. Moreover, the world of what Lewes calls "the Invisible," though of dominant importance to human life and psychology, is accessible only to scientific method or to a kind of visionary Intuition (ultimately analyzable to "sensations"). Holding, in the complexity of its myriad relationships, the primary elements of meaning and value, it remains obscure to all but the most passionate (and the passion is a condition for great scientific study) and assiduous investigators. Thus the ordinary world to which George Eliot's realist program was devoted and which would seem to be the center of empiricist epistemology begins to look like a world forever excluded from truth and moral acuity—ultimately, in fact, not even susceptible to direct representation. Although quantity tends to replace the traditional mysteries—"our problem," says John Tyndall, "is not with the quality but with complexity"[26]—there are still mysteries. The citizens of the ordinary world are incapable of understanding it without intuition; and the ordinary, with its organic filaments, is ultimately coextensive with the universe itself. "Every Real," says Lewes, "is the complex of so many relations, a conjuncture of so many events, a synthesis of so many sensations, that to know one Real thoroughly would only be possible through an intuition embracing the universe" (I, pp. 342–43). To penetrate the mysteries of the unknown without surrendering faith in the reality and validity of the material world and the empirical method was the object of both Lewes and George Eliot.

The closest approximation to the sort of intuition necessary for penetrating the mysteries comes, in George Eliot's later novels, in the voice of the narrator which, as we have seen, raises important problems about reliability. But within the novels proper, George Eliot's vision required that she move beyond the world of the "dull grey eyes," since the fullest moral action, dependent on the fullest knowledge, which is itself dependent on the deepest feeling, is available only to the exceptional people in her provincial settings. The moral superiority of the untutored Dorothea Brooke, even over the sensible and educated Mr. Farebrother (who, it turns out, is a bad scientist),[27] derives, for example, from her response to her own deep feelings, her intuitive recognition of "unapparent relations." It is this that leads her to support Lydgate. But Dorothea's moral imagination reflects the other truth— that she is an alien in a world that does not offer itself to common sense, either to Mrs. Cadwallader's or to Celia's. Such people, impelled by feelings issuing only from the experience of "direct relations," act and judge hastily. "There is nothing petty," George Eliot wrote as early as *The Mill on the Floss*, "to a mind that has a large vision of relations." But the question is, how does one achieve such a vision?

The answer, in Dorothea's case and in Lewes's theory, is at least partially clear: one must be capable of standing outside of oneself (of what might, indeed, be called an ecstasy, so rare and religious in tone does it become). It is to such an ecstasy Dorothea forces herself in the remarkable eightieth chapter of *Middlemarch*. Her immediate feeling of "direct relations"—particularly with Will Ladislaw, whom she has found in a compromised position with Rosamond—has led her for a moment to give up her generous mission to help Rosamond understand Lydgate and to soften the pain of that painful marriage. "How should I act now," she cries almost in prayer near the end of her night's vigil, "if I could clutch my own pain, and compel it to silence, and think of those three?" (p. 577). This familiar and moving sequence in Dorothea's history has its precise analogue in Lewes's evolving theory. It is also coherent with George Eliot's belief in the connection of feeling to knowledge, of knowledge to moral action. In her early review of Mackay's *Progress of the Intellect*, she noted that "we have long experienced that knowledge is profitable; we are beginning to find out that it is moral, and shall at last discover it to be religious."[28]

Dorothea struggles beyond the limits of self by virtue of the power of "feeling," the source, in Lewes's epistemology according to *Problems of Life and Mind,* of all knowledge ("by the Real is meant whatever is given in Feeling" [II, pp. 16–17]). The power of her own feeling allows her to imagine the reality of other people's feeling (Lewes: "by the Ideal is meant what is virtually given, when the process of Inference anticipates and intuites [*sic*] what *will* be or *would* be feeling under the immediate stimulus of the object" [II, p. 17]). We are in the presence here of what we have long recognized as George Eliot's "moral aesthetic," articulated frequently and less "scientifically" in the novels themselves. Obviously, in Lewes's theory and in George Eliot's fiction, the ideal, the making present to self of feelings literally present only to others, is achieved by virtue of the imagination, or, one might say, the power to create workable hypotheses. Only the facts given us by the narrator allow us to verify Dorothea's belief in Lydgate; for Dorothea herself, Lydgate's own explanation is the only evidence. But her hypothesis that Lydgate would not do what the town assumes he has done is a condition for useful action. Imagination seems, in the details of novelistic life, to *create* reality as much as it "penetrates" it.

But the imagination, in this view, is potentially more real than the observable external fact, the apparent relations; for the imagination can fuse together what the analytic mind has necessarily but arbitrarily separated. For both Lewes and George Eliot, organism was not a metaphor but a fact. Psychology was comprehensible only by bringing together the study of biology, of the organism in which mind is located, and of society, that larger organism—the "medium"—in which the smaller organism of the self exists by virtue of its myriad and complex relations. These conceptions were ultimately verifiable; indeed, the novels test their validity, and (putting aesthetic questions aside) justify themselves as hypotheses are justified—as imaginative constructs essential to the progress of knowledge (hence, of morality), but still only provisionally true. In Lewes's philosophy we find an attempt to construct a large unity of psychology (a discipline avoided by Comte because too focused on the individual) and sociology (the locus of "humanity"). In this construct the self and the other are not two things but one; the objective and subjective are indispensable to each other, are indeed merely different aspects of the same thing. There is no existence without relationship: "Nothing," writes Lewes in *Problems of Life and Mind,*

> exists in itself and for itself; everything in others and for others: *ex-ist-ens*—a standing out relation. Hence the search after *the thing in itself* is chimerical: the thing being a group of relations, it *is* what

these are. Hence the highest form of existence is Altruism, or that moral and intellectual condition which is determined by the fullest consciousness—emotional and cognitive—of relations. [II, pp. 26–27]

George Eliot herself, writing in 1868 her "Notes on Form in Art," reiterates this organicist view: "Forms of art can be called higher or lower only on the same principle as that on which we apply these words to organisms; viz. in proportion to the complexity of the parts bound up into one indissoluble whole."[29] Complex unity is the ideal, both in art and life. To sustain their tough willingness to acquiesce in the very changes that were fragmenting and desacralizing their worlds, Lewes and George Eliot had to incorporate as richly as possible the complexities which—to common sense—seemed to be shattering the unified vision of an earlier age, and which to Victorian culture as a whole challenged dangerously all the inherited traditions of religion and morality.

But we can see here that for Lewes and George Eliot, unity is transferred from God to organism, an entity that implies continuity and growth, through evolution, interdependence, and therefore self-denial, love, morality, complexity, and mystery. Altruism, a positivist ideal, becomes both a Christian moral imperative and a scientific one.

But here, the impulsion to unity—echoing in the traditional Victorian insistence on self-denial—has the further complication of threatening the very conception of selfhood. The self, in Lewes's view, cannot be understood as a thing in itself, but only as a set of relations. He speaks moreover, elsewhere in *Problems of Life and Mind*, of "mind" as an abstraction that names a process and a set of relationships, not as a stable thing that can explain anything. The self is both "the generalised abstraction of continuous feeling," and a series of "concrete discontinuous states" (II, p. 19). The self, then, is a sum of qualities forever in process. "Character too," says the narrator of *Middlemarch*, "is a process and an unfolding." The notion is put yet more strongly by Clifford. "The universe," he says, "consists of feelings. A certain cable of feelings, linked together in a particular manner, constitutes me. Similar cables constitute you. That is all there is"[30]

As a mere part of an "involuntary, palpitating life," Dorothea's self is almost an illusion and has its value in the larger fate of the species. Although, in accordance with George Eliot's realist aesthetic and her refusal to sacrifice immediate feeling and particularities to ideas, the image that Dorothea sees at the window is particularized, her vision is rapidly assimilated to larger significances. Her moral triumph entails the disappearance of the self and slips back from science to Carlylean self-annihilation. Similarly, the character of the "highest" (i.e., most "altruistic") beings in Eliot's novels is increasingly defined by the absence of what we traditionally think of as character. Where Hardy gives us a "man of character" in Henchard, Eliot gives us Daniel Deronda. That special self-identifying eccentricity, whether Micawber's lamentations or Casaubon's austere defensiveness, is a sign of a demanding self incapable of the necessary absorption in the Lewesian organism.

The austerely theoretic force that lies behind Dorothea's vision is more immediately recognizable in Eliot's poetry, where, as R. H. Hutton early remarked, "the rhythm and music drop a soft cloud over the moral detail of life, and fill her soul with the principles she has generalised from its study, rather than with the minutiae of its scenery."[31] There are no such minutiae at the end of *Jubal*, when the angel comes to console Jubal after his people have failed to recognize him as the godlike founder of music whom they celebrate:

> This was thy lot, to feel, create, bestow.
> And that immeasurable life to know
> From which the fleshy self falls shrivelled, dead,
> A seed primeval that has forests bred.

The grim affirmation here and in *Middlemarch* is too reminiscent of the near despair of Tennyson's famous complaint of Nature: "So careful of the type she seems, so careless of the single life." But in the positivist context, what drives Tennyson to despair constitutes the highest moral affirmation. As Lewes sees the problem in *Problems of Life and Mind*, it is only when one gets beyond the sense of reality available to ordinary perceptions (and thus, also, beyond the conventional sense of character) that one can begin to find the possibility of affirmation.

> It is true that our visible Cosmos, our real world of perceptions, is one of various and isolated phenomena; most of them seeming to exist in themselves and for themselves, rising and disappearing under changing conditions.... But opposed to the discontinuous Cosmos perceived, there is the invisible continuous Cosmos, which is conceived of as uniform Existence, all modes of which are interdependent, none permanent. The contradiction is palpable. On the one side there is ceaseless change and destruction, birth and death, on the other side destruction is only transformation, and the flux of change is the continuous manifestation of an indestructible, perdurable Existence [II, pp. 28–29]

"The discontinuous Cosmos perceived" is the Victorian world without God, Newman's living busy world that shows "no trace of my creator." The wider the vision of relations, however, and the more broad the range of imagination, the more beautiful the world becomes.

What Rosamond, with her narrow Middlemarchian mind, finds hideous and monstrous, her husband finds beautiful. "The invisible continuous Cosmos" offers not, of course, a "trace of my creator," but another object of verifiable empirical study—the organism. And organism, in late-century thought, almost displaces God, for its vital complexity can help explain phenomena that seem merely irrational and fortuitous. The organism offers an ultimately intelligible universe, and it banishes monsters. What appears as "destruction" becomes only "transformation," and what appears as the "flux of change" turns out to be "the continuous manifestation of an indestructible, perdurable Existence." Thus, within the same empiricist tradition by which Newman learned to make the leap from the limitation of sense experience to God, Lewes makes the leap from that limitation to science, and scientific method.[32] Progress, the diminution of evil, follows directly from the expansion of science beyond simple empiricism to an exploration of the "unapparent" by means of the refined instruments of hypothesis, imagination, and sheer intellectual energy.

In *Middlemarch*, Lydgate is on the verge of the imaginative genius required for true application of scientific method, and he is most directly engaged in the attempt to see "unapparent relations." In that brilliant passage, so easily read as a description of the novelist's art,[33] in which Lydgate's investigative ambitions are described, we learn that he values

> the imagination that reveals subtle actions inaccessible by any sort
> of lens, but tracked in that outer darkness through long pathways
> of necessary sequence by the inward light which is the last refinement of Energy, capable of bathing even the etheral atoms in its
> ideally illuminated space. [P. 122]

Every word here is alive with scientific or Lewesian implication.[34] This is no mere vague celebration of scientific hopes and tenacity, but a precise articulation of the dream of meaning, of the melding together of object and subject, self and other, thought (or spirit) and matter. It is where Lewesian empiricism, in its later phases, desired to go. It may be, as the narrator remarks, that Lydgate has asked the wrong questions in his investigations, but he is not far askew; and in this passage George Eliot implies Huxley's world governed according to rational laws and uniform principles. In it, all phenomena will be made comprehensible by a unifying theory.

Lewes's empiricism is almost Berkeleyan in its insistence on the perceiver or "feeler" of experience. "The universe to us is," he says in *Problems of Life and Mind*, "the universe of Feeling, and all its varieties are but varieties of Feeling. We separate them into object and subject because we are forced to do so by the law of Relativity" (II p. 19). The best scientist would be the most "sensitive," the most capable of the widest range and most intense registration of feeling. Such a scientist, we might say, would burn with a hard gemlike flame. Science depends on intensity for precision, and "precision is the one quality which impotent minds least appreciate" (II, p. 337). Thus Lydgate's "inward light" is the intense but disciplined feeling that allows imagination. "Light," contemporary science had shown, was, with heat, a product of energy, though more intense and more refined," moving its impulses through a matter so refined scientists named it "ether." But the light is also human consciousness, another even more refined product of material energy, though so subtle that no philosopher had been able to show its materiality. It is an energy that has no mass of its own. Thus it is also a subjectivity that allows for the construction of the ideal (hence "ideally illuminated space"), the process of inference that anticipates "what will or should be feeling under the immediate stimulus of the object." This light of scientific imagination thus follows necessary sequence," the continuing impact of cause and effect through the material world. The scientific imagination does not extend to vague guesses, extravagant as it may seem to become, but works within the limits of the real and is controlled by the "law and order" that become evident in all of nature.

The full explication of this passage in Lewesian terms would take the five volumes he required—nor could he really finish before his death. But its references are as precise and specific as in the word "ethereal," where we have not a vague Miltonic reference to the unearthly but a precise allusion to the then accepted hypothesis that ether was the medium in which electromagnetic waves propagated, the very space in which illumination was possible. It was "unapparent" but "real."

Ethereal, of course, carries with it its prescientific connotations, as well, and further implies that union between spirit and matter that is the object of Lydgate's search, and Lewes's. Both fictional and real scientist seemed to feel that the spiritual would be explicable in terms of matter, and Lydgate is, like Lewes, attempting to discover the "Physical Basis of Mind," is trying to "pierce the obscurity of those minute processes which prepare human misery and joy, those invisible thoroughfares which are the first lurking places of anguish, mania, and crime, the delicate poise and transition which determine the growth of happy or unhappy consciousness" (p. 122). Sadness, like madness, is a disease. The large vision of relations is perhaps the way to the cure.

But Lydgate fails, ironically, because he is not adequately "selfless." His attempt to banish the monstrousness of the "discontinuous Cosmos" for the impersonal immortality of the "continuous" one is flawed by the "spots of commonness" on his character. His uncommon, his Arnoldian "best self," which is properly distanced in his scientific work, is inadequately disciplined in his life. While the narrator watches his implication in the organism of Middlemarch, Lydgate fails to see beyond his immediate experience. He does not, in society, aspire to Dorothea-like selflessness that would allow him a full imagination of the paths of necessary sequence, nor does he understand, what George Eliot knew, that every biological issue has sociological implications.

Ironically, then, Dorothea is the better scientist, and the contrast between her success and Lydgate's failure raises directly a central aesthetic problem that arises from the aspiration to selflessness. The Victorian realist, we have seen, puts primary emphasis on character; and the shift of emphasis from character is part of the whole transformation away from realism. The beginning of the breakdown of the idea of the self is already visible in George Eliot, as traditional moral-religious concerns flow into scientific thought. It is, after all, the sheer force of selfhood through which Victor Frankenstein and Michael Henchard cast their monstrous shadows on the world. The resistance to that sort of titanic egoism is central to Eliot's work as a whole, and if *Daniel Deronda*, with its shifts in narrative mode, does not quite prefigure D. H. Lawrence's kind of fiction, with its turn away from "the old stable ego of character," it belongs in the same post-Darwinian celebration of the divine impersonality of vital energy. Deronda is described as a character whose

> early-wakened sensibility and reflectiveness had developed into a many-sided sympathy, which threatened to hinder any persistent course of action. . . . His imagination had so wrought itself to the habit of seeing things as they probably appeared to others, that a strong partisanship, unless it were against an immediate oppression, had become an insincerity for him. . . . A too reflective and diffusive sympathy was in danger of paralysing in him that indignation against wrong and that selectness of fellowship which are the conditions of moral force. [pp. 412–13]

The implication here, useful for our reading of conventional Victorian realism, is that "character" is largely created by moral definition. Our understanding of characters in Victorian fiction tends to be related to their moral energy, which means, among other things, their location among the social ideals and conventions. The moral crisis for the characters and the technical crisis for Eliot are that moral action seems to issue only from an intensely feeling ego such as Dorothea's (which, one might note, is one of the reasons Lawrence was so bitterly antimoralist in his fiction and criticism). In "Leaves from a Notebook," George Eliot places this kind of moral energy in a larger context: "No doubt the passionate inspiration which prompts and sustains a course of self-sacrificing labour in the light of soberly estimated results gathers the highest title to our veneration, and makes the supreme heroism. But the generous leap of impulse is needed too to swell the flood of sympathy in us beholders, that we may not fall completely under the mastery of calculation."[35] But the ego that moves us to generous leaps is also the obstacle to moral action. Deronda in his passive state has a large vision of relations, an almost scientific world view, but he lacks the energy to act, a "character."

This contradiction is of the first importance in Eliot's art. The well-known theme of vocation in her novels is an aspect of the contradiction, for selflessness, in depriving the self of motive, disentangles the knot that ties the self together—as John Stuart Mill discovered. Deronda is without motive except, almost literally, the desire to discover his own selfhood. In that suspended state, however, he is preparing himself for the conditions of good scientific experiment because he becomes capable of objectivity, of shifting his center "till his own personality would be no less outside him than the landscape" (p. 229). This is what the narrator of *Middlemarch* tells us we must do: "In watching effects, if only of an electric battery, it is often necessary to change our place and examine a particular mixture or group at some distance from the point where the movement we are interested in was set up" (p. 292).

In *Daniel Deronda*, however, it is a character, not the narrator, who makes the experimental shifts, and the world he inhabits begins to respond to his investigations as the world of Middlemarch responds to the narrator's. Putting his personality outside him like a landscape has the effect of making the landscape into the shape of his feelings. It is either selflessness, or, shifting our own vantage point, solipsism. The novel, by realistically describing the "invisible history" (p. 202) and "unapparent relations" and fusing the material and the ideal, knowledge and feeling, self and other, becomes what we may for shorthand convenience call a "romance." The complexity of reality as George Eliot imagines it makes for a reality unimaginable in traditional realistic forms.

The changing form of Eliot's fiction is reflected in her dramatic imagination of the kinds of characters who can achieve the condition of the "highest" organism, having "the most varied group of relations bound together in a wholeness which again has the most varied relations with all other phenomena." Such characters must maneuver through the complexities of relationship, and while approximating in an *engaged* way the vision of the narrator who can look with scientific detachment on the action, must yet remain "characters." The most obvious protagonists, like Adam Bede or Felix Holt, have about them an artificial clarity that is dramatically unconvincing. Even as Eliot tries to complicate our sense of their moral rigidities, their characters still seem too close to being fixed in marble. And their moral clarity makes them too obviously the centers of value.

But the Deronda kind of character, usually slightly off center stage, seems to me to represent George Eliot's richest response to the world view I have been discussing, not because he is dramatically successful but because he is not quite. It is as though Hardy had tried to put his dramatic emphasis on Farfrae. Such a character represents a dramatic risk almost the reverse of the risk Hardy takes in actually putting it on Henchard. Such characters cannot be what the novels most value, but they are capable of an openness and complexity that almost paralyzes. These characters, in particular Philip Wakem, Will Ladislaw, and Deronda, are sophisticated, skeptical, directionless, and unable to define themselves except in relation to a woman who provides motive for action. They fit rather neatly into J. Hillis Miller's description of the "victim" of Matthew Arnold's "modern spirit": that "victim" is "forced to conduct [himself] according to inherited institutions, beliefs, laws, and customs which no longer seem at all appropriate to actual conditions, [in] doubt of the possibility of ever finding the proper form of life."[36] (These characters, too, have much in common with their attenuated cousins in Walter Pater's fictions, figures whose sensibilities are also too complex to allow engagement.)

While it is the narrator of George Eliot's novels who understands and tests the laws of invariable sequence, these characters, within the narrative, bear an unusually heavy burden of responsibility for seeing with the narrator's range and minuteness. Like the narrator, they are aliens in their communities, literally so for physical reasons, or reasons of birth, but metaphorically so because they feel more variously and sensitively. In their alienation, they point away from fictions like *Adam Bede*, and from the norms of Victorian domestic realism, to the kinds of narratives that, in following out the most extreme implications of the realist program, undercut realism finally. Like young Hanno in Thomas Mann's *Buddenbrooks*, they cannot survive in the world realistic fiction is obliged to create.

Thus, from Will Ladislaw to Joseph Conrad's Martin Decoud, there is a much shorter step than at first seems possible. They are both creations of the scientific-empiricist world view we have been discussing, and the parallels in their careers (across continents and thirty-two years) are striking. The difference in literary modes and the difference in their fates are in part the results of the ramifications of the empiricist view that translates reality into sensation, and sensation into the motion of matter, and matter into attenuated waves of energy. The transition from Middlemarch to Costaguana is the transition from George Eliot's saving "organism" to Tyndall's threatening "mechanism": "No matter how subtle a natural phenomenon may be, whether we observe it in the region of sense or follow it into that of imagination, it is in the long run reducible to mechanical laws."[37] Costaguana takes us from Lewes's creative organism to the manufactured monster. Conrad follows out to its gloomiest recesses the implications of Tyndall's "materialism," and never entertains the organicist optimism of Lewes's theories.

Will Ladislaw lives in a world whose creator is participating in a struggle to transform a growing materialism into the ideal shapes of an organic and meaningful world, a world in which subtle relations seem to spin out into consciousness. Decoud, on the edges of civilization, is forced to direct confrontation with a mechanical world which is constructed, arbitrarily but adamantly, out of a primal mindless energy that belies his selfhood. The distance between him and Ladislaw can be seen as no more than the distance between two metaphors with which the new science was being shaped, and "reality" was being transformed.

IV

Although it is useful to see Conrad in the context of the scientific-empiricist tradition we have been discussing, in his work "ideas" are not as central as they are in George Eliot's. He was not, as Ian Watt remarks, "a philosophical novelist in the way that George Eliot, Thomas Hardy or George Meredith are."[38] In his earliest critical manifesto, the famous Preface to The Nigger of the "Narcissus," he distinguishes the artist from the "thinker and the scientist" (p. xi). His task as artist is to focus on the particular, seeing it through his own temperament and "in the light of a particular mood." He attempts not to work within a system but to examine "fragments" rescued out of the "remorseless rush of time" (p. xiv). The basis of art, Conrad could have said, was not the "idea" but the sensation. In a letter to William Blackwood in 1902, he talks of the "action" of his story, "observed, felt and interpreted with an absolute truth to my sensations (which are the basis of art in literature)."[39]

But "ideas" have their significance for Conrad, and Royal Roussel fruitfully abstracts from his work a "metaphysics of darkness."[40] Conrad was an intellectual of sorts. As Watt shows, he "was fairly well informed and, unlike most of the other great modern writers, he neither doubted nor discounted the findings of natural science."[41] His writing invariably reflects his peculiar, but not altogether uncharacteristic, perception of the way modern thought described the world. Certainly, he absorbed much of the tradition variously articulated by such men as Lewes, Clifford, and Tyndall, and almost contemporaneous with his earliest fiction, the later Huxley. He knew of the continental extensions of scientific knowledge into various kinds of idealist metaphysics: Eduard von Hartmann's investigations into the "Unconscious," and Frederick Lange's *History of Materialism*. But Conrad's commitment to the "truth of his own sensations," although it echoes with the aesthetic ideas of the impressionists, belongs with late-century aestheticism allied to the empiricist tradition. Even his instinctive recognition that "ideas" and "experience" are governed by different ordering principles reflects the empiricist belief that logic and syntax of language, as Lewes had argued, have an internal coherence inconsistent with that of the nonverbal universe. Conrad believed that to make language "real," to make us "see," he had to force it out of its conventional molds and scrutinize the rescued fragment" with analytic intensity. Then, perhaps, language will have a "magic suggestiveness," created through care "for the shape and ring of sentences." His refusal to reduce experience to some intellectual framework, or to any of the literary theories of his time, is certainly consistent with the skeptical empiricists' emphasis on the primacy of experience. Empiricism itself, under such Conradian scrutiny, can become questionable, and any idea or hypothesis expendable.

Conrad's rejection of "realism" as a method has behind it the very tradition of empirical analysis that had led George Eliot in her later novels beyond the realism she had originally imagined, and, with Lewes, to see the compatibiltiy of "idealism" and "realism."[42] In a letter to Arnold Bennett, for example, Conrad complained, "You stop just short of being absolutely real because you are faithful to your dogmas of realism. Now realism in art will never approach reality."[43] The "unseen universe" had, by Conrad's time, become a fact that made realism's preoccupation with surfaces irrelevent to "reality." Moreover, the registering of a sensation does not guarantee the reality of the object that ostensibly caused it. We have seen our sensations. In Conrad we can see how "empiricism" and "materialism" pointed directly to psychology, because, as I earlier pointed out, "matter" comes to us only as sensation" or "feeling." To talk about matter—assuming that it exists—one must talk about sensations.

Indeed, the empiricist tradition seemed to be calling all of external reality into question at the very moment that it was celebrating what Lewes, Spencer, and Comte called the "positive" stage of human development, in which society was moving beyond the earlier phases of myth and metaphysics. Pater, writing of that "thick wall of personality through which no real voice has ever pierced on its way to us, or from us to that which we can only conjecture to be without,"[44] is only poeticizing the point Clifford makes: "We can have no experience to know that some of our sensation is not supplied by ourselves." Literary realism is a self-contradictory program in part because empiricism is self-contradictory, leading to questioning the very experience that is supposed to be the source of our knowledge.

Reality will not hold still for a label. It does not hold still for common sense or for representational language. Much of the famous Conradian style, in its attempt to get beyond the surface of things, can be seen as an attempt to register the mystery of experience, our consciousness of the incompleteness of sensation, and of the evanescence of whatever offers itself to us as solid and objectively there. In a letter to Hugh Clifford, in which he offers an extensive stylistic critique of one of Clifford's books, Conrad is emphatic about the importance of words, in which "things 'as they are' exist." He complains of Clifford's use of abstractions that fix and define the experience that should be rendered dramatically. If a scene is presented, such words as "frightened" to describe an emotional state are "inadequate" to express the true state of the character's mind: "No word is adequate."[45] Given the disparity between the simplifying abstraction of the label and the complicating and diffusing particularity of the thing, all a writer can do is avoid labeling and attempt to render the sensation, the experience, in its particularity. Meanings can then emerge from the fact as the reader experiences it, free from the bullying of labels.

The distance between realism and reality had not only to do with "sensationalism," or the separation of language and brute reality, but with the incommensurability of appearance and reality: solid matter, we have seen, turns out to be insubstantial, a thing, as Conrad saw it, of "inconceivable tenuity through which the various vibrations of waves are propagated." This is the world of Lydgate's "ethereal atoms." But whereas to Lydgate and, presumably, George Eliot, the likelihood that all the world was composed of this obscure matter was an occasion for exuberant investigation, for Conrad it is an occasion for profound late-Victorian pessimism. Lydgate and Lewes seek among the atoms for consciousness; Conrad is appalled that this stuff of inconceivable tenuity vibrating through the universe gives "birth to our sensations—then emotions—then thought."[46] If for Lewes the discontinuous world is "monstrous" until understood in terms of the "continuous" world, for Conrad the continuous world turns out to be yet more monstrous, mere automated matter (since organism can be reduced to machine), arbitrary, blind, remorseless.

Conrad's response to the materialism of modern science seems to be precisely what the Victorians who resisted the science feared for themselves. Whereas the most impressive popularizers and investigators devised ways to avoid the depressing conclusions to which crude materialism and mechanism might have driven them, a great many writers found no consolation in Spencer's Unknowable, in Clifford's "mind-stuff," or Lewes's theory of "emergence," or in Huxley's enthusiasm for patient study of all the multitudinous aspects of nature, and his late more qualified belief that man might "subdue nature to his higher ends," and have "a certain measure of success" until the dooming "cosmic process" finally reasserts itself.[47] Against the theory of a continuously evolving uniform nature, in which there are no abrupt breaks and into which there are no intrusions of divine spirit, the objectors invariably raised the question of how immaterial consciousness got in. The horror of Darwinian uniformity was that it suggests that all things emerged from a primary undifferentiated stuff, and that humanity itself was merely a product of the more or less accidental working out of the laws of differentiation, no more special than the apes, the birds, or inorganic matter. Despite Huxley, that is, the objectors insisted on an intelligent direction of the universe (as Samuel Butler returned to a kind of Lamarckianism to affirm the consequence of will and intelligence in the evolutionary process), or they argued the absolute difference, not only between man and beast, but between organic and inorganic.[48]

Here is one of the most intelligent of Victorian critics, R. H. Hutton, rejecting evolutionary theory as an explanation of the differences between rational vital beings and irrational or inorganic entities. The target here is certainly Spencer, and might well also be Huxley, who lectured on the impossibility of drawing a clear line between the animal and the vegetable kingdoms.

> It is a mere self-deception of philosophy to accept the graduality of the stages by which life ascends, from the gravitating force of inorganic matter to the highest pinnacle of human reason, as any sort of evidence that the universe was all implicitly involved in its earliest stage. There can be no reason in assuming, contrary to all evidence, that all forces and all organisms, and all life, and all reason, lie shut up implicitly (i.e., without any manifestation or possible symptom of existence) in that which seems possessed of no force and no organism, and no life and no reason. If this assumption be not made, then, as we know only of one great power totally escaping sensible analysis and yet able to effect sensible changes—the power of mind—the natural assumption is that the actual and sensible additions to existence came out of that power. What is gained by showing the graduality of the transition from one creative process to another?[49]

As a man of traditional religion, Hutton could find no value in a Darwinian world stripped of value and of God. A uniform nature, bounded by the limits of unaided humanity, itself bounded by the limits of the laws of physics and chemistry, was not for Hutton what it was for George Eliot, a place hallowed by "the choir invisible" and by the human history within it. He cannot in any case imagine intelligence emerging from unintelligent and inorganic nature. Such a vision gives us a degraded world from which the highest possibilities of the human are excluded,[50] and gains us nothing in intelligible explanation. The explanation simply displaces God with an inexplicable and unhallowed humanity.

Huxley himself, objecting to a Spencerian "ethics of evolution," comes by the end of his career to find the merely human unattractive. Huxley's position is of great importance in relation to Conrad. It anticipates much in Conrad's work and also makes comprehensible Hutton's kind of need for a traditional religious view that gives to the natural world a sanctioning spirit and value. The position Huxley takes in the Prolegomena to "Evolution and Ethics" rejects Spencer's naive faith in evolution as a process toward perfection, and with it all those ethical systems built on arguments that transform Darwin's descriptions into moral prescriptions. The paradox Huxley announces, although he elaborated it in a way that averts the worst Victorian fears of the implications of an entirely uniform nature, governed by principles science has discovered, echoes in uncanny detail in the world of Conrad's *Heart of Darkness.* This most pessimistic of Huxley's writing builds on the paradox that the practice of what is ethically best (goodness or virtue) involves a course of conduct which, in all respects, "is opposed to that which leads to success in the cosmic struggle for existence" (pp. 81–82).

The "Harlequin," who, with his sailor's manual, resists the absorbing force of the jungle, is testimony to Conrad's sympathy with Huxley's idea. Indeed, *Heart of Darkness* opens with a vision precisely parallel to that which opens Huxley's Prolegomena—the vision of England before the coming of Caesar:

> "And this also," said Marlow suddenly, "has been one of the dark places of the earth!"

"It may safely be assumed," says Huxley suddenly, "that, two thousand years ago, before Caesar set foot in southern Britain, the whole country-side visible from the windows of the room in which I write, was in what is called 'the state of nature'" (p. 120). Marlow, thinking of "when the Romans first came here, nineteen hundred years ago—the other day," imagines the early colonists moving over "sandbanks, marshes, forests, savages—precious little to eat fit for civilized man," experiencing "cold, fog, tempests, disease, exile, and death," and "all that mysterious life of the wilderness that stirs in the forest, in the jungles, in the hearts of wild men."[51] Huxley's colonists faced a land in which "native grasses and woods" fought against "the drought of summer, the frosts of winter, and the furious gales which swept, with unbroken force, now from the Atlantic and now from the North Seas" (pp. 1–2). For Huxley, "nothing is more certain than that, measured by the liberal scale of time-keeping of the universe, this present state of nature, however it may seem to have gone and to go on for ever, is but a fleeting phase of her infinite variety" (pp. 2–3)—"the other day," says Marlow.

Moreover, the model Huxley uses to explain the necessity for ethical man to combat the "state of nature," and its evolutionary energies, is the model of the colonist. How would the perfect administrator of man's affairs successfully engage in the struggle for existence? First, he would have the colonists "clear away the native vegetation, extirpate or drive out the animal population, so far as may be necessary, and take measures to defend themselves from the re-immigration of either. . . . Under the conditions supposed, there is no doubt of the result, if the work of the colonists be carried out energetically and with intelligent combination of all their forces." On the other hand,

> if they are slothful, stupid, and careless; or if they waste their energies in contests with one another, the chances are that the old state of nature will have the best of it. The native savage will destroy the immigrant civilized man. . . . In a few decades, all . . . traces of the settlement will have vanished. [Pp. 16–17]

Here the comparison with Conrad's early story, "An Outpost of Progress," is irresistible.

The efficient administrator—strikingly missing from Conrad's Congo—would, on the other hand, repress all internal division, would "restrain the self-assertion of each man within the limits required for the maintenance of peace" (p. 18). But the establishment of "an earthly paradise, a true garden of Eden, in which all things should work together towards the well-being of the gardeners" would create new problems; the "struggle for existence" would reassert itself in the greed of men within a population growing precisely because of its success in defending itself from the savagery and wilderness outside. What is required, then, of the "efficient administrator" is an unsentimental brutality which systematically destroys or exploits that part of the population dangerous to the polity as a whole.

Huxley, of course, is appalled by the imagination of such a leader, such a "Saviour of society." He understands, moreover, that society is "kept together by bonds of such a singular character that the attempt to perfect society after this fashion would run serious risk of loosening them" (p. 24). He is as appalled by such saviors as Conrad is appalled by the figures of Kurtz, or the Professor in *The Secret Agent,* or Peter Ivanovitch in *Under Western Eyes,* or more ambivalently, Charles Gould in *Nostromo.* Such characters are the idealists and dogmatists who haunt and threaten Victorian realism from Thackeray on.

Finally, Huxley's "Evolution and Ethics" offers us an almost Kurtzian vision of humanity, profoundly unflattering and unsentimental. Mankind is an animal whose innate desire is to enjoy the pleasures and to escape the pain of life, and, in short, to do nothing but that which it pleases them to do, without the least reference to the welfare of the society into which they are born:

> That is their inheritance (the reality at the bottom of the doctrine of original sin) from the long series of ancestors, human and semi-human and brutal, in whom the strength of this innate tendency to self-assertion was the condition of victory in the struggle for existence. That is the reason of the *aviditas vitae*—the insatiable hunger for enjoyment—of all mankind, which is one of the essential conditions of success in the war with the state of nature outside; and yet the sure agent of the destruction of society if allowed free play within. [p. 27]

In *Heart of Darkness* Conrad surely shares this vision, and Huxley's solution to the problem is precisely the opposite of the one Kurtz finally takes. Kurtz lapses into "unspeakable rites" which must include cannibalism,[52] and moves to the heart of that human darkness which is—in Huxley's terms—the powerful pleasure-seeking self-assertion making both a "necessary condition" for the origin of human society "and the sure cause of its destruction." In Spencerian ethics, evolution moves man to a higher and higher moral condition because there is no incompatibility between the surviving "fittest" and the morally "best." They are the same. In Huxley and Conrad, the fittest and the morally best are contradictions.

"Every child born into the world will still bring with him the instinct of unlimited self-assertion," says Huxley. George Eliot certainly agreed: "We are all of us born in moral stupidity." What is required, as Huxley says, and as Eliot and Conrad would have argeed, is that the child learn "the lesson of self-restraint and renunciation" (p. 44). The community is the human ideal, and can survive only through the curbing of Spencerian individualism and of the appetite of the "ape and tiger." But the problem of self-restraint moves us to difficulties that seem insoluble. For society both requires the ape and tiger's energies, and will be destroyed by them. A Christian self-denial and turning of the other cheek are, for Huxley, as incompatible with human survival as is animal rapacity. Suffering from "the malady of thought" (p. 54), man cannot achieve happiness, but he can achieve morality—most of the time, and until the cosmic processes reassert themselves.

Conrad's Huxleyan world, modified or extended by Hartmann's kind of cosmic pessimism, elaborates on the tension between civilization and ape in a way that required a movement off the stage of domestic realism. The "ape and tiger," which Huxley could not help invoking from Tennyson's great poem, move onstage. Evil in Conrad is not merely—as it tends to be in Eliot—the force of primitive egoism self-deceived, but the direct rapacious assertion of human origins, the simple truth of nature. Huxley's Roman colonists were, in their attempt to conquer the earth, attempting to set up a garden, doing battle with nature. But for Marlow, sitting on the edge of the twentieth century in the darkness of the Thames from which ships of empire move frequently, "the conquest of the earth, which mostly means the taking it away from those who have a different complexion or slightly flatter noses than ourselves, is not a pretty thing when you look into it too much" (pp. 50–51). Here, one of the major devices of realism throughout its history is employed: the reduction of the romantic to the banal by means of the translation of a rhetorically inflated cliché into a set of unattractive details. But the stage is too large for Victorian realism; indeed the monstrous is overtly present on it. The questions are both cosmic and of large international political consequence. And the bitterness is not that of the quiet and sad disenchantment, mildly comic in implication, that we begin to find in Catherine Morland or Emma Woodhouse, or, more pathetically, in Maggie Tulliver and Dorothea Brooke.

The passage, moreover, sustains the intensity of romance by almost contradicting itself. For, says Marlow, "What redeems it is the idea only. An idea at the back of it; not a sentimental pretence but an idea; and an unselfish belief in the idea—something you can set up and bow down before, and offer a sacrifice to" (p. 51). Here again is the incompatibility between human consciousness and the evolutionary forces that are its source. Hutton's question returns: how to account for the presence of a phenomenon that seems irreducible to the physical. It is consciousness of a certain kind—an idea—that can redeem animal behavior from its merely animal brutality, as Charles Gould tries to redeem the inorganic silver of the mine by means of *his* idea.

Conrad did not try very hard to account for it. A dominant empiricist tradition, from Darwin into the early twentieth century, was that, on the whole, it could not be accounted for. Tyndall, for example, had said that "the position of the 'materialist' is stated as far as that position is a tenable one" only in "affirming that the growth of the body is mechanical, and that thought as exercised by us, has its correlation in the physics of the brain"[53] The nature of the correlation or any explanation of the connection remains a "mystery." Hutton, articulating another position, had not been puzzled, because he found the postulation of God both necessary and sufficiently explanatory. G. H. Lewes had simply put it negatively, in a perspective similar to Tyndall's. According to *Problems of Life and Mind*, since probability points to a physical basis of mind and since there is no experienced manifestation of mind without body, the burden of proof is on those who insist that there are nonphysical explanations: "If we can decompose the organic into the inorganic, this shows that the elements of the one are elements of the other; and if we are not yet able to recompose the inorganic elements into organic matter (not at least in its more complex forms), may this not be due to the fact that we are ignorant of the proximate synthesis, ignorant of the precise way in which the elements are combined?" (II, p. 11). The more skeptical way of putting it was the more usual among those scientifically inclined. Tyndall, for instance, had concluded this way: "The problem of the connexion of body and soul is as insoluble in its modern form as it was in prescientific ages."[54] This seems at once to justify Hutton's kind of objection to the gradualist explanation, and to dismiss it. Scientific skeptics, indeed, shared believers' distrust of the conclusiveness of scientific evidence. Samuel Butler put the problem succinctly: "Two incomprehensibles: You may assume life of some kind omnipresent for ever throughout matter. This is one way. Another way is to assume an act of spontaneous generation, i.e., a transition somewhere and somewhen from absolutely non-living to absolutely living. You cannot have it both ways. But it seems to me that you must have it both ways."[55]

Conrad's skepticism, however, was of a different sort from this; Butler's points to a kind of Erewhonian comedy,[56] a playful exploration of alternative possibilities through which traditional ideas and institutions are radically questioned. Conrad, too, questions radically, but he does so by accepting the second alternative of Butler—i.e., the undirected transition from nonliving to living. The mindless tenuous stuff of inorganic nature vibrates, and in its vibrations knits "time, space, pain, death, corruption, despair and all the illusions."[57] The skepticism here—"and nothing matters," says Conrad—undermines all thought, which is necessarily illusion, and indeed the very self, which becomes a mere "cable of feeling," or less. Thus, when Conrad concludes this extraordinarily painful letter, he can mockingly "admit however that to look at the remorseless process is sometimes amusing." But the tone, despite the Butlerian form, is anything but playful. The mockery, indeed, seems aimed at himself, and the language is full of contempt for the detachment the vision requires.

And detachment, of course, is required, since any attempt to interfere seriously with the mindless knitting machine of a universe is doomed to disenchantment and destruction, and slavery at the hands of the monstrous and mindless forces. Thus, as artist, Conrad seeks and admires skepticism. Survival depends, as he will say in another extraordinary letter, on protection of his thought intact against the terrible reality outside of thought.[58] The model of skepticism is indeed a kind of god, a creator, strangely like the very knitting machine that in its mindlessness weaves the world. "Scepticism," he writes to Galsworthy, "is the tonic of minds, the tonic of life, and agent of truth—the way of art and salvation."[59] Scepticism, that is to say, allows the detachment that can protect the "idea" from hopeless engagement with a mindless reality.

Thus, he tells Galsworthy, as a writer he must be merciless to his characters, must maintain toward them the kind of detachment and indifference that the mindless waves of energy maintain toward all of us. "In a book," he says,

> you should love the idea and be scrupulously faithful to your conception of life. There lies the honor of the writer, not in the fidelity to his personages. You must never allow them to decoy you out of yourself. As against your people you must preserve an attitude of perfect indifference, the part of creative power. A creator must be indifferent; because directly the "Fiat!" has issued from his lips, there are the creatures made in his image that'll try to drag him down from his eminence.[60]

But the heart of the Conradian paradox is implicit here if we read this against his own fictions. That stance of indifference is allowed only to the "creator" himself, and perhaps not even to him. Any character who seeks this Conradian disengagement, this skeptical and detached vision is, like Decoud in Nostromo, bathed in rhetorical scorn. The human condition imagined in Conrad's novels is one that requires the risk of the "conception," of the "idea," even with the larger knowledge that the risk is doomed. The idea, which is an alien element in the diffusely material universe, is the force that makes solidarity possible and that might briefly reunite mankind with its cold, detached, indifferent source. The implicit relationship here is rather like that between Frankenstein's monster and his creator. For the monster, dead matter suddenly infused with a spark of life, finds itself cut off from its true source. The "creator" rejects with horror his own creation as the monster seeks to be reunited with him. Alien and hence destructive, it invites the only connection possible with its creator, the connection of hostility. Ultimately, it must be reabsorbed into the inorganic, as it can never be in harmony with its source while it retains consciousness.

V

Conrad's special preoccupation with the relation between consciousness and brute reality puts him in the pessimistic phase of the scientism I have been discussing in this chapter. With Hardy, he feels the anomaly of consciousness in the world; with the later Huxley he imagines man's relation to the large evolutionary process as antagonistic. Not surprisingly, the intuitively pessimistic image of Frankenstein emerged occasionally as analogue or metaphor in discussions of the subject at the time, and these images help indicate further the continuous traditions of thought and art in which Conrad's ostensibly "alien" art develops. His transformations of realism are not erratic or eccentric, but part of a movement, alive in England as well as on the Continent, which was finding the conventions of realism increasingly inadequate.

In one of the most remarkable discussions of the relation between consciousness and matter, an essay of 1874 called "Body and Mind," W.K. Clifford attempted to avoid what was to be Conrad's deepest fear, that man was a mere mechanism or automation.[61] "We are," says Clifford, "to regard the body as a physical machine, which goes by itself according to a physical law, that is to say, is automatic." "But," he insists, "it is not *merely* a machine, because consciousness goes with it." And here Clifford plays some tricks with language that save the mechanical metaphor from its gloomiest implications. For, he says, freedom of the will, "that property which enables us to originate events independently of foreign determining causes," really means that we are automata, "that is, that we go by ourselves, and do not want anybody to push or pull us."[62]

The traditional objections are stood on their heads: "The objection which many people feel to this doctrine is derived . . . from the conception of such automata as are made by man. In that case there is somebody outside the automaton who has constructed it in a certain definite way, with definite intentions."[63] We are not, says Clifford, like the monster, for "as a matter of fact, we were not made by any Frankenstein, but we made ourselves." What is frightening is not mechanism but absence of control over our fates and incompatibility with our creator. That, says Clifford, would be the case if we were *not* automatic: "If there is a certain point where the law of causation does not apply, where my action does not follow by regular physical causes from what I am, then I am not responsible for it, because it is not I that do it. So you see the notion that we are not automata destroys responsibility."[64] The scientific vision, in liberating us from the myth of a Divine maker, becomes for Clifford an occasion not for despair, but for a new celebration of our dignity and of our origins. We are what we have made ourselves.

This was not Conrad's way of feeling about the idea of mechanism, nor was it, by the turn of the century, the direction philosophers were taking.[65] Nor was so brilliant and Butlerian a working out of paradox typical in the first decades after the publication of *The Origin of Species*. Huxley's lecture on animal automata, for example, though wonderfully clever itself, seems already ripe with awareness of how threatening the full implications of the argument for mechanism might be.

The essay "On the Hypothesis That Animals Are Automata, and Its History," to which Clifford's essay is in part a response, asserts firmly that animals are "conscious automata." Like Clifford, Huxley finds no incompatibility between the automatic and the conscious. "The consciousness of brutes," he says, "would appear to be related to the mechanism of their body simply as a collateral product of its working."[66] But he easily glides into blurring the distinction between animals and humans. "The soul," he says, "stands related to the body as the bell of a clock to the works, and consciousness answers to the sound which the bell gives out when it is struck." The soul, then, "is an indirect product of material changes."[67] However complicated, humans are machines, and Huxley's refusal to accept the labels "fatalistic, materialistic, or atheistic," which people think are the logical consequences of this belief, is, I think, at least mildly disingenuous, although there is no doubt about the authenticity of his skepticism and the force of his scientific refusal to proclaim a fact (e.g., the nonexistence of God, or even the existence of matter) without verifiable evidence. In the passion of his Victorian commitment to truth, which connects the whole enterprise of post-Darwinian science with the enterprise of Victorian realism, he could say, Damn the consequences of doctrines. "Consequences will take care of themselves." The only test of doctrines is their truth.[68]

Huxley's language is unequivocally "mechanical"; and although he agrees that mind is not material, but only a by-product of molecular action, he does not avoid the inference of other temperaments that the difference between machines and people is, on his scientific account, merely one of complexity. As Hutton correctly pointed out, the argument from gradual evolution does not get around the problem. Butler's paradox remains in force. At some point there is *no* consciousness. At the next point, there is.

In his long section on animal automatism, in *Problems of Life and*

Mind, Lewes argues that animals are a kind of "mechanism," but that it is important to distinguish between organic and inorganic mechanisms. The "mechanical" view of biology is, says Lewes, an artificial technique of science necessary for analysis but incomplete without the supplement of "subjective" truth as well. The application to nature of the model of the machine is, Lewes knows, merely metaphorical. His elaborate antithetical definitions of organism and machines (III, pp. 59–61) deserve full quotation, especially in that they also can be taken as metaphors for two different ways of seeing and writing fiction. But I will confine myself here to his last point. The way "organism" implies for both Lewes and George Eliot redemption in a desacralized world is illuminated by this discussion:

> Another marked characteristic of the organism is that it has a connexus of action, the simultaneous affect of a continuous evolution, appearing in stages and ages. In the animal organism there is a *consensus* as well as a *connexus,* through which there is evolution of Mind; and in the Social Organism an evolution of Civilisation.

In Lewes's theory of automatism and consciousness, he introduces a third element, community, which implies a radical difference, ignored by both Clifford and Huxley. God may not be a force in Lewes's world either, but consciousness, which can be a product only of organism, not of mechanism, plays the role of God. For consciousness grows from human solidarity, and from the intimate nexus of all elements (considered as separate elements only artificially for scientific purposes) within the system. It is organism that allows growth; mechanism only repeats itself. The body is thus a compatible home for mind, as society is for the collective mind. And that terrible alienation and distance that Conrad inferred from the mechanisms of science, Lewes knew was—for a moment—thwarted. The conditions for such a way of seeing were gone by Conrad's time; yet the aspiration to community and solidarity implied by Lewes's scientific metaphysics was in Conrad as well, though for Conrad unconnected to anything in which he could logically believe. "Evolution not Revolution," writes poor Razumov, doomed to self-destruction among revolutionaries and counterrevolutionaries. The voice of Schopenhauer, requiring the death of the will (which is consciousness, as biologists like Huxley were demonstrating), before man could be reabsorbed into his source, echoes gloomily over the science Conrad allowed himself to accept.

Those rare moments in Conrad, as Roussel points out, when consciousness and matter are harmonious, when, as in Sulaco, an idea has made for peace, are invariably followed by the reabsorption of consciousness into matter, or, as Huxley would put it, by the return of the "state of Nature." Consciousness in Conrad is the morally indisputable curse, what Hartmann called "the great mistake of the Universe." That it exists, there is no doubt; how it exists, Conrad, with his scientific predecessors, cannot explain; that it is as incompatible with the nature that produced it as Frankenstein's monster was with his creator, is a certainty Conrad needed no scientist to argue. As Conrad wrote to Cunninghame Graham:

> Yes. Egoism is good, and altruism is good, and fidelity to nature would be best of all, and systems could be built and rules could be made,—if we could only get rid of consciousness. What makes mankind tragic is not that they are victims of nature, it is that they are conscious of it. To be part of the animal kingdom under the conditions of this earth is very well,—but as soon as you know of your slavery, the pain, the anger, the strife, the tragedy begins. We can't return to nature, since we can't change our place in it. Our refuge is in stupidity, in drunkenness of all kinds, in lies, in beliefs, in murder, thieving, reforming, in negation, in contempt,— each man according to the promptings of his own particular devil. There is no morality, no knowledge and no hope: there is only the consciousness of ourselves which drives us about a world that, whether seen in a convex or a concave mirror, is always but a vain and floating appearance.[69]

So despairing a reading of the findings of science in the last half of the nineteenth century necessarily had other than intellectual causes. And it would not be difficult to argue that this version of Darwinism (for that, among other things, it surely is) corresponds closely to Conrad's sense of his own position—a stranger in a strange land, cut off from his origins, speaking a language not his own, loyal to the cause of his country *(une cause absolument perdue)*—but unwilling and unable to return to it. In such a personal context, ideas must seem at once absolutely ineffectual and essential to his own moral redemption. But this is another and longer story. The point is that Conrad's temperament was ripe for the international intellectual movement toward cosmic pessimism. And as Conrad would have said, his work as artist was to register the truth with absolute fidelity to his own sensations.

Thus we can see in Conrad how the enterprise on which Lewes embarked, which in the character of Edred Fitzpiers had already become an object of mockery, failed absolutely. Conrad's pessimism may have been extravagant and idiosyncratic, but his vision of experience, from which, for the great novelists, language had been hopelessly severed, can be taken as largely representative. All around Conrad, the certainties of science, as of traditional religion and morality, were dissolving into multiple and indeterminate possibilities. The organism may imply a saving intention, but the metaphysical questions would not be resolved and their insolubility filtered down out of philosophy into culture's experience. If scientific thought developed, as Huxley earlier argued, by imagining a uniform nature, it pursued its investigations into Butlerian paradoxes and relativity. The double and mutually exclusive theories of the nature of light might well imply two natures. Non-Euclidean geometries all imply different kinds of universes.

Chance had entered the universe in a way that began to invalidate both Clifford's and George Eliot's invariability of sequence. As Noel Annan points out, "Darwin introduced the idea that *chance* begets order. Fortuitous events, not planned or rational . . . result in a physical law: the process of 'natural selection'"[70] (against which, of course, Butler was so wittily passionate). That principle invalidates what Annan calls the "principle of internal determinism," that is, the notion that each species is permanent and its behavior is determined by its intrinsic nature. Not only does the world move into flux—and a mindless one, at that—but the notion that alternate worlds, alternate machines, are not only possible but might well one day exist, depending on the workings of chance, becomes a serious one. What staggers Conrad, as he describes it in another well-known letter to Garnett, after he has watched an X-ray machine at work, is precisely this arbitrary possibility of alternatives:

> The secret of the universe is in the existence of the horizontal waves whose varied vibrations are at the bottom of all states of consciousness. If the waves were vertical the universe would be different. This is a truism. But, don't you see, there is nothing in the world to prevent the simultaneous existence of vertical waves, of waves at any angles. . . . it follows that two universes may exist in the same place and in the same time.[71]

Conrad was sufficiently struck by this to write a novel of the fourth dimension with Ford Madox Hueffer. But the point here is only to suggest how Conrad's skepticism is pushed, by this "science," to further subversions of the possibility of meaning and value. He was moving toward that condition of doubt implied in Butler's paradox, and in so much of the late-century writers' ease in turning the traditional world on its head.

Earlier, in another exuberant essay pointing with confidence toward further unfoldings of truth, W. K. Clifford had urged his readers to accept the limits of their own knowledge: "I am driven to conclude," he says, "in regard to every apparent universal statement, either that it is not really universal, but a particular statement about my nervous system, about my apparatus of thought; or that I do not know that it is true. And to this conclusion . . . I shall . . . endeavour to lead you."[72] Clifford was precociously ready for doubt. In Conrad's hands this way of seeing was a way to despair. The only truth is truth to one's own sensations. The world—that strange set of vibrations that we call matter—is inimical, unintelligible, in constant flux, indeterminate.

Against this world, in the manner of the later T. H. Huxley, Conrad inconsistently struggled to assert the merely human. The "impression," as he implies in his Preface to The Nigger of the "Narcissus," may somehow create a solidarity, a community of the sort which George Eliot and Lewes were seeking with more confidence in the power of mere intelligence. When read in the light of the tradition of Darwinian and empiricist thought, in the light of the despair the cosmos seemed to evoke from him, the Preface becomes more coherent. "Confronted with the same enigmatical spectacle" as confronts the scientist and thinker, says Conrad, the artist "descends within himself, and in that lonely region of stress and strife . . . he finds the terms of his appeal." Those terms, it seems, are the terms of consciousness itself, for the artist speaks to the "invincible conviction of solidarity and knits together the loneliness of innumerable hearts, to the solidarity in dreams, in joy, in sorrow, in aspirations, in illusions, in hope, in fear, which binds men to each other, which binds together all humanity—the dead to the living and the living to the unborn" (p. xii).

It is no accident here—however inflated and perhaps disingenuous this rhetoric is—that there are echoes of George Eliot's way of thinking and feeling. We can almost hear that positivist "choir invisible," as we detect many elements of a kind of humanist theology. Conrad's fiction creates its tensions from such an invincible conviction of solidarity as he speaks of here, a conviction held against the evidence of the universe. Trapped within his own sensations, each individual shares the loneliness of the self and responds to his awareness of that loneliness in another. That the community of mankind is built on the unreal constructions of consciousness is for Conrad inevitable. For what distinguishes mankind from the rest of creation is, precisely, the consciousness that creates pain and illusion. What gives dignity to mankind is not withdrawal and detachment from the illusions of consciousness, but engagement in them.

The Preface, then, is a manifesto of combat with the world that logic and science require us to accept.[73] The "warlike condition of existence" keeps the artistic temperament out of sight, but that temperament is both the possibility of human solidarity and the source of all meaning. The "state of Nature" is a meaningless state; but the "subtle and resistless power" of the temperament "endows passing events with their true meaning." That is, all meaning is human-created. And consistent with the empiricist tradition out of which this transcendent solipsism and radical skepticism grows, the appeal of the temperament in art must be primarily "to the senses." Conrad's "modern" manifesto turns out to be, like George Eliot's less rhetorically intense (perhaps because more confident) manifestos, the articulation of a moral aesthetic. Art, for Conrad, is not the nearest thing to life, as George Eliot put it, but the condition for value and meaning in life. In George Eliot, art can "imitate" life—because life is organically coherent—and expand our sense of it as a consequence. In Conrad, since life itself is so determinately attenuated, so mechanically inhuman, and because life refuses to be "true,"—that is, have meaning—art essentially creates life. The attenuated substance becomes an endless possibility of significance, but language must create all the possible significances itself, none of which can, finally, be verified by anything but the sensation and temperament of the perceiver who hopes invincibly, like Lord Jim, for the reality of another perceiver.

13

The Hero as Dilettante
Middlemarch *and* Nostromo

*I*n life, it is the present moment, the present fact, which is important; the
*moment which preceded, the facts which went before it, borrow all their interest
from their relation to it. The mind, indeed, must "look before and after," but it
stands upon the "now" and the "fact" with which it has to deal. We are
but too apt, in our impatience, to neglect the present moment, casting longing
glances backward on the days that are gone, and longing glances forward
to the days that are to come, as if the former had not been, and the latter
will not be, simple presents. We fail thus to enjoy the present, and to
estimate the event or the man that is with us; we let the
irrecoverable opportunity slip by, to regret it when it is gone.*

G. H. Lewes, *Problems of Life and Mind*

*Every moment some form grows perfect in hand or face; some tone on the hills or
the sea is choicer than the rest; some mood of passion or insight or intellectual
excitement is irresistibly real and attractive to us—for that moment only.*

Walter Pater, Conclusion to *The Renaissance*

*To arrest, for the space of a breath, the hands busy about the work of the earth,
and compel men entranced by the sight of distant goals to glance for a moment at
the surrounding vision of form and colour, of sunshine and shadows; to make them
pause for a look, for a sigh, for a smile—such is the aim, difficult and
evanescent, and reserved only for a few to achieve.*

Joseph Conrad, Preface to *The Nigger of the "Narcissus"*

I

The three quotations in the epigraph to this chapter, one from a
scientific treatise, one from a book about art, one from the preface to a
novel, may suggest something of the community of vision amid the
most disparate enterprises and attitudes created by the diffusion of
scientific knowledge in the last quarter of the nineteenth century.
Lewes, who is in fact urging moral ardor, sounds like an aesthete. Pater,

accused of decadent aestheticism, is also proposing a way to live, a moral program. Conrad, like the others intensely aware of the glory of the moment, of its transience, of the difficulty of focusing upon it, writes a liberating literary manifesto that seeks community in the particular. Between the George Eliot who was ironic alike about the near-sighted and about the farsighted, and the Conrad who struggled to find meaning in the immediate moment, there is a continuity and community of attitudes that persist through all the radical differences. The moment had become less stable, yet more important. Firmness of conviction and of idea had to give way before the wonder of immediate experience.

The distance between *Middlemarch* and *Nostromo* is thus by no means absolute. Seen together, in the light of the tradition I have tried to sketch in the preceding chapter, they can provide a focal point for a last look at the transformation of the conventions of Victorian realism and of the moral aesthetic into the materials of modernism. (Ironically, there are even irrelevant connections between George Eliot and Conrad, as for example, that the Blackwood firm thought of Conrad's *Youth* as "the most notable book we have published since George Eliot.")[1] *Middlemarch* and *Nostromo* are the most ambitious enterprises of their pseudonymous and late-blooming authors; separated by thirty-two years, they are both encyclopedic "histories" and imaginative articulations of the late-century scientific vision, the one still hopeful about the possibilities of discovery, the other more than disenchanted. While *Middlemarch* attempts to see the ideal in the real and charges each moment with the significances of multiple perspectives, *Nostromo* sees the real in the ideal while multiplying perspectives beyond the possibility of significance.

The case for seeing these books as discontinuous and not comparable is made most lucidly as Edward Said. (Although his reference is actually to *War and Peace*, his arguments are surely meant for books like *Middlemarch*, also.) His three main reasons are that "*Nostromo* aspires to no authority on matters of history and sociology"; it does not "create a normative world that resembles our own"; it is "assuredly not the product of a great established literature."[2] But unless we take *Nostromo* as a completed assertion rather than as a process in "the remorseless rush of time," and disregard the tortuous narrative, it is misleading to claim that the novel does not "aspire" to authority. That it fails to achieve authority does not absolutely distinguish it from *Middlemarch*, a novel almost equally engaged with the problem, which yet struggles to find a language for a rapidly diffusing reality, and which leaves the issue almost as problematic as at the start.

Under the scrutiny to which modernist critics subject it, *Middlemarch* begins to look remarkably unstable and "unauthoritative."[3] Relationships in it turn out to be extremely difficult to define precisely, without something like the artificial conditions of scientific experiment, with microscopes, shifts of perspective, controls. If it seems to adhere to the convention of chronological sequence, the chronology is greatly complicated by multiplications of narratives, by retrospects that "account for" the present moments, and by carefully contrived echoes and parallels among the divergent narratives. Scientific control is both artificial and elusive; for *Middlemarch* to achieve authority, as I think we are expected to believe Dorothea achieves it in her assistance to Lydgate at the end, it must leap beyond the calculable and controllable.

The distinction between the two texts is further blurred by the idea of the "normative." Although the very title of *Middlemarch* suggests a world that "resembles our own," the book encompasses an extreme, almost Dantean, imagination of the world, by which the surface of realism is informed with a mythic energy. Midway in our life's journey, we descend into a kind of hell; the "normative world turns out to be filled with vampiric relations, Faustian overreachers, voices from beyond the grave.[4] Conversely, the conventions that govern the geographically remote world of Costaguana are those of folktales or romantic adventures, but *Nostromo* reasserts the normative in the midst of extremes: it builds, like *Middlemarch*, a recognizable community within which dwell capitalists, industrialists, petty officials, hostelers, dockworkers, journalists, traders, and peasants. And if we expect extremes under *Nostromo*'s tropical sun, it comes as a shock how much violence, psychological and physical, is incorporated in the little world of *Middlemarch:* murders, riots, blackmail and briberies, political rhetoric, deaths. Moreover, at a moral center of both books there is an inescapable analogy between Charles Gould, making his silver bear the burden of the ideological as he succumbs to its material power, and Nicholas Bulstrode, justifying his wealth by providence, and killing to preserve it.

There are enough such possible parallels to suggest a similarity in the raw materials of the two novels. Both are large historical fictions that attempt to create entire societies and—in the established tradition of Walter Scott—to read the fates of characters in the context of larger social and national movements from which they cannot withdraw. Both are preoccupied not only with Said's "authority" in personal, political, and literary senses, but with the relation among "feeling," idea, and action, with the way skepticism impedes, but is a condition of, intelligent action. As multiple perspectives layer and qualify each experience, history—even in *Middlemarch*[5]—seems strangely unprogressive and nonchronological. In *Middlemarch*, the universe becomes a "tempting range of relevancies,"[6] full of connections too subtle for ordinary consciousness. As Lewes was writing at roughly the same time in *Problems of Life and Mind*: "Every Real is the complex of so many relations, a conjunction of so many sensations, that to know one Real thoroughly could only be possible through an intuition embracing the universe" (I, pp. 342–43). A struggle for such an intuition seems to mark the achronology of *Nostromo*, where true connections remain yet more obscure.

I am not discussing similarity in order to argue identity. Nor am I claiming any direct influence (though it would be surprising if Conrad had not read *Middlemarch*).[7] Literary history is a complex of continuities and discontinuities, rarely more than in the implicit history that connects and disconnects these two novels. The facile compartmentalization of "modern" and "old-fashioned" cannot suffice. Recent emphasis in criticism on originality, newness, or belatedness has its uses, and it is particularly useful to imagine, as Said's analysis requires, the absoluteness of all beginnings: "With regard to what precedes it, a beginning represents . . . a discontinuity."[8] But discontinuity is comprehensible only in terms of some posited continuity, and both of these novels, although again they might fail, are self-consciously searching for "origins" in the context of scientific thought that was making origins unthinkable.

Middlemarch, for example, represents a continuity: it marks, as Henry James put it, "a limit to the development of the old-fashioned novel."[9] But it is also a beginning, particularly of the self-conscious attempt to imagine a secular-scientific community in a world cut off from traditional continuities implied by earlier fictions. Conversely, *Nostromo* is impelled by an explanatory energy to overcome the discontinuities of its style. Why, otherwise, are there so many attempts to make clear when each event took place (e.g., "rather more than a year later"; "a year and a half later")?[10] Why do we return to various actions to fill out our sense of what actually happened, as with the wonderful chapter describing Decoud's suicide, an event about which the primary fact is its absolute solitude? Who but a desperately explaining narrator could know or let us know about it? Alert to the literary conventions they can no longer sustain, both novels struggle within the realist tradition that seeks to get beyond literature into the real, now to confront the large threats of a universe latently hostile, monstrous and inhuman. One aspect of *Nostromo*'s narrative is its effort to make itself continuous with the tradition to which *Middlemarch* is so closely allied; it makes what we might call a "final" gesture at the possibility of registering the real within conventions of representation that *Middlemarch* itself calls into question.

II

The point where the problems of discontinuity and relationship and validation of authority most sharply focus is in the intersection of the narratives dealing with Will Ladislaw and Martin Decoud. The perspective of analogy once suggested, the dramatis personae of both novels may seem to blend into each other, as though Conrad had taken George Eliot's raw material and given Mr. Brooke—or his intellectual counterpart, Captain Mitchell—the responsibility of the narration. Charles Gould, the Bulstrodian idealizer of wealth in one aspect, becomes, in his relation to Emilia, a Casaubon in relation to Dorothea: monomaniacal, cold, tended to by a self-sacrificing wife who accepts his psychological betrayal of her. Emilia certainly occupies a Dorthea-like position in the novel, but Dorothea's qualities are manifest also in Antonia Avellanos, whose ineffectual father—like Dorothea's inadequately avuncular Mr. Brooke[11]—takes direction of a political newspaper.

As a preliminary example of how such analogies might illuminate each other, we can take the case of Charles Gould. His idea of making the mine a means to a generous and humane order in Costaguana incorporates with all their moral and intellectual ambiguities the large idealisms of Lydgate and Casaubon, whose ambitions critics have always seen to reflect each other. But the Gould enterprise suddenly juxtaposes these to Bulstrode's, forcing us to see that like him, the others, apparently less hypocritical than Bulstrode, are also imposing ideal structures on resistant materials. Their stories explore how far the ideal is consonant with the facts of experience. We see that achieving an adequate explanation of things is for all three a means to power even though they all disclaim a desire for power. And all four fail because their explanations are not adequate to encompass their relations with women. The women call the ideal structures into question and, in effect, undermine their power. (All of these narratives point to the larger problem of fiction's explanatory powers, and the possibility of the consolation of meaning for the loss of a beneficent God.)

In achieving a larger-than-life national ambition, Gould suggests the very large implications of the ironically treated protagonists of *Middlemarch*. Charles Gould is given the "medium" of which Dorothea Brooke is, among the provinces, deprived, and in it is allowed the scope of what the narrator of *Middlemarch* calls "an epic life" (p. 3). Yet his reform of a nation, within the scope of epic or romance traditions, is not free of bitter ironies. Here, too, sustaining an ideal enterprise against the compromising demands of circumstance is virtually impossible. Although *Nostromo* sets the problem against a nature "placid" and ruggedly indestructible, Gould is impeded as much by the conditions of a restricting society as is Lydgate or Bulstrode.

The problem of compromise in an ideal pursuit will return in Ladislaw's narrative, but the constructed, civilized selves of Lydgate and Casaubon are based in biological (i.e., "natural") drives and limitations that turn out to be more significant that their drives to order. (Lydgate's intellectual failures have a precise parallel in Jude Fawley's, who is partly thwarted by his own sexuality.) The natural, too, imposes itself on Gould—most overtly, in that he penetrates the mountainside with more passion than he can spare for Emilia (note, too, how all the marriages remain childless until after the narratives are effectively ended. Rosamond does have four children after the Lydgates' departure from Middlemarch and Dorothea goes through a difficult childbirth in the last pages). These characters all imagine that they possess the intelligence to make an idea operate on society or in nature. They suffer from the fantasy of control and are ultimately dominated by materials beyond any "idea." The knowledge required for a full mediation between external facts and man's capacity to impose (or discover) order must belong to other sorts of ambition.

To put it more accurately, one might say that it belongs only to those without ambition. I have already tried to suggest, in my discussion of Thackeray's *Pendennis*, that the less than ideal figure who refuses both dogmatism and idealism has a place in realistic fiction more important than his moral laxity might suggest. Without Victorian science lurking ominously in the background of his narrative, Pendennis is imagined as a character who remains undogmatically open to a wide variety of experience by virtue of his refusal to engage himself seriously. His progress is from romantic dream to appreciation of the possible, and narratively, he belongs in a novel that resists the climactic moment, the imposition of structure on the streamingness of experience, as long as possible. *Middlemarch*, of course, is a much more rigorously intellectual construction, but the direction of its thought is toward a reality that streams and blends and fuses and reflects; the novel's apparent largeness and looseness represent an attempt to find a means to reflect George Eliot's and Lewes's sense of the primacy of the immediate moment, the focusing of all past and present there. Those who attempt to force their shaping desires and ideas on such a world are doomed to suffer. Henchard would suffer in Middlemarch as he does in Casterbridge; but Farfrae would thrive there, too. The difference would be that George Eliot would continue to seek the ideal in the character of lesser intensity. Bulstrode is the Henchard of *Middlemarch,* the man with the secret, the man with ambition, the man who attempts to impose his ambition and his ideal on society itself. Ladislaw, to stretch a point, is the Farfrae, a jack-of-all-trades with a skill for living—open, undogmatic, and potentially the figure to mediate between external fact and the ideal. In the later realism, the dilettante not the doer seems to bear the burden of the real.

Conrad, like George Eliot with Ladislaw, explores the possibilities of refusing engagement and ambition, particularly with the character of Decoud. In what follows, I want to examine more extensively the roles of these two figures in narratives and in worlds inimical to the ideal, using the same technique of achronological playing back and forth between texts as I employed with Charles Gould and his analogues. Without the concentrated ambitions of a Gould or a Bulstrode, Decoud and Ladislaw come much closer to representing the diffuseness and complexities of the texts they inhabit and of the physical worlds they watch. They are outsiders who, by some perverse workings of a medium resistant to ideals, achieve what can be achieved.

Both Ladislaw and Decoud are described as dilettantes, and they are also, in Matthew Arnold's sense of the word, aliens. Like the young Arnold, who played the role of dilettante-dandy and surprised even his family with the seriousness of his poetry, they allow playful cynicism to keep them disengaged from the demands of social and political life. In both cases, the triviality of their lives defends them from a gravity they must ultimately face. Decoud's sense of friendship, for instance, has George Eliot-like qualities. Friendship means to him "the frank unreserve as before another human being, of thought and sensations; all the objectless and necessary sincerity of one's innermost life trying to react upon the profound sympathies of another existence" (p. 191). Ladislaw is slighter than Decoud, and as Henry James says, there is evidence of too great an indulgence and predisposition toward him on George Eliot's part, so that, while she does indeed treat his lightness ironically, "the impression once given that he is a *dilettante* is never properly removed." But James too recognizes that in George Eliot's conception, Ladislaw is meant to show "a large capacity for gravity."[12]

Whatever seriousness may be discovered in them later however, at their points of entrance into their novels one notes only their diffuseness and disengagement. Both of elaborately mixed blood that marks them as rootless, they find themselves drawn into political journalism not by conviction but by accident. Decoud "had studied law, had dabbled in literature, and hoped now and then in moments of exaltation to become a poet." To "pass the time," he had "condescended to write articles on European affairs for the *Semenario*" (p. 134). Ladislaw is as aimless, with a fine "sense of the ludicrous." Just back from Heidelberg, he now, as Mr Casaubon accurately and contemptuously describes him, "wants to go abroad again, without any special object, save the vague purpose of what he calls culture, preparation for he knows not what. He declines to choose a profession" (p. 59).

Conrad's rhetoric about Decoud is hostile; George Eliot's about Ladislaw is only affectionately diminishing. "As a matter of fact," says Conrad, Decoud was an "idle boulevardier," and his "cosmopolitanism" was "in reality a mere barren indifferentism posing as intellectual superiority" (p. 134). George Eliot, like her Dorothea, is more indulgent than Conrad; but as narrator she is far more negative than Dorothea. Dorothea says of Will before she really knows him that people such as he "may seem idle and weak because they are growing. We should be very patient with each other" (p. 61). "Will," remarks the narrator with an irony not far from Casaubon's, "had declined to fix on any more precise destination than the entire area of Europe. Genius, he held, is necessarily intolerant of fetters" (p. 61). Described as someone who had experimented with everything from opium to lobster, Will is sharply placed: "Nothing greatly original had resulted from these measures." And with an irony usually reserved in George Eliot for the egotists who will destroy themselves or others, she notes that he had "a generous reliance on the intentions of the universe with regard to himself. He held that reliance to be a mark of genius" (p. 61).

Ladislaw's cynicism is often a youthful failure of self-understanding, while Decoud's is a conscious construction. Refusing to take life seriously, Decoud and Ladislaw maneuver into a better position to understand the irrationality of life's demands and the possibilities of a satisfying way of being. To achieve this understanding is the condition for any meaningful action, and requires a complex sensibility. Ladislaw is regularly described as Shelleyan (with its implications both of rebelliousness and sensibility), and Decoud lives and dies "faithful to the end to the truth of his own sensations" (p. 194).

But because the more complex and various the organism, the "higher" and the more implicated with other organisms, for George Eliot, as for Lewes, the self exists only when the biological organism is part of a social organism. Thus Decoud and Ladislaw cannot remain disengaged, must become "characters," and eventually pay the price of life. The very complexity of their sensibilities guarantees engagement; and the way they are enticed into life constitutes the central paradox of their positions in the novels.

The similarities in the narratives describing this progress are striking. Decoud is invited by Don José Avellanos to "take the direction of a newspaper that would 'voice the aspirations of the province'" (p. 139).

Decoud comes to Costaguana, but, as his sister says, only because "you want to see Antonia" (p. 137); for the sake of remaining he writes trashy political rhetoric in a journal called *Porvenir* ("Future"). Ladislaw is invited by Mr. Brooke because "the political horizon was expanding,"the journal he has purchased might "clear the pathway for a new candidate," and Ladislaw had the power "to put ideas into form" (p. 215). "Why not?" Will asks himself, "and he studied the political situation with as ardent an interest as he had ever given to metres or medievalism" (p. 337). Ladislaw remains in Middlemarch to be near Dorothea. He writes trashy political rhetoric (Brooke calls him another Burke) in a journal called the *Pioneer*. Both characters find themselves, then, in a losing political cause; yet we are meant to believe that Ladislaw goes on to serious politics, and that Decoud becomes a founder of the nation of Sulaco.

Sexual energies really create their vocations.[13] This sort of narrative, apparently as traditional as Don Quioxte's quest for Dulcinea, is assimilated here into the tradition of evolutionary thought. Life draws Decoud to Antonia as it had drawn Lydgate to Rosamond. Moreover, Decoud carefully distinguishes, in what he calls his "sane Materialism," between the "friendship" he can feel for his sister, and the sexual attraction he feels for Antonia (p. 191). Seeing his situation with a cynical-scientific detachment he thinks of his preoccupation with Antonia as "a ridiculous fatality" (p. 137).

In that their most meaningful actions are accidents of sexual relations, neither seems to live by an authentic principle of moral life, or with a coherent imagination of experience. For both, the private and public seem gratuitously related, and the authority for the connection rests with a woman whose intensity of engagement makes the men seem mere facile scribblers. Antonia is solemnly committed to the nation implicitly mocked in Decoud's excessive support for its "reform" government. Dorothea is humanitarian rather than politician and does not believe in political reform before one has done one's best to make life better for those for whom one is immediately responsible. Her moral position, that is to say, once she gets over the farsightedness of her early career, is akin to the commitment to the present urged by Lewes, and is the moral counterpart of Ladislaw's almost Paterian aestheticism.

The couples thus enact a clash between intelligence and feeling that both texts attempt to reconcile, and this clash is intrinsic to the world that the myth of contemporary science was opening. The men are, in the texts, "completed" by women whose intensity of feeling requires action. In George Eliot's world, "Feeling is a sort of Knowledge,"[14] as in Lewes's more systematic epistemology, we remember, feeling *is* knowledge—the source of all that can be known. But Antonia and Dorothea not only evoke feeling, they imagine the feeling of others and thus cannot be satisfied without relieving pain. Dorothea's obsession with this becomes something of an affectionate joke. But Ladislaw is infected by feeling and transforms himself from dilettante to politician, "an ardent public man." Yet the intelligence that holds the men aloof at the start returns in the voice of the narrator herself, whose "masculine" intelligence reminds us that Ladislaw's cause, Reform, had, forty years later, made little difference in the quality of life in the land.

The narrator's irony in *Middlemarch* is implicit in Antonia's story in *Nostromo*. Like Dorothea, Antonia cannot bear to "abandon" her countrymen, "groaning under oppression" (p. 418). Having seduced Decoud into morality and feeling ("I have erected my passions into duties," he thinks [p. 409]), she becomes his antagonist after his death. To help those Costaguanans suffering under oppression, she proposes the reunification of Sulaco with Costaguana: "I am convinced that this was from the first poor Martin's intention" (p. 418). Under the pressure of feeling, she transforms Decoud's text. As he was forced to engagement in life, so—with the sanction of Antonia's feeling—Sulaco, the artificially detached, will be reabsorbed into the country from which Decoud had separated it.

But the ironies in these women's relation to the men they complete do not work toward satire; rather, this disparity between humans and the world they inhabit has been called the "cosmic joke." The disaster that issues from Decoud's relation to Antonia implies the impossibility of validating ideas through action, of moving coherently from observation to action, from thought to feeling. Yet the movement redeems Decoud—for a moment at least—from the intensely hostile rhetoric of the narrator. We learn that Decoud adopts as a disguise of genuine feeling what was, until his return to Antonia, his true being. In Costaguana, Decoud "can no longer dismiss their tragic comedy with the expression, 'Quelle farce!'" (p. 153): "He was surprised at his own sensitiveness." At last, to defend himself from the pain to which his "infatuation" for Antonia was exposing him, "he soothed himself by saying he was not a patriot, but a lover" (p. 153). Decoud will later think that the word *patriot* "had no sense for cultured minds, to whom the narrowness of every belief is odious" (p. 162). While the narrative seems to endorse Decoud's attitude toward politics and belief because it is confirmed by events, he finally acts as though he were a patriot (he is outraged by the weakness of the council determining to surrender to Montero), and he is accepted as one by Sulacan society.

III

The complication here is analogous to the insight of George Eliot that the more sensitive is always defeated by the less; and this suggests that we need to consider more extensively the nature of the "sensitiveness" that comes upon Decoud as a surprise. With scientific (or semiscientific) support, we return to the position implicit in Thackeray's *Pendennis:* the sensitive literally sense most and will therefore be most apt to see the complexities that might impede action. To adopt a "theory," an idea, a "maxim" is to impose an ideal structure that must radically distort reality. But at the same time, George Eliot and Conrad see both that the idea must be corrupted and "lose its 'virtue' the moment it descends from its solitary throne to work its will among the people,"[15] and that belief is indispensable to human existence. Here is the central Conradian paradox that makes him so available to modernist reading: one cannot live without illusions as one cannot live with them. George Eliot's world comes close to anticipating this paradox, for the narrator's wisdom extends beyond the deliberately limited vision of her most ideal characters. It is perhaps because the narrator knows too much that George Eliot sets her fictions back at least a generation, to a time when it remained possible not to know, when one might be "sensitive" and not impeded.

Ladislaw, in any case, is too alert to believe that an absolute can be embodied in action. He, like Decoud, argues against a "theory of political purity" (p. 158). Like Decoud, he argues for action knowing the inadequacy of the act: are we "to try for nothing till we find immaculate men to work with?" (p. 341). Here, Ladislaw argues against one of Middlemarch's idealists, Lydgate, one who is entrapped in the "small solicitation of circumstance" and driven from his idea. But Ladislaw, like the realist novelist, asserts the complicating energies of a "mixed reality as he attempts to change it, through language, which is the medium of the ideal.

As Decoud and Ladislaw are enmeshed in compromise and the ideal at the same time, they are allied most closely with their creators. Ian Watt has pointed out that Decoud's motive in writing to his sister before he embarks with Nostromo on the lighter is "one of the two main personal motives behind Conrad's writing in general": "a desire to leave a correct impression of the feelings, like a light by which the action may be seen when personality is gone, gone where no light of investigation can ever reach the truth which every death takes out of the world."[16] Decoud is one of the most obviously autobiographical figures in all of Conrad, more clearly so because of the extreme distance from which the narrator tries to see him. As Gustav Morf suggests, Decoud is "nothing less than the exact picture of what Conrad thought would happen to him if he returned to his native country."[17] This can be taken as another way of saying that Decoud tests the novelist's sense of what happens when the novelist, instead of writing about experience, lives it. Decoud commits suicide.

The autobiographical aspect of Decoud is underlined in a letter of Conrad's: "If one looks at life in its true aspect then everything loses much of its unpleasant importance and the atmosphere becomes cleared of what are only unimportant mists that drift past in imposing shapes. When once the truth is grasped that one's own personality is only a ridiculous masquerade of something hopelessly unknown the attainment of serenity is not very far off."[18] Royal Roussel says that this attitude underlies "the ironical stance of Decoud in *Nostromo*."[19] But this detachment is also condemned by the fiction, and it implies the other side of Conrad: the very Victorian passion for "solidarity," as Conrad calls it.[20] Decoud's death results from too great a fidelity to his own sensations, from absence of faith during sensuous deprivation, and from solitude; his life acquires meaning only through "language," friendship, the expression of feelings to another—through the novelist's art. For Conrad, then, the realist engagement with the moment, when it is the sole mode of perception, is as destructive as "belief" or "illusion."

Conrad's engagement with Decoud is paralleled by George Eliot's with Ladislaw. "The author," says Henry James wickedly, "is evidently very fond of him."[21] Speculation has variously turned him into G. H. Lewes and, more recently, John Cross.[22] But the major point is that he carries a heavier burden of authority than his lightweight dilettantism would seem to justify. He represents an aspect of George Eliot that appears no more often in her actual letters than the spokesman for solidarity appears in Conrad's. Ladislaw has precisely the qualities necessary for the novelist, except that he too is drawn into experience.

His sensitivity, however ironically treated, becomes the precondition for genuine art or genuine action. In a famous passage, in which he responds to Dorothea's question, will he "be a poet?" his answer is accurate in a way the rest of the text endorses: "That depends, To be a poet is to have a soul so quick to discern that no shade of quality escapes it, and so quick to feel, that discernment is but a hand playing with a finely-ordered variety on the chords of emotion—a soul in which knowledge passes instantaneously into feeling, and feeling flashes back as a new organ of knowledge" (p. 166). "But you leave out the poems," Dorothea replies, apparently undercutting Will's Paterian intensity. But not really. The implicit criticism of Ladislaw here is similar to that of Decoud: his ideas do not issue in action. But neither do the ideas of the novelist, except in the action of writing. And the quickness of discernment to which Ladislaw aspires might make action based on feeling compatible with intelligence—as it does with Dorothea in her relations to Rosamond and Lydgate. Through Will and Dorothea, *Middlemarch* as a text aspires toward the possibility of this sort of continuity, despite the likelihood that it will be trapped in the dualism of aesthetic versus moral that leads, in Conrad's world, from feeling into despair.

There is other evidence of the narrator's endorsement of elements in Ladislaw that might seem frivolously light. A few pages earlier, the narrator had told us how much easier it was for Dorothea to dream of devotion to Casaubon than "to conceive with that distinctness which is no longer reflection but feeling—an idea wrought back to the directness of sense, like the solidity of objects—that he had an equivalent center of self, whence the lights and shadows must always fall with a certain difference" (p. 157).[23] Moreover, this power to shift perspectives is one of the qualities that accompanies Will's lightness: "Will, too, was made of very impressible stuff. The bow of a violin drawn near him cleverly, would at one stroke change the aspect of the world for him, and his point of view shifted as easily as his mood" (p. 284).

Will here foreshadows the more solemn Daniel Deronda whose almost Christlike selflessness threatens to issue into Decoudian aimlessness. That selflessness, as I earlier discussed it, points to a literal loss of character. It also makes action impossible: "strong partisanship, unless it were against an immediate oppression, had become an insecurity" for Deronda. As for Decoud, a strong "belief" is invalidated by the nuanced particularities sensed by a poet's, or novelist's, imagination.

The distance between George Eliot's moralism and Pater's aestheticism shrinks to nothing here. We are in the borderland between Victorian empiricist epistemology, ethical theory, art, and social action. Deronda, Ladislaw, and Philip Wakem, of *The Mill on the Floss,* belong in the tradition that has its most notorious representatives among Pater's sensitive protagonists, Arnold's aliens, and James's artists. Philip Wakem, the crippled aesthete of the midland flats, represents the problem most touchingly; alienated from work and society by his hump back, too sensitive for the midland world, he explains to Maggie why he is not a painter:

> I think of too many things—sow all sorts of seeds, and get no great harvest from any one of them. I'm cursed with susceptibility in every direction, and effective faculty in none ["You leave out the poems," says Dorothea to Will, cursed not by his back but by his un-Englishness.] I care for painting and music; I care for classic literature, and mediaeval literature, and modern literature. I flutter all ways, and fly in none. [II, ch. 35, p. 286]

This incapacity to live, paradoxically, is the enabling condition of the writer, and it is no accident that the sensibility of the narrator of *The Mill on the Floss* is closer to Philip's than to any other character's. (Consider, for example, the opening vision from the armchair, and the closing perspective.[24] Withdrawn from engagement in large human action, the artist's one possible action is the articulation of sensibility. Philip is forgiven because he is crippled, and because his sensibility expands into active compassion, a true moral rather than merely literary solidarity.

Ladislaw's position is more complex, and the burden of moral responsibility George Eliot placed on him seems incongruous with the way he is allowed to be in the *Middlemarch* world. The problem he is invented to resolve or mediate is a risky one, threatening to push the writer into a crippling aestheticism or a despair of moral action. On the tightrope, Ladislaw is saved by his apparent triviality. Eugene Hollahan's summary of Ladislaw's intended role in *Middlemarch* can help explain this: "He manages to avoid the consequences of . . . visionary excess by embodying a medley of admirable traits such as are found scattered in other characters." He avoids "onesidedness," and unlike Mr. Brooke, who has "gone into" everything, Ladislaw is capable of "combining a worldly smattering of various bits of knowledge with a constructive power for envisioning a primary unifying involvement in a single field of activity."[25] Perhaps.

This defines Will's role in the context of the large intellectual system of *Middlemarch*. Avoiding one-sidedness has its dangers, however; and Raymond Williams defines Will's role analogously but more positively. Ladislaw, he says, "is a free man in the way the others are not; a free mind with free emotions; a man who is wholly responsive." Will's social alienation, as much as his emotional openness, is essential to the sort of freedom he embodies: "Coming from 'nowhere,' belonging 'nowhere', he is able to move, to relate and so to grow in ways that the others are not."[26] Will is thus a critical figure in the change in George Eliot's art which had taken her from the sort of reverence (if subtly qualified) for society and the past that we see in *Adam Bede* to the revulsion from society so clearly evident in *Daniel Deronda*, but also there in *Middlemarch*. Will, of course, has the capacity to "feel" intensely and, as is demonstrated in his feeling for Dorothea, to revere the past and whatever is best in society. But he is spared the hardening into commitment by his freedom from a defined social position and from property. For this reason, it is crucially important that he not accept Bulstrode's offer and that he never get his just inheritance from Casaubon.

The social implications of Will's peculiarly disentangled state might be further illuminated by exploring further the idea that he is a novelist *manqué*. The virtues of novelist and scientist were, for both Lewes and George Eliot, very close. As I earlier suggested, it was a consistent point of Tyndall and Clifford and Lewes himself that the imaginative activity of the scientist and that of the poet were similar. In her early essay on Mackay, Marian Evans defended the erudite researcher against the "practical thinker" who is

> often beset by a narrowness of another kind. It may be doubted whether a mind which has no susceptibility to the pleasure of changing its point of view, of mastering a remote form of thought, of perceiving identity of nature under variety of manifestation—a perception which resembles an expansion of one's own being, a pre-existence in the past—can possess the flexibility, the ready sympathy, or the tolerance, which characterizes a truly philosophic culture.[27]

It may be that Will never achieves philosophic culture, but he obviously has the qualities to achieve it. *Middlemarch* demonstrates how the qualities of such a "philosophic culture" have been fragmented among Lydgate, Casaubon, and Ladislaw. But the former two are, in different ways, hardened beyond redemption. Only Will has the elasticity to grow, and it is surely growth that the narrator of *Middlemarch* most strenuously seeks in a calcifying culture.

The connection between Will and the scientific enterprise is even more clearly suggested by a remarkable essay of W. K. Clifford's, "On Some of the Conditions of Mental Development," delivered as a lecture in March of 1868. Describing there the way the mind develops the "notion . . . of a thing being real, existing external to ourselves" by virtue of its "active power," which "binds together all its boundaries," Clifford takes this activity as one that "goes on as long as we live." The mind develops reciprocally with its environment so that new experiences become more rapidly assimilated. The well-developed mind, then, grows "more and more into accordance with the nature of external things." This action amounts "to the creation of new senses," as Will Ladislaw's "poet" develops a "new organ of knowledge" or the narrator seeks the power to conceive ideas with "the directness of sense, like the solidity of objects." Clifford continues in language strikingly akin to George Eliot's:

> Men of science, for example, have to deal with extremely abstract and general conceptions. By constant use and familiarity, these, and the relations between them, become just as real and external as the ordinary objects of experience; and the perception of new relations among them is so rapid, the correspondence of the mind to external circumstances so great, that a real scientific sense is developed, by which things are perceived as immediately and truly as I see you now. Poets and painters and musicians also are so accustomed to put outside of them the idea of beauty, that it becomes a real external existence, a thing which they see with spiritual eyes,

and then describe to you, but by no means create, any more than we seem to create these ideas of table and forms and light, which we put together long ago.[28]

The condition for this sort of creative power (for Clifford is consciously talking about creation that feels like representation) is growth.

And the idea of growth, emphasized by Raymond Williams as well, marks the final stage of the argument about Ladislaw's value in the structure of *Middlemarch*. Clifford is directly to the point here as well. "The first condition of mental development is that the attitude of the mind should be creative rather than acquisitive." Mr. Brooke's mere gobbling up of disconnected facts constitutes neither development nor knowledge. The "negative condition" requisite to the creative mind, says Clifford, is "plasticity: the avoidance of all such crystallization as is immediately suggested by the environment." The reverberations throughout *Middlemarch* of this idea are astonishing, and surely the failure of Lydgate, Casaubon, and Bulstrode can be described as the result of premature crystallization under the pressure of "environment." "A mind that would grow," continues Clifford,

> must let no ideas become permanent except such as lead to action. Towards all others it must maintain an attitude of absolute receptivity; admitting all, being modified by all, but permanently biassed by none. To become crystallised, fixed in opinion and mode of thought, is to lose the great characteristic of life, by which it is distinguished from inanimate nature: the power of adapting itself to circumstances.[29]

Here is perhaps the clearest articulation of the ideal that Ladislaw is imagined to approximate. The danger of the ideal in life is precisely the danger of Ladislaw's character—triviality and disengagement, the failure to fulfill in action the growth that absolute receptivity (and here Deronda is the more obvious exemplar) allows. The narrative problem of *Middlemarch* is, in a way, to combine this vital receptivity with engagement—something that always required crystallization. And this, of course, as we shall see, is Dorothea's role in relation to Will; in Conrad, Decoud's suicide dramatizes the failure of that combination.

But Will's freedom and vital receptivity distinguish him from all the other major figures in the novel. He is a counterforce to the "narrowness" of ideas and can seem to Middlemarchers genuinely subversive, although the text implies, rather, that he is creative. His relation to the enterprise of Lydgate and Casaubon is like Philip's to the obsessed activities of Mr. Tulliver and of Tom, and like Decoud's to Gould's idealizing of the mine. Both Ladislaw and Decoud are embodiments in the text of an ironic vision of human attempts to impose a single mythic structure on the complexities of experience. But J. Hillis Miller goes too far when he suggests that Will is "the spokesman" for George Eliot's "demolition" of the theory that history is purposive and progressive.[30] Both Will and Decoud can be seen as exponents of a Darwinian theory of life and history, a theory stripped—as it is in Pater's essay on Coleridge[31]—or unifying metaphysical additions. The world evolves; "progress" is an ideal imposition on a neutral evolution. The primary "scientific" difference is that although Will accepts comfortably the incongruity between the human ideal and the lived actuality, he inhabits a world in which there is a crude correspondence between the laws of cause and effect and morality. Will believes that purposive reform is possible, and he becomes a reform politician.

It would be a mistake to dismiss as an irrelevant sentimentalism the narrator's talk, at the end, of "the growing good of the world." The wise (and almost cynical) narrator knows that political reform (as opposed to Antonia-like revolution) is deceptive; history does not follow the purposive intellectual grooves of its most alert people, but changes develop organically and biologically, through the incremental inheritance of the qualities developed in the characters of such "diffusively" good people as Dorothea, and through her in her husband, her children, and the people upon whose lives hers has impinged. Such qualities are literally inherited.[32]

Science and ethics, pointing toward the value of detachment, join another tradition of disengagement, nicely articulated by John Morley in a review in Pater's *Renaissance;*

> The speculative distractions of the epoch are noisy and multitudinous, and the first effort of the serious spirit must be to disengage itself from the futile hubbub which is sedulously maintained by the bodies of rival partisans in philosophy and philosophical theology. The effort after detachment naturally takes the form of criticism of the past, the only way in which a man can take part in the discussion and propagation of ideas, while yet standing in some sort aloof from the agitation of the present.[33]

The connection of Pater to Arnold implicit here suggests a similar relation in this tradition of Conrad to George Eliot. Pater's withdrawal extends beyond Arnold's quest for closure because, in Pater, the possibility of objective understanding has been replaced by the ultimate logic of empiricism: since all experience is "sensation," the best we can do is remain faithful, Decoud-like, to the truth of our own sensations. What one analyzes is not the object as in itself it really is, but the conditions of the "impression."[34]

Arnold's moral ideal is aestheticized into a temperamental ideal, for the greatest sensibility is susceptible to the finest "shade of quality," as Ladislaw had put it. This is all scrupulously "scientific," but really one of the mythic forms of the new science. The pervasiveness of the scientific underpinning of the new aestheticism is manifest everywhere. Take, for example, a passage from one of Henry James's critical essays:

> Experience is never limited, and it is never complete; it is an immense sensibility, a kind of huge spider-web of the finest silken threads suspended in the chamber of consciousness, and catching every air-borne particle in its tissue. It is the very atmosphere of the mind; and when the mind is imaginative—much more when it happens to be that of a man of genius—it takes to itself the faintest hints of life, it converts the very pulses of the air into revelations.[35]

Recognizably Paterian, with echoes of Ruskin in the first two clauses, and our old friend, the metaphor of the web, in the third clause, this passage also draws directly on what any interested layperson would have been absorbing from science at the time. The Paterian emphasis on experience—"not the fruit of experience, but experience itself is the end"[36]—is an outgrowth of empiricist epistemology. But, as I have tried to show, empiricism was teaching also that one could never perceive everything, even of what seems to be given before you, and that all experience, like all matter, is in constant motion. Our sensations then work like Pasteur's experiment, in which he discovered that air was full of microscopic floating solid particles,[37] retrieving some of the infinitesimal matter of our experience. The "pulse" of the air is literal scientific fact, the appalling truth that Conrad discovered when being shown an X-ray machine, that all life was the wavelike movement of matter so fine and attenuated as to be invisible. The true scientist, like the true artist, experiences the subtlest motions of matter, and imagines and hypothesizes worlds on the basis of the minutest suggestions.

Here is a conflux of the various elements of the tradition to which Ladislaw and Decoud belong: science, matter, a theory of knowledge, sensibility, and experience. Whatever the cut of their clothes or the banality of their "characters," they are both a long way from the mid-century conventions of the ordinary that dominated realism. The condition of the fullest understanding is withdrawal from the hubbub, not disenchanted engagement; the effect of the refined sensibility that might achieve full understanding turns out not to be—as Arnold dreamed—a transformation of culture, but as Conrad saw it, the writing of books. To be sensitive is to be crippled.

IV

I have been trying to suggest that the striking but apparently accidental similarities between Ladislaw and Decoud actually reflect certain historically important similarities in the world views of George Eliot and

Conrad. In his public stances, and even in the voice of Marlow, Conrad draws as much as George Eliot on the Victorian Carlylean tradition of hard work and rigorous self-discipline: unself-conscious work is a sign of health; the pursuit of happiness is chimerical. "Work while it is called Today," Carlyle endlessly quotes, "for the Night cometh wherein no man can work."[38] George Eliot also agreed with Carlyle that the disciplined denial of desire and personal ambition is a condition for the richest life in a world where pain is the norm and the self is insignificant.[39] For her, too, as we hear it from Adam Bede and Felix Holt and Caleb Garth, work is the condition of moral salvation. Yet in Ladislaw and Decoud, both writers imagined characters who belonged to an alternative, anti-Carlylean, tradition, built by Pater out of Arnold's Hellenism.

The differences between these characters, and the way they are managed by their narrators, signify important changes in the tradition. They maneuver through a world of more or less obsessed idealists very differently, although for both, integrity depends on alienation, and alienation leads to further expulsion. Decoud's story points finally to what Ladislaw's story attempts to avert: the writer's expulsion from the community in the very act of fidelity to those sensations that might allow some secret solidarity—some Wordsworthian communion—with others.

Compared with Decoud, Ladislaw is a child. He is allowed a childish exuberance, a rebelliousness, a susceptibility "without any neutral region of indifference in his nature, ready to turn everything that befell him into the collision of passionate drama" (p. 586). His melodramatizing imagination manifests itself at first only in the flittering dilettantism we have already noted, but the narrator's indulgence undercuts much of the irony implicit in the narrative. Indeed, the most negative comments come from James Chettam and other members of the community whose shallowness we know. But Decoud's indifferentism comes to us in a bitter rhetoric that implies not only Conrad's hostility to the necessary strategy of withdrawal, but also Decoud's painful disenchantment. Cynicism is invariably the disguise of a frustrated moral idealism. Decoud, the narrator tells us, had "pushed the habit of universal raillery to a point where it blinded him to the genuine impulses of his own nature" (p. 135). Yet, unlike Ladislaw, Decoud is admired if not liked by most of the people with whom he has to work. In *Middlemarch*, it is the narrator who provides the wisdom that requires us to value Will's excesses of feeling, despite the judgments of the community. In *Nostromo*, neither the character nor the narrators are equal to the complex nature of Decoud. We can note, in his interview with Mrs. Gould, the "tremendous excitement under the cloak of studied carelessness," which is followed in a moment by this: "But already there was something of a mockery in Decoud's suppressed excitement" (p. 183).

Although it is important to recognize the moral intensity of the narrator of *Middlemarch* in the struggle to create a more complex kind of unity out of the shattering of traditional unities, George Eliot's voice is often the voice of disenchantment. It impresses on us the failures of history, the littleness of the self, the pervasiveness of death. Yet she struggles against the wisdom of her own insight to authorize Dorothea's quest (and Dorothea is yet another of those ambitious myth-hunting idealizers) for a binding theory. Whereas in *Nostromo*, we are told that Decoud dies because he cannot sustain an illusion, in *Middlemarch* what Decoud would have thought of as illusion carries with it the authority of science. And it is the same science that, in Conrad's world, makes *all* ideas illusion. It is reality read, as Conrad would have been the first to acknowledge, through another "temperament." But, as we can see by looking at the condition of George Eliot's temperament during the writing of *Middlemarch*, even here the difference from Conrad is not great.

The letters at the time are marked with a deep new awareness of death. Her experience of the painful dying of Lewes's twenty-six-year-old son, Thornton, haunts almost every letter for a year. Suddenly she is full of consciousness of death's approach and seems almost to be welcoming it. There is, indeed, a Schopenhauerian quality to these letters, anticipating the unmistakable presence of Schopenhauer in Conrad, a recognition that only the death of desire can bring peace. To Mrs. Richard Congreve she wrote, for example: "My strong egoism has caused me so much melancholy, which is traceable to a fastidious yet hungry ambition, that I am relieved by the comparative quietude of personal cravings which age is bringing."[40] One of Ladislaw's functions in the novel is to quench this Casaubon-like ambition.

The particularity of Thornton's death was intensified for her by the Franco-Prussian war, a subject that dismayed her and threatened any progressive sense of history. She speaks of Prussian brutality (at the start of the war she had sided with the Prussians) with cynical bitterness as "the regression of barbarism from that historical tomb where we thought it so picturesquely buried—if indeed we ought not to beg pardon of barbarism, which had no weapons for making eight wounds at once in our body." She ends the letter on the subject of dying, which "has no melancholy for me, except in the parting and leaving behind which Love makes so hard to contemplate."[41]

Surely such experience impressed forcefully on her the inadequacy of optimistic progressivist history like Comte's positivism, or Herbert

Spencer's "evolutionary" theory. The "onward tendency of human things," as she talks about it in *The Mill on the Floss*, becomes, with this barbaric "regression," terribly suspect. *Middlemarch* is significantly full of comments that imply ironically the failure of moral progress through history. One can detect an almost Decoudian tone, as when the narrator remarks, "As to any provincial history in which the agents are all of high moral rank, that must be of a date long posterior to the first Reform Bill" (p. 250).

Another element in Eliot's letters at this time seems to connect her with Decoud. Conrad talked of his personality as "a ridiculous and aimless masquerade." Eliot assimilated humanist positivism with Christian self-denial to see each self as a minute element in the species. In *Middlemarch*, we have seen, Dorothea learns this littleness by recognizing the self's impersonal participation in an "involuntary, palpitating life." But there is also, in letters at this time, a new sense of the insignificance of self that implies something of the pervasiveness of death, Eliot talks of striving for the "impersonal life" through which we may "gain much more independence, than is usually believed, of the small bundle of facts that make our own personality."[42] Ultimately Decoud achieves this kind of impersonality, but it turns out to be death, not improvement of the species. Alone on the Great Isabel, he is drawn out of the masquerade of personality back into its material and unindividuated source—the sheer matter of the Golfo Placido, which accepts his body "untroubled."

Obviously, in George Eliot's novels we are not ready for such a conclusion; the personal recognitions in *Middlemarch* are transformed into a quest for Dorothea's Lewesian "binding theory" that "could illuminate principle with the widest knowledge" (p. 16). While writing *Middlemarch*, she was preoccupied not only with death and the disasters of history, but with Lewes's Lydgatian attempt to bind spirit with matter, to develop a metaphysics of science, a coherent theory of "life and mind." George Eliot could say, in January, 1871, "my interest in his studies increases rather than diminishes."[43]

Decoud and Conrad were to give up on such a binding theory, what Decoud would have called a characteristic of Englishmen, who "cannot act or exist without idealizing every simple feeling, desire, or achievement" (p. 184). But Conrad does not endorse the refusal to idealize, any more than he endorses idealization. Decoud's death is a consequence of the refusal, and he merges "into the world of cloud and water, of natural forces and forms of nature"; the narrator tells us, in true Carlylean tradition, that "in our activity alone do we find the sustaining illusion of an independent existence against the whole scheme of things of which we form a helpless part" (p. 409). But the critical phrase is "sustaining illusion," which places us and the narrator in an impossible and very modern position. It is not the same thing as the remark of the *Middlemarch* narrator in discussing Will, that "our sense of duty must often wait for some work which shall take the place of dilettanteism and make us feel that the quality of our action is not a matter of indifference" (p. 338). The self is, as in Conrad, affirmed through work; but the affirmation is not an illusion.

Decoud could survive only if he were wrong about the world, or if he chose consciously to behave as though he were wrong. Work, Carlyle's salvation, serves in Conrad only to keep us from seeing the truth; the novelist's work—and Decoud's, too, as he talks to Mrs. Gould or writes to his sister—is to reveal the truth, a suicidal activity protected from suicide only by the activity of articulation itself. There is no other possibility for a pure materialist empiricism. Decoud's remarkable sensitivity and perceptiveness as a recorder of impressions are the other side of the belief that "ideas" are incompatible with experience. His intellectual audacity, as the narrator calls it, is precisely in his rejection of all traditional ways of making connections. Near his death he sees the world "as a succession of incomprehensible images" (p. 409), as Dorothea first saw the paintings in Rome. And if Decoud is trapped by his intellectual audacity, the complementary story of Nostromo reminds us that "disenchanted vanity" is "the reward of audacious action" (p. 412).

In Eliot's terms, however, Decoud is not so much a bad man as a bad scientist. Solipsism, the Paterian reading of Victorian empiricist thought, is necessary only if one does not have the scientist's faith in, first, the uniformity of nature, and second, what Eliot calls the "invariable law of consequence." On the strength of such a faith, one can make great imaginative leaps, reading, as Henry James suggests, "revelations" in the finest particle of experience. Here Conrad's quest for solidarity returns, and here Eliot gives her faith. Neither her science nor her morality had entered an age of indeterminacy.

Ladislaw, by means of his faith in Dorothea, is allowed the larger faith by which *Middlemarch* implies an ultimate coherence to human experience; Antonia's relation to Decoud differs from Dorothea's to Ladislaw in that—in keeping with a Schopenhauerian misogyny that marks Decoud if not Conrad himself—she becomes an occasion for an "illusion." Dorothea becomes a means to truth beyond the limits of common sense. Her test is a trial of faith in Ladislaw. Worse than the misery of being despised by a lover is "to think ill" of him (p. 593). She achieves a refinement of feeling that Lewes, in *Problems of Life and Mind*, called Knowledge: "a vision of relations that are not directly felt"

(II, p. 23). The world of *Middlemarch* is made coherent by a vast sum of "unapparent relations" that make the cosmos "continuous."

In *Daniel Deronda* this transformed reality transforms realism into something else. These unapparent relations become realities to the mystic hypothesizing of Mordecai, and the world of ordinary common sense itself becomes suspect, the object of contempt and cynicism. It happens, too, in *Middlemarch,* where coincidences are explained as belonging to the same sorts of causal links that account for more obviously inevitable events. The law of consequence works everywhere: "To Uriel watching the progress of planetary history from the Sun, the one result would be just as much of a coincidence as the other" (p. 302). Through an intuition built out of Jamesian experience Dorothea recognizes Lydgate's innocence; and in this, as Michael Mason has shown, the more scientific Farebrother turns into a bad scientist.[44] Dorothea "disliked this cautious weighing of consequences, instead of an ardent faith in efforts of justice and mercy, which would conquer by their emotional force" (p. 537). Mere sentimentalism to Decoud. But validated reality in *Middlemarch.*

The ultimate division between the two writers may come down to their perception of the relation between desire and reality. The structure of *Middlemarch,* almost as much as the structure of *Daniel Deronda,* is the structure of educated desire. The various events, which are no surprise to Uriel and have their scientific justification in the complexity and minuteness of unapparent relations, offer us a world in which "feeling" and "desire," emerging from a sensibility so fine that it must hold itself tentatively for a long time, provide some sort of rough justice. And they exercise a continuing and refining influence on the slowly evolving course of the world. Dorothea's "justice and mercy," by the testimony in George Eliot's next novel, can be transformed from desire into fact, can be made incarnate.[45]

In *Nostromo,* the structure of desire is the structure of fragmentation and disaster. The idea of justice and mercy is scattered with the pages of Don José's *Fifty Years of Misrule* during the Monterist revolt. Decoud's incapacity for faith is justified by the effects of Antonia's. For with her, faith is the misperception of unapparent relations. Her longing for justice issues in more injustice. *Nostromo* leaves us at a point George Eliot transcends through the union of Ladislaw and Dorothea: where the idea and the fact coexist without touching. Decoud becomes a fact in the untroubled waters of the Golfo Placido; Antonia becomes the idea that is the final ironic commentary on Decoud's own ironies. The writer of *Nostromo* seems the only one—and then for only as long as he is writing—to be able to hold the two together. Conrad said in one of his most moving letters that he himself remains outside of political action because, "je dois—j'ai besoin,—de garder ma pensée intacte comme dernier hommage de fidelité à une cause qui est perdue."[46]

The most poignant image in *Nostromo* of the difference between Conrad and Eliot comes in a scene whose images and characters echo resonantly with the world of Dorothea. Toward the end, the revolution over, the separate state of Sulaco rich and powerful, Mrs. Gould sits in her garden, resembling "a good fairy, weary with a long career of well-doing, touched by the withering suspicion of the uselessness of her labours, the powerlessness of her magic" (p. 427). Like Dorothea, disenchanted in the Lowick garden, chained to Casaubon's dream of a Key to All Mythologies, Emilia Gould has sought—and failed to find—a coherent faith linked to a coherent action. Charles has deserted her for his idealized mine, and she protects him from his own corruption by the incorruptible silver in their fruitless marriage, as Dorothea struggles to protect and satisfy Casaubon. But at that moment of disenchantment, it comes into Mrs. Gould's mind "that for life to be large and full, it must contain the care of the past and of the future in every passing moment of the present. Our daily work must be done to the glory of the dead and for the good of those who come after" (p. 427).The one apparently incorruptible figure in *Nostromo* thinks in the language of George Henry Lewes and of George Eliot, whose heroines share this desire exactly. They move to such a vision on a path of pain leading to disenchantment. The shattering of a dream opens a reality that requires recognition of one's implication in a world larger than the self. "If the past is not to bind us, where can duty lie?" Maggie Tulliver cries in her final rejection of Stephen Guest in *The Mill on the Floss* (VI, ch. 14, p. 417). Maggie, however, dies before paying the price of the past. Casaubon dies and spares Dorothea the worst. Emilia lives on with the burden.

Knowledge marks Emilia's behavior. "There was," she thinks, "something inherent in the necessities of successful action which carried with it the moral degradation of the idea" (p. 427). This echoes Conrad's nonfictional writing as well as Decoud. Whereas Dorothea infects Ladislaw with faith, Decoud has infected Emilia with disbelief, and the disbelief isolates her as much as it does Decoud. Yet the narrative grants her, in her survival with knowledge and with no novelist's opportunity to protect her idea, a kind of heroism: "An immense desolation, the dread of her own continued life, descended upon the first lady of Sulaco. With a prophetic vision she saw herself surviving alone the degradation of her young ideal of life, of love, of work—all alone in the Treasure House of the World" (p. 428). Her marriage is infertile; they are the last of the Goulds.

Dorothea is ultimately fertile, although she has difficulty in childbirth, and she ends believing in the work of her husband, while she herself is an ironic commentary upon it. At the last, we hear of her unhistoric acts (which have become part of the unapparent relations) responsible for the "growing good of the world." The elaborations and complexities and multiplying of perspectives of her novel are affirmed by a binding theory that replaces the dying mythology of Christianity and common sense. The possibility of bringing knowledge and action together, of moving from Ladislaw to Dorothea, of moving from self to other, turns out to be incompatible with the mode of the realistic novel, which dwells, like Decoud, in ironies, and resists ideas and feelings in favor of particularities.

With Emilia Gould we are in the presence of yet another sort of novel. The last we see of her is in "the only moment of bitterness in her life," when she has heard Nostromo's secret and finds Decoud's cynicism confirmed once more. She tells the heartbroken Giselle, weeping over the dead Nostromo, "Console yourself, child. Very soon he would have forgotten you for the treasure" (p. 459). Emilia, then, is the only character in the novel with full knowledge. She has heard from Decoud of her husband's "sentimentalism" and knows the real motive of Decoud's separatist politics (p. 183); she knows herself desolate and alone; she knows that the ideal is "degraded" in action; she knows the corruption of the incorruptible Nostromo. Her position is so powerfully imagined because it represents an alterantive to Decoud's suicide, an alternative yet closer to Conrad's own. Her knowledge, though it produces bitterness at least once, never issues in "barren indifferentism." Unlike Decoud, whose sensitivity is protected by his dilettantism, Emilia faces the illusoriness of her life, and yet she thinks as George Eliot thought, after all.

She is in the paradoxical position of the novelist who recognizes that writing is the only possible action, but knows that the only idea that writing can affirm is that ideas have no connection with the reality they purport to describe. She is different from the novelist, however, because when Nostromo offers to tell her about the hidden silver, she refuses to hear. Moreover, when Dr. Monygham asks what Nostromo has told her, she lies: "He told me nothing." The novelist may not refuse to hear, and may not lie. And Emilia, in order to sustain the ideal in action and fulfill her responsibility to past and present and future, must be corrupted. Like Marlow at the end of *Heart of Darkness*, she must lie to protect. Like the realist novelist of the great Victorian tradition she must hold out until the end against the monster she knows is there. For the modern novelist this is no option, and the Victorian consonance between the real and the moral is hopelessly smashed.

The progress these two books mark out, then, is progress toward the centrality of the disengaged figure, the writer himself. And the continuities are clear. In *Middlemarch* the world of "common sense" becomes monstrous, one to which the best must refuse unreflecting commitment. Ladislaw is right to stand at its edges and is horrified at the disaster caused by Dorothea's premature faith. In *Nostromo*, not only is the world of "common sense" monstrous, but there is no common sense. Behind the absurdities of greed and desire played out in the revolutionary politics of Costaguana lies a world of unapparent relations yet more monstrous—in its absolute, indifferent unintelligence. The faith of Dorothea pierces through to an ultimate coherence by imposing desire on reality; the wisdom of Emilia detects only the triumph of "material interests." *Nostromo* is a world in which all ideas are corrupted and hence one in which language may have no external reference. Only outside the pulsating world, in the imaginative constructions of fictions, can language thrive. Within it, with Decoud's suicide, the moral-aesthetic tradition implicit in Whately's review of Jane Austen becomes, irrevocably, two traditions.

Epilogue
Lawrence, Frankenstein, and the Reversal of Realism

A thing isn't life just because somebody does it. This the artist ought to know
perfectly well. The ordinary bank clerk buying himself a new straw hat isn't "life"
at all: it is just existence, quite all right, like everyday dinners: but not "life."

> By life, we mean something that gleams, that has
> the fourth-dimensional quality.

D. H. Lawrence, "Morality and the Novel"

Having begun with monsters, I return to them at last. The texture of
Conrad's fiction, in the deliberate absurdity of its central actions, in its
rapid movement to extremes, in its extraordinary psychic resonances,
in its disruptions and its constant confrontations with the ineffable,
seems only a more sophisticated development of the texture of *Frankenstein* itself. Like *Frankenstein*, it projects psychic landscapes as much as
literal ones. In the early *An Outcast of the Islands*, the too confident,
moral, and righteous Lingard, whose business seems the re-creation of
wastrels and derelicts, leaves Willems, the outcast, with a speech that
might well be a gloss on Frankenstein's relation to his monster:

> "You shall stay here," continued Lingard, with sombre delibera-
> tion. "You are not fit to go amongst people. Who could suspect,
> who could guess, who could imagine what is in you? I couldn't!
> You are my mistake. I shall hide you here. . . . You are not a human
> being that may be destroyed or forgiven. You are a bitter thought,
> as something without a body that must be hidden. . . . You are my
> shame."[1]

Conrad not only reflects the pattern of *Frankenstein*, while making its
psychic implications more centrally dramatic, but anticipates his own
richer and far more complex narratives, in which he more completely
disembodies the protagonists' "shame." Willems is Lingard's double,
his monstrous self, subject to uncontrollable passions and degradations. Beyond him lies Lord Jim, Marlow's double, who yet has

his own inescapable, recurring shame. And beyond him there is
Razumov, bearing the shame of his betrayal of Haldin and intimating a
reality that the narrator-Professor will not allow himself to face.

Conrad's is an art of extremes that, in disrupting the conventions of
the ordinary upon which nineteenth-century realism built, remains at
least consistent with the realist's need to point beyond literature, to
locate a reality beyond the conventions of language. The reality he
finds, or intimates, is a world in which the surfaces with which realism
was preoccupied and which it largely tried to take as the reality itself
merely disguise the truth, or repress it. His fiction is redeemed from
despair only by that art that marks separation and allows disengagement and clarity of vision. When he leaves Emilia Gould refusing the
full knowledge she has achieved, he implies both his continuities with
the tradition of Victorian realists, and his entire, self-conscious separation from them. There is, of course, no "growing good of the world"
beyond Emilia's unhistoric acts. Instead, there is the recognition that
the implicit fear of the Victorians was justified: when the monstrous
energies kept at bay by society and tradition were released they could
lead only to destruction and despair. Conrad intimates the other side of
Victorian realism: the inhuman reality that lies behind the humanly
organized and imagined world.

Conrad's fiction provides evidence of the pervasiveness of the developing empiricist view that since we know not external reality but only
our own sensations of it we must shift our focus from the physical to the
psychological if we wish to know the truth. But in addition he seems to
act out the consequences of the withdrawal of significance from the
external world. The psychological life of Conrad's protagonists, like Jim
or Razumov, goes on almost regardless of the relentlessly inhuman
physical realities in which they move; insofar as there seems to be a
connection it is the connection of discontinuity or disruption. The self
as focus becomes its own world in which human meanings are constantly disrupted by inhuman energies. That world is full of the drums
that beat in the heart of darkness, of the shadows of betrayal, of uncontrollable and incomprehensible fears and appetites. The self contains its own monsters.

Despite the uniqueness of Conrad's art, his way of feeling and imagining was characteristic of much late-century fiction in that it implied
the primacy of the artist's role. And yet it did so with an ambivalence
that registers once more the realist's dissatisfaction with anything but
the fullness of human experience. The disengagement implied by such
figures as Philip Wakem and Will Ladislaw becomes an essential quality of value and survival. As he wrote to Cunninghame Graham, Conrad's watchword in the midst of the universality of meaningless de-

pravity and the inevitable corruption of ideas by experience was *"garder ma pensée intacte comme dernier homage de fidelité à une cause qui est perdue."* Art was the means to that protection, but within his art Conrad pushed as far as he could to the full imagination of what it meant *not* to protect his thought. In the no-man's-land between those mindless millions who rot behind the banalities of their language and their spaciously ordered lives and the heroic but agonized few who burn in confrontation with the full "horror" of reality, Conrad set up his camp, vulnerably, amid the defenses of fragile language that implies both his desire for and fear of burning. It is surely no accident that he tended to break down both physically and psychically after each major book, each prolonged imaginative foray into the world where thought was not protected. And after *Under Western Eyes,* his fullest investigation of betrayal and redemption, he suffered his most severe breakdown and could never quite regain the artistic powers that forced him to imagine the monstrous experience at the edge of language.

Conrad's art leads us, then, to an almost ultimate reversal of the realist's position. Seeing with George Eliot the pervasive, perhaps irredeemable corruption of society, he cannot imagine for his characters a Deronda-like vocation in a world just beyond this one. The work to do in the world becomes only an illusion and, indeed, the world that had been the realist's subject has become all illusion as well. The realist's desire to get beyond literature ironically turns Conrad self-consciously back to literature, to the act of writing itself, as the only means of intimating a world that cannot be contained in language, and of reaching beyond the "thick wall of personality," through which no human voice ever penetrates, to some sort of tenuous community of feeling. Realism, from such a perspective, becomes itself merely conventional: it is a false construction deluding us into ignoring for a moment the insurmountable distance between idea and experience and the horror that hides beyond language. In reaching this impasse, Conrad takes us to where the Victorians feared they might be driven.

But to see the world as Conrad saw it was not necessarily to feel it as he did. And in the curious progress of the novelist's attempts to get at the real and even confront the shadowy monster who was emerging once more, we can find yet another reversal. After having finished writing *Sons and Lovers* in 1912, D. H. Lawrence wrote, "I can't forgive Conrad for being so sad and giving in."[2] The judgment implies that Lawrence's rejection of Conrad, whose work did impress him, resulted not so much from seeing the world differently as from refusing to "give in" to the horror that they mutually saw.[3] In Lawrence, to give in is to accept the reality of the realist's novel, or, Conrad-like, to accept the despairing consequences of discovering the banality and emptiness of the realist's world. Like Conrad, Lawrence saw the world as "rotting," heard the drums of the heart of darkness beating in his own breast, felt the dissociation of language from being. But Lawrence refused to obey the watchword *"garder ma pensée,"* to be the disengaged and crippled artist. Around each novel he built nonfictional structures reminiscent of the prose of the great Victorian sages. While, like Conrad, he made himself an alien, he never gave up the hope in his fiction and out of it of rebuilding a knowable community. And while despising the rot, as Conrad did, he did not fear to burn.

In Lawrence, Frankenstein returns again (almost literally), but Lawrence's reading of the tale constitutes an almost total reversal of the culture's and of Conrad's implicit in his terror of the heart of darkness. *Frankenstein* is not frightening because it imagines the release into the world of irrational energies and the destructive hidden impulses of humanity. The book is instinctively right that those energies *will* be released and are always there; but the energies are destructive because Victor Frankenstein had dreamed that the world is rational and comprehensible. He has built his monster on the assumption that there is no mystery in vitality, nothing sacred in life. Lawrence locates the peculiar modernity of *Frankenstein*—the absence from it of any theological or metahuman possibilities. The monster is evil not because he is irrational, but because he is constructed entirely out of rational, mechanical principles. He is the embodiment of the idea that mind can control matter, that thought is more important than flesh, and he is the revenge of the flesh on the arrogant mind.

Frankenstein turns up once more in Lawrence's *The Rainbow*, a novel that seems continuous with the nineteenth-century tradition of the family chronicle, large, loose, baggy, and intrinsically realist in method. But of course, *The Rainbow* is as visionary as it is realist, as patterned as a romance, and it reaches beyond the possibilities of realism both in substance and in technique. It refuses causal explanation in its attempt to get close to the instinctual life that realism, perforce, had slighted. Almost unnoticed among the many other signals that *The Rainbow* has mythic as well as realist aspiration, a "Dr. Frankstone" appears as Ursula Brangwen's instructor in the college laboratory where they are studying the structure of the human cell. If the scene reflects Lydgate's enterprise in *Middlemarch*, it more obviously imitates Mary Shelley's preoccupation in *Frankenstein* with the connection between matter and life, and Lawrence delightfully removes Frankenstein's masculine mask to make Dr. Frankstone a woman. But she is true to Victor's vocation as, in her remarks, she demonstrates how Mary Shelley's myth of creation anticipated the direction modern science was to take.

In her one major speech in the novel she argues a position that in all but tone is close to Conrad's: science was revealing not only that there was nothing special about human life but that it was entirely explicable in terms of matter:

> I don't see why we should attribute some special mystery to life—do you? We don't understand it as we understand electricity, even, but that doesn't warrant our saying it is something special, something different in kind and distinct from everything else in the universe—do you think it does? May it not be that life consists in a complexity of physical and chemical activities we already know in science? I don't see, really, why we should imagine there is a special order of life, and life alone—[4]

Lawrence has turned directly to the metaphor of Frankenstein for his image of the modern tendency to substitute mechanism for life. Ironically, for a writer who was rejecting the work of the Victorians, he was in fact adopting that Lewesian emphasis on the saving nature of "organism" that we considered earlier. "Organism," for Lawrence as for George Eliot, is precisely what distinguishes life from simple matter. Seeing organism as no more than complex mechanism, Conrad is driven to the edge of despair: there is little difference between Decoud alive and alone and Decoud absorbed in the inorganic waters of the Golfo Placido. But for Lawrence, the "mystery" of the organic is not only a George Eliot-like reimagination of the secular in the language of religion, so that though increasingly complex, it remained ultimately accessible to human knowledge; for Lawrence, the mystery has the full power of religious imagination. And the effect of this new way of feeling and thinking about the materials of science is the reversal of both the Frankenstein metaphor and the objectives of realism that characterize his fictional quests.

Ursula cannot accept this modern tendency to read life as mechanism. In the passage that follows, she rejects such a vision while bringing to her examination of the cell the sort of passionate intensity we have already seen in both Victor and Lydgate; and in her questioning what she sees she brings science and religious forms together.

> Was she herself an impersonal force, or conjunction of forces, like one of these? She looked still at the unicellular shadow that lay within the field of light, under the microscope. It was alive. She saw it move—she saw the bright mist of its ciliary activity, she saw the gleam of its nucleus, as it slid across the plane of light. What then was its will? If it was a conjunction of forces, physical and chemical, what held these forces unified, and for what purpose were they unified? [P. 441]

Whereas traditionally, the narrative of *Frankenstein* was read as a drama of the domination of dark human energies over human thought and will, here Lawrence takes it as the drama of the domination of mental consciousness over the mystic vitality of the whole human organism. Ursula is on the verge of religious vision that, had Victor undergone it, would have sent him back to a sexual union with Elizabeth rather than on to the manufacture of his animated being, the Monster: "She could not understand what it all was. She only knew that it was not limited mechanical energy, nor mere purpose of self-preservation and self-assertion. It was a consummation, a being infinite. She was a oneness with the infinite. To be oneself was supreme, gleaming triumph of infinity" (p. 441). At this point Ursula feels a deep "dread of the material world" and turns to "the new life, the reality," which is her relation with Skrebensky.

In a way, what Conrad had "given up" was this visionary faith. Had he looked at the X-rays that so shook him and discovered a divine energy instead of mere hostile mechanical and mindless movement, his art and his life would have been radically different. In Lawrence's view, one must risk what Lewes called the world of unapparent relations. One must risk accepting the mysterious invisible energies that Western culture had variously protected itself from by naming them God, or, with God gone, by naming them "id," or by repressing them, or by imagining the possibility of explaining them. In his rejection of "mental consciousness" Lawrence is, in effect, declaring war on the realists who assumed that what was real was available to "common sense" or explicable in the value-laden language they tried to imagine was primarily objective. Conrad, Lawrence surely knew, saw the same primary reality of the inexplicable and indescribable. His fault as a writer was that he was afraid of it.

In his original essay on Benjamin Franklin, Lawrence further elaborates his reading of *Frankenstein*. "Mary Shelley," he writes, "in the midst of the idealists, gives the dark side to the ideal being, showing us Frankenstein's monster."[5] That is to say, she created a myth that demonstrated the monstrousness of the merely mental "idea" (a very Carlylean notion). It is monstrous precisely because, as Conrad would have put it, all ideas are corrupted in experience. No idea can connect directly to the ultimate nonrational reality it purports to describe, and imposing ideas on experience is merely destructive. The idea of Frankenstein could have emerged only from a culture that had imagined the perfectibility of humanity, or a French Revolution to bring about the perfection. The notion of perfectibility was, as Lawrence suggests, allied to the fresh sense of the power of man to shape men: "The ideal being was man created by man. And so was the supreme monster."

The dark side to the ideal being is, then, its rationalist, Godwinian side, and Lawrence talks as though Franklin himself were the monster: "If on the one hand Benjamin Franklin is the perfect human being of Godwin, on the other hand he is a monster, not exactly as the monster in *Frankenstein*, but for the same reason, viz., that he is the production or fabrication of the human will, which projects itself upon a living being and automatises that being according to a given precept."[6] The true monstrousness is not the raging id (which Lawrence translates into the "creative mystery") but the attempt of consciousness to impose itself on the world. That imposition, coming through morality and science, is an act of the very will that the Victorians invoked as a means to discipline their own irrational energies, and it is doomed like Frankenstein to failure. In creating his monster, Frankenstein named the world and imposed the structure of a machine on an organism.

The Frankstone episode, in its rejection of the notion that there is "nothing special" about the world, is another almost parodic reversal of literary conventions. Austen mocks the extremity and "specialness" of gothic heroines; Lawrence mocks the middlingness of realistic ones. The parodic structure of Lawrence's vision is evident everywhere, even if it tends to come without much gaiety and with some bitterness. His protagonists reverse the behavior of conventional heroes and heroines, and they do so without much explanation: Tom Brangwen decides to marry Lydia the moment he sees her; Birkin sells all he owns; Aaron flees from his wife; the woman rides away to ritual sacrifice. Lawrencian parody turns away from realism toward myth (an element that, like the monstrous, realism always tried to disguise but never quite managed to exorcise). The complex progress of Lawrence's art is through various sorts of mythic shaping that he hoped would correspond not to literary traditions but to the true shape of experience that underlay the banalities of the realist, the buying of a "new straw hat." He invents new myths, finds each of them wanting, and has the courage to abandon them; but near the end of his career he returns, if somewhat chastened, to the visionary possibilities of *The Rainbow*. In *Lady Chatterley's Lover*, he creates a work that resonates parodically with the now dead traditions of realism and that, in the very spirit of the dead tradition, tentatively gestures beyond literature toward another reality and toward a faith in and love for the life Ursula once imagined.

The enterprise of *Lady Chatterley's Lover*, as Lawrence described it in his "A propos of Lady Chatterley's Lover," is to move toward some kind of reunion between idea and experience. The dissolution of that union has been a common element in almost every novel considered in this study. It is almost the central subject of *Red-gauntlet,* and among the young dreamers of impossible dreams it becomes a commonplace. Henchard's will testifies to the hopeless contradiction between intention and effect, idea and action, that makes the earlier realist enterprise ultimately self-contradictory. For Lawrence, it is the intiating assumption:

> We now know the act does not necessarily follow on the thought. In fact, thought and action, word and deed, are two separate forms of consciousness, two separate lives which we lead. We need very sincerely to keep a connexion. But while we think, we do not act, and while we act we do not think. . . . The two conditions, of thought and action, are mutually exclusive. Yet they should be related in harmony.
> And this is the real point of this book.[7]

Such consciousness of the separation between language and life suggests why *Lady Chatterley's Lover* had to become such a naughty book to the culture Lawrence was trying to reach (despite his own contempt for the effort to shock or *épater le bourgeois*). It stands in parodic relation to the tradition of moral-aesthetic realism, while itself (good parody that it is) belonging to that tradition. It stands almost equally against the developing tradition that was transforming the hero into the artist. It is, at any rate, a novel that refuses to "give up," as one that struggles unevenly by reappropriation of old myths to destroy the conventions of language and society that stood between writer and reality. It is an immensely personal book, caught inevitably in the contradictions of language and art, in which Lawrence nevertheless comes close to succeeding in his quest to stand impersonally free of the frightened will both of his culture and of himself.

Necessarily, then, the novel is importantly about novel writing. Clifford Chatterly and Mrs. Bolton are Victorian realists. Both of them write gossip, as the narrator calls it, and the letter of Mrs. Bolton to Connie in Venice is really a virtuoso parody of the texture of much realist fiction. Clifford's stories are also gossipy, if more intellectual and analytic (as in a later phase of realism): "The observation was extraordinary and peculiar. But there was no touch, no actual contact. It was as if the whole thing took place in a vacuum. And since the field of life is largely an artificially lighted stage today, the stories were curiously true to modern life, to the modern psychology, that is."[8] Like the lovable Philip Wakem before him, Clifford is a cripple. His capacity to see with such minuteness and to register details so precisely derives from the incapacity to be engaged. He does, indeed, become the perfect representative of the modern writer as we have watched him being imagined by earlier writers.

But more important for my purposes here, Clifford brings together two images—one of the crippled and disenchanted artist seeing clearly by virtue of staying out of "touch," and the other of the merely created being. What we first learn about Clifford is that he was shipped back to England from the war "more or less in bits" (p. 47). Like Frankenstein's monster he is "more or less" put together again. For Lawrence he is no longer human, but merely pieced together mechanical fragments. Life is literally organic, and if Lawrence seems rather brutal and unfeeling about Clifford it is because he takes Clifford as a construction of modern civilization itself: an effect of the war, and a figure reduced physically to what the culture has chosen for itself in the person of those absurdly named intellectuals, Tommy Dukes (the best of them), Charlie May, Arnold B. Hammond, and Winterslow. He is mere mental consciousness. Tommy Dukes, who knows he is himself merely a "Mental-lifer," nevertheless knows as well the consequence of being one. What he says about the relation between ideas and life explains both Clifford's monstrousness and the critical importance of not being satisfied with the observer's stance in which one merely knows without touching: "Hate's a growing thing like anything else. It's the inevitable outcome of forcing ideas on to life, of forcing one's deepest instincts; our deepest instincts we force according to certain ideas. We drive ourselves with a formula, like a machine. The logical mind pretends to rule the roost, and the roost turns into pure hate" (p. 76).

Clifford's world is the world of the machine. In *Lady Chatterley's Lover* we have the final reversal of realism because in it the monster is not the irrational life-energy hidden in the woods beyond society, but society itself. The possibility of redemption lies in those woods, where society feared the monster lurked. All the time, Lawrence implies, it was itself the monster. Clifford is the Benjamin Franklin, that is, the Frankenstein of *Lady Chatterley's Lover,* and the satyr gamekeeper, of course, is the one figure that might restore life, who combines sexual vitality with tenderness and compassion and the capacity to articulate it. Thus, the world encompassed by the conventions of realism is merely an animated corpse; the world belonging to the irrational and mythic energies of nature, Tennyson's "ape and tiger," is the only truly human reality.

It is odd how, in pushing this reversal, Lawrence also signals certain continuities with the best Victorian fiction. In Victorian realism, one also finds a gossipy community too ready to apply general moral maxims and cruelly insensitive to the particular case. Maggie's position in *The Mill on the Floss,* another novel struggling to get beyond the crystallized conventions of a moribund society, is closely analogous to Mellors's and Connie's. Mellors, trapped by a brutal wife, is not very distant from Stephen Blackpool in *Hard Times*, trapped by his wife. Of course, in Lawrence the social regulations have no binding moral force as they have in Dickens, only the stupid force of convention. What Lawrence is determined on is the absolute severance (only partly completed in Hardy) between the social rule and the moral right. Indeed, the idea of "moral right" is irrelevant, and the language of moral convention is mocked and parodied. It is demonstrated to be dead.

For this reason, the whole narrative strategy of the novel seems an almost deliberate slap at our conventions of reading. The narrator is reckless with clichés, and for much of the first half of the book trivializes what should be dramatically powerful wtih hackneyed phrases that a Victorian novelist would have been embarrassed to use. The first sentence announces that this is a tragic age, but the last sentence of the first paragraph is reduced to "We've got to live, no matter how many skies have fallen." Clifford is "more or less in bits." Connie must "live and learn" (p. 47). Describing Connie's loneliness, the narrator says, "There's lots of good fish in the sea" (p. 75). Listening to the intellectuals, she must sit "quiet as a mouse" (p. 79). Describing the pretty color of the rock burned in the mines, the narrator sneers, "It's an ill-wind that brings nobody good" (p. 85). Such language disappears with Mellors, except when he himself uses it in bitter defensiveness. But the tone is aggressively cheapening as if to announce that all we conventionally value in narrative is merely trivial.

Such language is appropriate, we must feel, to the kind of novel the narrator describes in a very Victorian "intrusion" in chapter 9: "But the novel, like gossip, can . . . excite spurious sympathies and recoils, mechanical and deadening to the psyche. The novel can glorify the most corrupt feelings so long as they are *conventionally* 'pure.' Then the novel, like gossip, becomes at last vicious, and, like gossip, all the more vicious because it is always ostensibly on the side of the angels. Mrs. Bolton's gossip was always on the side of the angels" (p. 148). What one needs is a new language, for the language of realism has become only the language of gossip. "All the great words, it seemed to Connie, were cancelled for her generation: love, joy, happiness, home, mother, father, husband, all these great dynamic words were half dead now, and dying from day to day" (p. 107). So it is that Connie "hated words" because they came "between her and life" (p. 139); and so it is that as Connie begins to break out of the grip of Clifford's mental consciousness the text, in chapter 8, suddenly begins to overflow with literary allusions, strangled among clichés. To "touch" Mellors, Connie must purge herself of "words," and together, Lawrence and Mellors struggle to a new vocabulary, a vocabulary that might at least intimate the wonder of the impersonal organic life from which civilization fled as from a monster. It is for this reason that Lawrence touchingly dwells on "fuck" and "cunt," conscious of how they will disturb his audience, and anxious that they register, through that disturbance, the vitality that lies buried under conventional words and conventional social ordering.

In his rejection of the conventions of realism, Lawrence belongs nevertheless to that great struggle of the realists both to use and to reject literature and language, for the sake of a reality beyond language. He is trapped like those before him in language, though the terms have changed and though he rightly determines that what the Victorians used to register the complexity and streamingless of experience was not hardened and unreal. It was a literary and historical fact that the reality of the Victorian novelists had gone bad. The First World War had blown Clifford and realism to "bits," and in the effort to keep Connie herself from "going to pieces" (p. 63), Lawrence seeks a new vision and a new art.

The Victorian realists had put their faith in the "fact," and the fact had failed them. But the fact of Victorian realism remained beyond the particular surfaces and conventions of order, or disorder, we may find from novel to novel. We can hear in Lawrence's own comments, in *Lady Chatterley's Lover,* on the spirit of genuine fiction, echoes of the ideals and the achievements of the Victorians themselves. In the intensity of his moral engagement, in his radical attempt to reinfuse vitality and meaning into a world from which meaning had been withdrawn, in his quest to find a form that would honor the streamingness of experience without Thackerayan diffusion of plots, in his effort to find a new language to make a vital conjunction between art and experience, Lawrence was perhaps the last of the great Victorians. This is not so clearly distinguishable from George Eliot, after all:

> After all, one may hear the most private affairs of other people, but only in a spirit . . . of fine, discriminative sympathy. For even satire is a form of sympathy. It is the way our sympathy flows and recoils that really determines our lives. And here lies the vast importance of the novel, properly handled. It can inform and lead into new places the flow of our sympathetic consciousness, and it can lead our sympathy away in recoil from things gone dead. Therefore, the novel, properly handled, can reveal the most secret places of life: for it is in the *passional* secret places of life, above all, that the tide of sensitive awareness needs to ebb and flow, cleansing and freshening. [P. 148]

"If art does not enlarge men's sympathies," says George Eliot, "it does nothing morally."[9] "Art is the nearest thing to life."

Lawrence rejects the realists to embrace the monster they feared. In so doing, he transforms, in the very spirit of realism, the language of fiction, the art of the novel. He leaves Connie and Mellors, however, still seeking that consummation implicit in the image of the Grecian urn I invoked at the start. Lawrence knows that he doesn't know, and lives with that knowledge. His language strains toward those "secret places" as Connie and Mellors lean undespairing toward each other.

Notes

Chapter 1

1. See, e.g., Terry Eagleton, *Criticism and Ideology* (London, 1976) and Frederic Jameson, *Marxism and Form* (Princeton, 1971). Insisting on a Marxist (and materialist) critical theory, both reject interpretation and close reading as the primary functions of criticism. Jameson sees such activity as part of the "liberal tradition," whose antispeculative bias encourages "submission to what is by preventing its followers from making connections" (p. x).

Eagleton sees the primary function of criticism as finding a ground outside of literature (scientific) by which to identify the sources to which literature itself must be blind (p. 43). Although sympathetic to these views, in part because of their insistence on a reality to which literature directly connects, I have discovered in the course of this study that the realist-empiricist tradition need not be antispeculative and fragmenting. The ideology lurking in the details of experience and of texts can emerge through the habit of attention and of encouraging the very liberal-humanist tradition of skepticism toward the big idea that may, indeed, lead to "submission." It can also encourage a dialectic between systems and particulars essential to humane and responsible thought. In a sense, this study attempts to trace such a dialectic through a century of fiction.

2. Gerald Graff, *Literature against Itself* (Chicago, 1979), esp. ch. 2. Graff's book appeared after mine was essentially completed. In his assault on the kind of criticism I allude to here, Graff is both detailed and persuasive, and would seem to provide much ammunition for my position. But in fact I find his lumping of an extraordinary variety of critics together as though they were all saying the same thing for the same reasons disconcerting and unfair. Moreover, salutary as is his attempt to confront this criticism and find a place for realism, he is too ideologically engaged to confront the epistemological substance of the arguments, a substance that challenges the very possibility of his more "humane" alternatives. For a more convincing and intellectually cogent critique of the deconstructionist position as argued by J. Hillis Miller, see William E. Cain, "Deconstruction in America: The Recent Literary Criticism of J. Hillis Miller," *College English* 41 (1979): 367–82. For Miller's most explicit statement on deconstruction, see Harold Bloom et al., *Deconstruction and Criticism* (New York, 1979).

3. *The House of Fiction*, ed. Leon Edel (Westport, Conn., 1973), p. 276.

4. "The Place of Realism in Fiction," *Selections Autobiographical and Imaginative from the Works of George Gissing* (London, 1929), p. 221.

5. *The Modes of Modern Writing* (Ithaca, 1977), p. 25.

6. In his now classic *Art and Illusion* (London, 1960), E. H. Gombrich shows how aesthetic appreciation begins only after the art object is pried loose from its practical context (ch. 4); George Lukács argues that "description begins when external things are felt to be alienated from human activity" (see George Lichtheim, *Lukács* [London, 1970], chs. 6 and 7).

7. For the classic analysis of this connection, see Harry Levin, *The Gates of Horn* (New York, 1963), esp. pp. 43–38.

8. For an interesting recent attack on the use of generic distinctions in criticism, see Nicolaus Mills, *American and English Fiction in the Nineteenth Century: An Antigenre Critique and Comparison* (Bloomington, 1973).

9. *The Metaphysical Novel in England and America: Dickens, Bulwer, Hawthorne, Melville* (Berkeley, 1978), pp. 2–3.

10. Eigner prefers to see such syntheses as attempts to discredit the realistic or empirical by means of the metaphysical.

11. "The Science of Fiction," *Life and Art* (New York, 1925), p. 87

12. See "Periodical Criticism: Reviewers Reviewed. The *Quarterly*," *Athenaeum*, no. 1, 2 Jan. 1828, p. 11.

13. The word seems to have been borrowed from the French in the 1850s, although the idea of *vraisemblance* was current in the 1840s. See Richard Stang, *The Theory of the Novel in England, 1850–1870* (New York, 1959), p. 145; and two essays to which Stang alludes, R. G. Davis, "The Sense of the Real in English Fiction," *Comparative Literature* 3 (Summer 1951): 200–217, and "Balzac and His Writings," *Westminster Review* 60 (July 1853): 199–214. The latter essay does not seem to assume a naive realism, but its brief discussion of the term is useful in suggesting the close connection between realism and romanticism.

14. *Fables of Identity* (New York, 1963), p. 36

15. See, for example, *Studies in European Realism* (New York, 1964). He objects, there, to "exact copying," and sees the great realists as creating "types" in which the fullness of human experience, private and social, is embodied.

16. See J. Hillis Miller, *The Disappearance of God* (New York, 1965) for the best-known recent discussion of the impact of the loss of transcendence on nineteenth-century English literature.

17. Ibid., p. 3.

18. *Past and Present* (Boston, 1965), ch. 2, p. 13.

19. *Sketches by Boz, The Works of Charles Dickens*, Gadshill Edition, ch. 1, p. 1.

20. "The Fiction of Realism," *Dickens Centennial Essays* (Berkeley, 1971), p. 124.

21. "Daniel Deronda: George Eliot's Struggle with Realism" in Alice Shalvi, ed., *Daniel Deronda: A Centenary Symposium* (Jerusalem, 1976), p. 92.

22. See, in addition to Gombrich, Linda Nochlin, *Realism* (Harmondsworth, 1971).

23. *Critical Essays*, trans. Richard Howard (Evanston, 1972), p. xvii.

24. *Beginnings* (New York, 1975), p. xiii.

25. Leo Bersani, *A Future for Astyanax* (Boston, 1976) sees realism as a strategy to serve society by "containing (and repressing) its disorder within significantly structured stories about itself" (p. 63). I would revise this view by adding that while it struggles to contain what it imagines as monstrous, it also devises the strategies to imagine and release it.

26. Frye, *Fables of Identity*, p. 27.

27. *Mary Barton* (London, 1906), ch. 6, p. 70.

28. Nochlin (*Realism*), in an attempt to modify the arguments of E. H. Gombrich, emphasizes the role played by observation in realistic art in the modifying of conventions.

29. *The Realist Novel in England: A Study in Development* (Pittsburgh, 1974), pp. x, 13.

30. *Problems of Life and Mind* (London, 1890), vol. 1, pp. 113–14.

31. *The Novels of Anthony Trollope* (New York, 1977), p. 40.

32. In an earlier draft of this book I used the word "dialectic" rather than the more general word "process" here and throughout. Because "dialectic" is used with unfortunate looseness and because my own use of it was subject to misinterpretation, I have largely eliminated the word. But what I am trying to convey throughout the book is that "realism" is not static but progressive. Its history is largely a dialectical one. That is, it moves from parody of a discredited literary mode (thesis-antithesis) to a new imagination of the real (in the pattern Levin has described), which might be described as a synthesis. This synthesis, however, quickly is perceived as conventional itself and thus subject to further parody. Part of the problem with the word dialectic here is that the kind of synthesis I am talking about (as we can find it in Conrad and later) is no longer safely called realism. It is another stage of the history of the novel, profoundly informed by the realist impulse, yet no longer realism in the sense that the nineteenth-century novel might be seen as realistic.

33. See *The Sense of an Ending* (New York, 1967). Kermode discusses how, in the writer's attempt to "make sense" of things, it is essential to great art that the "sense" not be too simple. Easy resolutions in narrative become merely "escapist" and unsatisfying.

Chapter 2

1. *The Madwoman in the Attic* (New Haven, 1979), p. 77. This study bears an obvious relationship to theirs, which appeared after my manuscript was completed. Like them, I begin with Austen and Mary Shelley. Like them, I imagine the ubiquity of the "monster," which might well be called, in my study as well, the madwoman in the attic. Yet my argument is that the "monstrous" is an aspect of *all* realistic literature, that the repression of it is part of the strategy of realism, not exclusively or even primarily of women's literature. Interestingly, Bersani, calling the monster "desire," detects the same pattern. I use *Frankenstein* as a metaphor for the strategies of realism, while Gilbert and Gubar take it as a paradigm of the woman's imagination of her position as a writer and victim in a patriarchal system. It is important to see, however, that the Victorian

cultural condition made it possible, even necessary, for men to imagine their monstrous doubles and to feel themselves in enclosed spaces that they had to accept even to the crippling of their desire and self.

2. "*Frankenstein* and the Traditions of Realism," *Novel* (Fall 1973): 14–30.

3. U. C. Knoepflmacher notes this pun in his "Thoughts on the Aggression of Daughters," in Knoepflmacher and George Levine, eds., *The Endurance of Frankenstein* (Berkeley, 1979), pp. 88–119.

4. Most criticism of *Frankenstein* has focused on its mythic or psychological implications. Although I am not concerned here to explore the psychobiological implications of the book, they are obviously of importance for a full understanding of it.

5. See Scott's own comment: "The author's principal object . . . is less to produce an effect by means of the marvels of the narrations, than to open new trains and channels of thought, by placing men in supposed situations of an extraordinary and preternatural character, and then describing the mode of feeling and conduct which they are most likely to adopt" ("Remarks on *Frankenstein*," *Periodical Criticism of Sir Walter Scott, Bart.*, [Edinburgh, 1835], vol. 2, p. 252).

6. See Ellen Moers, *Literary Women* (New York, 1976), pp. 91–100, and Knoepflmacher, "Thoughts on the Aggression of Daughters." Relevant, too, is Sandra Gilbert's work in feminist poetics, particularly, "Patriarchal Poetry and Women Readers: Reflections on Milton's Bogey," *PMLA* 93 (May 1978): 368–82.

7. "Night Thoughts on the Gothic Novel," *Yale Review* 52 (1962): 238.

8. *Ariel like a Harpy: Shelley, Mary and "Frankenstein"* (Letchworth, England, 1972), pp. 101 ff.

9. *Frankenstein*, ed. M. K. Joseph (London, 1971), p. 58.

10. *The Hero of the Waverley Novels*, rev. ed. (New York, 1968), p. 27.

11. Ibid., p. 36.

12. Ibid., p. 17.

13. *Some Words of Jane Austen* (Chicago, 1973), p. 18.

14. Richard Whately, Review of *Northanger Abbey* and *Persuasion*, rept. in Brian Southam, ed., *Jane Austen: The Critical Heritage* (New York, 1968), pp. 87–88.

15. Walter Scott, Review of *Emma*, rept. in *Jane Austen: The Critical Heritage*, p. 63; and Whately, Review, p. 88.

16. Whately, Review, p. 88.

17. Ibid., p. 90.

18. *Partial Magic: The Novel as a Self-Conscious Genre* (Berkeley, 1975). The thesis of Alter's book, that self-consciousness is characteristic of the novel form, and that Victorian realism is an aberration from that self-consciousness, is of direct relevance to my arguments, but badly underestimates the Victorians' awareness of the limitations of the novel as direct representation of reality.

19. Whately, Review, p. 91.

20. Ibid., p. 89.

21. Ibid., p. 94.

22. Ibid., p. 91.

23. Ibid., p. 95.

24. Ibid., p. 96.

25. Ibid., p. 98.

26. *A Reading of Jane Austen* (New York, 1976), p. 192.

27. *Jane Austen's Letters*, ed. R. W. Chapman (London, 1969), p. 443.

28. A. Walton Litz, *Jane Austen: A Study of Her Artistic Development* (New York, 1965), p. 115.

29. "What Became of Jane Austen?" rept. in Ian Watt, ed., *Jane Austen: A Collection of Critical Essays* (Englewood Cliffs, N.J., 1963), p. 141.

30. Walter Scott, "Essay on Romance," *Miscellaneous Prose Works* (Edinburgh, 1834), vol. 6, p. 127.

31. George Eliot, *Adam Bede* (New York, 1948), ch. 17, p. 178.

32. George Eliot, *The Mill on the Floss*, ed. Gordon S. Haight (Boston, 1961), p. 239.

33. W. M. Thackeray, *The Newcomes*, (Boston, 1884), II, ch. 2, p. 19.

34. See Alexander Welsh, *The City of Dickens* (Oxford, 1971), p. 10.

35. Ibid., p. 11.

36. *Conrad's Romanticism* (New Haven, 1974), p. 57.

37. Author's Note, *Within the Tides* (New York, 1924), p. viii.

38. For a discussion of this concept and of its relation to the tradition of English fiction, see Raymond Williams, *The English Novel from Dickens to Lawrence* (New York, 1970).

39. Joseph Conrad, *Under Western Eyes* (New York, 1924), p. 3.

40. *The Nigger of the "Narcissus"* (New York, 1924), pp. xiv–xv.

41. See Gillian Beer, "Beyond Determinism: George Eliot and Virginia Woolf," in Mary Jacobus, ed., *Women Writing and Writing about Women* (New York, 1979).

42. *Letters from Joseph Conrad, 1895–1924* (Indianapolis, 1956), p. 46.

43. *Modern Painters*, III (London, 1860), pt. 9, ch. 12.

44. *Joseph Conrad's Letters to R. B. Cunninghame Graham*, ed. C. T. Watts (Cambridge, 1969), p. 65.

45. C. B. Cox, *Joseph Conrad: The Modern Imagination* (London, 1974), p. 11.

46. *Letters from Joseph Conrad*, p. 292.

47. For Conrad's attitude toward "matter," see his letter on seeing an X-ray machine, ibid., p. 143. Royal Roussel, *The Metaphysics of Darkness* (Baltimore, 1971), p. 27. For the general late-century attitude, see Alexander Welsh, "Realism as a Practical and Cosmic Joke," *Novel* (Fall 1975), pp. 23–39.

48. Welsh's essay "Realism as a Practical and Cosmic Joke" explores this situation. See also Roussel, *Metaphysics of Darkness*: "Consciousness must always turn outside itself to find the source of its existence in some ground which does not share its own nature" (p. 10).

49. "Leaves from a Notebook," in *The Essays of George Eliot*, ed. Thomas Pinney (New York, 1963), pp. 450–51.

50. "Joseph Conrad: Alienation and Commitment," in Hugh Sykes Davies and George Watson, eds., *The English Mind* (Cambridge, 1964), pp. 257–78.

51. See Eigner, *Metaphysical Novel*, for a general discussion of this characteristic of writers in the realistic tradition.

Chapter 3

1. *The Novels of Jane Austen,* ed. R. W. Chapman (Oxford, 1923) ch. 1, p. 17.

2. Introduction to *Northanger Abbey* (New York, 1959), p. 16.

3. Among the interesting discussions of *Northanger Abbey* as "very much a novel," see Marilyn Butler, *Jane Austen and the War of Ideas* (Oxford, 1975), esp. pp. 178–81; Frank J. Kearful, "Satire and the Form of the Novel: The Problem of Aesthetic Unity in *Northanger Abbey,*" *ELH* 22 (1965): 511–27; Avrom Fleishman, "The Socialization of Catherine Morland," *ELH* 41 (1974): 649–67.

4. Fleishman, "Socialization of Catherine Morland," p. 650.

5. See Tave, *Some Words of Jane Austen,* on the importance of language as precise definer of things in Jane Austen.

6. Everett Zimmerman, "The Function of Parody in *Northanger Abbey,*" *MLQ,* 30 (1969): 53–63, argues that parody need not entail rejection of the things parodied, and does not in *Northanger Abbey.*

7. For a complex and important discussion, from the perspective of a modernist critic, of the way realism restricts and congeals experience, or, better, narrative possibilities, see Bersani, *Future for Astyanax,* esp. ch. 2. In a later chapter I use some of Bersani's arguments from this and other works, to argue almost the opposite: that the best Victorian novelists used realism as a means to break thorugh the congealing categories of morality and narrative conventions.

8. "Satire and the Form of the Novel," p. 27.

9. "'A propos of 'Lady Chatterley's Lover,'" *Phoenix II,* ed. Warren Roberts and Harry T. Moore (New York, 1968), p. 513.

10. For a remarkable piece of practical criticism in which the light of disenchantment is analyzed in several novels, see Barbara Hardy, *The Novels of George Eliot* (London, 1959), esp. pp. 189–200.

11. "A Note on Jane Austen," rept. in *Jane Austen: A Collection of Critical Essays,* p. 27.

12. *The Gates of Horn,* p. 47. Levin's is the classic discussion of the relation between realism and parody, but some of the titles of parodies here are my responsibility, not Levin's.

13. See Butler's (*Jane Austen and the War of Ideas*) discussions of the conventions Jane Austen played with from her earliest novels.

14. "On *Sense and Sensibility,*" rept. in *Jane Austen: A Collection of Critical Essays,* p. 44.

15. *The Action of English Comedy* (New Haven, 1970), pp. 211–12.

16. Julian Moynahan, "The Hero's Guilt: The Case of *Great Expectations,*" *Essays in Criticism* 10 (1960): 60–79.

Chapter 4

1. *The Spirit of the Age* (London, 1960), pp. 85–86.

2. *Romantic Narrative Art* (Madison, 1960), pp. 184–85.

3. See Welsh, *The Hero of the Waverley Novels,* who argues in his first chapter that in "Scott's lifetime the novel reverted to the romance, which expresses rather than criticizes the desires of the mind" (p. 9). This point, and his argument that Scott neither "practiced himself nor quite recognized the method of

posing fiction against fiction in order to pass, in Harry Levin's phrase, 'from the imitation of art through parody to the imitation of nature'" (p. 11) seem to me essentially right. But my argument about Scott throughout is that he worked casually in modes profoundly mixed.

4. In a MS essay, "Scott and the Dreaming Boy: A Context for Waverley," Jane Millgate traces Scott's relation to romance material and contemporary poetry, and shows that Waverley's story is not simply "the straightforward dramatisation of an awakening from youthful quixotism for which it is sometimes taken." But Millgate overstates the case in asserting that the novel "vindicates the life of the imagination."

5. See Scott on *Emma*: "Social life, in our civilized days, affords few instances capable of being painted in the strong dark colours which excite surprize and horror; and robbers, smugglers, bailiffs, caverns, dungeons, and mad-houses have been introduced until they ceased to interest" (*Sir Walter Scott on Novelists and Fiction*, ed. Ioan Williams [New york, 1968], p. 230).

6. Edwin Muir, "Walter Scott," in Derek Verschoyle, ed., *The English Novelists* (London, 1936), pp. 111–22. Muir denies Scott's influence on later writers. The argument is interesting but surely based on Muir's disappointment at Scott's refusal to live up to his best talents.

7. *Waverley*, ed. Edgar Johnson (New York, 1964), ch. 52, p. 387.

8. See Robert C. Gordon, *Under Which King: A Study of the Scottish Waverley Novels* (New York, 1969). Gordon emphasises the duality of Scott as a principle of form in the novels: "There is in most of Scott's work this sense of a conflict between past and present, ancient lawlessness and established law, passionate nostalgia and historical fact" (p. 10).

9. The problem of Scott's weak heroes is discussed by almost everyone from Scott to Welsh. Lukács finds the undistinguished hero a particularly valuable tool for the historical novel, a figure who can bring two opposing forces into the center of the novel, who "can provide a link without forcing the composition," (*The Historical Novel*, trans. Hannah and Stanley Mitchell [Boston, 1962], p. 37). Walter Bagehot makes a typical nineteenth-century criticism of Scott's heroes in "The Waverley Novels," *Literary Studies* (London, 1895): "Every one feels how commonplace they are.... They have little personality" (vol. 2, p. 119). Bagehot complains that they are all portrayed from the outside. For an excellent survey of nineteenth-century attitudes toward Scott, making clear how critical his idolaters could be, see J. H. Raleigh, "What Scott Meant to the Victorians," *Victorian Studies* 7 (1963): 7–34.

10. *Life on the Mississippi*, rept. in John O. Hayden, ed., *Scott: The Critical Heritage* (London, 1970), p. 538.

11. The three most impressive recent studies of Scott are all concerned with the distinction. See Welsh, *Hero of the Waverley Novels;* Francis Hart, *Scott's Novels: The Plotting of Historical Survival* (Charlottesville, 1966); Avrom Fleishman, *The English Historical Novel: Walter Scott to Virginia Woolf* (Baltimore, 1971). Hart is impatient with the problem: "There remains the hardy tendency to submerge or prejudice practical criticism in arid debate over whether Scott is Romantic or anti-Romantic" (p. 3).

12. Lukács, *Historical Novel,* p. 31.

13. James T. Hillhouse, *The Waverley Novels and Their Critics* (New York, 1968; orig. ed., Minneapolis, 1936).

14. "The Power of Memory in Boswell and Scott," in Norman Jeffares, ed., *Scott's Mind and Art* (New York, 1970), p. 253.

15. Bagehot, "Waverley Novels," pp. 113–14.

16. Pottle, "Power of Memory," p. 253.

17. Ibid., pp. 236–37.

18. Edgar Johnson points out in his note that "Sir Walter has made a number of variations from the original." Pottle interestingly discusses the inaccuracy of Scott's memory.

19. Originally printed in the *Quarterly Review* 16 (1817); rept. in *Sir Walter Scott,* ed. Williams, pp. 237–59.

20. See Alter, *Partial Magic:* the major tradition of the novel "has been enormously complicated by the writer's awareness that fictions are never real things, that literary realism is a tantalizing contradiction in terms" (p. x).

21. Pottle's comments are worth quoting in full: "Scott felt a clear distinction between the products of what I have called average or literal perception and those of constructive imagination, and derived the keenest pleasure from the juxtaposition of the two. No other English author, I should suppose, has ever taken such delight in exposing his *sources:* here are the real facts, here is what I made of them. Wordsworth furnishes a strong contrast. *The White Doe of Rylstone* is based upon matter precisely like that which Scott used in *The Lay of the Last Minstrel,* and, if it had been written by Scott, would have been accompanied by voluminous antiquarian notes, showing in detail just how the original history had been cooked. Wordsworth was rather angry when Scott offered to send him a batch of his material while he was at work on the *Doe.* . . . But Scott, having presented a romance, seems almost to feel under obligation to deflate it by parallel columns of history" ("Power of Memory," pp. 250–51).

22. See Samuel Johnson, "Preface to Shakespeare," rept. in *Johnson: Prose and Poetry,* ed. Mona Wilson (Cambridge, Mass., 1951), p. 503.

23. "Essay on Romance," orig. pub. 1824; rept. in Miriam Allott, *Novelists on the Novel* (New York, 1959), p. 49.

24. Introduction, *The Fortunes of Nigel* (New York, 1901), p. vi. This passage is also reproduced in Allott, *Novelists,* p. 50.

25. *The Bride of Lammermoor* (London, 1964), ch. 1, p. 26.

26. *Old Mortality,* ed Alexander Welsh (Boston, 1966), Conclusion, p. 361.

27. "Milton," *Critical and Historical Essays* (London, 1899), p. 3. Macaulay's essays are full of echoes of Scott's attitudes, e.g., "The truth is, that every man is, to a great extent, the creature of the age" ("Gladstone on Church and State," p. 485).

28. *Fables of Identity,* p. 36.

29. "Most 'historical novels' are romances. Similarly a novel becomes more romantic in its appeal when the life it reflects has passed away" (ibid., pp. 306–7).

30. *Sir Walter Scott* (New York, 1932), p. 348.

31. Frank Kermode (The Uses of the Codes," in Seymour Chatman ed., *Approaches to Poetics* [New York, 1973], pp. 51–80), rejecting certain aspects of structuralism, argues against current efforts to reject some past naiveté about

language: "People who believe in the simple specularity and transparency of novels are indeed very naive, and they are certainly prevented by their simplicity from reading texts in their textuality, narratives in their narrativity, and so on" (pp. 55–56); "Perhaps we need once again to remind ourselves that the theory of infinite structuration is historically part of the continuing French reaction against an atavistic academic criticism. This has entailed the false assumption that flexible, productive and plural reading is to be had only on the basis of new and revolutionary theoretical arguments. But those are circuitous routes to truths more readily accessible: The novel has long been aware of its chimerical potential; it is an authentic *faux-naif*, expert in the limitations of its own pluralities. *That* self-consciousness, rather than an unwilling symbolic permissiveness, is what preserves the *lisible* as something more than an imperfect herald of the truly modern" (pp. 78–79).

Frederick Jameson shows that "realism," in modernist criticism, is an invention that serves ideological purposes: "whenever you search for 'realism' somewhere it vanishes, for it was nothing but punctuation, a mere marker or a 'before' which permitted the phenomenon of modernism to come into focus properly. So, as long as the latter holds the center of the field of vision, and the so-called traditional novel or classical novel or realistic novel or whatever constitutes a 'ground' or blurred periphery, the illusion of adequate literary history may be maintained. But as soon as our critical interest itself shifts to these last, we become astonished to discover that, as though by magic, they also have every one of them been transformed if not all into modernists, at least into precursors of the modern.... It is with the modernists, indeed, a little like Goering and the Jews: they are the ones who decide what is modern and what is not, and the private term of realism is reserved for books they do not happen to be interested in at the moment" ("The Ideology of the Text," *Salmagundi* [Fall-Winter 1976], pp. 233–34).

32. Quoted from Lockhart in R. H. Hutton, *Sir Walter Scott*, English Men of Letters Series (London, 1884), p. 105. See Pottle, "Power of Memory," p. 253.

33. See Fleishman, *English Historical Novel*: "Scott conceived of history from the outset as a past that allowed itself to be made present without losing its unique character, and this sense of the historical novelist's double perspective helps account for the work's imaginative complexity and great success. It is both an entry into the past—often achieving an interior sense of past life—and a coherent interpretation of the past from a particular standpoint in the present" (p. 24).

34. "Sir Walter Scott," *Essays: Scottish and Other Miscellanies* (London, 1915), p. 66.

35. See Robert Caserio, *Plot, Story, and the Novel* (Princeton, 1979), for a strong argument against the modernist separation of the concepts of "plot" and "story." His book challenges with great intelligence contemporary critical attempts to divorce narrative from "meaning."

36. Note the following dialogue in the Introductory Epistle to *The Fortunes of Nigel*:

Captain: In short, sir, you are of opinion with Bayes—"What the devil does the plot signify, except to bring in fine things?"

Author [of Waverley]: Grant that I were so, and that I should write with a sense and spirit a few scenes, unlaboured and loosely put together, but which had sufficient interest in them to amuse in one corner the pain of body; in another to relieve anxiety of mind; in a third place, to unwrinkle a brow bent with the furrows of daily toil; in another, to fill the place of bad thoughts, or to suggest better; in yet another, to induce an idler to study the history of his country; in all save where the perusal interrupted the charge of serious duties, to furnish harmless amusement,—might not the author of such a work, however inartificially executed, plead for his errors and negligences the excuse of the slave, who, about to be punished for having spared the false report of a victory, saved himself by exclaiming—"Am I to blame, O Athenians, who have given you one happy day?" (p. xiii).

37. Carlyle, "Sir Walter Scott," p. 65.

38. Raymond Williams notes two aspects of Scott's kind of historical novel that influenced the Victorians; the "knowable community," in which "persons themselves can be wholly known" in and through relationships, and "at the other end of the scale . . . an increasing scepticism, disbelief, in the possibility of understanding society; a structurally similar certainty that relationships, knowable relationships, so far from composing a community or a society, are the positive experience that has to be *contrasted* with the ordinarily negative experience of the society as a whole" (*English Novel*, p. 15).

39. Welsh, *Hero of the Waverley Novels*, p. 22.

Chapter 5

1. Note Frye's comment on fictions not directed at "plausible content": "Removing the necessity for telling a credible story enables the teller to concentrate on its structure, and when this happens, characters turn into imaginative projections, heroes becoming purely heroic and villains purely villainous. That is, they become assimilated to their functions in the plot" (*Fables of Identity*, p. 27).

2. Hart, *Scott's novels*, p. 306.

3. See Hart's interesting discussion of the way history works in *The Bride*, ibid., esp. pp. 328–33.

4. Quoted in Donald Cameron, "The Web of Destiny: The Structure of *The Bride of Lammermoor*," in Jeffares, ed., *Scott's Mind and Art*, p. 186.

5. The prose is heavily sprinkled with passages that place a custom, a vicious habit, a particular grossness or strangeness in a time before the enlightened narrator. For example: "It is well known, that the weddings of ancient days were celebrated with a festive publicity rejected by the delicacy of modern times" (ch. 34, p. 321); "The desperate and dark resource of private assassination, so familiar to a Scottish baron in former times, had even in the present age [i.e., the narrative present] been too frequently resorted to" (ch. 4, p. 52); "The high and unbiassed character of English judicial proceedings was then little known in Scotland; and the extension of them to that country was one of the most valuable advantages which it gained by the Union" (ch. 14, p. 160).

6. See Scott's essay "On the Supernatural in Fictitious Composition and Particularly in the Works of Ernest Theodore William Hoffman," in *Sir Walter Scott*, ed. Williams, pp. 312–53. There Scott argues that the love of the supernatural has a rational foundation: "The belief itself, though easily capable of

being pushed into superstition and absurdity, has its origin not only in the facts upon which our holy religion is founded, but upon the principles of our nature, which teach that while we are probationers in this sublunary state, we are neighbours to, and encompassed by the shadowy world, of which our mental faculties are too obscure to comprehend the loss, our corporeal organs too coarse and gross to perceive the inhabitants" (p. 313).

7. Cameron ("Web of Destiny") argues: "The supernatural here resembles an inspired guess about the future, based on a sudden intuitive understanding of lines of force in another life, a heightened and deepened form of the parent's warning to the child: 'if you go on doing that kind of thing you'll kill yourself.' In the social sphere, an analogy to these private intuitions is afforded by the close relation between Scott's sense of history and what is very nearly the same thing, his sense of fate" (p. 189).

8. Hart, *Scott's Novels*, p. 329.

9. Ibid., p. 332.

10. A. O. J. Cockshut calls the last scene in *Redgauntlet* "perhaps the finest passage in all Scott's works" (*The Achievement of Walter Scott* [London, 1969], p. 211).

11. Advertisement, *The Antiquary* (Boston, 1893), p. vii.

12. "Scott's *Redgauntlet*," in Robert Rathburn and Martin Steinmann, Jr., eds., *From Jane Austen to Joseph Conrad* (Minneapolis, 1958), p. 47.

13. Welsh (*Hero of the Waverley Novels*) describes this typical figure: "About half of the Waverley Novels exploit the energy of an agent who is not totally depraved. This agent characteristically operates outside the law. He acts with deep feeling, and his intentions are 'good,' though fierce and mistaken. The reader can associate, to a greater or less degree, with his plight, which is that of a man outside society" (p. 59).

14. Daiches, "Scott's *Redgauntlet*," p. 45.

15. *Redgauntlet* (Boston, 1894), II, p. 331.

16. Hart (*Scott's Novels*) makes an ingenious argument about the centrality of Geddes to the thematic development of the novel. Though I do not find the argument convincing, it is worth attending to: "The central position throughout the novel of an appealing Quaker is proof of Scott's thematic awareness. Any praise of the novel should focus on Joshua's role, for he is not simply a complex and sympathetic depiction of what was for Scott a potentially comic religious extremism, but more, the chief exponent of the novel's governing values. When, after Darsie's capture, he fades from view until the end, he takes with him much of the book's promise of ultimate unity. The Byronic Jacobitism of Redgauntlet which takes his place seems a digression rather than a fulfillment" (p. 50).

Chapter 6

1. *Roundabout papers* (Boston, 1884), p. 208.

2. See John Loofbourow, *Thackeray and the Form of Fiction* (Princeton, 1964), pp. 5–6 and passim.

3. Introduction, *Thackeray: A Collection of Critical Essays* (Englewood Cliffs, 1968), p. 10.

4. *The Letters and Private Papers of William Makepeace Thackeray*, ed. Gordon N. Ray (Cambridge, Mass., 1946), vol. 3, p. 142.

5. Ibid., vol. 2, p. 772.

6. David Masson, "Thackeray," rept. in Geoffrey Tillotson and Donald Hawes, eds., *Thackeray: The Critical Heritage* (London, 1968), p. 346; W. C. Roscoe, "W. M. Thackeray, Artist and Moralist" in ibid., p. 270.

7. The quotation from Levin's *Gates of Horn* is used in relation to Thackeray by James H. Wheatley, *Patterns in Thackeray's Fiction* (Cambridge, Mass., 1969), p. 17.

8. See J. A. Sutherland, *Thackeray at Work* (London, 1974), pp. 113–15 and passim.

9. "The Other Freud," *Humanities in Society* 1 (1978): 35.

10. *Thackeray's Novels: A Fiction That Is True* (Berkeley, 1974), p. 234.

11. See Jameson "Ideology of the Text."

12. Bersani, "Other Freud," p. 36.

13. Rawlins, *Thackeray's Novels*, p. 200.

14. "Rebecca and Rowena," *Burlesques* (Boston, 1884), p. 321.

15. Bersani, "Other Freud," p. 36.

16. Ibid., pp. 36–37.

17. See Juliet McMaster, *Thackeray: The Major Novels* (Toronto, 1971), p. 57; Jean Sudrann, "The Philosopher's Property: Thackeray and the Use of Time," *Victorian Studies* 10 (1967): 359–88. This essay remains one of the best studies of Thackeray's use of memory in his fictions.

18. *A Future for Astyanax*, p. 10.

19. Rawlins, *Thackeray's Novels*, p. 134.

20. "Preface to 'The Tragic Muse,'" *The Art of the Novel*, ed. R. P. Blackmur (New York, 1934), p. 84.

21. There is even something Jamesian about J. J. Ridley. Cf. *The Newcomes*, II, p. 284.

22. See my discussion of the relation of Conrad's impressionism to realism in ch. 12 below.

23. *Thackeray* (New York, 1879), p. 183

Chapter 7

1. *The Gay Science* (New York, 1868), II, p. 218.

2. The classic description is in Ian Watt, *The Rise of the Novel* (New York, 1957), ch. 1.

3. *An Autobiography* (New York, 1923), p. 109.

4. *Aspects of the Novel* (London, 1927).

5. *English Criticism of the Novel, 1865–1900* (Oxford, 1965), p. 98. For an important argument that plot and story are indistinguishable, and for the primacy of story in narrative, see Caserio, *Plot, Story, and the Novel*.

6. For an interesting study of the contrast between romantic and realist uses of images, see Andrew Griffin, "Fire and Ice in *Frankenstein*," in Knoepflmacher and Levine, eds., *The Endurance of Frandenstein*, pp. 49–76; and ch. 10 below.

7. Cf. Loofbourow's discussion of Ethel Newcome and Diana, (*Thackeray and the Form of Fiction*, p. 68).

8. See Carol Christ, *The Finer Optic* (Yale, 1975), who shows how particularity corresponds to both severance from nature and a new way to integrate it— through the domestication of the symbolic.

9. See my analysis of the passage in *The Boundaries of Fiction* (Princeton, 1968), pp. 255 ff.

10. In effect, this is continuous with the tradition of realism described by Watt (*Rise of the Novel*), and by Erich Auerbach in *Mimesis*.

11. *The Exposure of Luxury* (Pittsburgh, 1972), p. 116.

12. Ibid., p. 117.

13. *Thackeray: The Age of Wisdom* (New York, 1972), p. 427.

14. Hardy, *Exposure of Luxury*, p. 117.

15. The connection between the two passages was first noticed by George Saintsbury in his *A Consideration of Thackeray* (London, 1931), p. 87. Carl Dawson, in *Victorian Noon: English Literature in 1850* (Baltimore, 1979), further discusses the connection in attempting to locate a "common feeling of isolation" among major writers of the day (p. 117).

16. See Rawlins's excellent discussion of this (*Thackeray's Novels*, p. 134).

17. See W. J. Harvey, *The Art of George Eliot* (Oxford, 1962), ch. 3.

18. See Wolfgang Iser's discussion of the narrator of *Vanity Fair* in *The Imperial Reader* (Baltimore, 1974).

19. Gordon Ray, *Thackeray: The Uses of Adversity* (New York, 1955), p. 277.

20. McMaster, *Thackeray*, p. 53.

Chapter 8

1. *Past and Present* (Boston, 1965), "Gospel of Dilettantism," p. 154.

2. *Thackeray: A Critical Portrait* (New York, 1941), p. 140.

3. Ibid., p. 141.

Chapter 9

1. Eigner (*Metaphysical Novel*) emphasizes Trollope's and Thackeray's refusal to take novel writing seriously. He quotes Thackeray's letter (*Letters*, ed. Ray, IV, pp. 158–59), in which he compares the novelist to the "pastry cook" serving up sweets when he prefers "bread and cheese."

2. *The Professor* (London, 1969), ch. 19, p. 140.

3. Author's Preface, ibid., p. xi. The Preface was written after *Shirley*, probably in 1849.

4. See John Romano, *Dickens and Reality* (New York, 1978).

5. *Autobiography*, p. 126.

6. *Trollope: A Commentary* (London, 1947), pp. 362–65; see R. C. Terry, *Anthony Trollope: The Artist in Hiding* (Totowa, N.J., 1977), ch. 1, who suggests that Sadleir overplayed the damaging effects.

7. *Thackeray*, p. 185.

8. *The House of Fiction*, ed. Leon Edel (Westport, Conn., 1973), "Anthony Trollope," pp. 101–2.

9. See Juliet McMaster, *Trollope's Palliser Novels: Theme and Pattern* (New York, 1978) for a valuable discussion of the way Trollope's novels find their structures through thematic organization. Robert Tracy, *Trollope's Later Novels*

(Berkeley, 1978), argues that Trollope's organization of novels is related to the double plotting of Renaissance drama.

10. Consider the subject of *Is He Poppenjoy?*—Lord George and adultery, the marquis and a possible illegitimate son.

11. See Alter, *Partial Magic,* esp. ch. 1.

12. *Novels of Anthony Trollope,* p. 40.

13. "Anthony Trollope," p. 111.

14. *The City of Dickens,* p. 214. See the final chapter, in which Welsh discusses the implication of closure for the Victorian novel.

15. See Kincaid's discussion of the dangers of "art" in *Novels of Anthony Trollope,* esp. p. 139.

16. *He Knew He Was Right.* (London, 1968), p. 35.

17. *Ayala's Angel* (London, 1929), pp. 33–43.

18. *Great Expectations* (New York, 1957), ch. 40, pp. 341–42.

19. *Is He Popenjoy?* (London, 1944), II, pp. 297–98.

20. See Kincaid's (*Novels of Anthony Trollope*) discussion of the way Trollope risks experience in the form and narrative content of his novels.

21. *The Vicar of Bullhampton* (London, 1924). pp. 158–59.

22. Recent criticism has emphasized how Trollope's narratives quietly subvert conventional moral judgments and complicate moral issues. See McMaster (*Trollope's Palliser Novels*) and Kincaid (*Novels of Anthony Trollope*) and Ruth apRoberts, *The Moral Trollope* (Athens, Ohio, 1971).

23. Kincaid (*Novels of Anthony Trollope,* p. 14) points out that Trollope's morality is tied to situations and the general moral rules are not carefully defined.

24. *Can You Forgive Her?* (London, 1968), p. 376.

25. Sadleir, *Trollope,* p. 391.

26. *Mr Scarborough's Family* (London, 1907), p. 240.

27. See Tracy, *Trollope's Later Novels,* p. 302, for such a reading.

28. *The Prime Minister* (London, 1961), II, pp. 320–22.

29. See my "Can You Forgive Him? Trollope's *Can You Forgive Her?* and the Myth of Realism," *Victorian Studies* 18 (Sept. 1974): 5–30. That essay was, in fact, conceived as a chapter of this book. Too extensive for inclusion, it can, however, provide a reading that substantiates the arguments made here.

Chapter 10

1. Ellen E. Frank, "The Domestication of Nature: Five Houses in the Lake District," in U. C. Knoepflmacher and G. B. Tennyson, eds., *Nature and the Victorian Imagination* (Berkeley, 1977), p. 92.

2. George Meredith, *Beauchamp's Career* (London, 1950), p. 4.

3. *Trollope,* p. 196.

4. See A. Dwight Culler, *Imaginative Reason: The Poetry of Matthew Arnold* (New Haven, 1960), for a discussion of how this pattern of geography runs through all of Arnold's poetry, as well.

5. "Fiction, Fair and Foul—I," *The Works of John Ruskin,* ed. E. T. Cook and Alexander Wedderburn (1908), vol. 34, pp. 271–72.

6. *Modern Painters, III* (volume 5 of *Works,* ed. Cook and Wedderburn), p. 235.

7. *Pictures from Italy* (London, n.d.), p. 101 ("To Rome by Pisa and Siena").

8. Ibid., p. 55.

9. See Derrick Leon, *Ruskin: The Great Victorian* (London, 1949), p. 93.

10. *Fables of Identity*, p. 31.

11. *Adam Bede*, ch. 17, p. 181.

12. *The Mill on the Floss*, IV, ch. 1, p. 238.

13. *The Playground of Europe* (London, 1904), p. 53.

14. *Cranford and Cousin Phillis* (Harmondsworth, 1976), p. 225.

15. *Under the Greenwood Tree* (New York, 1965), pt. IV, ch. 2, pp. 171–72.

16. I cannot find indication that Dickens read volume 4 of *Modern Painters*. Professor Philip Collins has kindly looked into the matter for me and finds certain evidence only that Dickens at one time read *The Seven Lamps of Architecture*. According to Derrick Leon, Dickens asked Ruskin to be allowed to dedicate *Master Humphrey's Clock* to him. But Ruskin obviously distrusted much of the young Dickens's zeal for the present and against the past. In any case, Dickens's sense of the potential gloom of mountains predates Ruskin's by many years.

17. See George Ford, "Felicitous Space: The Cottage Controversy," in Knoepflmacher and Tennyson, eds., *Nature and the Victorian Imagination*, pp. 29–48.

18. *Little Dorrit* (Harmondsworth, 1973), bk. II, ch. 1, p. 482.

19. Whatever ambivalence Dickens might have felt toward mountainous landscape (and to a certain extent he always took a tourist's pleasure in it), he almost always made mountains the site of extreme and dangerous action. In the late story he wrote with Wilkie Collins, *No Thoroughfare*, he and Collins pulled out all the melodramatic stops. The villain, Obereizer, spent his childhood in the mountain gloom; and in the Simplon pass he reveals his villainy to the hero and almost succeeds in killing him. There, too, the hero's dramatic rescue is achieved. It is true that Vendale marries his rescuer in the mountains. But as the wedding ends, Vendale sees Obereizer's funeral train. And the last words of the story are consonant with the tradition I have been tracing: "Then, looking back along the street, he sees the litter and its bearers passing up alone under the arch, as he and she and their marriage train go down towards the shining valley" (*No Thoroughfare*, in *Christmas Stories from "Household Words" and "All the Year Round"* [London, 1914], p. 574).

Chapter 11

1. *Daniel Deronda* (Harmondsworth, 1967), p. 876.

2. *The Woodlanders* (London, 1920), pp. 160–61.

3. J. Hillis Miller, *Thomas Hardy: Distance and Desire* (Cambridge, Mass., 1970), pp. xiii–xiv and passim.

4. *The Return of the Native* (London, 1920), p. 1.

5. The explicit discussion in Hardy of the cost of civilization is fairly common in the nonfiction. The most interesting instance is "The Dorsetshire Labourer," *Life and Art* (New York, 1925), pp. 20–47.

6. "The Profitable Reading of Fiction," *Life and Art*, p. 73.

7. Ibid., p. 69.

8. Florence Emily Hardy, *The Early Life of Thomas Hardy: 1840–1891* (London, 1928), pp. 193–94.

9. Ibid., p. 189.

10. Ibid., p. 225.

11. Ibid., p. 265.

12. "Candour in English Fiction," *Life and Art*, p. 76.

13. "The Profitable Reading of Fiction," p. 61.

14. See J. Hillis Miller's discussion of this problem in his Introduction to Hardy's *The Well-Beloved* (London, 1975).

15. Hardy, *Early Life*, p. 190.

16. (*Thomas Hardy* [Norfolk, Conn., 1964]) points out the connection between Henchard and *Lord Jim* (see esp. pp. 146 ff.). John Bayley (*An Essay on Hardy* [Cambridge, 1978]) also makes connections between Conrad and Hardy.

17. *The Mayor of Casterbridge* (Boston, 1962), p. 277.

18. See Knoepflmacher, "Thoughts on the Aggression of Daughters," pp. 88–119.

Chapter 12

1. *Methods and Results* (London, 1893), p. 66.

2. *Middlemarch* (Boston, 1956), p. 578.

3. Rev. of *Middlemarch*, rept. in David Carroll, ed., *George Eliot: The Critical Heritage* (London, 1971), p. 338.

4. Huxley, *Methods and Results*, pp. 60–61.

5. Ruskin's own argument that one has to *learn* to see nature contradicts the notion that there is such a thing. Gombrich's *Art and Illusion* provides the most extensive rejection of the notion.

6. Quoted in *The Genius of John Ruskin*, ed. John Rosenberg (Boston, 1963), p. 28.

7. William K. Clifford, *Lectures and Essays*, 2 vols. (London, 1901), I, p. 338.

8. Ibid., I, pp. 308–9.

9. See ch. 1, n. 13, above.

10. Rev. of *Modern Painters, III, Westminster Review* (1856), p. 343.

11. Huxley was an aggressive supporter of the use of hypotheses in scientific experiment, and all the scientific writers who moved in the George Eliot circle (especially Lewes) were convinced of the necessity of fictions. Alexander Welsh ("Theories of Science and Romance, 1870–1920," *Victorian Studies* 17 [1973]: 135–54) tries to establish a relation between changes in fictional structures and the increasing scientific acceptance of hypotheses, or "fictional models."

12. *Essays on the Use and Limit of the Imagination in Science* (London, 1870), p. 16.

13. *The Essays of George Eliot*, ed. Thomas Pinney (New York, 1963), p. 31.

14. *Methods and Results*, p. 60.

15. John Tyndall, *Fragments of Science for Unscientific People* (London, 1871), p. 47.

16. *Lectures and Essays*, II, pp. 58–59.

17. See "Experimental Method and the Epistemology of *Middlemarch*," (Ph.D. diss., Vanderbilt Univ., 1976); and his essay, derived from the dissertation, "G.

H. Lewes Revised: George Eliot and the Moral Sence," *Victorian Studies* 21 (1978): 463–92.

18. *Methods and Results,* p. 41.

19. *The Mill on the Floss,* bk. VII, ch. 2, p. 435.

20. *Skeptical Essays* (London, 1928), p. ii.

21. *Fragments,* "The Scope and Limit of Scientific Materialism," p. 123.

22. "Coleridge," *Appreciations* (London, 1922), p. 67.

23. Maurice Mandelbaum accepts Tyndall's description of himself as a materialist. See the excellent *History, Man and Reason: A Study in Nineteenth Century Thought* (Baltimore, 1971). Tyndall's materialism is, on his own account, little more than a faith that everything will ultimately be explicable in terms of matter; he makes no dogmatic claims for materialism or for its capacity to resolve traditional metaphysical issues.

24. *The Physical Basis of Mind* (London, 1893), p. xiii.

25. *Contemporary Thought and Thinkers* (London, 1894), p. 260.

26. *Fragments,* p. 61.

27. Michael York Mason, "Middlemarch and Science: Problems of Life and Mind," *Review of English Studies* 12 (1971): 151–69.

28. *Essays,* ed. Pinney, p. 45.

29. Ibid., p. 435.

30. *Lectures and Essays,* I, p. 346.

31. *Brief Literary Criticisms* (London, 1906), p. 186.

32. The interesting and important connection between empiricism and what seems a very unempirical leap of faith is suggested in Lewes's treatment of Hume in the *Biographical History of Philosophy* (London, 1852), pp. 513–20.

33. See for example Alan Mintz, *George Eliot and the Novel of Vocation* (Cambridge, Mass., 1978), pp. 98–102.

34. The question of whether Lydgate is being treated ironically even in his work, is a complex one. It is clear that he has asked the wrong question, as the narrator tells us. But the crux of the issue for criticism and for our sense of George Eliot's enterprise is whether the quest for a binding theory (whose actual manifestations *are* treated ironically) is not central for her. J. Hillis Miller, in two important essays, suggests that the dominant enterprise is toward the shattering of traditions of order, and of history itself. See "Optic and Semiotic in *Middlemarch*," in J. H. Buckley, ed., *Worlds of Fiction* (Cambridge, Mass., 1975), pp. 125–45; "Narrative and History," *ELH* 61 (1974): 455–73. Ingenious as these readings are and healthy as it is to demonstrate Eliot's critical and self-conscious relation to the traditions of narrative and language, the emphasis in these essays fails to indicate that against her own perception of discontinuities and disruptions, Eliot was laboriously engaged in attempting to reconstruct the fragments of experience and language into a coherent whole. For an excellent discussion of George Eliot's impulse toward particularity and away from abstract structures, see Elizabeth Ermarth, "Incarnations: George Eliot's Conception of 'Undeviating Law,'" *Nineteenth Century Fiction* 29 (1974): 273–86.

35. *Essays,* ed. Pinney, p. 451.

36. *The Disappearance of God* p. 11.

37. *Fragments,* p. 53.

38. *"Heart of Darkness* and Nineteenth-Century Thought," *Partisan Review* 45 (1978): 108.

39. *Letters of William Blackwood and David S. Meldrum,* ed. William Blackburn (Durham, N.C., 1958), p. 156.

40. See *Metaphysics of Darkness.* In ch. 1 Roussel lays out in detail the world view implicit in Conrad's sense of the incompatibility between consciousness and its source.

41. Watt, *"Heart of Darkness,"* p. 108.

42. See Lewes's *The Principles of Success in Literature,* originally published, beginning with its first number, in *The Fortnightly Review* (1855). Republished in book form. See, in the chapter "Of Vision in Art," the section "Idealism and Realism": "There are other truths besides coats and waistcoats, pots and pans, drawing-rooms and suburban villas."

43. G. Jean Aubry, *Joseph Conrad: Life and Letters,* 2 vols. (New York, 1927), I, p. 302.

44. *The Renaissance* (London, 1888), p. 248.

45. Aubry, *Life and Letters,* I, p. 280.

46. *Letters from Joseph Conrad,* p. 144.

47. *Evolution and Ethics and Other Essays* (London, 1911), pp. 83–84.

48. See Huxley, *Discourses: Biological and Geological* (London, 1894). In his remarkable essay "Biogenesis and Abiogenesis," Huxley connects the experiments on "spontaneous generation" with this large metaphysical issue. These experiments were, in fact, a focal point in the argument for the "physical basis of life."

49. "Science and Theism," *Theological Essays* (London, 1902), pp. 45–46.

50. "The Moral Significance of Atheism," ibid.

51. Joseph Conrad, *Youth and Two Other Stories* (London, 1924), p. 49.

52. For a discussion of Conrad and cannibalism, see Tony Tanner, "'Gnawed Bones' and 'Artless Tales'—Eating the Narrative in Conrad," in Norman Sherry, ed., *Joseph Conrad: A Commemoration* (London, 1976).

Fragments, p. 63.

54. Ibid., p. 64.

55. *The Note-Books of Samuel Butler* (London, 1903), p. 323.

56. See Dwight Culler's discussion of the form of Darwinian paradox, "The Darwinian Revolution and Literary Form," George Levine and William Madden, eds., *The Art of Victorian Prose* (New York, 1968), pp. 228–46. This "form" points also to the sort of indeterminacy already implicit in the notion that there is more than one possible way to describe the phenomenon of light, and in the profusion of non-Euclidean geometries that W. K. Clifford was bringing to the attention of the scientific and lay public.

57. Aubry, *Life and Letters,* I, p. 216.

58. Ibid., p. 270.

59. Ibid., p. 301.

60. Ibid., pp. 301–2.

61. See Conrad's famous letter in which he compares life with a "knitting machine," ibid., I, p. 216. For a better text, see *Joseph Conrad's Letters to R. B. Cunninghame Graham,* ed. Watts, pp. 56–57.

62. *Lectures and Essays*, II, p. 34.

63. Ibid., p. 35.

64. Ibid., pp. 36–37. This argument, paradoxically stated, has a long history in the nineteenth-century discussion of determinism. Only an ordered and sequential universe makes education and choice possible. Those who insist on freedom are implicated in the argument for inconsequence. For a discussion of this relation to George Eliot, see George Levine, "Determinism and Responsibility in the Works of George Eliot," PMLA 77 (1962): 268–79; K. K. Collins's dissertation, pp. 59–63; and Beer, "Beyond Determinism: George Eliot and Virginia Woolf."

65. See Bertrand Russell's famous manifesto, "A Free Man's Worship," in *Selected Papers of Bertrand Russell* (New York, n.d.), pp. 1–15. For an interesting discussion of these attitudes in relation to "realism," see Welsh, "Realism as a Practical and Cosmic Joke."

66. "On the Hypothesis that Animals are Automata, and its History," *Methods and Results*, p. 240.

67. Ibid., p. 242.

68. Ibid., p. 244.

69. Aubry, *Life and Letters*, I, p. 226.

70. *Leslie Stephen: His Thought and Character in Relation to his Time* (Cambridge, Mass., 1952), p. 165.

71. *Letters from Joseph Conrad*, p. 143.

72. *Lectures and Essays*, I, pp. 335–36.

73. For an extensive discussion of the intellectual background of the Preface, see Ian Watt, *Conrad in the Nineteenth Century* (Berkeley, 1979), esp. pp. 79–81. Unfortunately, this book appeared after mine was completed.

Chapter 13

1. *Letters of William Blackwood*, ed. Blackburn, p. 172.

2. *Beginnings*, p. 110.

3. It is interesting to note an important conflict in views on this matter. While J. Hillis Miller, in "Narrative and History," argues that in *Middlemarch* George Eliot sees history as "an act of repetition in which the present takes possession of the past and liberates it for a present purpose, thereby exploding the continuum of history" (p. 471), a reading that is there "for those who have eyes to see it," Steven Marcus seems not to have the eyes. Against Miller's view, argued in "Optic and Semiotic," that the narrator in *Middlemarch* pulls the ground from under herself by working several different kinds of totalizing metaphors, ultimately self-contradictory, Marcus complains that Eliot's insights into the relativity of knowledge tend to stop with herself. The narrator is allowed to achieve an objectivity not possible *within* the world of the novel and is allowed therefore to create a novel with a firmly historical narrative. For Marcus, Eliot's narrative is not only historical, but "historical narrative as existing in hypostatic, not to say reified form" ("Literature and Social Theory: Starting in with George Eliot," *Representations: Essays on Literature and Society* [New York, 1976], p. 187).

Obviously Marcus is closer to Eliot's concern with "binding theory"; yet if it is misleading to focus on the deconstructing energies of *Middlemarch*'s narrative, it is equally misleading to ignore the way Eliot complicates the notions of cause and effect, of progress, of the distinction between self and other, idea and feeling, feeling and action. The "authority" of her narrator is always tentative, but the narrator is given the authority possible to the scientist—incomplete yet the best attainable.

4. See David Carroll, "*Middlemarch* and the Externality of Fact," in Ian Adam, ed., *This Particular Web* (Toronto, 1975), pp. 73–90.

5. For an important study of the way history is woven into the texture of *Middlemarch*, see Jerome Beaty, "History by Indirection: The Era of Reform in *Middlemarch*," *Victorian Studies* 1 (1957): 173–79.

6. *Middlemarch* (Boston, 1956), ch. 15, p. 105.

7. *Letters of William Blackwood*, ed. Blackburn, p. 155: Here Conrad, in one of the two direct references I have found to her in his letters, misspells her name as Elliott. But Conrad's familiarity with Victorian literature was great and, if only in deference to the firm of Blackwood, he calls her one of the "great names."

8. *Beginnings*, p. 35.

9. Review of *Middlemarch* in *The Galaxy* (1873). Rept. in *The House of Fiction*, ed. Edel, p. 267.

10. *Nostromo* (Harmondsworth, 1863), pp. 77, 118.

11. U. C. Knoepflmacher, "*Middlemarch*: An Avuncular View," *Nineteenth Century Fiction* 30 (June 1975): 53–81, interestingly discusses the weakness of the uncle figures in *Middlemarch* as an expression of the breakdown of traditional authority; this works well in *Nostromo*.

12. Review of *Middlemarch*, p. 263.

13. See Mintz, *George Eliot*: Mintz argues that in George Eliot the romance plot is displaced by the quest for vocation.

14. Thomas Pinney, "More Leaves from George Eliot's Notebook," *Huntington Library Quarterly* 29 (1966): 364.

15. Conrad, "Autocracy and War," *Notes on Life and Letters* (New York, 1924), p. 86.

16. "Conrad's Preface to *The Nigger of the Narcissus*," *Novel* 8 (1974): 114. Cf. *Nostromo*, p. 196.

17. *The Polish Heritage of Joseph Conrad* (rept. New York, 1962), p. 131.

18. *Letters from Joseph Conrad*, p. 46.

19. *Metaphysics of Darkness*, p. 26.

20. Through all his criticism of Conrad, Ian Watt has insisted on this more affirmative aspect of Conrad's writing. In addition to the essay on the Preface, see "Joseph Conrad: Alienation and Commitment," "*Heart of Darkness* and Nineteenth Century Thought." A similar position is taken by David Thorburn, *Conrad and Romanticism* (New Haven, 1974).

21. Review of *Middlemarch*, p. 262.

22. Richard Ellmann, "Dorothea's Husbands," *Golden Codgers* (New York, 1973), pp. 17–36.

23. In *Problems of Life and Mind*, Lewes defines the Ideal as "what is virtually given, when the process of Inference anticipates and intuites [*sic*] what *will* be or *would* be Feeling under the immediate stimulus of the object," (II, pp. 16–17).

24. I am grateful to two former graduate students for their subtle and convincing arguments about the centrality of Philip's vision to the book: Helen Cooper and Stephanie Pinson.

25. "The Concept of Crisis in *Middlemarch*," *Nineteenth Century Fiction* 28 (1974): 457.

26. *The English Novel*, p. 93.

27. *Essays*, ed. Pinney, p. 29.

28. *Lectures and Essays*, I, p. 109.

29. Ibid., p. 116.

30. See n. 3, above.

31. The connections are there not only in the passage quoted earlier, but in others, such as these: "To the modern spirit nothing is, or can be rightly known, except relatively and under conditions. The philosophic conception of the relative has been developed in modern times through the influence of the sciences of observation. These sciences reveal types evanescing into each other by inexpressible refinements of change" (p. 67). Or note this: "Man's physical organism is played upon not only by the physical conditions about it, but by remote laws of inheritance, the vibration of long past acts reaching him in the midst of the new order of things in which he lives" (pp. 67–68). This latter is connected to the kind of influence Dorothea is supposed to exercise on us through her unhistoric acts.

32. Even Darwin probably believed in this kind of inheritance. Bernard Paris, *Experiments in Life* (Detroit, 1965), makes excellent use of the relation of Lewes's ideas to George Eliot's. He points out that there is such a thing as inherited characteristics in Eliot. See Lewes's discussion, passim, esp. *Problems of Life and Mind*, I, p. 219.

33. The Editor [John Morley], Review of Pater's *Renaissance*, "Mr. Pater's Essays," *Fortnightly Review* 13 (1873): 470.

34. *The Renaissance*, p. xi.

35. *The House of Fiction*, ed. Edel, pp. 31–32.

36. *The Renaissance*, p. 249.

37. See Huxley's "Biogenesis and Abiogenesis," and Tyndall's "Spontaneous Generation," in *Fragments*, II.

38. The most famous occasion for the quotation is at the conclusion of "The Everlasting "Yea" chapter of *Sartor Resartus*.

39. Ironically, for so intellectual a writer, George Eliot frequently explored the possibility that *not* knowing is healthier than knowing. The most extreme form of this is in "The Lifted Veil," where the capacity to know other's thoughts is a moral and psychological disaster.

40. *The Letters of George Eliot*, ed. Gordon S. Haight, 9 vols. (New Haven, 1955–1979), V, p. 124.

41. Ibid., IV, p. 135.

42. Ibid., IV, p. 107.

43. Ibid., IV, p. 135.

44. See Ch. 12, n. 27, above.

45. "Second-sight is a flag over disputed ground. But it is a matter of knowledge that there are persons whose yearnings, conceptions—nay, travelled

conclusions—continually take the form of images which have a foreshadowing power: the deed they would do starts up before them in complete shape, making a coercive type" (*Daniel Deronda*, p. 527).

46. *Letters to Cunninghame Graham*, ed. Watts, p. 65.

Epilogue

1. *An Outcast of the Islands* (Harmondsworth, 1976), pt. IV, ch. 5, pp. 225–26.

2. *The Letters of D. H. Lawrence*, ed. Aldous Huxley (London, 1932), p. 66.

3. For an interesting discussion of the shared elements in Conrad and Lawnce, see K. K. Ruthven, "The Savage God: Conrad and Lawrence," *Word in the Desert* (London, 1968), pp. 39–54.

4. *The Rainbow* (New York, 1961), p. 440.

5. "Benjamin Franklin," *The Symbolic Meaning* (New York, 1964), p. 34.

6. Ibid., p. 35.

7. "A propos of 'Lady Chatterley's Lover,'" *Phoenix II* (New York, 1968), p. 489.

8. *Lady Chatterley's Lover* (London, 1960), p. 59.

9. Eliot, *Letters*, ed. Haight, III, p. 111.

Index